THE DREAD HEIGHTS

THINKING FROM ELSEWHERE

Series editors:

Clara Han, Johns Hopkins University

Bhrigupati Singh, Ashoka University and Brown University

Andrew Brandel, University of Chicago

International Advisory Board:

Roma Chatterji, University of Delhi

Veena Das, Johns Hopkins University

Robert Desjarlais, Sarah Lawrence College

Harri Englund, Cambridge University

Didier Fassin, Institute for Advanced Study, Princeton

Angela Garcia, Stanford University

Junko Kitanaka, Keio University

Eduardo Kohn, McGill University

Heonik Kwon, Cambridge University

Michael Lambek, University of Toronto

Deepak Mehta, Ashoka University, Sonepat

Amira Mittermaier, University of Toronto

Sameena Mulla, Emory University

Marjorie Murray, Pontificia Universidad Católica de Chile

Young-Gyung Paik, Jeju National University

Sarah Pinto, Tufts University

Michael Puett, Harvard University

Fiona Ross, University of Cape Town

Lisa Stevenson, McGill University

THE DREAD HEIGHTS

Tribulation and Refuge after the Syrian Revolution

BASIT KAREEM IQBAL

FORDHAM UNIVERSITY PRESS NEW YORK 2025

Fordham University Press also publishes its books in a variety of electronic formats. Some content that appears in print may not be available in electronic books.

Visit us online at www.fordhampress.com.

For EU safety / GPSR concerns: Mare Nostrum Group B.V., Mauritskade 21D, 1091 GC Amsterdam, The Netherlands, gpsr@mare-nostrum.co.uk

Library of Congress Cataloging-in-Publication Data available online at https://catalog.loc.gov.

Printed in the United States of America

27 26 25 5 4 3 2 1

First edition

CONTENTS

Introduction: God Grants Relief 1

1 Refuge 29

The Ruin of Community, 30 • Translating Muslim Humanitarianism, 38 • Abstemious Images, 47 • Pedagogy in Exile, 53 • No Refuge from God but God, 63

Threshold: Natality 69

2 Tribulation 78

Accepting, 82 • Reckoning, 100 • Distributing, 114 • Disclosing, 125 • A Grammar of Tribulation, 144

Threshold: Ambivalence 150

3 The Heights 158

Woe to Our Condition Here, 159 • Brutal Tyranny, 163 • As Though It Were Yesterday, 171 • If the Horizon Breaks, 184 • The Dread Heights, 192

Afterword: Eternity Has Fallen 200

Acknowledgments 205

Notes 209

Bibliography 259

Index 281

God glorified and exalted made us forget [our covenant] in order to test us, because this world is the abode of trials. We must keep faith in the Unseen from the beginning: had we remembered that [primordial moment], our test would have ended and there would have been no need for the reminder of the prophets, upon them blessings and peace. Whatever one forgets does not invalidate its binding nature, nor does it provide an excuse. God the exalted has said about our deeds that *God has reckoned, though they may have forgotten* (Q. 58:6), and He has told that He will requite and reward us.

—MULLA ʿALĪ AL-QĀRĪ, *GIFTS OF THE BLOOMING GARDENS*

INTRODUCTION: GOD GRANTS RELIEF

CROSSING THE HUMANITARIAN BORDER

In the summer of 2018, the Syrian regime and its allies attacked the southern province of Daraa, then under local rebel control, and tens of thousands of people fled for the borders with Israel and Jordan. There they camped under the sun, without adequate latrines or medicines, foodstuffs or water; there they desperately appealed for relief and succor. Images of masses of people seeking shelter in the bare desert spread across news media. They made videos of their supplications and imprecations. "O world, O Muslims, where are you?" They pleaded to cross to safety.

I had been doing fieldwork with refugees and relief workers in Jordanian towns and settlements near the border with Syria. Black smoke billowed during the day, and the night horizon was lit orange and white with the flashes of Russian bombs.

The border stayed closed. The Jordanian government refused to allow any more Syrians into the country, declaring that it had its own challenges to face.

I had a meeting scheduled that week with an international relief organization in Amman. Given what news had dominated the headlines for days, I expected them to cancel the meeting or to delay it, assuming they would be too busy attending to the aid crisis to meet with an anthropologist who had cold-called them. Instead, they were expecting me when I arrived and ushered me in to have tea with their country director. I asked him my usual questions—about the programs they ran, about what motivated their work, about how their infrastructure liaised (if at all) with local charitable associations—but then I could not help asking what this large nongovernmental organization, with its massive budget and busy offices, was doing for the hundred thousand people hiding in the desert and foraging for food to the north.

The director was surprised that I asked. "Look," he answered, "we can't do anything for them. They are on the other side of the border, which means that they fall under the mandate of our Damascus branch." (I knew the Damascus branch had become defunct over the course of the war. More broadly, policy literature had amply established how the Assad regime weaponized access to humanitarian assistance.)[1] "If the borders do open, then we'd be able to help get them emergency aid, but until that time . . . if we could help them it would have to be through the Jordanian military, and that would run counter to our principles."

He gestured to the four glossy posters hanging above the leather sofa he was sitting on. They featured the following English words in large type: neutrality, independence, universality, humanity. "These are our humanitarian principles," he said. "They require that we deliver the aid ourselves or coordinate with one of our established partners."

The media affairs manager had joined our meeting. "I heard there were some weapons smuggled to the rebels through an aid caravan," she added.

"There we have it," the director gesticulated. "We already know that there are anti-regime militia hiding among the IDPs [internally displaced people]. What would happen if they did open the border and terrorists escaped while civilians were rushing in?"

At the same time as we were meeting, thousands of people across Jordan had started sending aid to the north of the country. Clothes, blankets, umbrellas to protect against the sun, cases of water, bakeries sending trucks of bread, diapers, medicine—all sent to be piled in heaps in an empty lot in the border town of Ramtha (see figure 1). It kept coming, sent by families and small businesses watching the news and hearing the appeals. One of my longtime interlocutors, the director of an Islamic charitable organization based in Amman, held a series of meetings with Jordanian government officials. In the span of a day or two, Shaykh Zāyid had worked out an arrangement with the government (under the auspices of the national Jordan Hashemite Charity Organization) in which the privately gathered aid would travel across the border in Jordanian military trucks. Even if the government refused to open the border to the displaced Daraawis, the director of this charitable organization saw the space to maneuver an improvised response. After a

FIGURE 1. Aid is collected at Pilgrims' Square, Ramtha, Jordan. Basit Kareem Iqbal, 2018

press conference in Ramtha, he circulated appeals for emergency relief across his network of pious donors. "May God grant them relief," he concluded.

Another of my interlocutors, an imam from Daraa, had family among those fleeing the Syrian regime. Bilāl posted publicly on Facebook that week: "Their terrorizing the people is intentional. This terrible turmoil is what they want! Through this all, the believer has certainty in the saying of God the exalted, *say, naught befalls us, save that which God has decreed for us* (Q. 9:51). You want what you want and I want what I want, and God does as he wills." He both affirmed the vicious nature of the regime's violence and took recourse to the divine fate and the ethical virtues of reliance (*tawakkul*) and steadfastness (*ṣabr*).

When I came to visit him the next day in Ramtha he took me to the Daraa border crossing. "Look, there: Syria." But our taxi turned back before the first checkpoint and ducked into a large parking lot. "This used to be the old pilgrims' square," Bilāl explained. "In Ottoman times the pilgrims going for Hajj would stop to rest here as they traveled south." The square was full of activity: dozens of men shouting and calling to each other, heaving cases of bottled water onto trucks, unloading private vehicles and open-backed jeeps. Delivery vans with boxes of food, garbage bags in heaps, blankets wrapped together, baby formula, everything piled high. Through the pandemonium, the trucks were being loaded and unloaded. Behind the square, a slim minaret in the Turkish style was silhouetted against the setting sun.

Bilāl greeted some young boys who had come to shake his hand. *Shlōnak shaykhnā*, they asked how he was. He started recording a video on his cell phone to send to his Syrian friends in Syria and elsewhere in Jordan:

> Praise God, Lord of the worlds. We thank the Jordanian brethren, who have not forgotten us. Praise God, Lord of the worlds. In the last two or three hours, their hearts full of concern for their religion and their brethren, a way opened for them to contribute. Syrian and Jordanian alike, they gathered for their neighbors. God protect this land, God protect our brethren at the border, God protect our brethren inside. O God, Your succor, which You have sworn . . . [he panned to show the highway in the panorama]. On this blessed day the trucks have been arriving from around Jordan—from Mafraq, from Irbid, from Jerash. This is like the hadith of the Prophet: "no one believes while his neighbor lies hungry."
>
> We ask God to relieve the afflicted, to accept our martyrs into paradise, to shield the vulnerable, to reward our Syrian and Jordanian brethren. There is no division among the hearts of the faithful, in their mutual mercy. The hearts of the faithful extend across these borders where we are standing. [Tears sprung to his eyes.] This is the meaning of the prophetic hadith about the Muslim Community (*umma*): "the faithful are one body; when a single limb feels pain, the entire body aches with sleeplessness and fever." [The camera shook.] See this bakery that has donated bread, may God reward them. See the Muslims responding—the people who strive with their souls, some with their wealth, some with their prayer, whatever aid they are able to offer. All this has been gathered in just a few hours, praise God. [The camera panned across a boy carrying his younger sister, watching the aid being loaded into the trucks.] God reward the people of Ramtha, the people of Jordan, God reward every Syrian here

who is a free refugee, who helps the brethren inside, God bless all of you. [The camera paused on a long line of men passing cases of water, one to the next, onto a large truckbed.] God bless you, God bless you.

This reminds me of the time at the very beginning of the siege [in Daraa], how the people would give comfort to one another, how they would divide up a single piece of bread, how they would connect the houses, one to another [by smashing holes in their adjoining walls, to avoid being exposed to sniper-fire on the street].

Praise God in every condition: there is still goodness in this Community (*mā zāl al-khayr fī hādhihi l-umma*). O God, we ask Your relief for this Community. O Most Merciful of the merciful! By Your mercy we ask You, we seek Your succor. Enfold the hearts of the believers in mercy and mutual compassion. Even now they are coming here bringing donations or supplicating in their homes, praising God. Sixteen truckloads so far—this proof of fraternity, generosity, virtue.

■ ■ ■

In summer 2018, as tens of thousands of people in rebel-held Syria fled south under regime bombardment, international humanitarian organizations in Jordan refused to violate state sovereignty by delivering aid five kilometers across the northern border. The very principles that were meant to ensure humanitarian integrity (neutrality, independence, universality, humanity) here in fact prevented the provision of humanitarian assistance. Meanwhile, local Islamic charitable organizations in Jordan were already gathering food and medicine. They agitated for admitting the fleeing Syrians abandoned to the desert; then they negotiated Jordanian government delivery of this aid into Syrian territory. On both sides of the border, Muslims prayed for relief and cursed the cruelty of territorial politics. On the Day of Judgment, they swore, all betrayals and faithkeeping will be settled.

This apocalyptic scene does more than allegorize the political and ethical failures of humanitarianism. In a world of brutal sieges and mass displacement, my interlocutors insist that God is the one who grants relief. Their invocation defamiliarizes the primal scene of humanitarianism, in which a compassionate spectator is moved to address distant suffering. It likewise unsettles the political reason of humanitarianism, which rests on the institutionalized frameworks of nation, state, and territory. But it also displaces the coordinates of the humanitarian frame altogether. The discourses and practices of my interlocutors lead elsewhere, away from the moral economy struck between benefactor and beneficiary and away from the social imaginary oscillating between emergency and endurance. Humanitarianism grounds its procedures and protocols in the concept of the human, which (so it claims) lies prior to politics and culture and provides the locus for humanitarian compassion and critiques. The eschatological reference of my interlocutors instead disperses that logic and opens to the incommensurable.

"There is still goodness in this Community," Bilāl had ended his voiceover narration, citing an apocryphal hadith in which the prophet Muhammad foretold that so it would remain until the Day of Resurrection. The gathering of emergency supplies in Ramtha thus has an intimate relation to the gathering return of everything to God (*al-maʿād*). Between the recognition of goodness still obtaining among the Muslims and the promise of God's awful justice emerges Bilāl's prayer: *allāhumma farrijhum*, O God, relieve them.[2] This supplication admits our insufficiency not only in a world of closed borders and bureaucratic alibis, but also from the insistent vantage of the coming Hour. God, grant relief: this phrase, a refrain across the sites of my fieldwork, expresses the fundamental orientation of creational existence. It is indifferent to the designations of politics and culture (citizen or refugee, benefactor or beneficiary) in marking an essential vulnerability to the divine decree. The verse Bilāl had cited continues, *Say, "Naught befalls us, save that which God has decreed for us. He is our Master, and in God let the believers trust"* (Q. 9:51). The discourses and practices of my interlocutors seek to inhabit this position. Attending to their texture and vitality shows how contemporary Islamic traditions respond to devastation.

This book takes its title from the Quranic topos of the Heights (*al-aʿrāf*), an eschatological figure of the lacuna between paradise and hellfire, whose denizens are frozen in place, bearing witness to the saved and the damned through their reiterated supplications for relief:

> And there will be a veil between them. And upon the Heights are men who know all by their marks. They will call out to the inhabitants of the Garden "Peace be upon you!" They will not have entered it, though they hope. And when their eyes turn toward the inhabitants of the Fire, they will say, "Our Lord! Place us not among the wrongdoing people!" And

> the inhabitants of the Heights will call out to men whom they know by their marks, "Your accumulating has not availed you, nor has your waxing arrogant. Are these the ones concerning whom you swore that God would not extend any mercy?" "Enter the Garden! No fear shall come upon you, nor shall you grieve." (Q. 7:46–48)

Although the Quranic commentators offer differing explanations for who might these people be "who know all by their marks," no less for what these marks may be or what fate awaits them, this passage explicitly elaborates a relationship between their position and the striking lucidity it affords. They hope and fear between Garden and Fire; they endure the possibility of relief; they call out to their Lord. Academic and policy literature has established that displaced populations are suspended between national orders and thereby become objects of humanitarian concern. But the discourses and practices of my interlocutors bring a different suspension into view: a form of life whose key gestures (supplication, submission, insight) are illuminated by the Quranic figure of the Heights. These gestures convene a recursive temporality: in dread apprehension of what is to come, which has already been decreed and whose judgment has already shaped the present.[3] The same gestures emerge across otherwise disparate sites as they reflect the same fundamental lesson: you want what you want and I want what I want, and God does as he wills.

To be clear, this does not ignore that my interlocutors are violently displaced across territorial borders in this life, nor does it identify one place or another with the Garden or the Fire. Nor, of course, am I suggesting that displacement is the only historico-political condition giving rise to such an existential condition today. Rather, I show how my interlocutors' form of life is reflected in this Quranic figure of undecidable dislocation. Meanwhile, their gestures fold an intemporal dimension into the moment, underscoring the essential asymmetry between God (*allāh*) and creation (everything other than God, *mā siwā allāh*). ("Theology" is a name for the discourse that concerns itself with that asymmetry.) As in the image by Syrian artist Tammam Azzam that graces the cover of this book, what appears to be a road extending to a distant vanishing point is brought up short. The horizon is strewn with rubble, and some kind of garbage has blocked the way. More radically, the viewer's gaze encounters a limit and is drawn upward: horizontal extension is interrupted by a vertical plane. The journey through the fields and fences of this life does not deliver the observer to a destination beyond the hills; rather, the journey is revealed to be precisely the opening onto a vertical expanse whose vagaries are just as urgent and subtle as the former had seemed. In the image, this confounding is expressed through the interaction between surface and form: the rough uniformity of the asphalt (below/around) against the color and ambiguous depth of the image plane (above/ahead). This insight redoubles back onto the viewer, since it turns out that she is already located on the road whose coordinates have now shifted. That is, the collision between vertical and horizontal extension also encompasses the observer, who does not stand apart from the image or sovereign over her regard. Instead, she is implicated in that scene. This anamorphic procedure emphasizes not one element or another in the field of vision (given proper perspective or its lack) but a limit that cuts up representation.[4] Such an encounter with a limit is exemplary of the insufficiency of creation, for everything that exists was created for *a term appointed* (Q. 46:3).

My research initially took place at Muslim charities and community organizations involved in Syrian refugee support and resettlement. Then it expanded outward, following interlocutors into other spaces. I attended theology classes in a refugee camp in the Jordanian desert and a summer camp for refugee children in Edmonton; I observed Ramadan dinners held in tent settlements at the Jordan-Syria border and financial literacy trainings for newcomer families in Canada. *The Dread Heights* is thus based on fieldwork with refugees, relief workers, and religious scholars, primarily in Jordan and Canada. My interviews started in 2015 and 2016, with eighteen months of concentrated fieldwork across 2018 and 2019, follow-up trips in 2023, and regular communication with my main interlocutors across those years. This fieldwork was focused at four relief organizations but also included supplementary interviews and participant observation at a dozen others, which covered the gamut of Sunni theological and political orientations and included some nonreligious and Christian organizations.

Muslim charitable and community associations have in recent years assumed an unprecedented role in refugee support services in Jordan and Canada (and beyond). And, as shown in the border crisis of summer 2018, they are effective in this field. But Islam is not only a new resource for humanitarian projects. My interlocutors' existential reckoning with their situations, including the uncertainty of the future and how to inherit the past, is shaped by the way they inhabit Islam. Whether refugees, relief workers, or religious scholars, they wonder what fate has brought them there; how exile affects the soul; how new contexts in Jordan and Canada should be traversed. Such questions are not exceptional to these sites, of course. They emerge as part of the everyday work of inhabiting a tradition through the struggles of creational existence. This is because tradition does not guarantee historical meaning but articulates its essential contingency. As explored in this book, tradition offers a space to encounter the unbearable and so becomes the site of an immanent transformation. In the shadow of the war, of displacement and devastation, indeed well beyond the limitations of the humanitarian order, Islamic traditions offer an orientation to the insufficiency of the present. God, grant relief!

ISLAM AND SYRIAN REFUGEE SUPPORT IN JORDAN AND CANADA

As narrated further in Chapter 3, in 2011 police arrested and tortured children who were suspected of scrawling anti-regime graffiti on a school wall in the southern Syrian city of Daraa. Security forces fired on several thousand protestors with water cannons and live ammunition; the protests spread to other cities across the country, with their revolutionary demands escalating from accountability and the removal of certain police chiefs ultimately to the fall of the regime itself. And that regime deployed collective starvation and indiscriminate bombardment, disappearance and siege.[5] Opposition factions splintered and militarized. The resulting displacements and migrations to Turkey, Lebanon, Jordan, and beyond reached a massive magnitude. During my fieldwork in Jordan in 2018, for example, there were about 650,000 Syrians registered there as refugees, although the total number of Syrians in the country was often described as well over a million. Today about 150,000 of these people live in refugee camps, with the rest mostly in northern cities, in Amman, or in informal tent settlements.

As I was preparing my fieldwork grant applications, I came across a 2014 report surveying the massive humanitarian activities of Islamic charities serving Syrian refugees in Jordan and Lebanon. The United Nations High Commissioner for Refugees (UNHCR) data portal reports yearly funding requirements of an average USD 1.1 billion over 2013–18 for its Syrian refugee regional response in Jordan—and an average USD 376 million shortfall over those same six years. There simply isn't enough funding to provide the health, education, cash support, and other programs that UNHCR seeks. "This gap in humanitarian assistance," the report states, "is being filled by Islamic charities and community-based organisations. Their procedures for humanitarian assistance programmes are simple and informal, and their assistance is easy to access—especially in villages or areas with security concerns."[6] Such local associations and organizations are often less formalized (and so have less bureaucratic overhead), have different forms of access to local networks (through religious neighborhood associations), and have access to different donor streams (charity and alms coming from the Gulf but also donors in the West and elsewhere). In 2013, for instance, a year when there was a 240-million-dollar shortfall for UNHCR programs in Jordan, Gulf organizations (based in Saudi Arabia, Kuwait, Qatar) provided nearly 140 million dollars of humanitarian assistance coordinated through local Islamic charities.[7]

Yet all this activity raised other questions for the international aid sector. The report continues, "Concern has been rising among both humanitarian actors and refugees that some of these charities not only offer humanitarian assistance, but also religious and political thought, or even make assistance dependent on the religion or political affiliation of refugees."[8] For example, drawing directly on Islamic legal precepts, many such organizations have special allocations for the families of the martyred and the disappeared—namely, the widows and children of those killed or detained while protesting or fighting the Assad regime. According to the stipulated impartiality and secularity of proper humanitarian work, such activities are both too political and too religious.

Islamic charitable organizations certainly do, as the report presents, "fill gaps" in international humanitarian assistance. For instance, the UNHCR-funded clinic in the north Jordanian town of Ramtha closed with only one week's notice, referring all its patients to the UNHCR-funded Caritas clinic in Irbid fifteen kilometers away. This left a local Islamic charity's health clinic the sole medical facility serving the tens of thousands of Syrians in the Ramtha area. Its director and staff nurse, a young thin man in a white medical coat, shook his head vigorously as he insisted to me in June 2018 that expecting these patients to travel to Irbid was simply unreasonable. Many of them had already traveled a good distance to the town from informal tent settlements along the border. The number of patients at his clinic had thus multiplied, though its funding had not proportionally increased. This funding was already strained, he had explained when we first met six months earlier. Jordanian government subsidies for Syrian healthcare had recently been drastically cut, meaning that Syrians would have to pay 80 percent (not 30 percent) of the "foreigner rate" to access public healthcare services in Jordan. No other organizations nearby were now covering services like blood transfusions, he said, but they continued to do what they could with the funding they had (mostly given by wealthy Muslim donors in Kuwait). By the time I visited in 2023, although Syrian refugees had been further integrated into the healthcare system, government support for some procedures had been cut entirely. Meanwhile, the health center had expanded its facilities to another floor of the building.

Every day the Islamic charity posted on its social media which services would be available the next day (based on which of its rotating roster of doctors would be on site). A typical listing read:

> Clinics on Thursday, June 14, 2018, God willing: General medicine. Neurosurgery, spine surgery (doctor: —). Internal medicine (doctor: —). Women's clinic (consultant: —). Urology (doctor: —). Oral and dental medicine (doctor: —). Physical and occupational therapy—for males. Ramtha: 50 meters south of the bus depot. For inquiries call ——.

They also circulated a list of the five to ten most urgent medical cases to their WhatsApp networks of pious donors, giving a brief description of the necessary treatment along with how much it would cost. The impressive work of this facility, long after the abrupt closure of the town's UNHCR-funded clinic, neatly illustrates how local Islamic charitable organizations in Jordan "fill gaps" in international aid.

Islam has also become important to Syrian refugee support on the other side of the world. Since its Immigration Act of 1978, Canada has uniquely allowed for privately sponsored refugee settlement alongside its government-assisted refugee programs.[9] "Private sponsorship" encompasses refugee sponsorship by recognized nongovernmental organizations; by groups of at least five Canadians who together pledge money and time to support the newcomer family; by community sponsors like family businesses; and, since 2013, by a joint program in which sponsor groups split the cost of refugee sponsorship with the government. Admissibility of the refugee applicant is straightforward at least in principle, requiring only medical, security, and criminal checks as well as a UNHCR determination of refugee status. And resettled refugees (whether government-assisted or privately sponsored) are guaranteed federal health coverage as well as twelve months of financial support.

Religion was always important to such private refugee sponsorship in Canada. In 1979, the first organization to sign a sponsorship agreement with the federal government was the Mennonite Central Committee. Through their church, my own Mennonite grandparents sponsored an Eritrean family to move to Saskatchewan and supported them through subsequent decades. Even today the vast majority of the 100+ Sponsorship Agreement Holder organizations are faith-based organizations (mostly Christian).[10] Since the Syrian war, however, as refugee support and resettlement agencies serve Syrian newcomers to Canada, many of these agencies have reached out to mosques and Muslim organizations across the country to provide "cultural and religious relevance." As in Jordan (if for different reasons), humanitarian offices have come to see Islam as a resource for Syrian refugee support.

In late 2015 the Syrian war's displacement of millions of people became an election issue in Canada. The so-called refugee crisis at the Mediterranean had made news headlines for months, and the United Nations had appealed for international assistance in resettling Syrian refugees. Then–Prime Minister Stephen Harper pledged that Canada would resettle 10,000 refugees from Syria and Iraq over three years—and added that the government would resettle an additional 10,000 refugees from persecuted minorities (Middle Eastern Christians and Yazidis) if the Conservative party were reelected. The opposition Liberal party's Citizenship and Immigration critic ridiculed this anemic response to the Syrian crisis as "lip service." With an election looming in late October, the Liberal party leader Justin Trudeau pledged to resettle 25,000 Syrian refugees by the end of the very same calendar year.

At the beginning of September 2015, the image of a Syrian toddler's drowned body on a Turkish beach flashed across the world. It quickly emerged that the child had a family connection to Canada and that their resettlement application had been dismissed based on bureaucratic factors. The Syrian refugee crisis was already an election topic but was galvanized through the broad recognition (and horror) that the government response could already have been otherwise.[11] The Liberal Party swept to power and began a concerted effort to resettle Syrian refugees to Canada. It took resettlement agencies four months, not two, to bring 25,000 Syrians to the country, but these efforts continued long past that initial campaign promise. They reached over 86,000 resettlements to Canada as of the 2021 census.[12]

My fieldwork in Canada began after that initial campaign in 2015, but the processes set in motion by that government project continued. In Edmonton, where I conducted most of my Canada-side fieldwork, I loosely based my interviews and observations at the Islamic Family and Social Services Association (IFSSA). Its volunteers and outreach workers drive newcomers to the mosque during Ramadan and to the hospital in emergencies; they host Eid dinners and hold a summer camp at an Islamic school; they handle paperwork for incoming families, coordinate with host families, and manage incoming donations. The support capacity of this organization had grown exponentially in response to the refugee crisis as it coordinated with other social service associations to welcome hundreds of Syrian newcomers. Indeed, its experience in providing refugee support eventually led it to seek (and, in 2019, to gain) Sponsorship Agreement Holder status of its own with the federal government, meaning that it could now sponsor refugees directly.

Yūnus, a real estate developer, explained to me in August 2019 that a confluence of factors had led to fall 2015 being a time of new opportunities. As an IFSSA board member, he had coordinated a resolution that the organization do what it could to join the refugee support effort. "There's no way in hell we can change the outcome of the Syrian war from here, from a city on the other side of the world. But we live in Canada, whose private sponsorship plan gives us a line to the government." According to the agreement he arranged, IFSSA worked with established Sponsorship Agreement Holder associations (Catholic Social Services and the Mennonite Central Committee), liaising with the Edmonton Muslim community and acting as the constituency group that would assist in refugee settlement and support. He trained volunteers to help complete sponsorship applications and met with sponsoring families to clarify the terms of their memorandum of understanding.

Since the resolution Yūnus coordinated, IFSSA had sponsored nearly four hundred refugees. He independently assisted in the sponsorships of hundreds more. Two Syrian newcomer sisters in Edmonton described him as their "angel": they told me that he spoke with them by phone as they were on a Turkish beach desperately preparing for a treacherous sea crossing. "Don't despair," he had pleaded: "we can bring you to Canada another way."

He has an aptitude for working with others (settlement workers at other agencies spoke of him in the highest terms) and a facility with bureaucratic niceties. "It all just rests on the art of presentation. Cross your Ts, dot your Is. [The Ministry of] Immigration will work with you, as long as you don't misrepresent yourself. We have a chance here to change people's lives, if we stop thinking only about ourselves." But as our conversation concluded, his determination turned grimmer. "Remember that hadith about the Prophet saying that when one part of the *umma* [Community] hurts, the rest of the body feels it? Where's that feeling today? Instead, our own leaders give our oppressors awards and honors. What a horrific situation." He referred to the United Arab Emirates awarding Indian prime minister Narendra Modi its highest civilian award even after Indian troops imposed a curfew and blackout on occupied territory in Kashmir. What elsewhere indicts Muslim charities—namely, that they are too partial, serving the *umma* instead of embracing a truly universal mandate—is not only *not* a cause for suspicion: it is solicited in Canada by a refugee support apparatus that, through the bureaucracy of Sponsorship Agreement Holder associations and the private sponsorship system, deploys Muslim charitable practices (including their *umma* discourses) for its own purposes.[13]

In both Jordan and Canada, if for different reasons, Islam has thus become a resource for humanitarian work. But speaking of "filling a gap" in relief programs (as in Jordan) or "providing cultural proximity" for Muslim newcomers (as in Canada) maintains the secular perspective of the international aid regime, perceiving only how Islam becomes available for humanitarian projects. In part for that reason, this book does not extend the trenchant anthropological critiques of humanitarianism to the charities at which I did my fieldwork. Scholars have shown that humanitarian interventions produce complex spaces of exception; divide humanity into a complex hierarchy of benefactors and beneficiaries; and in fact take disasters, epidemics, or conflicts as occasions for practicing a new type of government.[14] Although I have learned much from this literature, *The Dread Heights* does not repeat its arguments about Muslim organizations supporting refugees in Jordan and Canada. This is not to say that those organizations should be immune from such critiques; indeed, it is often difficult to tell what distinguishes so-called faith-based organizations from their secular counterparts (see Chapter 1), and important studies have helped us understand how such organizations are conscripted or even structured by powerful economic and political formations (neoliberalism, multiculturalism, governmentality). But this book seeks to understand something else: not how Islam fills gaps in the humanitarian order or is transformed in that process but how specific contemporary Islamic discourses and practices—their grammar of concepts—stage the struggles of creational existence. In revolution and war, at the very encounter with what is unbearable: God, grant relief!

TOWARD AN ETHNOGRAPHY OF THEOLOGY

I had begun studying the Levantine Islamic scholastic tradition in Damascus in 2004–5. I knew that following the Syrian revolution and the regime's repression many of my former teachers and friends had fled to Turkey, Jordan, and the West. I first came to this project seeking to follow the wartime interruption of that knowledge-tradition exiled from the institutions that had supported it. Some of the projects I engaged in my fieldwork were indeed formally structured toward inheriting sharia knowledge (whether Levantine scholasticism or Gulf Salafism); some of those efforts appear in this book. But I soon realized that the questions that drove my research belonged to a different genre. Rather than following how the war had displaced an Islamic tradition of knowledge, I wanted to understand the devastation of the war through that tradition.

Following a methodological distinction offered by Michel-Rolph Trouillot, then, this book draws on fieldwork conducted among Muslim projects of Syrian refugee support, not to empirically document such projects' vast range nor to discursively trace a genealogy of modern Islamic thought, but in order to follow how the Islamic tradition encounters the Syrian war. In Trouillot's terms, the former projects are my "object of observation" while the latter encounter is my "object of study."[15] Across the chapters to follow, *The Dread Heights* puts anthropological literature and critical theory into conversation with Islamic texts and practices rather than treating the latter merely as material to be analyzed. That is, I seek to conceptualize, not just contextualize, my ethnographic topics through Islamic grammars.[16] The analysis offered here is not an ethnographic contextualization of Islamic theology: the preposition in the book's subtitle ("*after* the Syrian revolution") does not signal a historical rupture in how "tribulation" and "refuge" are theologically conceptualized, nor does it promise a revolutionary political theology.[17] Rather, I examine the ways the Islamic tradition guides adherents as they traverse the devastations wrought by the war.

This approach does not presume that my interlocutors are paragons of piety or that their religiosity simply requires this field of reference. Here I follow a methodological recommendation for the anthropology of Islam famously advanced by Talal Asad in a 1985 lecture, when he offered "tradition" as an analytic category that might allow the anthropologist to perceive, among other things, the play of differing but overlapping temporalities and an aspiration to coherence in discourse and practice. This concept of tradition promised to avoid prioritizing either homogeneity or heterogeneity, to draw together past, present, and future in considering the apt performance of a practice, to include specific forms of reasoning and argument, and to account for the productions of power and styles of resistance.[18] A tradition, in the sense refined by Asad since then, "is a set of aspirations, sensibilities, felt obligations, and relationships of subjects who live and move in the multiple times of a common world—whence the possibilities for disagreement."[19] A tradition is not a self-enclosed domain. It is always inhabited variously and necessarily incompletely. Following this insight, the anthropology of Islam has included inquiries into contemporary Islamic ethics, law, politics, psychology, and more.

Inspired by these methodological sensibilities, *The Dread Heights* offers an ethnography of Islamic theology. By this I do not mean just that my fieldwork involved reading theological texts alongside certain interlocutors, that the political theology of modern humanitarianism deserves anthropological critique, or that theology is lived at the level of the everyday. Rather, I seek to understand how the Islamic tradition articulates the struggles of creational existence at my field sites. For example, the imperative to learn and teach the Quran led a civil-engineer-turned-sharia-student to stay in Zaatari Refugee Camp long after he could have resettled to Canada; at a financial literacy training session, Syrian newcomer women in Canada debated how best to practice trusting reliance on God. The articulation of such problems, returning to them, lingering with them, were routinely at stake in these sites. Such questions animate concern into the shape of one's life, the status of one's relationships, the future horizon—and do so whether one is a refugee or not, whether one is displaced or exiled or not, however sophisticated one's theological learning may be. Although many of my interlocutors were learned in Islam, it was clear that such questions were not the prerogative of religious scholars alone. Nor were their answers. Whether refugees, relief workers, or religious scholars (certainly overlapping categories), my interlocutors inhabit Islamic grammars in finding their way. Their work is neither legible to qualitative political science nor available to the methods of intellectual history. This inquiry is thus resolutely ethnographic: these discourses and practices cannot be taken for granted nor read as transparent, as though their force or significance could be perceived apart from the concrete singularity of one's life. My questions are (also) theological but resist the epistemological and ethical boundaries by which this term is conventionally circumscribed. Yet this is not merely a recourse to "folk categories": as Saba Mahmood writes, any adequate analysis must attend to "the terms of being, affectivity, and responsibility that constituted the grammar of [these] actions," not only for purposes of ethnographic description but because "attention to such terms and concepts is necessary to rethinking analytical questions."[20] (This is one way the method pursued in this book differs from the anthropological conceit of understanding a society "in its own terms.")[21]

As part of its disciplinary self-reckoning, anthropology has seen an increased reflexivity regarding its own methodological "atheism," including the sense that anthropologists ought to more seriously probe the limits, affordances, and capacities of theological discourses in making sense of realities "beyond the human horizon."[22] Following the critical anthropology of secularism, this developing disciplinary conversation has assayed an anthropology "within and without the secular condition."[23] It has provincialized the prevailing scholarly method that promises to release the anthropologist into historical consciousness through the secular critique of religion. From the perspective of the orientations traced in this book, such critical operations—assigning the discourses and practices of my interlocutors the appropriate historical frame of reference to make them legible as social and political subjects—in fact refuse their opening to the incommensurable. By contrast, the grammatical forms of the Islamic tradition revolve around the essential ambivalence of creational existence—where, for example, violence and abandonment can at once tear and open a life, whose meaning must finally be divinely disclosed. Islamic grammars of concept and practice insist on this possibility, which is illegible to modern humanitarianism and opaque to secular social science. The force and significance of both world-historical and intimate events are already inflected by the impersonal testimony of the Day of Judgment. To be clear, my effort is less to identify anthropology with theology than to, as Asad writes, "confront anthropology with theology, not to encourage the former to draw on the latter (still less, to translate 'religion' opportunistically) but to draw on the latter to provoke the former."[24]

As shown in this introduction, Muslims in widely different contexts describe their work as motivated by fellow-feeling toward the Islamic Community (*umma*), against the abandonment of the Community by Muslim state leaders—these interlocutors each citing the famous prophetic hadith that "the parable of the faithful in their affection, mercy, and compassion for one another is of a body; when a [single] limb aches, the entire body reacts with sleeplessness and fever." Rather than only assessing how their citations of this text make sense according to their respective contexts (an interpretive procedure that bears the burden of establishing a commensurability between these disparate citations), I already grant that they commonly engage an Islamic tradition whose contours are not simply a function of its historical present. A tradition, understood as "an argument extended in time," and however it may center the present in articulating past and future, is not defined by that present.[25] In citing this hadith, these aid workers are siting themselves within that tradition. As networks of citation, discursive traditions are not merely ideological reflections of their social contexts and material arrangements.[26] Instead, a discursive tradition is how the grammar of concepts is translated: "The open-ended passing on of behavior and styles of argument in which language and life across generations are intertwined," writes Asad. There, "temporality becomes essential to the ways meaning is made and unmade, where 'inside' and 'outside' are not permanently fixed, because the distinction has to do with what is taken for granted only in and for a particular time."[27] A tradition-oriented inquiry is a way of attending to the complex temporalities of such citations.

Trouillot's distinction between "object of observation" and "object of study" also explains the organization of my field sites in this ethnography. The bulk of my fieldwork took place with refugees, relief workers, and religious scholars in Jordan (primarily Amman, Ramtha, Irbid, and other towns and settlements in north Jordan) and in Canada (primarily Edmonton but also Ottawa, Toronto, and Hamilton), although I also conducted interviews with Canadian and Syrian aid workers in Lebanon and Turkey. Yet this book does not argue for or from the massive differences between these sites. When

Muslim relief workers in Jordan and Canada each cite the same hadith about the *umma* in explaining their commitment, then, I do not take this as an occasion to elaborate the material infrastructure or social ideology that would demystify their actions. This is not an inductive study of Muslim charitable practices in Jordan (context 1) combined with a study of Muslim charitable practices in Canada (context 2), directed toward offering a general statement about contemporary inflections of Muslim charity that would then be theoretically applicable to other contexts. Rather than a multi-sited ethnography, this book offers an ethnography of a multi-sited tradition.[28] Instead of making an inductive argument (maintaining the critical distance necessary to reason from particular contexts toward the general), my interlocutors push me toward abduction.[29] Instead of referring my interlocutors' respective concepts to their "historical and cultural environments," following Stefania Pandolfo, "I want to take them into account for what they can elucidate, for the worlds they make possible, within and in spite of the gap of translation."[30] I seek not to cut cleanly through the appearance of things to the reality hiding behind, but to attend to their opacity in a different sense: without trying to represent or capture the impossible, rather to allow for the possibility of impossibility. Hear, again, the refrain—in Jordan, in Canada, after the war and after this life: God, grant relief!

RELIGIOUS, SECULAR, POLITICAL THEOLOGY

On February 6, 2023, a series of massive earthquakes struck southern Turkey and northwest Syria. The ground heaved and buildings buckled. Over 60,000 people were killed and hundreds of thousands were made homeless. International humanitarian organizations quickly mobilized emergency operations—but not to the region held by the rebels in northwest Syria. Only one international border crossing had been authorized by the UN Security Council for entry into the rebel-held enclave, and even there, by three days later, only a small (previously scheduled) delivery of tents had crossed from Turkey. Raed al-Saleh, the leader of the White Helmets (the Syria Civil Defense rescue organization), denounced the international bureaucracy and territorial politics that left thousands of Syrians to die, trapped under concrete slabs and rubble. Of course, as he well knew, international bureaucracy and territorial politics had already long abandoned Syrians to die under concrete slabs and rubble. The exiled Syrian intellectual Yassin al-Haj Saleh called it "Syria's catastrophe upon catastrophe": "The international community—if one really exists—has for years passively dealt with the Syrian crisis as if it were a natural disaster, and it didn't change course when a real one struck."[31] He wrote:

> This catastrophe would not have happened were it not for the rest of the world normalizing death in Syria for so many years. State-centered international organizations like the U.N. have legitimized governments even when they are genocidal ones like President Bashar al-Assad's. His regime, which has been destroying homes and killing Syrians with barrel bombs and cluster munitions for years with the help of its Russian and Iranian supporters, is also the only channel through which these same people can get humanitarian aid. Earthquakes do not recognize national borders, but the U.N. does.

Al-Haj Saleh concluded with the compounding unreality of the situation:

> What hinders many people from making sense of the situation in Syria is that it really is unbelievable. The level of suffering transcends human measure in scale, in duration and in intensity. This is what Hannah Arendt called the "shock of reality" and "the stark, naked brutality of facts, of things as they are." It is unbelievable that more than 600,000 people have been killed since 2011, close to 15,000 tortured to death, more than 100,000 forcibly disappeared, 7 million made refugees in other countries—and now 90 percent of the population left in Syria is under the poverty line.

The son of one of my interlocutors in Jordan, who had refused to reconcile with the regime and accept its terms for an amnesty, was now a schoolteacher in the rebel-held region. He circulated an appeal for aid. Two weeks later, he sent a video of a South Asian aid worker who had arrived from Qatar with trucks of emergency supplies. In rapid and eloquent Arabic, this man declared:

> This earthquake is ordained by God the glorified and exalted: we accept it. But never the tyranny (*ẓulm*) that came with it: the delayed arrival of search-and-rescue teams and heavy machinery, which could have saved so many. Against all that, we see here nothing less than a model from the days of the [prophet's] companions: they would help one another,

> cooperate among themselves, however they were afflicted. The prophetic virtues, the Muhammadan qualities, which we read about in books—we see them realized here among the Syrian people, both Kurds and Arabs, together.

For al-Haj Saleh, the Syrian catastrophe confounds every "human measure"; the suffering is "unbelievable" because of its scale, duration, and intensity; and the history of international responses to the regime's brutality has blurred the philosophical demarcation of natural and moral evils. For the South Asian aid worker, the relevant distinction is between the divine decree and human tyranny, which has demanded the enactment of prophetic virtues (generosity, hospitality, mercy) in the midst of the affliction. Read together, and however else they differ, these two responses to the 2023 earthquake present a stark delimitation of humanitarian logics. As with the Jordan-Syria border crisis in 2018, an adequate response to human suffering will not be obtained from cleaving again to humanitarian principles (humanity, neutrality, impartiality, independence). The actually existing international humanitarian regime, understood from rebel-held northwest Syria after the 2023 earthquake, is deeply imbricated in the same modern system of sovereign brutality and human tyranny that it claims to address.

Ironically, it is another earthquake, the leveling of Lisbon in 1755, that is routinely cited by scholarly literature on humanitarianism as the first modern disaster: the event that gave rise to a social scientific attitude, the emergence of a notion of brute suffering (to be rationally understood and alleviated), and ultimately the humanitarian discovery of a secular value for life. More directly, that earthquake's devastation is said to have shaken the ground of eighteenth-century theological optimism, inaugurating a new world released from the hold of religious theodicy.[32] The world-historical status of the Lisbon earthquake may be overstated across these references, but the cultural historian Marie-Hélène Huet observes that nonetheless "the selection of Lisbon as a modern disaster is . . . a judgment on the way we think of the time in which we live: an age when uncontrollable disasters always threaten the fragile order we have imposed on chaos."[33]

What was once an extraordinary event, Didier Fassin writes of the Lisbon earthquake, has become an "element of our everyday experience. We are used to the global spectacle of suffering and to the global display of assistance. Images of disasters, famines, and wars, of aid organizations and relief operations, have become familiar to us. They form the moral and emotional landscape of the age of humanitarianism in which we live."[34] Such images are variously mediated to distant observers for their practice of sympathy, although the political force of these moral sentiments is always modulated by the protocols of the current visual rhetoric.[35] Whatever sympathy is made available through humanitarianism—that is, the political traction afforded by broadcasting such images—is ironically compromised by its own exposure. In other words, when the virtue of universal benevolence is explicitly thematized as extending across distance, we should not be surprised if that distance proves difficult to breach.

The philosopher Charles Taylor celebrates this sensibility as a distinctly modern achievement: "We routinely grumble about our lack of concern and note disapprovingly that it requires often spectacular television coverage of some disaster to awaken the world's conscience. But this very critique supposes certain standards of universal concern. It is these which are deeply anchored in our moral culture."[36] He describes modern humanitarian sensibilities as indebted both to the Christian notion of universal love and to Enlightenment critiques of Christianity. By this account, humanitarianism rests on how to understand human suffering: it is driven by a secularized problem of theodicy. Yet for some commentators, tracing the historical and structural relations between Christianity and humanitarianism poses a "mortal threat" to the latter's "very identity."[37] Given its conceit of being a "force" of this-worldly "salvation," remarking the political theology of modern humanitarianism in this way fundamentally undermines its legitimacy.[38]

A century after the Lisbon earthquake came the 1859 Battle of Solferino (a French-Sardinian victory over Austria), whose carnage comprises the other origin point commonly identified for modern humanitarianism. The Genevan businessman Henry Dunant's bestselling testimony to the abandoned soldiers' suffering sparked a mass European campaign that by 1863 had created the International Committee of the Red Cross.[39] Distinct from earlier acts of compassion in that it is "organized and part of governance, connects the immanent to the transcendent, and is directed at those in other lands,"[40] modern humanitarianism from Lisbon, Solferino, and beyond is "co-dependent" with the world it has shaped.[41] Analytically, Michael Barnett writes, this "revolution in the ethics of care" cannot be understood through the story it tells for itself—not least because (like other bourgeois revolutions) it is "a matter of faith": "humanitarianism begins and ends with faith, it sustains and is sustained by faith. But faith is not one of a kind."[42]

In contrast to humanitarian "faith," Fassin proposes a general logic of "humanitarian reason."[43] As more than one element among others of the modern social imaginary, Fassin writes that the generalization of moral sentiments into a frame of reference for political life ("humanitarian government") is the "distinctive feature of contemporary societies."[44] The concept of the human inherited from the Enlightenment divides the person into biological life and political life, a division that grants two principles: "that all lives are equally sacred and that all sufferings deserve to be relieved."[45] The universalist politics produced by these principles thus includes the absolute imperative to maintain bare life but also the utilitarian imperative to alleviate suffering. The first of these is indifferent to how life is qualified, but the second requires a decision on which suffering is gratuitous and which redemptive. Humanitarian government declares the sacredness of life and the redemption of suffering. Thereby it "prolongs and renews the Christian legacy" as it confronts what is "intolerable about the state of the contemporary world."[46]

Yet humanitarianism's mode of confrontation refuses the unbearable. It insists rather on its recuperation and deployment: as the (Christian) heart of contemporary politics, humanitarian intervention and government here acquire a salvific power.[47] "By saving lives, it saves something of our idea of ourselves . . . by relieving suffering, it also relieves the burden of this unequal world order." Although Fassin himself does not elaborate this conclusion, the promise of humanitarian reason offers a melancholic yearning for a community "beyond any obligation," for relations between subjects "beyond any subjection."[48] Humanitarian reason for Fassin finally delivers us to the desire (long familiar from Christian political theology) for a human community of grace, released from the bonds of division and law. This is not incidental: Asad observes that, given the first theological usages of the term "humanitarian," the word "carries traces of the Christian idea of redemption, of Christ the Redeemer of humanity. Reaching out compassionately to another's pain (or sin) not only redeems individuals who are endangered but also elevates humanity as a whole."[49] These "traces" are not historical curiosities or evidence of incomplete secularization; they activate a redemptive power within the secular rhetoric of modern humanitarianism.

From humanitarianism as the secular repudiation of Christian theodicy and the discovery of a secular value for life to the desperate thought that humanitarian faith may be nothing other than the renewed inheritance of Christianity, the political theology of modern humanitarianism is essentially marked by a problem of legitimacy. The theorists and critics of humanitarianism anxiously establish its proximity to or distance from Christianity, its proper universality, its ambivalent relation to religious traditions of charity and refuge.[50] My interlocutors are not sequestered away from this humanitarian world: indeed, much of Chapter 1 of this book investigates how they engage the secular grammar of the international humanitarian regime. As shown there, the practices of secular humanitarianism and religious charity cannot always be neatly distinguished. Meanwhile, the polemical demands made of this research project, as of my interlocutors, routinely hinged on disarticulating religion and politics (rehearsing a secular operation within the terms of analysis).

By contrast, this book relinquishes both the liberal goal of establishing the humanitarian legitimacy of Islamic charities and the critical-theoretical ambition of establishing structural analogies or historical filiations between these projects.[51] Rather, it follows how Islamic grammars foreground the insufficiency of creation. This tradition does not refuse the unbearable by recuperating the present.[52] Instead, it impresses upon us the grave reminder that *everything is perishing except His Face* (Q. 28:88). This does not mean my interlocutors are politically quietist, of course. Rather, their styles of action are shaped by this truth. Whether refugees, relief workers, or religious scholars, they struggle to hold on to this lesson in revolution and war, displacement and refuge. God, grant relief!

IF DEATH IS NOT THE END

In her final publication, the late Saba Mahmood reflected on death as the limit of humanist conceptions of flourishing. She then observed that the devastation of Syria divulges the inadequacy of humanitarian reason, whose relational approach to the death of the other is meant to spur political change:

> When I look around at the inaction of world powers to stop mass starvation, rampant in Yemen today, for example, or the genocide conducted

in Aleppo and Raqqa recently, I doubt that these failures of action resulted from a lack of a proper ethical orientation. While some may have not been moved by the images the media projected to the world, there is no lack of empathy among most of the world's inhabitants for these catastrophes. These events unfolded owing to political reasons that require a different analytic than one focused on our lack of care for the other.[53]

This book responds in some fashion to Mahmood's invitation to seek out a different analytic for approaching a situation of mass violence—not just to particularize the universality of humanitarian reason but to recognize (as she also knew) that death is not the end. My interlocutors lead us away both from simply confirming global failures of empathy and from merely critiquing human finitude. I elaborate their discourses and practices within the terms of the Islamic tradition, not according to a generic vocabulary that is available to be abstracted and transposed to other sites or contexts, or that can be mobilized as an alternative "theory" of displacement or refuge.[54] The position of the dread Heights offers an awful lucidity that obtains recursively across the search for refuge, the cleaving of community, the variegations of life's trials, and the ultimately enigmatic divine decree.

This introduction has presented a methodological statement of the project. The remainder of the book proceeds along distinct modes of argument: Chapter 1 variously stages a confrontation between the anthropology of humanitarianism and the anthropology of secularism; through juxtaposing four distinct articulations, Chapter 2 ethnographically develops the tropics of a theological figure; Chapter 3 traces the texture of a singular struggle. Between the chapters of this book lie "thresholds" which insist that politically different forms of life are implicated in zones of indistinction. Rather than marking an exceptional problem of passage for displaced refugees, that is, these thresholds underscore the common dis/orientations of creational life. The brief afterword was composed after the Assad regime fell in December 2024.

Chapter 1 ("Refuge") traces how Islam shapes certain Muslim humanitarian projects in Jordan and Canada. The first section complicates the politics of religious solidarity. It locates contemporary relief work against historiographical and political-theological debates over how to conceptualize the Muslim Community. The second section troubles the acts of secular translation that generally mediate humanitarianism and religion. It examines how the director of one activist organization insists on locating charity and humanitarian aid within the same moral economy. The third section explores the problem of representing suffering in Muslim humanitarian spaces. The powers of the image and expressive form are contested across different media. The fourth section traces how the object of Islamic pedagogy in these sites is often less imparting information about religion than shaping the character of the exiled. A concluding section then gathers these four fields together, with a view to how they convene the patient work of making refuge. Whether practicing solidarity, translating responsibility, representing suffering, or transmitting the tradition, these spaces of refugee support are thoroughly infused by Islamic discourses and practices.

The first Threshold begins with a theatrical production by a Syrian playwright now living in Canada, in which, after the main character's young son drowns in the sea crossing to Europe, she returns to Aleppo, a city now in ruins and populated by the ghosts of life before the war. For many of my interlocutors, such a possibility of a new beginning, which Arendt famously called natality but which here has an eschatological referent, is something to be constantly endured, neither altogether relinquished nor celebrated.

Chapter 2 ("Tribulation") develops a "grammar" of tribulation. Each of its four major sections pursues one permutation of this theological figure, grounding key interlocutors' articulations of the ordeal (*fitna, ibtilā'*) of the Syrian war in their temporal sensibilities and ethico-political commitments. The primary interlocutors of this chapter are each engaged in projects of communal repair; they each understand the catastrophe of the war as marking an existential corruption. But how they respond to the divine trial expresses very different political and ethical relations. To be clear, admitting a divine trial does not give security against its ravages or its pain, but it can allow for an ethical engagement with the unbearable—opening a confrontation where one's very existence is at stake. For the director of an Islamic education program in Zaatari Refugee Camp, witnessing the divine trial requires the acceptance of sacrifice and distinguishing between degrees of affliction. For a Salafi exile whose revolutionary television program taught rebel fighters the law of jihad, engaging the divine trial yields a strenuous reckoning with the corrosive drift of idolatry. For activists at an Islamic charity serving refugees in Amman, the divine trial is the secret means by which God distributes the worldly occasions of good or ill. And for a teacher at an Islamic school in Edmonton who embraced Sufism decades ago in Damascus, the divine trial is disclosive: not of a single rule or divine habit but of the evanescent dynamic of outer meaning and inner reality. Taken together, these interlocutions offer an ethnographic constellation of contemporary Islamic theology, with the Syrian war debated respectively by a pragmatic pedagogue, a Salafi scholar, a lay activist, and a Sufi mystic. The final section of this chapter then gathers these articulations together to formally consider their distinct orientations.

The second Threshold sketches the alternating horizons of one of my interlocutors in Zaatari Refugee Camp: between returning to Syria, resettling to Canada, or remaining in Zaatari. Despite the difficulties of daily life in the camp, it was there that he rediscovered religion. His ambivalence about where to go has less to do with realigning his psychic topography than with the melancholic spatialization of a temporal schema in which the present (Zaatari) holds in tension—without ever fully eclipsing—encounters with a destroyed past (Syria) and an abandoned future (Canada).

Chapter 3 ("The Heights") lingers in the borderland between Jordan and Syria, in the hiatus between violence and repair, where boundaries and limits turn porous and disorientating. This chapter presents one man's testimony of the violence that has torn his life and opened it to new forms of care, which then redouble into traumatic returns. Once an imam in Daraa, at the mosque celebrated as the birthplace of the Syrian revolution, then tortured and hunted by the Syrian regime, he now serves as steward of an orphanage funded by an Islamic charity. His practices of care and memory—the movements of gentleness—bring into stark relief the force of the essentially enigmatic divine decree. His testimony expresses, with an unsentimental lucidity inseparable from his dislocation, the fundamental gestures of creational existence: encountering the limit and insufficiency of creation, turning again and again in search of succor (for only God is *al-ghaniyy*, the sufficient). Here every guarantee is withdrawn, refuge is made and unmade, and no single articulation of the divine ordeal is adequate. He is left with his reiterated entreaties for relief: the position of the dread Heights.

1

REFUGE

The Muslim refugee support efforts I observed across my fieldwork in Jordan and Canada included winterization campaigns and financial literacy classes, Quran education and iftar dinners. Some of those programs are outlined in this chapter, albeit with a view not to cataloguing this transnational sector but to developing some of its themes: solidarity (community in question), translation (universal vs. particular humanitarianisms), representation (contested depictions of suffering), and pedagogy (transmitting a tradition of obligation). At stake across these themes is precisely the contemporary form of Islamic traditions of refuge, for both refugees and others. In presenting such ethnographic complexity, this chapter stages a confrontation between the anthropology of humanitarianism and the anthropology of secularism. The critiques advanced here precede the more radical departure from a humanitarian frame of analysis in the following chapters.

The ethnographic engagements in this chapter are frequently based at the Jamʿiyyat al-Kitāb wa-l-Sunna (The Association of the Quran and Prophetic Practice), one of the Islamic charities at which I conducted my fieldwork in Jordan. This organization established itself early in Syrian refugee support: for example, in 2013, the year that the number of registered Syrian refugees in Jordan doubled from under 300,000 to nearly 600,000, this organization distributed USD 50 million of aid to 350,000 people (over 45,000 families).[1] It had already been active as a revivalist organization long before the Syrian crisis (see Chapter 2), but rapidly developed its support capacity as these needs increased. (By 2024 and 2025, meanwhile, it directed some of its funds to supporting soup kitchens in Gaza under Israeli bombardment.) Over the course of my fieldwork in 2018 and 2019, I spent many hours with the association's director, Zāyid Ḥammād, a slim man with sharp blue eyes, of moderate height but muscular frame. We would always meet in his office in the Ḥayy Nazzāl neighborhood of East Amman, where I would ask him questions over tea (usually just for me, because he would be fasting) punctuated by phone calls, often from individuals asking if there was any aid available, which he would direct to one branch or another of the organization—or, most frequently, would reply that they should quietly come to the office and receive 20 JOD ($40) for immediate expenses. Although I was impressed by his articulation of the themes pursued in this chapter (solidarity, representation, obligation), to be clear, these were not exceptional to him or his organization. Yet I draw on my fieldwork at the Jamʿiyya repeatedly in order to demonstrate what Talal Asad calls "an aspiration to coherence" in inhabiting a tradition.[2] As noted in the introduction, my aim is not to locate such Muslim organizations of Syrian refugee support outside the humanitarian world but to show how they variously encounter its grammar.

THE RUIN OF COMMUNITY

The academic and policy literature on Muslim humanitarian projects is frequently concerned with whether these Muslims are properly (impartially) serving bare humanity or whether they are parochially (selectively) serving the *umma*, the community of the faithful. This section considers methodological problems raised in social-scientific efforts to grapple with the *umma*, for historians and social scientists have argued that the language of *umma* has been thoroughly transformed by the grammar of the nation-state, such that "*umma*" has been recoded to align with the modern categories of "nation" or "Islamic society." By this account, continued use of the rhetoric of *umma* that ignores such transformations is historically naïve and has dubious implications for contemporary politics. In contrast to that approach, what is of interest to me is not the impersonal voice of history (which tracks the transformation of *umma* from the realm of theology to the modern science of secular geopolitics, for instance) but a set of relationships between speaker and addressee, convened through the act of enunciation, and how they articulate past and future. My interlocutors recognize themselves as part of the Muslim *umma*, as those who follow a certain path or way. And they raise the question of the *umma*—of its mutual accountability, relation, and authority—in terms that are explicitly extraterritorial, international, and intratemporal. What is the *umma* after the demise of its political institutions, the colonial division of its law into state sharia courts and national civil codes, and the postcolonial consolidation of new territorial borders?

The Arabic word *umma* lexically refers to a way, a course, a manner of conduct, and by extension the people of that way; the collective body that follows a certain course, and hence a community.[3] The Quranic sense of *umma* is generic: every community (*umma*) has received a divine "messenger" (Q. 16:36) or "warner" (Q. 35:24) who reminds them of the divine promise and threat before judgment comes to them: *Thus have We made the deeds of every community seem fair unto them. Then unto their Lord shall be their return, and He will inform them of that which they used to do* (Q. 6:108). Communities can disregard the truth of their own deeds, requiring a divine disclosure. And they may be internally divided, as when some from a community heed the divine message while others do not. Yet despite their fraction, they ought to cleave together: *Humankind was but one community, then they differed* (Q. 10:19). Among the multitude of communities, each with their *appointed term* (Q. 10:49) and with their set *rite* (Q. 22:34), the final dispensation distinguishes the believers. The *surrendering community* (*ummatan muslimatan*) fulfills the supplication of Abraham (Q. 2:128) in *calling to the good, enjoining right, and forbidding wrong* (Q. 3:104). Rather than simply being one community among others, the community here divinely addressed inherits, through the finality of the Quranic revelation, a singular mission: *Thus did We make you a middle community, that you may be witnesses for humankind and that the Messenger may be a witness for you* (Q. 2:143).[4]

These themes—unity and the inheritance of a divine mandate, witness, and justice—course through Muslim humanitarian sites. But the emphasis on the *umma* as a political body is not simply the result of postcolonial *ressentiment*, that is, a reaction to the postcolonial division of the world and the secular division of religion from politics. Even in early Islamic history such verses had clear political traction. Ovamir Anjum traces the historical trajectory of this "Community-centered" vision, in which the caliph is accountable to the Community, against a "ruler-centered" Islamic political thought that emerged under the Umayyad dynasty and a "Sunna-centered variant" synthesizing elements of each.[5] (Eventually Sunni political thought effectively "disappeared" the Community from the "political equation," such that a deep cynic of worldly politics like al-Ghazālī could cling to the symbolic necessity of a caliph, regardless of his justice or injustice.)[6] When my interlocutors insist on the political role of the Community, then, they are not simply inventing an Islamic version of popular sovereignty. Instead, they can be understood to recall (now in a postcolonial and globalized world) aspects of the early, Community-centered political vision.

Modern inquiries into the *umma* often survey Quranic or early Islamic articulations and then turn to the contemporary situation. Is the *umma* a fact or an aspiration?[7] It certainly provides an "affective symbol" for modern Muslim politics, idealizing unity in the face of dispersive differences. Yet it is also variously invoked and manipulated by states and nongovernmental bodies. As follows, my effort to consider competing figures of the *umma* in my field sites avoids a diagnostic mode of analysis that would oppose the concept of the *umma* ("ideal") to its political instrumentalization ("reality").

Even translating *umma* as "community" is a complex operation because it cannot be readily located. On the one hand, as a body in symbolic relation to a historical institution (the caliphate), it was implicated in an ethico-juridical regime whose inherited mission was nothing less than the discovery of the divine law. On the other hand, the Islamic juridical categories applied to territory did not correspond to the *umma*'s sociological limits, instead opposing the abode of war (*dār al-ḥarb*, where Muslims do not have the modicum of security that someone will not murder them in their sleep or rob them of their possessions) to the abode of Islam (*dār al-islām*, where God's law is enforced).[8] This legal regime was thus both personal and territorial, in that it applied to conduct between Muslims wherever it occurred and to conduct with anyone if on territory claimed by the Muslim ruler. The further territorialization of Islamic law itself came much later, with some historians dating this achievement as late as the Ottoman integration into the international family of nations.[9] The postcolonial fate of Islamic law (especially in its relation to territory) was often raised by my interlocutors in considering the present state of the *umma*.

The effort of locating the *umma* emerges through multiple conceptual and historical translations of law, theology, and politics. These negotiations resist the methodological realism of social science. For instance, Cemil Aydın insists that *umma* is a properly theological term that today only perpetuates the "illusion" of geopolitical Muslim unity. Aydın argues that *umma* cannot be read to mean the globalized Muslim world—for, he declares, the latter did not exist before the mid-nineteenth century. Living in *dār al-islām*, practicing Islam, even belonging to the *umma* was never a primary identity; instead, he writes, it was always mediated by "imperial ties and local realities."[10] By this account, the concept of *umma*—"an abstract religious term and ideal" whose "permutations were many and endlessly varied"[11]—properly belongs to a nonpolitical domain of diverse religious sensibilities. Faisal Devji makes a similar argument, finding the idea of a single Muslim *umma* not only disingenuous (mystifying its ineluctable politics) but dangerously anti-political (alienating Muslims from politics they could otherwise engage).[12] And Olivier Roy writes that the globalization of Islam has deterritorialized the religion so that neo-fundamentalists seek a purified "new *umma*."[13] A similar association between a "virtual" (because deterritorialized) *umma* and militancy runs through the security and humanitarian policy sectors—for example, in arguments that suicide bombers commit acts of terror against their neighbors because they believe they are virtually helping the *umma* elsewhere.[14]

Yet it is not clear to me that the *umma* discourses across Muslim humanitarian sites simply betray the concept to geopolitics, although certainly its grammar must now account for territorial sovereignty in unprecedented ways. This has already long been the case: earlier in the archives of Islamic reform, the prolific Syrian revivalist Rashīd Riḍā (1865–1935) serialized his book *The Caliphate, or the Supreme Imamate* as a response to the Turkish government's evisceration of the authority of the Ottoman Caliphate. In propounding a doctrine of the caliphate that was adequate to the exigencies of his age, he identifies the electors of the caliph (lit. "those who loose and bind," *ahl al-ḥall wa-l-ʿaqd*) with the "chiefs of the Community and those prominent in rank, in whom the great majority has placed their confidence, so that whomever they choose will be assured of their submission and serve to organize their affairs, secure from their disobedience or rebellion."[15] Riḍā again makes the caliph accountable to the Community. He explicitly attributes coercive power to the *umma*, not the ruler: "True obedience is due only to God, and worldly authority belongs to the body (*jamāʿa*) of the Community. The chief (*raʾīs*) is only a representative of its unity."[16] Importantly, the authority of the *umma* over the ruler is neither "self-originating" nor "self-authorizing" but is a (divinely) "ordained right" (*ḥaqq mashrūʿ*).[17] Although the caliphate gives the *umma* political unity, the authority of the *umma* precedes that political institution.

My interlocutors active in Syrian refugee support repeatedly recommended that I read Riḍā's work: a century later, they remembered his insistence that the unity of the *umma* was both divinely mandated and had to be historically cultivated. And they recalled his involvement in the struggle for an independent Syria. "This is the consciousness (*wa'iyy*) we still need today," one of them said.

As seen across this chapter, my interlocutors were deeply vested in the possibilities of the Muslim *umma* flourishing under postcolonial conditions of state and market. But they differed widely in how they regarded the contemporary situation, as well as in how to inherit the terms of Islamic legal traditions to which they were committed. To be sure, their discourses often reflect what Aydın describes as the "major themes" of pan-Islamism: a notion of Islamic civilization, the reinvention of Islam as universal world religion, a historical decline narrative begging heroic renewal, the positing of longstanding conflict between Islam and the West, a new spatial appreciation for the global reach of Muslims and their number, and an anticolonial, intersectional internationalism.[18] Thus my interlocutors often agreed, despite their differences, that the West was at war with Islam, that the loss of caliph had clouded the political present, that Muslim societies were collectively weakened but could rise together, and more. But their engagements also demonstrate the complexity of the question, showing how the language of *umma* has been conscripted into the geopolitical grammar of a "Muslim world." Talal Asad once wrote about the *umma*-concept and about facile analyses of it as an "imagined community" along the model of a nation that "the crucial point therefore is not that it is imagined but that what is imagined predicates distinctive modes of being and acting."[19] And of being undone. As the *umma* is invoked, lamented, and accused across the sites of my fieldwork, then, I seek not to expose its ideological function but to attend the specific sense of its reference. My interlocutors do not ignore the historical diversity that historians deploy to undermine the idea of a Muslim world. Indeed, it is their affective attachment to the *umma* in all its diversity that accounts for the pain they feel at the constitutive destruction of the world.

▪ ▪ ▪

I had asked Shaykh Zāyid Ḥammād of the Jam'iyyat al-Kitāb wa-l-Sunna about the *umma* in earlier conversations, but at a meeting in March 2018

I specifically mentioned a saying of the Prophet likening the believers to one body. I was remembering the scholarly literature on Islam and humanitarianism, which routinely mentions this hadith as a touchstone for how religion can incite transnational attachments that then are condensed into the figures of the militant, the medic, and the fighter.[20] The hadith is ubiquitous across contemporary Muslim discourses; it was often cited by my interlocutors of varying political and religious commitments in both Jordan and Canada. The report is found in the canons of al-Bukhari and Muslim: "The faithful in their mutual kindness, compassion, and sympathy are just like a body. When one of the limbs suffers, the whole body responds to it with sleeplessness and fever."

Shaykh Zāyid knew the hadith I referred to when I mentioned it; he finished it for me when I forgot the precise phrasing at the end. He supplemented it with another hadith about the *umma*: "My community (*umma*) is like rain: you know not which of it is best, the first of it or the last of it." When I asked how to understand the notion of the *umma* being like a single "body," he laughed a little and said that it is easy to understand, in our time of trials. "The hadith already says what it means: the faithful have mutual concern for one another. But what people don't usually understand," he continued, "is how to practice their obligations to each other." He noticed I was confused. "Unfortunately," he said, "even the Islamic activists (*islāmiyyūn*) don't perceive how their responses to this suffering can be compromised." The hadith describes a situation of affliction, but contemporary forms of response have their own corruption built into them. "Humanitarians don't always respect the dignity of the person they assist, for example."

"What do you mean?" I asked. I wanted him to further explain his perspective on Islamic Community. "I'm also thinking of the Quranic verse that says that *you* (Muslims) *are the best community* (*umma*). . . ."

He continued the verse: *The best community drawn forth from people* (Q. 3:110). "Listen," he said, "we need to finish reading to the end of the verse. It goes on: *you enjoin what is right and forbid what is wrong.* Do you know the Egyptian shaykh al-Sha'rāwi? He has one of the subtlest understandings of this verse. He comments that the first phrase is conditional upon the second, so that the meaning is, you *will be* the best of communities, *if* you enjoin what is right and forbid what is wrong. It does not happen on its own. Consider the other hadiths about *umma*: 'the trial (*fitna*) of my community is wealth.' 'The destruction of my *umma* is in killing one another.'

And then look around the lands of the Muslims: we have wealth but live in poverty; we are one *umma* but have sanctified the Sykes-Picot borders and are killing each other. We can't even stop massacres happening fifty kilometers away."

I was struck by his contrast. How these hadiths are read here clearly marks a difference from both what academics have called the robust pan-Islamism of the early twentieth century and the exhausted market democracy of post-Islamism in the late twentieth century. The abode of Islam (*dār al-islām*), as the home of the *umma*, is rendered radically vulnerable to factors both internal and external. The threats to its integrity are not only from the abode of war (*dār al-ḥarb*) but include the trials of wealth and the destruction of murder. Shaykh Zāyid certainly invokes the discourse of pan-Islamism, but he also departs from it in significant ways. He immediately coupled the hadith of the *umma* being like an aching body with the hadith about the Muslims being like rain, meaning that his narrative of Islamic Community is not simply one of betrayal and loss—Muslims are not here fashioned into an exemplary victim whose suffering is redemptive[21]—but is also an account of unanticipated mercy, of which rain is a paradigmatic Quranic figure.

One of the discursive innovations of pan-Islamism enumerated by Aydın was a new spatial appreciation for Muslims across the world, conceptualized as a global, international, and interconnected space. He had argued that the idea of a "Muslim world" is a secular concept that belongs to the modern science of geopolitics. Although that may well be, the spatialization of the *umma* in Shaykh Zāyid's account is distinctively characterized by corruption and pain. "The Quran tells us we could be the best community among humankind," Shaykh Zāyid laughed bitterly, "if we commanded good and forbade evil. But in their absence we have neither justice (*'adl*) nor flourishing (*i'mār*)." The forms of action available are ruined, and yet we persist among them.

Instead of conceptualizing *umma* at a grand scale, Tahir Zaman writes, scholars should look for it in the neighborly practices of building Islamic community through mutual aid. "The *ummah* manifests itself locally rather than globally—in the establishing of relationships with neighbors."[22] As expressed through the aid work of IFSSA in Canada or the Jam'iyyat al-Kitāb wa-l-Sunna in Jordan, for instance, the efficacy of the *umma* is hard to deny. Islamic Community is here practiced within the space of the humanitarian world, not opposed to it, in a world whose terms are largely already defined (territoriality, border politics) but the closure of whose grammar is far from complete.

The hadith about the believers being like one body was traditionally read as an example (*mathal*) and simile (*tashbīh*) encouraging solidarity in good works. The Levantine scholar Yaḥyā bin Sharaf al-Nawawī (d. 1277) writes in his hadith commentary that reports like this "explicitly amplify the rightful claims of Muslims upon one another and urge them toward mutual compassion and solidarity in whatever is free of sin and not reprehensible."[23] This explains why Shaykh Zāyid immediately passed from the affective image of one body to the obligations it implies, specifically among the fraternity of the faithful. The hadith is ubiquitous across Muslim humanitarian sites, which amplify appeals to the unity of the Islamic Community. A language of unity thus suffuses the domain of Islamic politics and charity today, but its field of reference is ambiguous. The force and significance of its symbolic forms are difficult to distinguish from their evacuation. Yet rather than the community guaranteeing the life of tradition, these forms of destruction ("sleeplessness and fever") are revealed to be a mode of the life of tradition, which finds expression even through the rending of the community. Shaykh Zāyid had noted the possibilities of renewal mortified at every turn through the tribulation of wealth and the devastation of murder as much as by the imposition of colonial borders and civil war. Ruin is a figure of its present life.

As news of Russian bombing campaigns and horrendous torture emerges from Syria into the sites of Muslim humanitarian practice, claims of Islamic unity seem farcical. But then, too, the ruin of community discloses another vantage from which to view the devastated present. "Just like those who came before us," Shaykh Zāyid had concluded, echoing the Quranic injunction to travel through the land to encounter the ruins of those who came before. *Have they not journeyed upon the earth and observed how those before them fared in the end? They were greater than them in strength and left firmer traces upon the earth; yet God seized them for their sins, and they had none to shield them from God* (Q. 40:21). To see the Community ruined is to recognize its place—one's own place—alongside the other peoples who have passed from the face of the earth, destroyed in the end by God against whom there is no other refuge. Maurice Blanchot writes, "Through death the eyes turn back, and this return is the other side, and the other side is the fact of living no longer turned away, but turned back."[24] To see the Community ruined is to occupy the future anterior, to see in its present life how it will have passed from the realm of the living, and so to glimpse in its "cadaverous resemblance" what is already the case. *All things perish, save His Face* (Q. 28:88).

My interlocutors inherit the sensibilities of Muslim unity, their fellow-feeling (as in the hadith) leaving them aching with sleeplessness and fever when one limb suffers. They agree that the Community lacks a sovereignty proper to it, or even the ability to protect its own integrity. Rather than simply discounting the discourse of religious solidarity as a rhetorical device of ideological identification or demonstrating the manifold ways an ideal of Muslim unity is thoroughly undermined, it is more productive to revisit the affective figures of pain and loss through which its fellow-feeling is articulated. In the collective aching body of the Muslims, responsibility is due the believers, indifferent to sovereign borders. The authority of the *umma* is now diffuse, and perhaps it always was so; but it is defined simply by mutual affection, by its practice of complaint in the face of contemporary destruction. The *umma* here traverses territorial borders without presupposing or precluding them. Without justice (*'adl*) or flourishing (*i'mār*), in the wake of the vigorous projects of pan-Islamism and the divergent confessions of post-Islamism, the Community takes the form of its loss. Its incapacitations by murder and wealth, civil war and colonial division, make its continuing disappearance the contemporary mode of its appearance.

TRANSLATING MUSLIM HUMANITARIANISM

Although mentioning Islam at local charities often led to discussions of theological concepts or religious practices (see Chapter 2), doing so at international humanitarian organizations repeatedly resulted in the careful sequestration of religion to its proper (ethical) domain. Though I might gesture toward the religious themes and terms emblazoned on their uniforms and their logos or to the exhorting hadiths prominent in their own promotional material, these interlocutors would clarify that Islam informed their values without making the organization "Islamic." These interlocutors implied that I had misread the acts of translation at play in the humanitarian field in presuming that these words referred to a theologico-political tradition rather than a set of abstracted ethical values.

In one such interview, the program manager for one of the largest NGOs working in Syrian refugee support in Jordan was keen to have me know that they were not a religious organization. She insisted that they were identical to secular relief organizations; the implementation of their programs was held to the most rigorous international standards. "Only our mission was inspired by Islamic values," she qualified. We were sitting in her office behind whose glass walls I could see one of her colleagues finishing his afternoon prayers. Religious terms featured prominently in the brochures of the organization, and she had just explained to me how they allocated zakat funds. Clearly Islam did more than provide the original inspiration for its mission. But what?

The country director later joined us, and I asked if they could explain those Islamic values. He listed them in English and then translated them for me, five values corresponding to Islamic virtues to guide the organization's humanitarian practices: sincerity (*ikhlāṣ*), excellence (*iḥsān*), compassion (*raḥma*), social justice (*ʿadl*), and custodianship (*amāna*). "By ensuring that our work abides by these values," he said, "we ensure international humanitarian principles: impartiality, independence, humanity, neutrality." To uphold "sincerity" and "excellence," he explained, "we have to remember it's not just between us and the beneficiaries. It's also an action directed to God glorified and exalted, all according to the intention (*ḥasb al-niyya*)." What the organization calls "social justice" and "compassion" map onto the humanitarian principles of impartiality and humanity, he said, while "custodianship" entails responsibility to every living thing (neutrality). These values are drawn from Islam, and they inspire the organization to safeguard international standards.

At around the same time, in March 2018, I visited another organization called United Muslim Aid, an organization started in the United States whose Jordan chapter I visited a few times. Their brochures are glossy and are typical of the rhetorical form of international aid organizations, featuring dusty children with big eyes looking seriously at the reader. The first brochure panel proclaimed the prophetic hadith about the believers being like one body united in its suffering. At the end of a long interview with two of their program managers, as I was packing up to leave with the brochures in hand, I asked about their name. Given my interest in the present life of the *umma*, I was curious about the term "united" in the phrase "United Muslim Aid." But they looked at me quizzically. "I'm not sure," one of them began. "Maybe it's *united* because we're doing this together?"

"I think it's *united* because the organization started in the *United* States," the other offered. These aid workers were skeptical about any substantive connection between the mandate of their NGO (or even its name) and the hadith leading their brochure.

As noted earlier, much of the literature on Muslim humanitarianism seeks to gauge just how secular or religious Muslim organizations are. Following that approach, one might conclude that the institutional cultures of the two organizations recounted here have been effectively secularized (insisting on the abstraction of Islamic ethical values, conscripted into the service of generic international humanitarianism). They certainly do, as Marie Juul Petersen writes, "confine religion to specific and well-defined functions and spaces, acceptable primarily in the form of underlying values and 'ethical references,' inspiring and motivating people rather than shaping organizational activities and structures in concrete and visible ways."[25] Yet such a conclusion would also lose the enmeshment of these secularizing articulations within the social relationships that give them form.

In reaching such conclusions, moreover, this diagnostic mode remains struck between the Islamic and the secular. While recognizing that the secular grammar of international humanitarianism structures the conditions of legibility of such international faith-based organizations, the secular translation of religious virtues into abstract ethical values is itself a productive intervention into Islamic discursive traditions of charity and aid.[26] Key here is that secular power (inciting certain articulations and not others) is not somehow "outside" Muslim practices today. Rather, it is integral to the form they take.

In academic analyses structured by a binary between Islam and the secular, the task of social science is to account for modern Muslim life through the tropes of rupture versus continuity, modernity versus tradition, secularity versus religion. In contrast, the anthropological analytic of "tradition" developed by Talal Asad can methodologically skirt the triumphalist history of the secular. The final section of his *Formations of the Secular* is devoted to exploring secularizing reconfigurations of law and ethics in colonial Egypt. Asad criticizes those orientalists who lament these developments as a betrayal of Islamic tradition: he insists that it is not their job to authorize certain historical articulations against others. He writes that the concept of "orthodox Islam" with which many orientalists approach Islamic law is "misplaced," for it properly belongs to a "religious dispute" between those "committed to doing certain things *to* what they regard as the essential tradition."[27] The orientalist rendition of historical difference as the modern invention of tradition is here displaced; modernity and colonial secularity are not the outside of Islam. Instead, Asad concludes, "aspects of shari'a reform [were] both the *precondition* and the *consequence* of secular processes of power."[28] This approach to modern Islamic forms of life does not methodologically inscribe a spatial division ("inside" versus "outside" the tradition). Rather, "the use of the figure 'inside' and 'outside' by someone [seeking to inhabit that tradition, that is, one] who aspires to coherence, is an expression of experiential tensions; the use indicates *temporality* rather than spatiality. . . . A discursive tradition is not a bubble in which one is located but a set of aspirations, sensibilities, commitments, and relationships of subjects who live and move in the different times of a common world.'"[29] Rather than deciding whether one set of Muslim humanitarian practices is more or less secular, more or less Islamic, than another, the anthropologist should instead consider the force of secular power in modulating (not determining) the experiential tensions of those acting—as the country director at the NGO put it—"according to their intention" (*ḥasb al-niyya*). He had quoted a famous hadith before I left: *fi kulli kabidin ratbatin ajr*, "there is [divine] reward for serving every animate being." Hence, as he saw it, his Islamic commitment to the four humanitarian principles enshrined by the UN Office for the Coordination of Humanitarian Affairs.

■ ■ ■

In my first meeting with Shaykh Zāyid of the Jam'iyyat al-Kitāb wa-l-Sunna, I described my research topic as being the relationship between religion and humanitarianism (the shorthand I often used with aid organizations). He immediately forwarded to me something he had already prepared on the topic, which he said would answer my questions. He had developed this analysis with two audiences in mind. For practitioners in the secular humanitarian sector, this presentation was directed at assuaging their concerns that faith-based organizations such as his were instrumentalizing charity for dubious religious or political ends. For practitioners working at Islamic charitable organizations, this presentation was directed at establishing the centrality of a humanitarian mission in the sharia. He delivered different versions of this presentation in various venues, emphasizing certain aspects as appropriate. A year later (in February 2019) I heard him give an abridged and extemporaneous rendition at a meeting bringing together government agencies, humanitarian organizations, and think tanks, after which he noted how the representative of a Christian charitable organization had been impressed with his emphasis on prophetic mercy. "Now maybe he won't be so worried about our beards," he joked to me.

In locating humanitarian work within the paradigms of Islamic sharia and international humanitarian law, this presentation also provides a basis for critically translating between them. It is a PowerPoint presentation of nearly thirty slides, some more detailed than others, titled "The Work of Islamic Charitable Organizations in the Light of Islamic Shari'a and International Humanitarian Law" (*'amal munaẓẓamāt al-khayriyya al-islāmiyya 'alā ḍaw' al-sharī'at al-islāmiyya wa-l-qānūn al-duwalī al-insānī*). The PowerPoint begins with Q. 21:107: *And We have not sent you (O Muhammad) except as a mercy to the worlds.* This slide glosses "world" in a few ways: it quotes the twentieth-century Egyptian scholar Muḥammad al-Sha'rāwī (1911–98) to cite the classical definition of the "world" (*'ālam*) to which the Prophet brought mercy as being "everything other than God"—namely, the realms of angels, jinn, humans, even animals, plants, and minerals; it quotes the twentieth-century Syrian scholar Rātib al-Nābulsī (b. 1939–) to say that the Prophet was sent as a mercy to the faithful and to infidels and to hypocrites, to all the children of humanity, men, women, children, and to birds and animals alike. Subsequent slides enumerate authorities and roots of humanitarian principles (*mabādī' insāniyya*): first the *fiṭra*, the divinely established human nature; then the various religions (*adyān*); then national and international laws; and finally, principles of utility or public benefit. The next slide lists ethical principles for humanitarian work (humanity; sanctity; responsibility and legitimacy; dignity). The presentation proceeds like this, establishing the conceptual space of humanitarianism, before shifting into a comparative mode: one slide has two columns, the first defining international humanitarian law and the second defining international humanitarian law *in Islam*. There is little substantive difference between the two columns; each is directed toward human protection and the maintenance of human dignity, but they invoke different archives (international treaties/conventions and sharia, respectively). The next slides abandon this explicitly comparative effort, instead offering Islamic reasons for specific humanitarian principles and then discussing the purpose and types of charitable action.

The comparative mode returns on a slide titled "areas of charitable work in Islam and their equivalent in the West" (*majālāt al-ʿamal al-khayrī fī-l-islām wa mā yuqābiluhā fī-l-gharb*), but curiously its vector has shifted: it first lists the fields of charity writ large in "Islam," then gives their counterparts in "the West" (in English translation), and then provides a direct Arabic translation of the latter concepts. Not only has the direction of the comparison changed (from an Islamic term to a Western one, rather than the other way around), but there are three columns, not two, and some of these translations end up more awkward than others in passing from a regime of virtues (e.g., *al-rifq bi-l-ḥayawān*: kindness to animals) to a regime of rights ("protection and promotion of animal rights"). The Islamic practice of "enjoining good and forbidding evil" (*al-amr bi-l-maʿrūf wa-l-nahy ʿan al-munkar*), for instance, is rendered into English as "civic action," and then into Arabic again as *al-mumārasa al-muwāṭiniyya*.[30] And this is explicitly conducted as a translation between "Islam" and "the West" (*al-gharb*; the international humanitarian apparatus is explicitly figured as Western).

What makes Muslim humanitarian practice distinct, Shaykh Zāyid concluded in conversation when we discussed this presentation, is that it affirms the natural disposition (*fiṭra*) of humanity. (The *fiṭra* was by his account the most basic foundation from which humanitarian principles are drawn.)[31] And because the principles and practices of Muslim humanitarianism accord with this nature, being also a means of upholding personal and collective duties to God, it urges humanity, it spurs it on, it develops the capacity of humanity.[32]

Amira Mittermaier has described Islamic practices of giving in postrevolutionary Cairo as exhibiting a "nonhumanitarian ethics." These practices may bypass the humanitarian fetish for spectacular suffering, as people are moved to act by a divinely imposed obligation (not simply by compassion for a generic suffering Other). Nor is the scene of such charity determined by the asymmetrical relationship between benefactor and beneficiary, for God is a mediating third party who makes the relation between "benefactor" and "beneficiary" reversible (in that the "beneficiary" is the one who occasions the practice/possibility of the "benefactor's" piety in the first place).[33]

While Shaykh Zāyid's presentation takes such an ethics for granted, it also—in explicitly relating to each other humanitarian fields in "Islam" and "the West"—engages the secular grammar of the international humanitarian regime. We can thus understand his argument for the legitimacy of Islamic charitable work to pedagogically address (or itself interpellate) an Islamic counterpublic within the space of the humanitarian world—approaching counterpublic not, with Nancy Fraser, as a kind of subaltern opposition to bourgeois discourse, but rather with Charles Hirschkind as a set of discursive practices that structure the rationalities, sensibilities, and aims of the Islamic reform movement. Hirschkind writes that this counterpublic is structured precisely by the institutional divisions of modern politics (public and private, state and society) that it configures toward its own ends. He explains,

> As mosques in Egypt over the last fifty years became the site for new kinds of social and political organization and expression, everyday practices of pious sociability gradually came to inhabit a new political terrain, one shaped both by the discourses of national citizenship and by emerging transnational forms of religious association. In the course of this shift, forms of practical reasoning tied to the tradition of the virtues became oriented not simply toward a notion of moral community (an *umma*) but toward what we would recognize as a public as well: the practice of the virtues and the deliberation of issues of public concern were fused together in a unique manner.[34]

In the Islamic Revival (in Egypt and elsewhere), *da'wa* (calling to God) has "provided the conceptual site wherein the concerns, public duties, character, and virtues of an activist Muslim citizen have been most extensively elaborated and practiced."[35]

Here, then, lies an answer to my question about how activist groups like the Jam'iyya articulate their activities of social reform (Quran study programs and pilgrimage trips) with their activities of refugee support (winterization campaigns and cancer treatment). For one of the final slides of Shaykh Zāyid's presentation reorganizes the earlier table listing the fields of charitable work, now demonstrating a logical hierarchy that was more ambiguous when they were listed serially in columns. Here the outermost circle (filled in grey) includes "kindness to animals" and "concern for the rest of creation." The middle circle (filled in orange) includes "enjoining good and forbidding evil," "supporting the oppressed," "solicitude for guests and aiding the needy," and "maintaining family ties." And the innermost circle (filled in green), is "calling to God" (*al-daʿwa ilā-llāh*). The core of charitable work in Islam, as conceptualized by Shaykh Zāyid, is *daʿwa*. This does not mean that charity is merely the outer edifice behind which these Islamist activists advance a proselytizing agenda (for that only begs the question of what comprises *daʿwa*, and in what situations)—but it does demonstrate the common denominator between the Jamʿiyya's Quran circles in the early 2000s and its funding of Syrian refugees' cancer treatments in the 2010s.

According to a common academic typology of Salafi movements, the Jamʿiyya is a "reformist" (activist) rather than a "purist" (nonpolitical) or "jihadist" (militant) group. But rather than translating *iṣlāḥ* conventionally as "reform," Shaykh Zāyid's theorization of *daʿwa* as the inner heart of Islamic charitable action (just as it is the founding practice of the Islamic Revival's counterpublic) allows retranslating *iṣlāḥ* as "repair." For Quran education and cancer treatments can each then be seen as reparative activities: two species with a common genus, that is, of reprising a social body (*mujtamaʿ*, *umma*) that has been variously corrupted by poverty, fractured by displacement, afflicted by illness, and incapacitated by ignorance. Reading *iṣlāḥ* as "repair" dispenses with the burden of having to establish the commensurability of varying practices under the same organization's mandate. It also locates the activism of the charity against the rending of the Islamic community.

Although I had described an earlier slide of the PowerPoint as *comparing* the fields of humanitarian activity in Islam and in the West, such comparison should not be understood as the abstraction of similar cultural practices between "Islam" and "the West" (e.g., abstractly translating "enjoining good and forbidding evil" as "civic action" or vice versa). That model of conceptual translation, following Dipesh Chakrabarty's distinction between analytical and affective histories, relies on a mediating measure of general equivalence. Understanding Shaykh Zāyid's PowerPoint in the register of analytical history would yield a secular social-scientific analysis evacuated of nonhuman agencies, in which a universal category of "culture" explains historical or ethnographic difference between separate contexts. Yet Shaykh Zāyid clarified that non-Islamic humanitarian practices—those of the Christians who feared Salafi beards, those of the secular NGOs with whom his Association coordinated—are *also* based in the divinely given human disposition (*fiṭra*). These are not two discrete contexts, each with their own distinct logic, mediated by "culture": the fundamental ground of humanitarian work is shared in that the *fiṭra* is itself established by divine agency. Rather than a process of generalized exchange, then, Shaykh Zāyid's conceptual translation between "Islam" and "the West" is better considered in the register of affective history: a "barter exchange" where different practices, "although porous to one another," are not "exchangeable through a third term of equivalence."[36] That is, the *fiṭra* does not commensurate different practices through a process of interpretation. Instead, in the universalist idiom of Shaykh Zāyid's account, it grounds the practice of difference.[37] But because non-Islamic humanitarian practices are not centered on *daʿwa*, Shaykh Zāyid continued, because their work is not ultimately seeking the divine pleasure, they disproportionately focus on beneficiaries or benefactors, or exploit beneficiaries along the way, or are driven by enthusiasm and not serious commitment. Islamic activists also fall into these pitfalls, he admitted, but can at least take recourse to the tradition of Islamic moral reasoning to escape them.

The secular grammar of international humanitarianism structures the conditions of legibility of charitable organizations. This is one of the discursive regimes Shaykh Zāyid engages as he insists on the religious and political legitimacy of Muslim humanitarian work. Yet his argument proves instructive well beyond the suspicious and hesitant audiences he addresses. Rather than reinforcing the normative secularity of humanitarianism or ignoring it altogether, he translates humanitarianism for an Islamic counterpublic, back and forth between the paradigms of Islamic sharia and international humanitarian law.[38] The methodological implications of such critical translation extend well into humanitarian sites with a more ambiguous relationship to religion. They leave me pessimistic about answering such questions as, on the one hand, "What is so Islamic about Islamic humanitarianism?" or, on the other hand, "Do Muslim humanitarians really work for humanity?" The first of these questions suggests that, given the isomorphism of aid programs in our neoliberal world, humanitarianism offers fundamentally secular forms of practice beneath the dross of whatever religious language is used to justify or articulate it. The second of these questions suggests that Muslim charitable and humanitarian practices—suffused as they are with the language of Muslim unity, the *umma*, and Muslims aiding other Muslims for the sake of God—are not sufficiently impartial to properly meet the standards set by the international aid industry. As variously argued in this book, these questions, whether implying too little or too much religion, are methodological traps. They enact the difference that they purportedly seek to analyze.

One of the insights of the anthropology of secularism has been that if social scientists approach contemporary Muslim practices with a view to separating what is properly secular from what is properly religious, then they have already committed themselves to a secularist analysis. (Muslims themselves, of course, regularly ask the question of what is properly Islamic, but in doing so they engage their discursive tradition with authoritative criteria that may or may not be shared with the social scientist—who presumably is not seeking to intervene into that tradition.) And one of the insights of the anthropology of Islam has been that identifiably secular logics (here, e.g., rendering *al-amr bi-l-maʿrūf* as "civic action"; invoking the concept of "humanity") can rearticulate Muslim forms of life without these somehow becoming less Islamic for the anthropologist.

Contemporary Muslim humanitarian practices are certainly marked by neoliberalism and globalization—but these do not entail universalization. Rather than analyses that decide (according to a universal set of terms) whether one set of humanitarian practices is more or less secular, more or less Islamic, than another, scholars might consider the force of secular power and corresponding acts of translation that modulate (not determine) the forms of Islamic charity today. This recalls Chakrabarty's insistence that analytical histories, in which a universal category (culture, economy, religion) translates between particular contexts, are not sufficient. Instead, such accounts need be interrupted by affective histories, which retain, among other factors, heterotemporal horizons and nonhuman agents. The register of affective history offers a way to trace the entanglement of distinct projects without sublating one into the other or abstracting them into a third term offering general equivalence. In doing so, such critical translations "act as our grounds for claiming historical difference."[39] The relationship between Islamic charity and international humanitarianism cannot be cleanly parsed by the secular mediation of religion or by the division of particular from universal. The entanglement of these discourses instead speaks to the asymmetries of global power that structure sites of urgency and aid.

ABSTEMIOUS IMAGES

The pain of belonging to the *umma* today is registered in and conveyed from one heart to another. This presumes that pain is not necessarily a thought-destroying event: it can be shared. Pain is a public relationship, not something essentially private. It depends on the responses of others. Social suffering is a condition of specific relationships; it is a mode of living a relationship. And "as a social relationship, pain is more than an experience. It is part of what creates the conditions of action and experience."[40] The pain of belonging to the *umma* extends across the Community as it is divided by borders and disposed by capital. But how then is such pain to be conveyed? If *umma*-consciousness is lacking among the Muslims today, as some of my interlocutors vociferously held, what are the protocols and means of exciting such fellow-feeling? Through words, through images?

The visual rhetoric of human rights organizes social and political relations according to the conventions of humanitarian government, distributing agency and consolidating identities.[41] Some of the Islamic charities at which I did my fieldwork certainly participated in that visual field. The archives of their pamphlets and brochures are telling. Some boast children with dusty faces and dirty clothes gazing stolidly at the viewer, a hand clutching a sweetmeat. Others are more modest (and less practiced in graphic design), as when the UK-based charity I discuss in the first Threshold simply showed images of smiling pilgrims from its last successful trip to Mecca. But beyond their instrumentalization in humanitarian fundraising, images are also recognized for their witnessing power. This section briefly considers alternative ways this witnessing power is modulated in Muslim humanitarian sites.

On a chilly evening in February 2018, I went to an art exhibit staged by a Scandinavian NGO working in refugee support in Jordan. These were paintings by Syrians in Azraq Refugee Camp, a huge, desolate, and remote site of some 35,000 residents. The artists themselves were not at the event (they were still sequestered in the camp), but representatives of the NGO at this upscale restaurant in the Jabal Amman neighborhood spoke about how art gave refugees the means for self-expression and a kind of healing. Proceeds from their sales went directly to the artists, we were assured. The audience mulling over these paintings was mostly composed of European expatriates, speaking English and French and accepting finger-food from silent waiters. We drifted around the hall, taking in the range of the images. Little cards gave the name of the artist, the title of the piece, and its price. The symbolism of the paintings themselves was explicit. In one, a mother bird came home to an empty nest. Another featured a seated woman holding an hourglass while a dark figure on the horizon froze under a diving warplane. In another, children on the seashore wave to boats with white sails on the horizon, and a white dove takes flight. In the painting I purchased, a large square canvas in orange-brown tones, a shadowy figure reaches from sharp rocks for a ladder ascending to an open book—but the bag it carries has fallen open, and whatever was within has scattered. "We are helping them tell their own stories," the man at the microphone concluded, "by using the resources of art therapy." Refugee art workshops are popular within refugee camps, where they alleviate tedium; and refugee art sales are popular among largely expatriate, socially conscious consumers.

A few weeks later, in March 2018, the *New York Times* ran a story titled "The Real Face of War? It May Be This Boy in a Pink Sweater."[42] The face in question was that of Jad Allah Jumaa, a toddler smiling at the camera, leaning on a sofa with a pudgy hand. He had recently been killed in a Russian airstrike on eastern Ghouta. We only learn that fact at the end of the article, which readers reach with a growing sense of dread. Ghouta was one of the remaining areas of free Syria, a suburb of Damascus subjected to an extermination campaign by the Assad regime and its Russian ally, an assault of napalm and chemical weapons and more. There is compassion fatigue among Western observers, the article comments, while the regime discredits the images of the suffering it has caused. The author then writes that at one time, such images still held the power to move us, but no longer. He wonders if it is because victims in Syria are brown and Muslim or because of the scale of the war there. He concludes, "Maybe we need to stare at a simple, everyday family snapshot to remember what binds us."

These examples indicate two ways the witnessing power of images is mobilized in the humanitarian field. For the Scandinavian NGO that organized the painting workshops in Azraq camp, images have the power to bear witness to traumatic experience—and making such images is a type of therapeutic expression. For the *New York Times* article, too, images have the power to bear witness—only that it is undermined by political conditions and affected by other elements of the visual field. These two senses of the testamentary function of images (the redemptive promise of art and the depleted power of the image) are shared across the humanitarian field in which anthropology participates, insofar as it too is shaped by faith in the power of witness and by faith in the symbolic work of culture to resist anomie or the manipulation of state and market.[43] This section now turns to an alternative modulation of images' power: an argument made by the

Jamʿiyyat al-Kitāb wa-l-Sunna's Shaykh Zāyid, in the Jordanian press and also in person to me in May 2018, which confronts the disciplining apparatus of the visual rhetoric of humanitarianism.

Shaykh Zāyid prepared a short article on the spectacularization of suffering he saw as endemic to humanitarian projects. He warned that indulging in such visual practices might be sentimentally effective but also threatened to undermine the religious merit of this charity. No matter the sincerity of the activist or volunteer's intention, he told me, they had also to take responsibility for the forms of action they took up. His critique was directed at the producers of an Emirati television show called "My Heart Assuaged" (*qalbi iṭma'an*), in which a man (his face obscured) visits impoverished people and inquires into their conditions—and then doles out the cash or equipment they need. Before each episode ends the camera lingers with the faces of the beneficiaries: they tear up in gratitude, they supplicate in thanks. Although his critique was addressed to this television program, Shaykh Zāyid said as we discussed it, it had far broader relevance, given the media saturation of modern life. He published his commentary on a reformist website and distributed it across his online networks, including to the volunteers and employees of his charity.[44]

The text begins with a parable from early Islamic history. The first Caliph, Abū Bakr al-Ṣiddīq, would daily, after the dawn prayers, journey to a tent on the far side of Medina. One day ʿUmar bin al-Khaṭṭāb followed him to learn the secret of that place. There he discovered an elderly blind woman and orphan children whom Abū Bakr would serve, sweeping their house, milking their sheep, preparing their food, and sometimes washing their clothes. Seeing the commander of the faithful (*amīr al-mu'minīn*) setting this high standard, ʿUmar exclaimed, "You exhaust the caliphs after you!" To this day, Shaykh Zāyid wrote, no one knows the name of that woman—nor would the woman have ever known that it was Abū Bakr who served her, except that ʿUmar wished to compete with him in doing good works.

If you fear God glorified and exalted, Shaykh Zāyid continued, do not expose the faces of the poor and needy before millions of people. Preserve their dignity (*karāma*)! These images and video clips will be saved in an online archive, available there for the perusal of any who wants to return to them. How would a young woman feel when she seeks marriage—when the story of her family's impoverishment was already exposed to millions of people? If a young man did marry her, would he not use this against her at the first disagreement between them? And the same, of course, is true for a young man seeking marriage. Nor is this limited to the marital domain but has implications for all sorts of social, psychological, economic, and cultural relations.

There are ways that the producers of this television program could at once preserve the specificity of the needs they addressed and avoid publicizing the identity of their beneficiaries, Shaykh Zāyid offered. These included obscuring their faces, as the program already did for its narrator-protagonist who traveled to these scenes of need. Another alternative would be presenting only the voice of the beneficiary after the charity has been disbursed—that is, not lingering on the affected face of the other but letting his or her voice recount the tragic situation and utter the praise and gratitude occasioned by the gift. Another solution would be having the program host or someone else describe for viewers the effect (happiness and joy) of the charity—or even to have actors play the role of the beneficiary, by which the aim of the episode (eliciting compassion from the audience) would likewise be reached.

I am fully aware, concluded Shaykh Zāyid, that such television programs depend crucially on showing the reaction of the needy beneficiaries; that is what accounts for their popularity. But it is also perfectly clear that such shows can find ways to preserve the dignity of the poor and, at the same time, promote the television program in an appropriate manner and, in so doing, spur others to aid the poor and needy. One who says that poverty is not something to be ashamed of, a defect to be resolved—well, these days, poverty has become a crime. So fear God regarding the poor and the needy, orphans and widows: be the hand that raises distress from them and illuminates their path. Preserve their dignity and humanity.

When we met later that week, Shaykh Zāyid was still disturbed by the spectacularization of suffering he saw overtaking even the sector of Islamic charity. He was not against photography per se, but the uses of images in humanitarian settings required greater care, especially now when digital technology meant that their depiction of immiseration and poverty would be preserved out of time. Anyone could peruse these images later on, rendering these people's lives a form of entertainment. His brief article paraphrased here had engaged other questions as well: by opening with the story of Abū Bakr and 'Umar, he implicitly established that good deeds done in secret were more meritorious than those done in public. Charity given in secret deflects divine wrath, he told me—it can be an expiation, a shield. But in the course of his comments he recognized that it was precisely the public (or at least exposed) play of emotion solicited by the gift that yielded the surplus affect that in turn accounted for the show's popularity—and perhaps offered a route for encouraging others to likewise do good. In suggesting that actors could play the beneficiaries to the same compassionate ends, he showed that he was not invested in the representational authenticity of that affect. He was not against manipulating that emotion, given the televisual instrumentality that the program was based upon. Indeed, he recognized that the image offers only a screen whose essence is always withdrawn.

His broad pragmatism extended to other scenes of suffering. I mentioned images of torture that had been smuggled out of Syria and how some of my interlocutors regarded their dissemination as a kind of jihad because these could expose the crimes of the regime. But in the face of the constant stream of images from Syria, video of bombardments and pictures of torture, of dead bodies and wounded children, of displacements and of cruelty, I continued, the images themselves are painful. They exceed whatever forensic use to which they might be put. What more public exposure could be needed now, when the reporting already suffices? (Of course, such images are not always painful. Bilāl's photographic archive engaged in Chapter 3 depicts scenes of utter violence, yet his repeated return to these images is neither voyeuristic nor sensational. Instead, they provide a site for his mourning and his practice of witness. Such harrowing images can thus also be disclosive.) Some other interlocutors held that such images should not be spread at all. Preserve the dignity of the dead and the living, I remembered one of my interlocutors in Edmonton insisting—do not display their wounds or demean their bodies by making them available to be seen. Shaykh Zāyid admitted the validity of both arguments but said that a single rule could not answer what is to be done. The ethics of representation depend on the situation and what good such depictions could afford. Thus, in his commentary on the television show, his concern lay with its effects on the lives of the beneficiaries as well as with how it reconfigured the scene of charity.

Shaykh Zāyid's critique emphasizes the force of images in sites of charity and displacement. But rather than celebrating images' power or lamenting their depletion and misuse (the Scandinavian NGO vaunting art therapy as a form of testimony, the *New York Times* article recalling its audience to political solidarity), it urges a kind of restraint. For Shaykh Zāyid, the exercise of images playing on sentiment may indeed yield a compassionate response—perhaps even a political one. But he warns that imaging technology also bears unintended consequences for those caught on screen, which may in fact evacuate the ethico-spiritual merit of such compassion. Images are central to his work: for example, Shaykh Zāyid appeals to his donor network for funding to pay for refugees' cancer treatments by circulating pictures of signed documents stating the name, type of cancer, and treatment cost. But these are not images of the needy patient. He tempers enthusiasm for the witnessing power of the image by recalling the noncoincidence of appearance and being and by warning against how this force can be turned against those who are depicted in such images and those who consume them. The abstemiousness of these visual practices is informed by Islamic sensibilities and is not readily reflected in the spectacular rhetoric of contemporary humanitarianism.

PEDAGOGY IN EXILE

Displaced from the religious institutions that sustained the Levantine Islamic scholastic tradition, many of my interlocutors keenly felt the need for appropriate religious education. (There is a certain irony to the fact that these Islamic charities articulate a pressing need for appropriate religious knowledge, when the policy literature suspects precisely these charities for being "immoderate.") Rather than simply spreading information about Islam, these educational programs are directed toward inculcating the sensibilities that would allow the students to bear the challenges of their lives without lapsing into despair or fury (each of which betray a lack of tempered religious knowledge). Such religious education classes for and by Syrians have proliferated through the war. Whether for children or adults, whether in rebel-held areas inside Syria or among displaced communities in Jordan, Lebanon, Turkey, or the West, the curricula of such programs range in degree of formality; they are often improvised from internet sources and audiovisual recordings and are based on the Islamic knowledge of the teachers. But they do not offer exclusively religious education. For example, the weekly schedule at the Jam'iyyat al-Kitāb wa-l-Sunna's enrichment sessions included Arabic, English, nutrition, and math—and the occasional museum or swimming pool field trip. The Islamic organizations facilitating such remedial education programs in Jordan, Lebanon, Turkey, and elsewhere are often also engaged in orphan support and food and emergency cash distributions. They frequently coordinate with national and international aid organizations and neighborhood charitable associations. As also seen earlier in this chapter, their work confuses a principled division between humanitarianism and religious activism. This section introduces two sites detailed later in this book (children's education in east Amman and at an orphanage in Ramtha), now with a view specifically to examining their pedagogical projects.

▪ ▪ ▪

Only three children came to the Jamʿiyyat al-Kitāb wa-l-Sunna center in Amman that day in March 2018, which confused the counselors (there were usually at least five times that number). Following a series of phone calls, they worriedly discussed how one of the children had been assaulted on the way home from school two days earlier. Although the event happened on the other side of the neighborhood, rumors had spread among the Syrian families, and the parents of most of the children had kept them home that morning. But three kids had come, and so as a smaller group we turned to Q. 105, "The Elephant."

> *Hast thou not seen how thy Lord dealt with the masters*
> *of the elephant?*
> *did He not make their scheming go astray,*
> *and send against them birds in swarms,*
> *pelting them with stones of baked clay,*
> *such that He made them like devoured husks?*

We all knew how to recite the sūra already, so instead of working through reciting the individual verses together we illustrated them. Khulūd distributed markers for us all to contribute and wrote the sūra's name in the center of a large sheet of paper. She muttered the first verse to herself as she drew a bright yellow sun and clouds with faces looking down. "So who was coming to attack?"

"The unbelievers!"

"That's right! And who was their chief?"

"Abhara the Ethiopian."

"Not quite—his name was Abraha, and he was a king in Yemen, not Ethiopia. But this sūra came as a sign to the Prophet Muhammad, that you have a great blessing. Look, they came to attack the House of the Muslims, the House of God, the Kaʿba. And you know what they had with them? Elephants!" She squinted at the elephant she had just drawn and laughed, commenting to me that it looked like a tangled garden hose more than the great mammal she had intended.

One of the boys added stick figures lined up behind the elephant. "How big were they?"

"Have you ever seen an elephant in real life? No? But you've seen pictures—and can you imagine them being destroyed by birds? Think—how did God send the pellets? Here, color in these pellets under the birds [she handed the boy to her right a dark red marker]. How would a bird be able to carry them?"

"In its beak!"

"That's right, it would just have to remember not to swallow [they laughed]. Three pellets from hellfire: one in each of its talons and one in its beak. And just like that, all the warriors and their forces were demolished—*like devoured husks*." She drew the elephant and stick figures all rolled onto their side and gestured that the children color them in. One of the boys added blood seeping from each of the prone figures as the divine flock flew away.

"What do we understand from this? God has power over every oppressor, no matter their army or air force." I thought of the news I had just read that morning: 12,000 people fleeing eastern Ghouta, the suburb of Damascus under regime air strikes. "I'm not afraid of anyone, that's what it teaches us. I can face anything in supplication."

Later that week, in March 2018, after the counselors promised to call the parents when the children had safely arrived at the center and to lock the door for the duration of the sessions, attendance had risen to a dozen children again. Their mood having returned to the center was boisterous, a far cry from how quiet the previous days had been. Two boys scuffled. Another teased his cousin for wearing shorts. The counselors held a contest to see who could recite the two final sūras most precisely. Three kids sidled up to join my team before Khulūd gestured them back to their own group. We stood and repeated the verses in turn, following a reciter on the television screen. Anytime someone made a mistake they had to sit down.

Say: I seek refuge in the Lord of the daybreak
from the evil of what He has created
from the evil of the darkness when it enshrouds
. . .

The counselors looked around, wondering why someone hadn't recited it. "Whose turn is it?"

A ten-year-old blushed. "Me—but I can't read."

"That's okay, repeat after me," Khulūd said.

from the evil of those who blow upon knots
and from the evil of the envier when he envies. (Q. 113)

Before they turned to the next sūra, the counselors described them both. "You see how they both start with the same phrase? *Say: I seek refuge in the Lord. . . .* We take refuge in God from the devil every time we recite the Quran, because God is greater, more powerful, than anything in the universe. Right? He created the lion, the whale, the fruits we eat. So we seek His aid anytime we are scared of something. Hey, are you listening? So at night if we're scared, we go to mama, we go to baba. It's the same with God. You see?" Khulūd turned to the young boy next to her, Ibrāhīm. "What are you scared of?"

"Well—my neighbor is a kid with a white dog. He scares me." She clucked her tongue sympathetically and recommended the boy keep his distance from the neighbor if he could.

"I'm scared of my teacher," another child offered. "He beats the students with a stick."

Khulūd sat up sharply, her tone less playful. She asked for more details, how many students were in the class, what he beat them for. (Some children had only fourteen others in their class. Others had fifty.) She was clearly uncomfortable with such corporal discipline, especially when it scared the other children. She could not intervene directly but still tried to give some practicable advice. "When the teacher tells you all to be quiet or he'll hit you, why is he doing it?"

But the children clamored in: "To hit us! That's why he is telling us—he wants to hit us!"

"Look . . ." Khulūd paused. "I don't think hitting is right, and certainly not in school. We don't support hitting in this center, not us hitting you or you hitting each other. But what can you do when someone is threatening you?" She tried to make the point general again.

"You should hit him first and run away!" The children giggled.

She smiled too. "But what if he is faster than you? Stronger than you?"

A large boy smirked. "You can trick him: tell him you have a chocolate or a sweet to give him, then push him from behind." He raised laughs at the prospect.

"Okay, okay." Khulūd brought their attention to a poster the counselors had prepared and taped to the wall. Its first column listed "sources of fear": the police; strangers; animals (dogs, snakes); the war; blood; the street; fire; the dark. The second column noted "where I feel the fear in my body." The third listed "what I do to work on my fear." That last column was filled with practical advice but emphasized avoiding the fearful situation altogether if possible: trying to avoid being seen and being polite but firm to escape the police; fleeing and telling one's parents if strangers approached them; reciting the evening litany (*adkhār al-masā'*) and joining one's parents or siblings in bed when afraid of the dark.

"See this verse, *from the evil of what He has created* (Q. 113:2). We take refuge in God from the evil of what God created, of every created thing (*makhlūqāt*), because God created things that can hurt us. Like bears."

"Yeah! Bears—like pandas!" interjected Ibrāhīm, with a bear on his red tracksuit.

"That's silly," an older boy scoffed, "pandas don't eat people. Nor do elephants."

"But an elephant could still step on us!!" The youngest child there was adamant, her eyes wide.

"I once saw a horse kick a man," commented a boy in my group.

"Wow, okay." One of the other counselors came to join our group. "God protect us from all these things, all these evils human and jinn and animal." As we returned to reciting the sūra the children kept listing things they had been afraid of. One was still scared of the dark. Another used to be scared of the moon until he got used to it. The "blowers on knots" mentioned in the verse are the practitioners of black magic, which led into an elaborate debate over whether werewolves truly drank blood and whether vampires exist. We ran through the sūras two more times before playing a game of musical chairs.

■ ■ ■

A visiting organization had recently come to the orphanage to offer some English language classes to the children, Bilāl told me when I visited in mid-June 2018. (See Chapter 3 for a full account of this site and the depth of Bilāl's ambivalence.) He rubbed his forehead. "I can't decide whether I should accept their offer. I probably will. But what kinds of programs would actually be beneficial for the children? And whom should we ask for help? You know that even the organizations who help us Syrians in Jordan sometimes don't—they sometimes don't reflect the principles they talk about. They'll get funding to do this work and then use it to pay their own officials. We don't want to support their corruption, we only want to work with those that have integrity. The responsibility (*mas'ūliyya*) is overwhelming." Bilāl recognized the double standards and hierarchies of the humanitarian sector; he was keenly aware that even an innocuous request would be factored into the calculated metrics of aid organizations.

The magnitude of his responsibility had to do with the weight of making decisions that affected two dozen families and the futures of their children; but it also had eschatological implications for his own eternal fate. "It is Islam that gives this weighty sense of responsibility," he continued; "that is what makes you feel obliged. Someone without religion (*dīn*) would not care about such things. Why should they?" He insisted that one is necessarily obliged to others (to God, humans, nonhumans) already by virtue of one's creaturely existence. But one can live heedless of these obligations; one can be careless with one's life. Islam is what teaches one to live in obligation (*taklīf*)—and that is the beginning of ethics and indeed of justice (*'adl*), which means giving each their due, bearing one's life and livelihood as a trust (*amāna*) for which one is accountable. Talal Asad writes,

> The individual's acquisition of appropriate agency and its exercise are articulated by responsibility, a responsibility not merely of the agent but of the entire community of Muslims severally and collectively. If religious behavior is to be defined in terms of responsibility, then we have here a case of behavior that acquires its sense not from a historical teleology but from a biographical one in which the individual seeks to acquire the capacities and sensibilities internal to a religious tradition (*al-sunna*

al-dīniyya) that is oriented by an eschatology according to which he or she stands alone on the Day of Judgment to account for his or her life. In this tradition the body-and-its-capacities is not owned solely by the individual but is subject to a variety of obligations held by others as fellow Muslims. There is therefore a continuous, unresolved tension between responsibility as individual and metaphysical on the one hand, and as collective and quotidian on the other—that is, between eschatology and sociology.[45]

How does one learn to live in obligation—not least in times of war, when one is displaced from one's home and its institutions of social reproduction? This question is raised across the lands of estrangement (*bilād al-ghurba*) to which Syrian refugees have fled. As I was told time and again in the course of my fieldwork, we are bound together simply by virtue of living alongside each other. But such mutual obligation does not automatically translate into living lives obliged. The displaced families knew that all too well, having been variously interpellated as international objects of pity and fear. Turned into strangers (*ghurabā'*), expelled from the towns and villages where (so they insisted) a modicum of moral integrity had still obtained before the war, the years since their displacement had abandoned them to *ghurba*. Exile voided community—they experienced its dissolution—and suspended the force of moral obligation between kin and neighbors.[46]

Fostering that countervailing sense of obligation was the task Bilāl set himself. He held religious sessions for the children at the orphanage every other day, which included memorizing the Quran, studying the hadith, discussing ethical questions that arose in daily life, and learning the jurisprudence of daily worship. He hoped that these lessons, which took place after the dusk prayers, would provide a basis for the children to counter the fear and suspicion dominating life all around. "Even here, on the border with Syria, our own neighbors were afraid of us at first," he explained. "They were suspicious of us, either for being [religious] extremists or for taking their jobs." Jordan had faced dire economic straits already before the influx of hundreds of thousands of Syrians displaced as a result of the war. "But now our relations have improved," he continued, attributing this improvement to his religious instruction.

We need to offer these lessons because—speaking frankly—people's thoughts have been polluted in Syria, between the apostatizing (*takfīr*)

> [by which some rebels deemed it licit to attack other Muslims] and the blatant repression (*ẓulm*) [of the regime and its sycophants]. Our effort here is to give the children a different approach, a different ethics.

Building a sense of obligation, even in the lands of exile (*bilād al-ghurba*), is what could prevail against the refugees' abandonment and the corruption of the world.

It was a warm night, finally comfortable after the day's heat. Music from a wedding some distance from Ramtha reached us in fits and starts. A dozen children (this session was for older boys, eleven or twelve years old) gathered under the metal trellis in the complex courtyard. There was the faint scent of jasmine on the air, which Bilāl had told me he planted there so that the children would associate its fragrance with their religious lessons. "The Prophet was sent with the message of mercy (*raḥma*)," he began. "The mercy to the worlds. Can we enumerate them? The world of humans, the world of animals, of angels, of jinn. Each has its own language, its own life. Remember the ants which fled under the hooves of Solomon's army—and how he heard their complaint." He reminded them of the hadith of the woman condemned to hellfire for starving a cat. "But wait, who here prayed the dusk prayer?" Nine of the boys raised their hands. "Good, good." He nodded to the three who had not. "And good for your honesty as well. Honesty is the basis of virtue, really." Even though these boys had not prayed, he did not lecture them. In fact, he commended their honesty.

They reviewed the sūra they had been memorizing that week (Q. 75, al-Qiyāma, "Resurrection"), each of the boys reciting a section, with Bilāl correcting them as needed. Then he asked them to recite what they had memorized from Imam al-Nawawī's compilation of forty hadiths. They went around the circle, each having to recite a different hadith with its chain of narrators. "Actions are but by intention, and everyone will have what they intended . . ." "Religion is sincerity. . . ." "None of you believes until he wishes for his brother what he wishes for himself. . . ." After they had each presented one hadith (he helped remind them if they had forgotten), he presented the stories of four early paragons of virtue (Ṣuḥayb Rūmī, Bilāl bin Rawāḥa, Salmān al-Fārisī, and Najāshī) before turning to practical ethics.

> We are here as Syrians, as strangers (*ghurabā'*). This is a proverb for us: *yā gharīb kun adīb*, o stranger, be well-mannered. Right? We need to be good neighbors. Remember the hadith about the smell of food cooking

annoying those who are not eating? Invite others to eat, be generous. Love for each other what you love for yourself.

The homily lasted an hour. Then he sent some of the boys to clean up the square in front of the building, to clean up any rubbish that had fallen. Before he dismissed them, he led them, laughing, in a one-footed race, from one side of the square to the other, as I sat under the trellis and finished my notes. His eldest son brought us a tray of watermelon and a pot of sweet tea before the night prayer, and I left again for Amman.

A year later Bilāl sent me a file he had prepared. Its funding fast depleting as the war drew to a close, the Islamic charity that funded their building had shut down yet another of their orphanages. He was anxious that their building would be next. The Jordanians think the war is over and the Syrians should return, he explained, but the situation is more complicated. He sent these suggestions to the charity and circulated them to anyone he thought might be able to help stave off the threatened closure of these buildings.

He wrote that life under the Syrian regime was still nightmarish and that conditions in Jordan (outside the shelter of these orphanages) were still desperate. Then he offered some suggestions for how to garner more funding, to be circulated among those who might be able to help stave off the threatened closure. His appeals emphasized the religious value of the lessons he offered, arguing that there is great divine reward (*ajr ʿaẓīm*) for supporting the livelihood of orphans and widows, but also further reward for supporting their religious education. He implied that although other sites were similarly deserving, his pedagogy set this orphanage apart from other sites of humanitarian need, making donations to his building all the more imperative. He emphasized that what was truly at stake in his teaching, beyond the particular religious texts he taught the children, was the formation of their sensibilities. These are integral to the effort of inheriting Islam in our time, he reasoned, when the world is characterized by corruption and abandonment. Such corruption has drifted even into our knowledge of religion, he continued, and the displaced Syrians were abandoned between the extremism of sectarian militias on the one hand and the sycophancy of the religious establishment on the other.

In framing his appeals to prospective donors in this way, Bilāl hoped that the value of his religious lessons would have instrumental (even economic) traction outside the ethical field in which they took place. He thus risked the instrumentalization of his Islamic pedagogy for the sake of its material-economic conditions of possibility. In the face of abandonment, he insisted that—given enough time and enough material support—the children could learn to be obliged.

▪ ▪ ▪

These two programs engaged dense theological issues and social problems through their pedagogy. Khulūd insisted that the God who created the evil of created things was greater and more generous than that evil. Thus, through her Quran lessons she sought to give the children resources to deal with their fear—of the police, of war, of the dark. Maybe, too, of werewolves. Meanwhile, facing precarity, poverty, and uncertainty in the shadow of the ongoing war, Bilāl sought to clarify the true conditions faced by Syrian refugees in Jordan to donors whose generosity might flag. His "recommendations" for keeping the buildings open emphasized the religious value of the lessons offered there. Each of these programs was under strain (financial and otherwise). By the time I returned to Jordan in 2023, for instance, the Jamʿiyya's children's program had shut down for lack of funding, while the orphanage was overcrowded with a new influx of families. Nonetheless, each program asserted the importance of inculcating the sensibilities of Islam as the means of modulating (if not resolving) those tensions. As Bilāl had said, inhabiting those sensibilities is how one learns to be obliged. Exile here is borne of a dislocation, a displacement from the cultural and religious contexts that would allow for the integrity of the community. Here tradition, specifically through the ethical work of charity, neighborliness, and etiquette, offers the resources to disarticulate oneself from the effects of destruction and so to emplace oneself again. It also thematizes exile (*ghurba*) as part of this pedagogy. These projects seek a slow, intimate rehabilitation, which (so they insist) is possible through therapeutic recourse to the ethical tradition but requires time to take hold.

Each of these two efforts demonstrates how those working in Muslim humanitarian sites turn to the archives of Islam for resources to implement a pedagogy of character. This emphasis on forming sensibilities is integral to their projects of inheriting Islam, for it is required by the corruption that has swept the world. Such corruption has even drifted into knowledge of religion, these interlocutors lament. Whether the refuge promised by Community has been interrupted, or the Community has been abandoned by its leaders, or it has been ruined, the *umma* does not offer shelter, and its members do not feel obliged by its pain. These pedagogic initiatives are thus activities of repair (*iṣlāḥ*): they insist that different collective formations of body, soul, and intellect are possible. The Islamic tradition offers a recourse precisely because it is exposed and torn.

NO REFUGE FROM GOD BUT GOD

As noted earlier, the academic literature on Islam and humanitarianism is thoroughly exercised by problems of identity and difference. Without acceding to that problematization, this chapter has located Muslim efforts of Syrian refugee support within (not outside of) the humanitarian world. But it has also gestured to what more is at stake at these sites, beyond secular frames of conception. Whether seeking to conceptualize the place and condition of the *umma* after the division of the world into territorial states, translating between Islamic charity and international humanitarianism, modulating the witnessing power of images, or working on the ethical sensibilities of the exiled, following the patient work of making refuge shows that Muslim humanitarian sites are spaces of theological debate and deep reflection.[47] I have emphasized these encounters not merely to argue for a more expansive analysis. Rather, I seek to admit into the arguments of this book itself how the Islamic tradition orients one to the insufficiency of history and politics. This insufficiency is what confounds humanitarian reason. Meanwhile, the questions animating my interlocutions are not exceptional to sites of displacement or refuge. This much is clear from the recursivity of the analyses pursued in this book: God is the one who grants relief (in the Syrian border crisis of 2018, as beyond); refuge is found or made in and through religion (by refugees and others); tribulation is elemental to creation (in Jordan and Canada and beyond). As seen in this final section, refuge is only ever ambivalent—it rests on the divine pleasure.

■ ■ ■

In June 2019, two events were held in northwest Canada a bare few hundred meters apart. Each engaged religion and Syrian refugees, but to dramatically different effect. The first was a demonstration against Syrian regime brutality organized outside Edmonton City Hall by Syrian newcomers to Canada, an event at which Islamic chants of protest and mourning commingled with humanitarian appeals. The second was the municipal celebration of World Refugee Day, an event coordinated with Christian and Muslim refugee-sponsoring religious organizations and inaugurated at City Hall by the mayor. In their distinct confrontations with the devastation of the Syrian war, they each disclosed alternative itineraries of violence and hope.

The first event, called simply "Protest the War in Syria" and advertised on Facebook and by word of mouth, was attended by nearly one hundred people in Edmonton's Churchill Square. We milled about greeting acquaintances and friends until a stocky young man in his early twenties took the microphone. He told the story of his displacement from northern Syria to Turkey, and then on to Egypt and then refuge in Canada. He led the crowd in some chanting in unison—"Thank you, Canada!"—but then his tone grew grimmer. "Thank you for bringing us here. Thank you for taking refugees. But this is not enough," he said. "We need the war to stop." Most of the gathered throng were Syrian newcomers themselves, alongside a few of their friends and a couple of journalists. They were carrying the Syrian revolutionary flag and placards bearing printed images of shrouded children. (The Syrian regime and its Russian ally had launched a campaign against Idlib province in recent months, attacking hospitals and schools with cluster bombs. The protest's circulated announcement stated, "Many of the families who now live in Edmonton come from Idlib. In the last few weeks—during the blessed month of Ramadan—they have lost family members, friends, many of their parents have lost their homes and are now either on the road, or have found shelter in olive tree groves, away from the bombings but exposed to the elements, with no sanitary installations in place.") "Look at our kids!" exhorted the speaker. "They are dying, they are being killed! Please, bring peace!" His voice cracked. The crowd parted, and a dozen children approached the speaker, carrying prop coffins made of plywood and cardboard (see figure 2). They led the gathered protestors in a march a few times around the square while the speaker shouted slogans of mourning and anger. "Peace in Syria! Stop killing our kids!" And, in Arabic, *Ḥurriya li'l-abad/ghaṣban 'annak yā asad!* (Freedom, forever/against your will, O Assad!) *Lā ilāha illā llāh/al-shahīd ḥabīb allāh!* (There is no god but God/the martyr is the beloved of God!) The parents of the children carrying the coffins pushed them toward the dais for the journalists to take pictures. They stood there awkwardly, giggling. It was unclear how the event was to end.

FIGURE 2. Protest the War in Syria, Edmonton, Canada. Basit Kareem Iqbal, 2019

The speaker came forward again. "Please," he pleaded. This was a scene of pathos, in that the addressee of his demand was ambiguous. "If you do not stop the war—if Assad stays in power—we will lose everything. Our beliefs, our world. Thank you, Canada."

As the crowd dispersed, I made my way toward City Hall, on the eastern side of the square. Some of the Christian and Muslim organizations with whom I had conducted fieldwork were co-sponsoring this event. I entered the building and was taken aback by how full the atrium was—full of music and color. A line of people getting third-wave coffee, bannock, and fruit snaked around the rows of chairs facing a podium. The event began with a choir singing Chinese, Algerian, and Indian songs and an announcement of the event's global hashtag (#withrefugees), a land acknowledgment, and an Indigenous smudging. The mayor of the city then welcomed everyone, joking that his trim blue suit was the traditional garb he had found for this multicultural service. "What we have in this city is very easy to take for granted. But it's really through the eyes of newcomers, especially refugees who have lost everything, that we see how special it is. And we see this as we have welcomed so many Syrian families here over the years. We understand, instinctively, the value of welcome." Each of the sponsoring organizations and offices had a speaker on the program, often represented by someone who had herself come to Canada as a refugee or was descended from one. "On this day we remember every man, woman, and child who is forced to leave their home. . . ." began one. "So many have found a new life here in Canada, due to the actions of our government and everyday Canadians. . . ." said another. "Our province is a beacon of hope . . . and how fortunate it is for us that their search brings them here," commented a third. The speakers recounted the history of private sponsorship of refugees in Canada and lamented the unprecedented numbers of displaced people around the world. The event ended with a call to action from the Canadian Council for Refugees and concluded with a round dance.

The contrast between these two events held a few meters apart stayed with me over the next months—a contrast that was all the sharper for their parallels. Both made a place for religion in refugee support programs; both included appeals for aid to sites of emergency and need. But in register and mood, they stood far opposed.

When I had coffee with ʿAmmār, the speaker from the former event, the following week, I was struck by both the depth of his bitterness and the lucidity of his despair. I met him along with one of his family's refugee sponsors, a professor at the local university. He had been eager to leave Syria six years prior, ʿAmmār said, after nearly being killed in the bombardment of his village—but his insomnia began shortly after he left. He would watch videos of the regime's chemical attacks and of the regime thugs stepping on the stiff bodies of their victims. He would weep and then could not sleep. "Why is this happening to us? They are kids, what did they do, that they should die?" It started to make him doubt his own religion, he said. At the very least he could see how everyone—the regime and others—used religion as a cover for their own desires for comfort, luxury, and power. ʿAmmār had wanted to return to Syria to fight the regime—but then ISIS took over his part of northern Syria, and it was hard to see what fighting could do, he said. "People were dying for no reason. I don't know. I don't know." He started to see the present ruin as the result of abjection across the generations. "If we had been raised differently, maybe we would have been different—but we did everything for the wrong reasons, because our fathers and grandfathers did just the same. In Syria, the violence of the regime subjected everyone. We were afraid, jealous, and betrayed each other. We did the work of devils. And here, we hate each other just as much. We haven't been freed." He had started to really, truly pray three years ago, as he never had before, and now he could see how servility crept into the soul.

I asked, How did you feel about the protest? It was nice to gather like that, yes? I had seen two stories covering it in the local news. "I'm sad," 'Ammār immediately replied. "The media just reports what it wants. I had spoken about Russia attacking us, about Canada's relations with Russia, but none of that was shown. They only reported that there were dozens of protestors there, though I counted 75 adults and 50 children. But it was pathetic: we have 4,000 Syrians here in Edmonton. What if they had all come? If the protest was ongoing? If we'd had a camp-out for twenty days, while the regime and Russia were attacking us in Ramadan? That would *do* something." Instead, some of the Syrian families he had reached out to had excused themselves, saying they had meetings or appointments—which he found out later had been lies. The professor sitting with us commented gently that maybe some of them had been afraid of repercussions to their families in Syria. "That is happening already." 'Ammār shook his head. "The regime is not waiting for news from Canada to target our families. Every day we hear who has been killed, or wounded, or starved." He paused. "And as for those who did come, many of them just wanted to be seen on TV."

As our conversation wrapped up, it took on an eschatological tenor. "Sometimes I look around at everyone here—Syrian, Canadian, it does not matter—and see them like they are drunk. Do you know that verse?" He referred to Q. 22:2, which describes the awful scenes of destruction auguring the divine Judgment: *On the day you see it, every nursing woman will forget what she nurses, and every pregnant woman will deliver her burden, and you will see mankind drunk, though drunk they will not be. Rather, the punishment of God is severe.* "That's how they are, already in this life. It doesn't matter what it is that they gorge on—if it is pills, or drink, or women, or something else. We don't actually care for anything but ourselves. And so God has punished us. When I see them dying, in Syria, I think and I think—and I know that we would stop it if we all actually cared. But we don't, and so we don't."

Here the *umma* is not a noble community that would offer refuge to the oppressed had its history not been interrupted by colonialism, or had its leaders not abandoned their posts because of corruption, or had it not been ruined. Instead, its multitudes are nothing but froth on the sea. (Despite your great number, the Prophet Muhammad had famously replied about a day when the nations set upon to devour the Muslims, "you will be as scum upon a torrent.") The Quranic image ʿAmmār offered for global indifference to the destruction of Syria threw into stark relief the difference between the two events on World Refugee Day. The meager attendance at the former—even the motivations of those who did show up—cast a kind of judgment on the bright and affirmative mood of the latter. (I had already remarked that the protest was notable for who was absent—namely, the usual crowd of stalwart Edmonton leftists, the people I remembered organizing with in high school and college against the occupation of Palestine and the invasions of Afghanistan and Iraq—but whose parochial anti-imperialism blinds them to any political formations outside the West.) His critique extended outward, encompassing the generations in Syria who had done the work of devils and the backbiting Syrian newcomers in Canada. At his local mosque, he noticed an old man refusing to give up his chair to an even older man—he heard teenagers who should know better joking during a funeral prayer—he saw women whose veils barely covered their breasts. The destruction of the world spooled outward, eviscerating the relations between neighbors and kin, between Muslims and their god. And nightly, as the hour grew late, he watched videos of the regime's violence, and he wept.[48]

The destruction of the earth approaching the Hour of divine judgment afflicts everyone indiscriminately. Its fear and shock are indifferent to the just and the unjust. The Quran depicts the violence of that quaking: women will forsake their nurslings and miscarry, people will lurch about in terror. This is what ʿAmmār already sees, in measuring the course of his everyday life against the violence of the world. In that eschatological image, the "drunk" will be driven out with horror also at what they have themselves wrought. The Quran continues—*that is because of what your hands have sent forth, and because God wrongs not His servants* (Q. 22:10).

In this perspective, the constriction of the world retains a saving recourse only to the very one who is *Witness over all things* (Q. 22:17). What refuge there is, is always heteronomous. It is not made in this world: as in Q. 9:118, *the earth, despite its breadth, closed in upon them, and their own souls closed in upon them, and they deemed there to be no refuge from God, save with Him. . . .*

THRESHOLD

Natality

An invisible line separates the right and left halves of the stage, whose sets mirror each other except that the right side is lit more brightly and its birthday cake has one candle, not two. The play opens with Hagar seated on the left side and holding her swaddled child, singing to him: "O sea, for the sake of your waves / don't disturb those who sleep / O sea, for the sake of your tides / ebb quietly, lest you wake tender hearts / O sea, whose waves swing / in time with the moon / My dreams have been lost / and my wounds are laid bare to the waters." She rises from the rocking chair, walks to the right side of the stage, and places her son, Jamāl, in his crib. Then she calls a man to negotiate her escape to Europe from Aleppo via Mersin, a port city in southern Turkey. Gunfire picks up outside, which she curses: "I hope God destroys you. Don't you get tired of all this? You've made us hate life." Then she addresses Jamāl: "I envy you, little angel; you don't know what is happening. It makes me feel better that you're not afraid."

Explosions rock the set, and Hagar starts speaking to the sandbags piled against the window, naming them and inviting them to her son's birthday party. She continues arranging the apartment, talking to the sandbags and her sleeping son in turn, whispering her dreams and her fears. Her phone eventually rings; she chooses not to answer when she sees that it is her ex-husband, who abandoned her for another woman. Then the smuggler raises the price again, and in desperation she calls Nazeer, a successful businessman who had always wanted her. He agrees to lend her the money if she gives in to his desire. She resists, again and again, but then apologizes to her son and starts unbuttoning her shirt as the lights go out. Next, on the left side of the stage, she narrates her escape: the foreign fighters who insulted them at a checkpoint, her stay at a hotel in Turkey, the forty people floating in an overcrowded rubber dinghy. A huge wave overturned it as she was trying to give Jamāl some water and she lost him to the waves. She swam searching for him for three hours until the Turkish coastguard picked them up and returned them to Izmir. Her final lines are, "May God be with you. From now on, the sea is your crib and the waves are your swing. Today is your second birthday. No one is invited. Like last year and like every year, I will blow out your candles alone." As she addresses him a final time, she unwraps the swaddling blankets from the baby she had been carrying and consoling through the whole play. The swaddled form was no baby at all, the audience sees, but a bright life jacket that she lays gently on the sand. She blows out the candles, and the stage goes black.

The playwright, Aksam Alyousef, immigrated to Canada in 2016, at the height of the so-called refugee crisis that became an election issue in Canada that year. Exile and refuge are consistent themes of his work. His third play, "Hagar," is a solo performance, a one-woman play set in Aleppo in 2014 and 2015.[1] At the festival performance my wife and I attended in summer 2019, which was also directed by Alyousef, the lights came back on to the audience weeping. The local paper gave it 4.5 stars out of 5, writing that the main character "pushes with sadness and uncertainty and vulnerability as the audience's hearts break with her."[2]

The mood of the play is laden with sentimentality; it relies on exposition to reify tropes of foreign fighters and hypocritical European states; it flattens the political specificities of the Syrian war, giving its violence a generic quality. Yet these criticisms aside, it effectively emphasizes the interpenetration of multiple times. This extends beyond standard dramatic uses of analepsis or prolepsis to how the stage itself is organized, where each of its halves depicts the same house in Aleppo and the same objects are turned to different uses. This juxtaposition is both temporal and spatial: in recounting her exodus to Turkey, Hagar says, "I could tell you Izmir is a beautiful city. But I wasn't a tourist, I was a refugee and the sights meant nothing to me. We passed buildings, gardens, schools, and factories. In my mind, all I could see was the wreckage of Syria, our ruined homes. I saw blood everywhere, on the walls, on the curbs; body parts hanging on electricity lines." Although she left Aleppo for her son's sake, that he could have a different future, she could see nothing except the ruin of Syria, which she carried with her.

She crosses from one side of the stage to the other multiple times in the play, but because it is framed at beginning and end with her on the left side—namely, after her son's drowning—the performance as a whole expresses how her present is haunted at every turn by his death. She inhabits her loss and cannot escape it, even though the immediacy of the war has passed from her door. Every character of the play is vile: only her son was innocent and pure, and her desperation had been to shelter him from the "monsters" that she said have been "unleashed on the land." She implies that war has destroyed the living and that all that remains are memories of the virtue and integrity of the last generation, on the one hand, and hope and fear for the next generation, on the other.

The same theme animated a conversation I had in March 2018 with the regional director of an Islamic charitable organization that focused its efforts on those living in informal settlements on the Jordan-Syria border. Dr. Khālid explained their programs of medical aid, dry goods provision, and clothes distribution. (I later volunteered in one of its shoe distribution campaigns.) They donated livestock (goats, chickens, bees) to people living in these settlements, so that they would be able to use and sell any surplus goat's milk and eggs and honey. They were particularly concerned with prenatal care, offering free monthly checkups to pregnant refugees and paying for hospital deliveries, and then trying to provide regularly for those newborns and their families. But the main thing, the thing that drove their work, Dr. Khālid kept repeating, was the search for peace. And if the war hadn't ended yet, they had to make peace for themselves. They sent hundreds of children on *ʿumra*, the minor pilgrimage, and gave them daily peacebuilding lectures, telling them they "had to learn to live with [their] brothers, [their] friends." These lectures were one means of answering a question that Dr. Khālid raised: "How do you convince one people not to fight against another one?"

The protracted time of the war was straining the material basis of his organization's work, he explained, and eroding the buffer they tried to form between precarity and desperation. He continued, "We want them to forget the war. Maybe, God willing, as we hope, the war will stop. Then they can live in peace, live in a time when they can forget everything and live a life for themselves." I recalled a Nietzschean dictum about forgetting being the only release from historical cycles of violence.[3] I mentioned some friends who had to flee the regime and the difficulty I foresaw in convincing them to forget. He interrupted me. "Our only hope is if you can live without the war, if you can let it go." Life, in his account, is a fragile thing. His organization tried to shield the children from being exposed to the war, even from birth through the prenatal care programs he was proud of, offering those who lived in tent settlements clothes and shoes and livestock—all while knowing that what peace they could build through their pilgrimage trips and mutual exhortations could only be secured by the end of the war. And then by forgetting it.

Neither Alyousef nor Dr. Khālid had hope for the generation marked by the war, only for a future generation unscathed by its violence, free from both foreign interference and internal jealousy, released even from its memory—if the war ended and there was material funding enough to keep the babies safe as they grow. In this they echoed the anthropologist David Scott's exploration of the discontinuity between generations of memory. "It is the *transformation* of the 'affective force' of a traumatic event that concerns me," Scott writes, "the sense in which a founding experience can be inherited in ways that allow a succeeding generation to act upon it—or with it—differently than their predecessors did."[4] Loss may be inherited in different ways, and not all of them entail "embittered and melancholic fixation, at best in painfully ambivalent nostalgia and at worst in a blind desire for revenge." Scott observes a diverging "generational habitus" between the "profoundly traumatized and *disappointed* generation that lives the ruin of the Grenada Revolution as an absolute, irrevocable loss and a recurring, unending end" and that of another generation, "children of another era of expectation," one that is marked not by loss but by its aftermath. "The past, needless to say, has not gone away . . . but the cathexis that drives the search for its whereabouts is now disconnected from the temporal structure of revolutionary desire or (its sometime twin) revolutionary recrimination."[5] In short, loss can be animated by a different remembrance, affording alternate forms of politics and life.

Such discontinuity is what Dr. Khālid staked his charitable programs on: to tend to the living, certainly, but reserving "hope" for those unscathed by the war—however much they may have to live with its effects. It is also what Alyousef allegorized through Hagar's desperation on behalf of her son, to save him from the monsters this generation has become. They each affirmed the power of new beginnings (however obliquely) but also found their effective possibility to be marred by the devastation of the present. Hagar's son Jamāl ("beauty") was pure and innocent—her angel, she called him—but he drowned in the very effort she took to save him. Dr. Khālid shook his head as he spoke of the unsustainability of his programs—and he worried for what would come after. For both Alyousef and Dr. Khālid, the present had been hollowed out, and what hope there was lay in a future separated from this eviscerated present. Until that future arrives, with time suspended, the endless present offers only a geography of ruin (*al-kharāb*).[6]

Alyousef and Dr. Khālid's accounts of the suspended present were each articulated with reference to religion. In describing the work of his organization, for example, Dr. Khālid had described the religious ethics driving the need for integrity in humanitarian work. The funding of his programs came nearly entirely from British Muslims moved to act for their fellows in the *umma*.[7] For his part, Alyousef was ironic about the religious overtones of his play. Interviewing him in January 2019, I remarked its parallels with the Quranic story of Hagar in the desert. The two women share a name, an absent partner, and concern for a young son. Each story features sand and water. Each Hagar appeals to God for his mercy. Only, Alyousef's play does not feature a divine intervention; when Hagar sees Jamāl's lips parched and wants to give him water, like Hagar before her saw Ishmael's thirst and ran between the mountains Safa and Marwa in her desperation, the angel Gabriel did not appear to reveal the well called Zamzam. Instead that is when the wave comes to sweep her son overboard. "Maybe the time of miracles is gone," Alyousef said ruefully.

I shook my head, appreciating how deep his despair ran. Yet surely that kind of epochal rupture would depend on what counts as a miracle. I remembered ʿAlī (see Chapter 2), who celebrated machine technologies as modern miracles, comparable to examples from early Islamic hagiographies. And I remembered Bilāl (see Chapter 3), who insisted that it was a divine power that had shielded him from the Syrian security forces hunting for him house to house in Daraa at the beginning of the revolution. He had cited Q. 36:9: *And We placed a barrier before them and a barrier behind them and veiled them; so they see not.* According to the Islamic scholarly traditions ʿAlī and Bilāl had each studied in Syria, such miracles should be understood through the typology of events that break with the habitual order (*kharq al-ʿāda*), whether at the hands of the prophets (*muʿjizāt*, miracles that challenge and humble) or the saints (*karāmāt*, miracles that honor and ennoble). By such accounts miracles happen every day, and the divine agency is implicated in both the habitual order and its exceptions.

For their part, Alyousef and Dr. Khālid deferred worldly hope onto those of the next generation who could in fact take distance from the war. They insisted on this possibility, even if they were not optimistic about it obtaining. Hannah Arendt famously called that possibility of a new beginning "natality," and made it the central category of politics: "the new beginning inherent in birth"—the birth of Hagar's Jamāl and of the orphans Dr. Khālid supports, perhaps—"can make itself felt in the world only because the newcomer possesses the capacity of beginning something anew, that is, of acting."[8] There is already something miraculous about this possibility of a new beginning, which perhaps complicates Alyousef's ceding the time of miracles to history. At the end of her essay "What Is Freedom?," Arendt writes,

> If it is true that action and beginning are essentially the same, it follows that a capacity for performing miracles must likewise be within the range of human faculties. This sounds stranger than it actually is. It is in the very nature of every new beginning that it breaks into the world as an "infinite improbability," and yet it is precisely this infinitely improbable which actually constitutes the very texture of everything we call real.[9]

For Arendt, of course, such miracle and hope are brought into being through human speech and action (not divine intervention); and she is concerned with the "second birth" of participation in a public realm (not the birth of children, like Alyousef and Dr. Khālid).[10] And although her political action is the miraculous interjection of contingency into the linear time of human history, such action is still finite and constrained by that linearity.[11]

Alyousef and Dr. Khālid might well have agreed with Arendt, given their shared pessimism about the present.[12] But most of my other interlocutors in the following course of this book do not require that the touch of contingency have a human agent.[13] Indeed they would argue that contingency itself, however routine the miracle in question, expresses precisely an inhuman dimension. Nor would they yield the linearity of the time in which we live, instead insisting that it is cross-cut by parabolic vectors of repetition and redemption, renewal and ruin. They stand closer to Benjamin than to Arendt, as he (in terms distinct from Arendt's "natality") worked toward a concept of "the present as now-time shot through with splinters of messianic time."[14] Benjamin "proposed the vision of a history in which nothing is sacrificed, nothing is lost forever. If each moment of the past can be actualized, replayed under other conditions on a new stage, nothing in human history is irreparable. By the same token, nothing in the future is inevitable."[15] Yet this too yields melancholy, not optimism. For even in Benjamin's famous Thesis IX, whose angel of history—eyes wide, mouth open, wings spread—"would like to stay, awaken the dead, and make whole what has been smashed," the angel serves precisely to arrest the messianic promise it bears.[16]

For Alyousef and Dr. Khālid, and, too, for many of my other interlocutors in this book, the possibility of a new beginning is something to be endured, neither altogether relinquished nor celebrated. Meanwhile, the war continued. My Syrian friends and interlocutors in Jordan and Canada watched as the names of towns and villages were transmuted, through an expanding topography of devastation, into emblems of ruin (Daraa, Ghouta, Aleppo, Yarmouk, Daraya, Douma, Kafrnabel . . .). They overlaid multiple registers of loss in expressing the problem of natality in the ruined present: the loss of childhood, the loss of ethics, and the loss of Islam were interwoven in their articulations, including when considering the future horizon of a generation ("the children of the war"). Indeed, some of the most iconic and the most searing images of the Syrian war had to do with children (drowned on a Turkish beach, shell-shocked in an ambulance in Ghouta, miraculously rescued from rubble in Aleppo). These images were broadcast by citizen journalists and by some news media and on social media networks. They were one idiom of expressing the utter devastation of the present and of naming the ruin of the *umma*. Violence against children was already there at the beginning of the Syrian war, for the 2011 protests themselves were sparked by the arrests and torture of children in the southern city of Daraa (see Chapter 3). At one such protest in Daraa on April 29, 2011, security forces detained Hamza al-Khatib, a thirteen-year-old boy. His body was returned to his family nearly a month later with numerous broken bones, gunshot wounds, cigarette burns, and a severed penis.

Alyousef, the self-declaredly apolitical dramaturge living in Canada whose play *Hagar* spurred this threshold reflection on natality and contingency, described the time of the war as a fever-dream, a nightmare in which those under its sway lost their ethical judgment. "Maybe after the war they will wake up," he offered. He could not see himself returning until the regime had fully consolidated its rule and things returned to normal, he said, but then quoted the proverb, "If you have drunk from the water of Damascus you will always return to it" (*idhā sharibta min mā' dimashq sa-ta'ūdu ilayhā dā'iman*).

Inhabiting the ruined present, many of my interlocutors turned in their exile to memories of the sweetness of life in Syria. Bilāl, the imam from Daraa whose practices of memory and care I follow in Chapter 3, returned compulsively to the images of his orchard and his beloved Omari Mosque. Marjān, a professional seamstress who now taught sewing to other newcomer women in an IFSSA-sponsored program in Edmonton, described Syria to me in summer 2019 as a blessed land fragrant with culture, religion, and scholarship (*ḥaḍāra, dīn, ʿilm*). Its politicians may be corrupt and evil, she said, but its people are generous and gentle. History itself began in Damascus (Cain killed Abel on its Mount Qasyoun), and there history will end (for Jesus is foretold to return to its Umayyad Mosque). Even if she herself eventually had to flee, she was grateful to have lived there in her life. She halted her reverie to turn to me. "Basit, would you visit Syria again?" I remembered the affable reassurances of an American contractor in a Beirut airport lounge in February 2019, boasting that the bars and businesses of Damascus were hopping despite the war dragging on. Of course I would like to, I replied to her, but I'm not sure I would, now. It's complicated.

I thought of Bilāl living at the Syrian border and of the videos he had sent me that week. When I had left Jordan most recently, he had given me a small green booklet on the blessings of the Levant. Its final brief chapter exhorts readers not to disparage or demean that land by leaving for other parts of the world.[17]

Marjān smiled. "Yes—that complication is what we constantly consider now, as the war is ending. People have different circumstances: the mother of a friend wanted to die in Syria, not in Canada—so she went back, and she died there. I understand people have different reasons to go back—but I don't have those reasons now. Our exile (*ghurba*) is encompassing—we sorely miss the closeness and intimacy of life in Syria. But we need to remember God's bounty: Canada is a generous and free country, and you can find good and evil everywhere. What matters in the end is what kind of path (*ṭarīq*) God sets for you. And then, after Bashar, we will return, God willing."

In Islamic pietistic genres, despair (*ya's, qanaṭ*) is a sin. One must not abandon hope of God's mercy. A hadith even says that God "laughs at the despair of His servants and soon changes it," for the divine mercy is infinite.[18] Indeed such despair (constricting the divine beneficence and perfection) verges on unbelief: *He said, 'Who despairs of the mercy of his Lord, save those who are astray?'* (Q. 15:56). To be clear, the hope and despair of Alyousef and Dr. Khālid were limited to the grim social and political horizon: they were directed at the worldly lives of others, not their own eschatological fate. And they did not, like many of the other aid workers and refugees I encountered in my fieldwork and follow through the rest of this book, understand the Syrian crisis with reference to theological concepts of tribulation and trial (*fitna*, *ibtilā'*). The next chapter of this book elaborates these concepts in greater detail, tracing their variations and their implications.

2

TRIBULATION

The theological figure of tribulation was there at the beginning of the Syrian revolution. In March 2011, in the weeks immediately after the children were arrested in Daraa on suspicion of disparaging the president, with protests springing up in solidarity across the country, Syrian religious figures addressed the emerging crisis. For example, the traditionist scholar Saʿīd Ramaḍān al-Būṭī recognized that reform and repair (*iṣlāḥ*) were a religious obligation—but cautioned that these must not become an alibi for igniting civil strife (*fitna*). The mufti of the republic, Badr al-Dīn Ḥassūn, called for calm, for the protesters to return home, and condemned the "sermonizers of *fitna*" (namely, those scholars like Yūsuf al-Qaraḍāwī who urged all Syrians to oppose the regime). And a few months later, the exiled shaykh Muḥammad al-Yaʿqūbī appeared on Al Jazeera to argue for the religious obligation of opposing oppressive rulers. The hadiths in which the Prophet warns against *fitna* do not apply here, he declared, because "truth and falsehood are clear."[1] Each of these scholars evaluated the legitimacy of the Syrian uprising with reference to the term *fitna*, a figure of tribulation, of upheaval and unrest.

My interlocutors' discussions of the Syrian revolution and the war often engaged the same set of terms, analyzing their scope and their scriptural valences, arguing for which theological paradigm best fits a contemporary example, distinguishing between multiple senses and uses. In doing so, their contestations and citations, their styles of reasoning and forms of suasion, should be understood with reference to the discursive tradition of Islam.[2] More specifically, their arguments contributed to (even when they did not explicitly reference) the tradition of debate over the legitimacy of uprising against an established ruler, within which *fitna* "epitomize[s] all that is objectionable in an act of rebellion against the government: it mean[s] sedition, civil strife, the disruption of political and religious order, and a grave menace to the social fabric of the community."[3] But *is* that what it means? Does that concept apply to this case? What are its other, perhaps latent senses? What alternative terms are available? My own effort at understanding the grammar of tribulation often reflected their analytic habits. These terms were not static, of course; what my interlocutors meant by "tribulation" (whether *fitna* or the sense of trial imparted by *ibtilā'*) varied widely. Yet its substance in each case is not merely a polemical function of their respective politics. Nor does it simply reflect a theological doctrine.[4] As shown in this chapter, what my interlocutors mean by "tribulation" is worked out as they confront forms of affliction in the immediacy of their own lives.[5]

Balā, lexically a "trial, or a test," presents itself as a tribulation, an event that affects an individual for demonstrative purposes.[6] Likewise *fitna*, in the classical Arabic lexicons a "burning with fire, the melting of gold and silver in order to separate, or distinguish, the bad from the good," is "a trial, or probation, and affliction, distress, or hardship; or the trial by which the condition of a person may be evinced, in respect of good and of evil," hence often "a temptation."[7] But the Quran radically expands the scope of these terms. Indeed, the Quran builds the divine trial into the very nature of creation: *He it is who created the heavens and the earth in six days, while His throne was upon the water, that He might try you (li-yabluwakum) as to which of you is most virtuous in deed . . .* (Q. 11:7). Even though *balā* and *fitna* only appear in twenty-nine and twenty-one Quranic passages, respectively, it is difficult to delimit their range. The vernacular sense of a deprivation is certainly present—*And We will indeed test you with something of fear and hunger, and loss of wealth, souls, and fruits; and give glad tidings to the patient* (Q. 2:155)—but even the beauty of the earth is likewise a trial (Q. 18:7–8). And if death is a trial, so equally is life—*[God] Who created death and life that He may try you as to which of you is most virtuous in deed, and He is the Mighty, the Forgiving* (Q. 67:2)—with the exegetes commenting at length on the sequential priority of death over life in this verse. But the divine trial is not even restricted to afflictions within life or the play between life and death, for it includes the eschatological manifestation of secrets in the Last Judgment (Q. 86:9). Even in this fleeting life, *fitna* and *balā* animate the embryonic creation of humans (Q. 76:2), the difficulty of abiding by divine commands

(Q. 3:154; 5:94; 7:163), the differences that cleave community (Q. 5:48), the unequal distribution of provisions (Q. 6:53; 89:15–16), and both evil *and* good (Q. 21:35), both enjoyment *and* affliction (Q. 21:111; 39:49). The terms *balā* and *fitna* do not appear in the Quranic narratives of divine punishment, meaning that the Quran does not permit the causal association of suffering with sin.[8] No one is exempt from trials, not even prophets. All creation is a trial—indeed, creation itself is a trial. There is no escape from its ordeal.[9]

Read together, these Quranic passages render the meaning of experience fundamentally contingent, for they retract the equation of worldly success with otherworldly felicity. Across individual, collective, historical, and creational scales, experiences of contraction (*qabḍ*) and expansion (*basṭ*) participate in the disclosure of God as the one who contracts (*al-qābiḍ*) and expands (*al-bāsiṭ*). Wealth and want, defeat and triumph, sickness and health are each such trials of disclosure, for they convene singular and immanent confrontations with the insufficiency of creational existence. (Only God is *al-ghaniyy*, the self-sufficient.) These confrontations are impersonally demonstrative of good and evil, to be sure, but their final meaning is ultimately withdrawn.

To be clear, there are internal divisions across the ways the trial is configured. For example, some of my interlocutors distinguished between a *fitna* and an *ibtilā'* on the basis of their respective objects: the former affects the social body, while the latter affects an individual. Yet they also suggested a qualitative distinction to this difference in scale: a *fitna* is not simply the sum of multiple *ibtilā'āt*. The former operates according to a logic of contagion, spreading confusion and strife among people. The latter operates according to a logic of the limit, where even an ordinary event puts one to the test. Even for those interlocutors who insisted on the difference between these terms, as seen later, they may implicate each other. Commonly across these accounts, the locus of *fitna* as the spread of confusion and strife is not any social body (*mujtamaʿ*) but specifically the Islamic Community (*umma*), which it sets into upheaval. That is, they see this ordeal to implicate the Muslim Community writ large, not simply displaced Syrians as individuals or a national collective. Our conversations frequently passed from discussing the tribulation of the Syrian war to locating it as but one instance of the broader trial facing the Muslims today.

My first interlocutor in this chapter (pseudonym "Abū Bakr") is a teacher from Damascus who has a doctorate in Islamic law and legal theory (*fiqh*, *uṣūl*) from al-Azhar University in Cairo. He was displaced from the southern Syrian city of Daraa in the early days of the revolution and now directs the ʿAbdullāh bin al-Mubārak Program in Zaatari Refugee Camp. For Abū Bakr, it was only because the individual members of the Community were mutually implicated in solidarity that the divine interpellation put some to test. For him, witnessing the divine trial has meant the acceptance of sacrifice, a trait that also characterized the eponym of his sharia studies educational program.

My second interlocutor here (pseudonym "ʿUmar") is a Syrian exile who has lived in Jordan for decades. A scholar with a doctorate in Quranic sciences from al-Jazīra University in Sudan, he was also a regular commentator on revolutionary television and media. We met at his house in north Amman, having been introduced by a mutual acquaintance. For ʿUmar, engaging the divine trial has meant a strenuous reckoning with the corrosive drift of idolatry. For him, the vanguard of the Community is the protagonist in a preternatural struggle between good and evil.

My third interlocutor here (pseudonym "ʿUthmān") is an activist at the Association of the Quran and Prophetic Practice (*Jamʿiyyat al-Kitāb wa-l-Sunna*), one of the largest Islamic charitable organizations in Jordan. We met consistently over the course of my Jordan-side fieldwork. For ʿUthmān, the divine trial is the secret means by which God distributes the worldly occasions of good and ill. The journal of his organization in the poor neighborhood of east Amman had long argued that the Community was besieged by fracturing tribulations.

My fourth interlocutor here (pseudonym "ʿAlī") had worked at an Islamic aid organization and had studied the Islamic sciences for eight years in Damascus, which is where I first met him in 2005. He later moved to Edmonton, the city in northwest Canada where most of my Canada-side fieldwork was based. For ʿAlī, the divine trial is disclosive, revelatory, apocalyptic: not of a single rule or divine habit but of the evanescent dynamic of outer meaning and inner reality. For him, prior episodes of the history of the Community provided the means to understand the dynamic movement of the present.

The four versions of "tribulation" articulated in this chapter do not exhaust its political and ethical configurations. But the juxtaposition of these four accounts establishes the density of this figure and, too, its opacity. In the four sections to follow, I ground my interlocutors' arguments within their ethical-political practices and sensibilities. A brief fifth section then traces the "grammar" of these figures, with a view to formally comparing their affects and intensities.

ACCEPTING

The sky was hot and bright and utterly still. Ḥāmid, the portly guard who had accompanied me since having my permit confirmed at the camp administration building, declared we needed water before essaying back into the heat. He ducked into a large empty conference room emblazoned with maps and flags and messages of gratitude to sponsors. We were in Zaatari Refugee Camp, ten kilometers into the semi-arid steppe east of the city of Mafraq, at the southernmost edge of the plains of Hauran that topographically unite this region (now in north Jordan) with the Syrian governorate of Daraa. Further north, Hauran is arable—it produced grain for the Romans through the Ottomans—but here the basalt has given way to the yellow-red dust of the Syrian Desert. It sweeps across roads and rises in plumes behind vehicles. The low-lying camp first becomes visible as slips of white on the horizon. Its massive scale is difficult to grasp from the highway, certainly not from its entrance, which is manned by Jordanian gendarmerie checking identification and exit permits. Hundreds of Syrians, mostly young men, leave the camp every day to work as laborers nearby. I visited repeatedly in summer 2018, when the camp hosted nearly 80,000 refugees, six years after it had been opened under the auspices of the Jordan Hashemite Charity Organization (JHCO) in cooperation with UNHCR. The camp is divided into twelve districts, which are then subdivided into blocks.[10]

Ḥāmid dabbed sweat from his forehead as we left the administration stockade through another secured chain link fence. We walked down the main market street, named the Champs-Élysées (a homonym of Shām-Élysées, Heavenly Syria) after the French hospital that once stood at its head, passing restaurants and barbershops and bicycle repair stalls, a chicken squawking, children huddled over a kite.[11] Ḥāmid waved to a colleague in a van carrying members of a German NGO. His colleague pointed to the vehicle's air conditioner and gave us a big grin. "Next time you should bring a car, it would be much better for you," Ḥāmid sighed. The only other vehicles permitted in the camp were transport trucks that act as taxis. We squinted against the sun. He explained that tensions in the camp had eased in the last few years, as conditions improved and as the security forces built up some measure of trust. They had first given Syrians canvas tents rather than the metal trailers ("caravans") that now populated each of the twelve sectors. The tents were overcrowded, cooking fires started frequently, the water and sanitation system was unhygienic, the roads weren't paved so dust blew everywhere, sections flooded or steeped in mud when it rained. In a high-profile altercation that escalated over police arrests in 2014, panicking security forces shot at protesters, killing one youth. Facing these conditions, I thought, it was no wonder that the Syrians protested. "I was even hit by a stone to my temple," Ḥāmid said. Unlike Syrian refugees in Turkey or Lebanon, those in Zaatari regularly agitated against camp authorities, organizing sit-ins and blockades. The fractious encounters declined only once the UNHCR camp management started working with informal street leaders, recognizing their authority and making them "de facto partners in camp governance."[12] Ḥāmid pointed out stale bread spread on plastic sheets to dry, which camp residents sold to farmers nearby as animal feed.

We arrived at the first large mosque trailer we would visit that day, Jāmiʿ al-tawḥīd (The Mosque of Divine Unicity), which was cool and dark. Red carpet along the floors, a few short bookcases with Qurans, small windows shuttered against the heat. Three men sat inside, waiting for the hour of afternoon prayer. The next mosque we visited was named after the Prophet's cousin Jaʿfar al-Ṭayyār, who famously sought asylum with the Christian Negus of Abyssinia against the idolatrous Meccans who came to return the Muslims to enslavement and persecution.[13] (Much as the camp residents had sought asylum in Jordan against the Syrian regime's brutality, I thought.) This mosque trailer, unlike the first one, had some running water to make ablutions. A young boy sat against the wall, nodding his head in rhythm as he recited his Quran lesson. His memorization circle of fifteen boys met every evening after the dusk prayer, he said. As I visited more mosques over subsequent trips, I found that almost all had such Quran memorization groups, loosely coordinated through the ʿAbdullāh bin al-Mubārak Program.

Hospitality Politics

The ʿAbdullāh bin al-Mubārak Program sits on the far side of Zaatari Camp, away from the bustle of the market street and the school buildings. The site

FIGURE 3. Playground at the ʿAbdullāh bin al-Mubārak Program Site, Zaatari Refugee Camp. Basit Kareem Iqbal, 2018

is formed by white metal trailers facing each other with a sheet metal roof over a common courtyard. Its walls are painted in greens and blues, depicting riverine scenes and lush foliage, visions of paradise in strong contrast to the desert and dust outside. Water and reeds painted on the walls, flowers and walls, the floor bare and dusty (see figure 3). When I arrived at the site that weekend, the program director was already teaching. I waited with Zāhid, a young teacher at the institute, in the office trailer until his class ended. I sat in a plastic chair across from the director's desk. Other chairs lined the walls, facing a dark brown coffee table, with piles of photocopied books stacked against a printer. Printed charts and schedules covered a bulletin board hung against the far wall. The roar of the generator in the courtyard was barely shut out by the trailer door. It accompanied our conversations (and later made interview transcription difficult).

"I am your brother Abū Bakr," the director introduced himself. A large man with a deep voice in his late forties, he had studied sharia at al-Azhar University in Cairo and returned to Daraa with a doctorate in 2007, only to find that the mosques in Daraa already had enough imams and preachers. He served as a preacher (*khaṭīb*) for one year and then involved himself in a mosque construction program abandoned with the war. He came to Zaatari in July 2012, just after the camp opened. Unlike many other Syrians I met, who entered much later or who left as soon as they could, his perspective on the camp extended over its whole span. He found a vocation there.

> As I stayed here I found that I had to, as the scholars say, spend charitably from (lit. purify) the religious knowledge I had gathered—just as when a person has wealth, he withdraws zakat from it, it's the same thing with religious knowledge (*al-ʿilm al-sharʿī*). Here in the camp our family are in need of learning the religious sciences; praise be to God, we began the Program to this end, and we are continuing to expand its activities.

He spoke pointedly into my voice recorder, expressing his gratitude to the Kingdom of Jordan. "Thank God, they laid their trust in us, through everything that was happening. Here in the camp we had nearly weekly protests and scuffles. But then, praise be to God, we began to raise the consciousness between people." He acted as a moderator between competing factions and articulated residents' demands to the camp administration. "I mean, we are guests here [in Jordan]; it's not right for us to instigate protests or fights here while the brothers [in Jordan] are giving us food and drink. Eventually the protests stopped, praise be to God, and they allowed us to open prayer spaces and they established schools and hospitals and markets."

Abū Bakr was very aware of the tenuous status of Syrians in the country. When we met, the majority of UN-recognized refugees in the country did not have access to affordable healthcare[14] or reasonable basic education,[15] and even those who did manage to obtain a prized employment permit were mostly restricted to menial labor.[16] Syrians within formal refugee camps, of course, had healthcare and education coordinated through UNHCR, but the overwhelming majority of Syrians in Jordan lived outside these camps. The refrain of refugees in tent settlements and aid workers in Amman alike was that the camps are "like prisons." The likeness is not hard to make out: Zaatari and Azraq are completely fenced in chain link and barbed wire and are surrounded by moats, with soldiers guarding their perimeters. Azraq camp, which opened in April 2014 to accommodate "overflow" from Zaatari, has an even more intensive (and thoroughly digitized) "culture of political surveillance" and is more remote, deeper into the southern desert.[17]

The residency status of Syrians in Jordan is also suspended. Like its neighbors, Jordan is not a signatory to the 1951 United Nations Geneva Convention on Refugees. A 1998 Memorandum of Understanding between the Jordanian government and UNHCR permitted asylum seekers to remain in the country for six months, while articles of the Jordanian Constitution enshrined various protections for asylum seekers—but also granted the Ministry of the Interior the discretion to deport illegal entrants. The 1998 Memorandum was amended in 2014 after the massive influx of Syrians because of the war: it confirms the principle of non-refoulement (the principle forbidding returning asylum-seekers), but there remains no possibility of local integration despite the 2018 "amnesty" proclaimed for the 30,000–50,000 Syrians then estimated to live outside camps without permits to do so. Syrians in Jordan are officially referred to as "refugees" (a term that had previously been reserved for Palestinians) but also, broadly, as "guests," affirming a relationship of hospitality in which guest and host have clearly defined roles.

The Jordanian government has long inscribed the social obligation of *karam* (generosity) into a national (and commercial) mandate, in a construction that has been repurposed toward offering refuge to Palestinians, Iraqis, and now Syrians.[18] This discourse of hospitality bears its own risks. "The host must fear the guest" (*lāzim al-muʿazzib yikhāf min al-ḍayf*), in a Jordanian Bedouin proverb that the anthropologist Andrew Shryock explores, because "hospitality creates a momentary overlap of the inner and the outer dimensions of a house (a *bayt* or a *dar*)"—and so protracted displacement, meaning protracted hospitality, quickly rehearses a question of sovereignty.[19] Indeed, in Jordan, as in Lebanon and Turkey, hospitality has formed a "discursive strategy of socio-spatial control" practiced by governments and humanitarian agencies alike.[20] *Pas d'hospitalité*, writes Derrida, step of hospitality/no hospitality: "on the one hand, *The* law of unlimited hospitality (to give the new arrival all of one's home and oneself . . .) and on the other hand, the laws (in the plural), those rights and duties that are always conditioned and conditional."[21] The hospitality relation is aporetic. The scuffles and stone-throwing in Zaatari camp were demands in the name of hospitality, for a better hospitality, against the "conditioned and conditional" laws (and chaotic administration) of hospitality; yet they were also a breach of etiquette. In mediating those early conflicts, Abū Bakr sought to repair that breach while rearticulating (not relinquishing) the claims of the protesters.

Although he pointed to the status of Syrians as "guests" in Jordan, moreover, he also insisted on a relationship of brotherhood (*ukhuwwa*) that further complicated the hospitality dynamic. He introduced himself to me as "your brother"; he described the Jordanians as "the brothers" who offered them refuge; later on, he ended our conversation with greetings to "the brothers" in Canada. He spoke directly into my voice recorder:

> And we hope, if God wills, to meet them; we welcome any one of them to visit us, simply for the sake of our brotherhood, as in the hadith telling that a man visited his brother in another township, and God sent an angel in the form of a man on the road to ask where he was going. He said, I am visiting my brother for the sake of our brotherhood (*min bāb al-ukhuwwa*), without any claims of kinship. The angel said, do you have a need which you are going to fulfill in visiting him? He said, no. He said, I am a messenger from God to inform you—eh, what's the hadith?—that God loves you as you love him.[22]

This "brotherhood" is not outside the politics of hospitality, of course—but in extending his invitation to the Canadian brothers, to visit the Syrian brethren among the Jordanian brothers, Abū Bakr's rhetoric both indicates the reversibility of guest-host relationships and grounds this brotherhood in divine love beyond whatever claims of kinship and need.

The 'Abdullāh bin al-Mubārak Program

Abū Bakr's gratitude to the Kingdom of Jordan, notably, was not for the Jordanian brothers offering food and drink (for that much can rightfully be claimed by any guest), but specifically for the trust it placed in the 'Abdullāh bin al-Mubārak Program, when the government permitted the allotment of a site within Zaatari Camp dedicated to fulfilling a pressing need that the international aid community could not address. As Abū Bakr explained, man cannot live by bread alone. Religious knowledge (*al-'ilm al-shar'ī*) guides a person through life, safeguarding the individual from unknowingly falling into sin. However, the ʿAbdullāh bin al-Mubārak Program did not only provide religious guidance for individuals in the camp. It also served a communal function in creating a legitimate space for the exercise of religious differences at a time when the excesses of religious extremism were close to mind. A graduate of a sharia institute in Damascus later explained to me why such a program was necessary:

> We are from a society whose thought is evil, whose thinking has become excessive. . . . [After the war started] we encountered strange ideas we had never read about except as remarks in the ancient books: declaring others to be apostates (*takfīr*) and bombing them (*tafjīr*), accusing others of corruption (*tafsīq*), killing others merely due to suspicion. We seek refuge in God from these things!

The mandate of the program, then, was to attend the individual and collective need for religious knowledge, which would foster personal virtue but also allow for civil relations between people in the camp and beyond.

The infrastructure of the program supported three initiatives corresponding to distinct pedagogical objectives. The first of these initiatives was dedicated to specifically supporting orphans and widows (their fathers/husbands either imprisoned, disappeared, or martyred). In a video recording of a speech to prospective donors, Abū Bakr commented that through engaging orphans and widows, through pedagogy (*tarbiya*) and teaching (*taʿlīm*), they hoped to alleviate some of the psychological issues that had befallen them as a result of the Syrian crisis. The second initiative was the Usāma bin Zayd Institute for the Preservation of the Quran, open to students ages nine to fourteen. It focused on Quran memorization, jurisprudence of purity and prayer, and virtues of the Prophet's companions. The third initiative was named the Imam al-Shāfiʿī Institute for the Study of Arabic and Islam; it comprised four levels and was open to students fifteen years old and up. When I visited in summer 2018, there were 180 students enrolled in this institute—a substantial number but, the teachers told me, a far cry from the multiple series of around 500 students each who had gone through the program in earlier years. Men and women had separate teachers and classes (men on Saturdays, women on Wednesdays) but followed an identical program of study.

TABLE 1: Course of Study (Six-Month Terms for Each Level)

▪ **Level 1**	▪ **Level 2**	▪ **Level 3**	▪ **Level 4**
-jurisprudence -prophetic biography -creed -hadith -etiquette of seeking knowledge	-jurisprudence -prophetic biography -creed -technical study of hadith -grammar	-jurisprudence -principles of preaching -creed -Quranic studies -grammar	-jurisprudence -legal theory -Islamic history -creed -Quran recitation/ memorization -Quranic exegesis and its methods -grammar

After graduating from the Imam al-Shāfiʿī Institute, students may enter the Advanced Institute for Specialized Study. This, too, comprised several levels and focused on more advanced topics (e.g., jurisprudence of inheritance, criminal law).

The curriculum of each level was organized around key texts thoroughly in line with the scholarship of Jordanian/Gulf Salafism[23]—even though some of the program teachers were graduates of Syrian and Egyptian Islamic institutions that were staunchly antagonistic toward Salafism writ large. Indeed, some of the key contestations between the Syrian religious establishment and Salafi scholars took place in the late 1990s and early 2000s, while these teachers were themselves students at sharia institutes in Damascus and elsewhere.[24] The traditionalist scholars in Syria succeeded in thoroughly marginalizing their doctrinal rivals, meaning that the program curriculum's Salafist commitments were quite a departure from the teachers' own instruction.

Such religious education programs proved immensely popular in Zaatari Camp. A 2014 education needs assessment survey reports that 34 percent of children aged six to eleven and 40 percent of youth aged twelve to seventeen attended one or more such programs.[25] At roughly the same time as this survey was conducted, there were 120 orphans registered in the ʿAbdullāh bin al-Mubārak program's orphan support programs, 230 students enrolled in its Usāma bin Zayd Institute, and 560 students enrolled in its Imam al-Shāfiʿī Institute.[26] Religious education mostly complemented children's formal schooling, but (given how many more mosques than schools there are in Zaatari) these programs were also more accessible than the latter.

These programs were developed and implemented independently of the formal education programs whose curriculum, attendance, and pedagogy were coordinated and measured by international partners. The Zaatari Education Sector Working Group grew curious. "Despite the prevalence of educational programs run from mosques in Zaʿatari camp, little is known about them, and they were not included in the [previous year's needs assessment report]."[27] From a dedicated focus group, the working group gleaned the broad contours of the thriving religious education sector: news of these programs spread through word of mouth and at mosques; they were open to both girls and boys; they took place daily or on the weekend; they were funded by private charitable institutes and were free to participants (teachers received "symbolic sums"); they sometimes included general and vocational education; students received certificates and awards. Yet the generality of the information reported there speaks to the sheer lack of detail offered by focus group participants. The wariness of community leaders to participate at all—"It is important to note that [this focus group discussion] was conducted with three individuals only, due to participants cancelling or not attending, even after rescheduling"—suggests their reticence to expose the religious education programs to too much institutional scrutiny.

The program also evidenced a clear concern for bureaucratic rituals and the material infrastructure of higher education institutions. Videos the teachers shared of the "graduation ceremonies" of the various cohorts register the importance of formality. In these ceremonies, the covered courtyard that is the center of the program site is filled with hundreds of people sitting in neatly arranged plastic chairs facing the dais, which students approach in a steady line to receive the graduation certificate, shake hands with the program director, and pose for a photograph. The teachers here bore their mandate (to sow sound knowledge of religion) in terms of an institutional vision.

In describing the program to me in 2018, Abū Bakr left the future scope of its mandate undetermined, perhaps because of political sensitivity in talking to me, a stranger (albeit a brother) from Canada—but perhaps also because the course of the war had already dramatically shifted in favor of the regime, leaving few clear paths of return available to these Syrians in

Jordan. In contrast, when rebel groups had been winning substantial gains five years earlier, he addressed a gathering of Kuwaiti Salafis from the Jam'iyyat Iḥyā' Turāth al-Islāmī (Revival of Islamic Heritage Society) who were visiting Jordan on a charitable mission.[28] In a video recording of his speech then, still in the first few months of the program, he observed that people in the camp had their daily sustenance provided for, though they still needed paved roads and sanitary toilets. But these infrastructural needs aside, there was another dearth in the camp. It was 'Abdullāh bin al-Mubārak, he continued, after whom they had named their program, who had once said, "After prophethood, I know of nothing better than disseminating knowledge" (*lā a'lam ba'd al-nubuwwa shay' afḍal min bathth al-'ilm*). This is what they sought to do; and he described the purpose of the program as being

> to prepare the students, male and female, who come from more than fifty towns and regions in Syria: for when they return to their lands after the fall of the regime, they will be the ones to spread the knowledge (*yanshurūn al-'ilm*), to deliver the Friday sermons, to establish the circles of Quran memorization and the circles of knowledge, and to conciliate between people (*yuṣliḥūn bayn al-nās*); to be instruments of change, beneficial actions, in their lands and in their societies.

Abū Bakr remarked on the ambitions of the program:

> Some of our brothers were surprised at [the planned course of the sharia program], they objected to how much time it would take. To answer their objection, well, I recall the proverb, "work for Zaatari like you will live there forever, and work for Syria like you will return there tomorrow."

He chuckled at his own rendition of the proverb, "work for your worldly life (*dunyā*) like you will live forever, and work for your afterlife (*ākhira*) like you will die tomorrow." An exhortation to allow the imminent eschaton to order one's priorities, in Abū Bakr's paraphrase the brief duration of temporal existence was aligned with Zaatari Camp while the abiding destination of the refugees was, still, Syria. He explained:

> We take the approach that, while you are residing here, you should pursue knowledge, study, and concern yourself with religious knowledge—

> so that, God willing, you will be ready for the time after the fall of Bashar, by the will of God—and we ask God that that time come soon!

In similar terms, a UNHCR video that describes the ʿAbdullāh bin al-Mubārak Program as a "joint Jordanian-Qatari initiative" shows one of the teachers at the program describing its Quran memorization and religious education programs. "God willing," he concludes, "they [the program graduates] will be the ones who return to Syria," as lay activists (*duʿāt*) and mosque preachers (*khuṭabā'*).[29]

Such planning for the return to a free Syria aside, life in Zaatari already offered the possibility of practicing Islam differently than under the Syrian regime and its network of secret police. After the 1979–82 Islamist uprising in Syria, Hafez al-Assad severely curtailed nonauthorized forms of religiosity. "The regime relied on a two-pronged strategy to regain control of the religious field," writes Thomas Pierret. The first was, simply, coercion (locking mosques between prayer times and stipulating the contents of Friday sermons); the second was "sub-contracting" religious activities to loyal clerical networks.[30] This double strategy prevailed until the late 2000s, when Bashar al-Assad declared the need to preserve secularism, calling an end to the regime's policy of "indirect rule" of the religious scholars. Among other measures, he massively expanded the Ministry of Endowments, with the goal of integrating the *ʿulamā'* under state administration; arrested Islamic activists; shut down Islamic studies institutes; closed prayer rooms in public malls; banned wearing the niqab in universities; and prevented clerics from leaving the country without permission.[31] Public expressions of religious practice, which under the Baath regime had always been scrutinized, were now newly suspect.

The aforementioned video on the ʿAbdullāh bin al-Mubārak Program next shows a burly middle-aged man with curly hair and a thick salt-and-pepper beard slumped forward on a torn pillow in front of his tent. The camera pans just long enough to glimpse the UNHCR logo on the tent canvas covered in a thick film of yellow dust. The ground is rubble, dust and crushed pebbles. He has round glasses and is in a grey robe and barefoot, his plastic slippers set to the side, and he is reciting from a Quran. "Haytham is a pious man who came here with his family," a man with a British accent intones in voiceover. "At Zaatari, he reads Quran in public, which he never felt comfortable doing at home." Haytham then speaks into the camera, telling how he came to Zaatari after the regime started shelling the school building in which they were sheltering. "Ramadan here is difficult, yes, we don't have enough food, there isn't much meat, but at least we have peace (*hudū'*)."

Regardless of how distant the prospect of return to a freed Syria seemed as the war drew on, the program's preparatory work continued. After my interview with Abū Bakr we went to the program's mosque for the afternoon prayers. He stood at the pulpit and called up a young boy, eight or nine years old, in a spotless robe and skullcap and a fresh haircut. The boy hooked the wraparound microphone behind his ears and paused for a second, looking out over the three dozen youths and men in the congregation, his shoulders clenching. Then he began his oration with a Quranic verse, scanning the prayer hall: *O you who believe! Reverence God and speak justly, that He may set your deeds aright for you, and forgive you your sins. And whosoever obeys God and His messenger has achieved a great triumph* (Q. 33:70–71). Abū Bakr looked on, grinning, as the boy continued.

> The Prophet, peace and blessings of God upon him, said, The believer is one who knows the Quran and acts according to it; the parable of the believer who recites the Quran is that of a citron, its fragrance is pleasant and its taste is pleasant. The parable of the believer who does not recite the Quran [he hesitated] is that of a date, it has a sweet smell but—

Abū Bakr murmured something. The boy stopped and shot him a glance. The program director repeated a little louder, "It has no smell—" The boy nodded.

> —it has no smell but its taste is sweet. The parable of the hypocrite who does not recite—

Abū Bakr shook his head: "Who does recite." The boy looked out at us again.

> —who does recite the Quran is that of the colocynth—

Abū Bakr intervened again: "It's basil." The boy stuttered to a halt. Abū Bakr put his arm around his shoulder. "It's no matter! You did well, you did well. We'll try again later." He took back the microphone and elicited our proclamations, "*takbīr*!" The congregation chanted in unison, "God is great! God is great! God is great!" The boy returned to the second row, embarrassed. But although he had confused the hadith, it was clear that he had the makings of an orator; he had ably acquired the affective charge and the performative gestures of a Friday preacher.

After the afternoon prayers, Abū Bakr went to teach another class. I returned to the office trailer to speak further with the program teachers before I had to leave. They were curious with whom I had studied in Damascus, nearly fifteen years previous. I struggled to remember the names of certain shaykhs and mentioned a few they did not know. Then their ears pricked up. "Ha," laughed an older teacher from Idlib, with a grizzled face and a strong limp, "you studied with Shaykh Fulān? Do you know where he is now?" "No," I replied, suddenly cautious. "He stayed in Damascus, he's there still." "Oh?" I asked naively, "without any problems?" "Problems, what problems? He's supporting the regime. It's been seven years; if there are shaykhs still in Damascus now, it is because they are supporting the regime, they believe Bashar to be the rightful ruler and so legitimize anything he does." His eyes flashed bright and hard, and he soon left the room.

"For myself," Zāhid commented, "I think some people living their lives in Damascus have excuses for why they are still there, I will not condemn them all." I mentioned the cousin of a friend who was imprisoned for some time and who could not leave Damascus even after being released. "Yes," he said, "there are lots of people like that. Remaining there doesn't mean you support Bashar." The conversation in the office turned to the recent news that Russia was organizing conditional surrenders for those rebels who laid down their arms. Though Zāhid would not condemn everyone who still lived under the regime, he could not trust the promises of amnesty. "They're lying!" He raised his voice. "And reconcile? I'd rather die than reconcile." He raised a finger to the ceiling. "I swear by God I'd rather die."

Between Affliction and Tribulation

Before I left Zaatari on my final visit that summer, I asked Abū Bakr how he understood what had happened in Syria, which had driven him into exile. I mentioned that some of my other interlocutors described the crisis (*azmeh*) as a divine test (*fitna*) or trial (*ibtilā'*). But how so?

Abū Bakr agreed that the Syrian crisis was an ordeal, even that it could have a spiritually purifying effect, but he refused to specify its divine rationale. "We can say that the violence in Syria is a tribulation (*ibtilā'*) that should lead us to introspection, certainly. But what about the children who have been killed, who were innocent, had no sin upon them, who have been killed and injured and exiled? We have to distinguish between them, their families, and others—it's no divine tribulation for them, or for the elderly, or for vulnerable women." Rather, he argued,

> the Syrian crisis is a tribulation in the sense that there is an obligation for the entire Islamic Community to be united in solidarity: that we should stand shoulder to shoulder in the affliction (*natakātaf fī-l-miḥan*). As if there were a famine striking all the people, you should address it together; if there are wounded among you, you should open clinics and hospitals to cooperate in treating them—so it is here: a divine test for those who are able to feed their neighbors, who are able to shelter the displaced. Have they done so?

In the generous manner I had come to expect from him, he first affirmed "tribulation" as an appropriate term but then specified its scope, exempting the weak and vulnerable from its logic and directing it in fact toward those who were *not* afflicted by the worst.

Abū Bakr did not demand a singular response to the ordeal or prescribe how one might pass the divine test. Instead, he turned the figure of tribulation toward a question of capacity. "Someone who is incapable of doing anything more is excused before God; the one who has no power except supplication is excused [from doing anything more than supplicating]. We cannot burden anyone beyond his strength (*fawqa ṭāqatih*). But the one who is able to act and fails to do so? Certainly, it is a trial with respect to him (*ibtilā' fī ḥaqqih*) and he is not excused." There are those who can resort only to the power of prayer; that is the situation that God has put them in, he continued, and they are excused (*ma'dhūr*) before God; they will not be accountable for their inaction on the Day of Judgment.

But is one excused? What is one's capacity? How does one determine what lies within one's strength? In the absence of an external measure, one must ask oneself these questions, whether touched by the event directly or standing adjacent to it. The event convenes "a certain problematization," bringing one to the "thresholds of reflection."[32] As Abū Bakr elaborated the variegation of personal capacities, he was confident that the call (of the event of trial) could find response (by the constituted subject):

God does not burden a soul beyond what it can bear (Q. 2:286)—and besides, people are of different capacities. . . . Meanwhile there are a host of other calamities happening elsewhere, beyond Syria. There are devastating earthquakes, tsunamis, all around the world, right? Yet someone who has the ability to act cannot abandon the Community; one who does not have this ability, who is himself in need, he is excused. And God knows best.

This configuration of ability, obligation, and excuse was compelling, and I remain impressed by his articulation of how the divine trial in fact tests those *not* most severely afflicted. Yet I wondered if (perhaps for pedagogical reasons) Abū Bakr was not simplifying the exchange of call and response. I remembered Peter Singer's utilitarian hypothesis, where he insists that we have an obligation to aid distant strangers no less than a drowning child before us.[33] Abū Bakr insisted on the *umma*'s ability to respond to the obligation—however variegated that ability may be, however many are exempted as a result of their weakness, and however many betray their brothers by not acting.

According to this account, tribulation tests those around the event. *[God] created death and life that He may try you as to which of you is most virtuous in deed, and He is the Mighty, the Forgiving*, reads Q. 67:2. But if the trial produces a duty, how can one adjudicate between multiple duties? Abū Bakr recognized that there is more than one event, and so there may be "hierarchies of concern" and "competing moral obligations."[34] But he concluded by reiterating the need to act, if one has the capacity to do so.

For Emmanuel Levinas, it is this crowded ethical scene that requires justice—that is, "comparison, coexistence, contemporaneousness, assembling, order, thematization" of these multiple duties of care, "and thence also [their] copresence on an equal footing[,] as before a court of justice."[35] If there were only to have been responsibility toward one single other, "there would not have been any problem."[36] But a third party also calls; she deserves the same attention as the other while having her own relation to the other:

But how does responsibility obligate if a third troubles this exteriority of two where my subjection of the subject is subjection to the neighbor? The third party is other than the neighbor but is also another neighbor, and also a neighbor of the other, and not simply their fellow. What am I to do? What have they already done to one another? Who passes before the

> other in my responsibility? What, then, are the other and the third with respect to one another? *Birth of the question.*[37]

For Levinas, love would suffice for the other, but the call of a third requires justice beyond love. Derrida reads these impossible obligations as providing the passage from ethics (hospitality to the other) to politics (on behalf of the third). A politics based on ethics, which risks perverting ethics, is certainly necessary, "but must never forget, in any engagement, in any decision, that it is the singular relation to [the] mortality and vulnerability [of the other] that matters."[38]

Abū Bakr of course did not venture an answer to the conflict of love and justice. Instead, he had cited the Quran, which declares that the divine mercy supervenes over the divine wrath (e.g., Q. 6:54). In doing so, he deferred the Derridean problem of politics by making the question of discerning one's obligation in relation to one's ability itself already heteronymous, already bound up with the entreaty that God not impose a burden beyond one's strength:

> God tasks no soul beyond its capacity. It shall have what it has earned and be subject to what it has perpetrated. "Our Lord, take us not to task if we forget or err! Our Lord, lay not upon us a burden like Thou laid upon those before us. Our Lord, impose not upon us that which we have not the strength to bear! And pardon us, forgive us, and have mercy upon us! Thou art our Master, so help us against the disbelieving people." (Q. 2:286)

As he stayed in Zaatari Camp, he had said at the beginning of our interviews, he found that he had to pay dues on the religious knowledge he had acquired (*zakāt al-ʿilm*)—just like one must give charity from one's material wealth in order to purify it for one's own use (*zakāt al-māl*). He perceived his obligation as being to answer the need for religious knowledge and guidance in the camp, a need no less pressing than sanitary toilets or paved roads, a need few others beside him and his fellow teachers could or would fulfill. Certainly not the international humanitarian aid apparatus, despite its obsessive tracking of education outcomes and attendance in Zaatari schools. And so Abū Bakr stayed in the camp long after he could have left. Given his doctorate from al-Azhar University, the roster of wealthy donors and famous preachers who visited him at the ʿAbdullāh bin al-Mubārak program, and the ease by which he regularly left the camp for meetings or errands, he could have arranged to take up a teaching post elsewhere in the Gulf. Instead, he remained there. Rather than a humanitarian gesture of self-sacrifice,[39] I would suggest, Abū Bakr's reiterated decision to stay in Zaatari emulates the ascetic eponym of his program.

In later biographies and hagiographies, 'Abdullāh bin al-Mubārak (118–81 AH/736–97 CE) provides a multifaceted model of uniting knowledge (*'ilm*) and action (*'amal*): variously a pious merchant, a heroic warrior-pilgrim who renounced booty and renown, and a scrupulous hadith-transmitter who traveled in search of knowledge.[40] Apart from being a hadith transmitter, he was also one of the first to record the prophetic narrations in writing, making use of new techniques in preserving the traditions. His two most famous works, compilations of hadiths on jihad (*Kitāb al-jihād*) and on asceticism (*Kitāb al-zuhd wa-l-raqā'iq*), provide models of pious action that he himself reflected. The latter text, his magnum opus, comprises 1,627 thematically organized reports on self-purification. A section on the perils of knowledge echoes the "threshold of reflection" to which the experience of tribulation brought Abū Bakr. There Ibn al-Mubārak cites the Prophet's companion Abū l-Dardā': "The worst rank on the Day of Judgment is that of the scholar who did not benefit [others] through his knowledge." Or, again, "My greatest fear is to stand in front of God during the time of Judgment and have it be said to me: 'What did you do with what you learned (*fa-mādhā 'amilta fī-mā 'alimta*)?'"[41] Shortly thereafter he quotes Wahb bin Munabbih: "There is an exorbitance (*ṭughyān*) in knowledge, as there is exorbitance in wealth."[42] As Abū Bakr had told me, *zakāt* expunges the exorbitance in wealth, just as acting (*'amal*) according to knowledge (*'ilm*) and teaching it (*ta'līm*) expunges exorbitance in knowledge.

Abū Bakr's response to the tribulation discloses how truth demands putting oneself at stake in its pursuit.[43] His example recalls the non-renunciative asceticism of 'Abdullāh bin al-Mubārak, who lived in the world while detached from it, who valiantly fought the Byzantines, who was eager to inherit and embody prophetic knowledge. He demonstrated "the inextricability of ascetic self-(de)formation from the praxis of mimesis and poiēsis."[44] His example insists that even teaching and learning may be insufficient to excise the transgression (*ṭughyān*) that coagulates when knowledge lies inert. Yet, as a hadith declares, the prophets leave an inheritance of knowledge rather than of dinar or dirham, an inheritance that is passed among the generations by those who can bear it—that is, those who embody the integration of *ʿilm*, *ʿamal*, and *taʿlīm*. Exiled from the pedigreed institutions of Islamic learning that claim to guarantee this inheritance, then, Syrians in Zaatari Camp nonetheless have among them those who unite theory and praxis in strenuous search of the divinity that is anterior to true knowledge.[45]

Putting Oneself at Stake in Pursuit of Truth

I absentmindedly picked up a book from the office coffee table before I left the camp: a colorful hardback print of al-Tirmidhī's *al-Shamā'il al-muḥammadiyya* (The Muhammadan Qualities).[46] This famous third-/ninth-century text about the Prophet, authored by the compiler of one of the six Sunni hadith canons, is a collection of nearly four hundred narrations thematically divided into fifty-six sections. It inaugurated a genre of prophetic biography dedicated to elaborating his physiognomy, dress, habits, and virtues. Though provided without commentary or editorial interpolation, the collocation of these reports forms an ekphrastic portrait of the beloved messenger. "His face shone like the moon in the night of the full moon," reads one report. "He was taller than middling stature but shorter than conspicuous height. He had thick, curly hair. The plaits of his hair were parted."[47] Another report turns to his demeanor. "He was well acquainted with sorrow, much absorbed in thought, had little rest, was silent for long periods and did not talk without cause. . . . He honored each of God's signs of grace, even though it might be small, and never found blame in anything."[48] Taken together, these reports, which detail the prophet's gait and posture, his manner and his tone, offer a repository of gestures for lovers of the prophet to repeat and thereby inherit. It is through such a "gestural modality," writes Nauman Naqvi, that one can mimetically encounter the body of the beloved.[49]

A lengthy inscription in blue ballpoint ink caught my eye as I flipped past the book's introduction. I squinted at the penmanship. After standard opening invocations, it continued, "We began reciting this book *The Muhammadan Qualities* by Imam Tirmidhī on Saturday 8 Ramadan 1438/3 June 2017 with a license (*ijāza*) and a continuous chain of transmission [of its hadith reports] to the Messenger of God, peace and blessings of God upon him." I glanced up at Zāhid, surprised that these teachers were so circumspect about this text while their curriculum otherwise was not organized according to the traditional *ijāza* system of knowledge transmission. "Yes," he answered, "we [teachers] just finished reciting it for the third time in order to receive licenses to transmit it ourselves." The handwritten inscription ended with an entreaty, "asking the Protector exalted and glorified to honor us through its [the book's] recitation in its entirety, and to make it a proof for us, not against us [on the Day of Judgment] (*ḥujjat la-nā lā ʿalaynā*)."

Knowledge of religion is perilous because it can bear witness against its inheritors. If it lies inert, if it is betrayed or set aside, it coagulates and risks one's fate. The eschatological fate of the teachers in Zaatari Camp was already bound up in their kenotic effort to inherit the body of tradition. For Abū Bakr and those around him, where the thresholds of reflection clear a space between affliction and tribulation, witnessing the divine trial passes into affirming the abyssal unity of truth and obligation.

RECKONING

"No!" ʿUmar answered strongly. "The Quran can be a means of guidance for people, for bringing them from darkness to light in whatever situation they find themselves. That is what is important, not how precisely one can articulate its particles." The two older men were seated on sumptuous, gilded sofas across from each other. The thick window drapes in the formal sitting room were still mostly drawn. I was on a plush third sofa between them, watching their discussion escalate.

ʿUmar was in his mid-fifties, at least a decade younger than Abū Ḥasan. We were at the former man's house in spring 2018, in an upscale neighborhood on the northern outskirts of Amman. Though not an accomplished reciter like the latter, he had received a doctorate in Quranic studies from a university in Sudan. In Jordan, he had transcribed and edited personal recordings for multiple volumes of the Salafi scholar Nāṣir al-Dīn al-Albānī's fatwa encyclopedia; he spent two years at a publishing house preparing editions of Islamic texts under the respected hadith critic Shuʿayb al-Arnaʾūṭ. He had published two books of his own, each nearing 600 pages in length. The first, based on his dissertation, is a heresiographical typology of Quran interpretation (divided neatly among the deviant sects: al-Khawārij, al-Jahmiyya, al-Muʿtazila, al-Shīʿa, al-Bāṭiniyya, Ahl al-Kalām, al-Ṣūfiyya). The second is his own accessible redaction of Islamic jurisprudence, organized according to its typical order (from purity and prayer to crimes and juridical matters) but adduced solely through Quran and hadith—that is, without reference to the traditional Islamic juridical schools (*madhāhib*). And, most pertinently to our discussion, he was an early vocal supporter of the Syrian uprising.

Abū Ḥasan, the short, mild-mannered retired civil engineer sitting to my left, was himself a master of the ten modes of Quran recitation. Decades ago he and nine other reciters in Jordan formed a group of volunteers granting licenses (*ijāzāt*) in Quran recitation by teaching from verse manuals outlining the ten grand recitations (*al-qira'āt al-kubrā*); the initiative grew to a scale of thousands of students and was later adopted by the Jordanian Ministry of Endowments. He was also involved in a charitable organization dedicated to supporting Syrian refugees in Jordan as well as coordinating health and education programs in rebel-held areas within Syria.

Abū Ḥasan and 'Umar had both left Syria nearly four decades prior, among the wave of exiles (*muhājirīn*) from the Hafez al-Assad regime following the 1982 Hama massacre.[50] In the aftermath of the "events of Hama" (*aḥdāth ḥamā*), in which helicopter gunships bombarded the country's fourth-largest city in the name of suppressing an insurgency by the Muslim Brotherhood, the regime cracked down broadly on Islamist activists (whether Brotherhood members or not). The "pedagogy of violence" enacted at Hama, writes Salwa Ismail, among the terror and the thousands of fatalities, "inaugurated a model of violence and a frame of power relation" that scholars observe extended through the 2011 revolution. "Regime brutality in Hama was constructed as a template for the regime's anticipated use of violence to suppress opposition. It was understood as a lesson (*al-dars al-hamawi*)."[51] It was lessons of the Syrian revolution that we had met to discuss, but Abū Ḥasan and 'Umar's argument over the proportional attention given Quran recitation had taken precedence.

Between Form and Content

"I just read something relevant to this," 'Umar said; "let me get it." He returned to the room carrying a faded volume and paged through it briefly before paraphrasing it aloud: imagine a people who came upon a sign that read "Warning! Dynamite will explode in this area at 9 o'clock. Extreme danger. Leave immediately!" and who proceeded to chant and sing this dire warning in verse form, attending to its form yet heedless of its meaning. That is how we read the Quran today, the author wrote. Does it benefit a judge to precisely pronounce a law text without comprehending or ruling according to it? ʿUmar passed us the book, a collection of articles by the Salafi judge ʿAlī al-Ṭanṭāwī (1909–99). He opens his 1956 essay "Your Quran, O Muslims" by recounting a prayer he had recently attended at the Umayyad Mosque in Damascus, in which the imam recited Q. 69 (Sūrat al-Ḥāqqa, which describes the apocalyptic violence of the Day of Judgment) with all the melodious sing-song one might expect at a dramatic performance, lacking only raucous applause afterward. How can a Muslim chant this grievous revelation as though he were declaiming a ghazal, al-Ṭanṭāwī asks. No greater affliction has struck the Muslims, he continues: they move their tongues to utter the Quran's words, reciting it even with correct articulation (*tajwīd*), yet they do not consider the need to move their minds to understand its meanings. They deem the recitation an end in itself![52]

Abū Ḥasan shook his head. He still taught dedicated students (and me) daily in his neighborhood mosque, in a lower-income area on the eastern side of the city—teaching them correct recitation, not exegesis. "These positions aren't mutually exclusive," he responded mildly, "and need more time to elaborate. I hear what you are saying. Reciters need to consider the meaning of the revelation. I remember Ibn Taymiyya's statement in the final days of his imprisonment in Damascus, before his death, 'I regret losing most of my time not pursuing the meanings of the Quran.' But the Quran is not like a lawbook [from al-Ṭanṭāwī's analogy]. There are twenty-one *madd*s (extended syllables) just in the first sūra of the Quran. You have to pronounce them correctly: *wa lā ḍ-ḍāllīn* [he elongated each vowel in the final word from Q. 1:7 to four beats]."[53]

ʿUmar wasn't done. He pressed on. "Reciting is important. But it is only part of a bigger project. The Quran itself says, *recite of it what is easy for you* (Q. 73:20). If someone is virtuous, is trustworthy, completes his prayers, is dedicated in worship, enjoins good, and forbids evil—and hasn't even memorized a single long sūra, isn't that sufficient for him and his religion? We put so much importance on memorizing and articulating correctly, but not enough on the message itself! How much does reciting *wa lā ḍ-ḍāllīn* benefit without learning what going astray (*ḍalāl*) means? Really?"

Abū Ḥasan was not convinced. "But this position is not opposed to the other one. Meantime people regularly make clear and glaring mistakes in recitation (*tajwīd*). Al-Albānī himself held that it is necessary to learn to recite correctly, it's a religious obligation on each individual (*farḍ ʿayn*), to learn enough to recite in your daily prayers. Sorry this got far from your topic," Abū Ḥasan smiled at me and shifted into a more homiletic register. "We can't change anything of how the Quran is recited. Why? Because God is protecting it. So that's why we need to—"

"Exactly!" ʿUmar leaned in, interrupting him. "God is protecting His revelation. That means we don't need to be so concerned about mastering every articulation, and should focus on implementing its message! The most important thing about the Quran, the divine address, is that it came to separate truth (*ḥaqq*) from falsehood (*bāṭil*). Such attention to the form of things instead of actually hearing the address—it's what my shaykh al-Ṭanṭāwī was seeing in Syria in the 1950s. And it's what we can still see there now, but so much worse! In fact, that is why things have come to be as they are."

I pricked up my ears. Oh?

"Look," ʿUmar turned to me, "in Syria before the revolution, they were engrossed in the outer form of things. There was lots of religious knowledge but they would just treasure it [without practicing it]. They knew lots of hadiths but they would think that a house gained blessings (*tabarruk*) simply through having a copy of [the hadith canon] *Ṣaḥīḥ Bukhārī* [without practicing what it contained]. We have drifted so far from God's religion! Come [he invited us to stand], let me show you what I mean."

We followed him into his office lined with floor-to-ceiling bookshelves. We sat on two chairs opposite his desk, and he moved his computer screen so we could see. "This is idolatry (*kufr*) and clear deviation (*inḥirāf*) across the lands of Syria." He opened a computer folder containing dozens of subfolders, titled according to the topics of the Salafi polemic against Levantine Sufism: idolatry; body piercing; miracle stories; celebrating the Prophet's birth. . . .[54] "Look at this one," he said, "you must have heard it, it is everywhere." He double-clicked the top clip. The video panned across a large room, men sitting against its walls, nodding their heads to the rhythm of a chorus. The camera zoomed in to four men with microphones sitting at the front, two holding frame drums. I immediately remembered the melismatic ode, which I had sung in a Damascus mosque—and had to stop myself from nodding along.

yā imām al-ru-u-u-slī yā-ā-ā sanadī (ah!)	*o leader of the prophets, o my support*
anta bābu llā-ā-ā-hi mu-u-uʿtamadī	*you are the door of God, on whom I rely*
fa-bi dunyāy-a-a-a wa ā-ā-ākhiratī (i!)	*in this my worldly life and my afterlife*
yā rasūla llā-ā-āhi khu-u-udh bi-yadī	*o messenger of God, take [me] by my hand*

"Eh, you hear that? 'You are the door of God'?! This is love of the Prophet taken to the extreme! Now listen to this one." He opened another clip. The mosque hall in this video was full and resounding with song. He pointed to a grainy figure seated at a dais. "You see him? That is al-Būṭī, the regime's shaykh."[55] I could just make out his distinctive turban. "This is al-Būṣīrī's Mantle Ode (*qaṣīdat al-burda*). Let me find the worst section." He skipped ahead.

yā akram al-rusli mā lī man lūdhubihi	*Most noble of Messengers! To whom shall I turn*
siwāk ʿinda ḥulūli l-ḥādithi l-ʿamami	*but you, when the General Calamity befalls?*

"Al-Būṣīrī is saying that when the greatest of calamities befalls him, he can turn only to the Prophet. What kind of excessive enthusiasm is this—contradicting what God Himself says in the Quran, *And do not call upon any, beside God . . .* (Q. 10:106)?!"

fa-inna min jūdika d-dunyā wa ḍarratahā	*for this world and the next are from your bounty*
wa min ʿulūmika ʿilmu l-lawḥi wa-l-qalami	*and knowledge of Pen and Tablet are of what you know*[56]

"Then he says that this life and the afterlife are from the Prophet's generosity. But they belong to God, surely! And he says that the Prophet knows the divine mystery (*al-ghayb*)—the Tablet and the Pen—but that is preposterous. All of this is excessive and utter deviance. You see, [he turned to me] this was the heretical understanding of Islam across Syria. It was disseminated across the lands, it was proselytized from the highest pulpits." He sat back in his office chair. Abū Ḥasan shook his head but did not intervene. I waited for ʿUmar to connect the Sufi poetry in Damascus to the Russian air strikes in Douma. "Remember the verse of Sūrat al-Raʿd? *God does not change the condition of a people until they change what is in themselves* (Q. 13:11). Change (*taghyīr*) does not happen without a stick (*ʿaṣā*). For us to change what is in ourselves—it can only happen through force (*quwwa*). It is a way to correct (*taṣḥīḥ*) ourselves, for a revolution (*thawra*) in our way of thinking (*fikra*)."

ʿUmar turned to the shelf behind him, which was filled with small thick notebooks. He pulled a few down and opened one to its first page. A table of contents in neat handwriting listed a series of topics: Lessons from the Prophet's Migration. The Struggle between Truth and Falsehood. True Victory. Where is God? The Prohibition of Usury. Marital Rights. Jews in the Quran. The Shīʿite Danger. These were sermon topics he had developed against common mistakes and misconceptions, he explained, but the audience who needed to hear them extended far beyond the congregation of a single mosque. "When the revolution started, we found we had to do something. This was an occasion to instruct the youth, to teach them. I sat with many of the youths of the Free Army (*al-jaysh al-ḥurr*) and was shocked to find that they were ignorant even of the basic pillars of the religion. They were farm workers, you see, or laborers—certainly uneducated—and had become warriors with little religious training. In fact, they thought they were free to do anything in the war, that the rules of jihad don't apply if they are fighting the Nuṣayrīs [i.e., Assad's ʿAlawite regime]. But our religion doesn't let us do that."[57]

When Is the Victory of God

ʿUmar's accessible manual of jurisprudence, which he gifted to me when we rose to leave, includes a lengthy chapter on jihad: its definition, merits, obligation, and rules of conduct, as well as stipulations pertaining to booty and non-Muslims. There he spells out the purposes of military jihad, which are not bloodshed or aggression but the purification of God's slaves, the lifting of oppression, defense against tyranny, returning the rights of those who have been deprived, and freeing Muslim captives. He cites the Companion Abū Bakr's counsel to an army heading toward Syria: "I charge you with ten things: Do not kill women or children or the elderly infirm; do not cut down fruit trees or destroy a habitation; do not slaughter sheep or camels except for food; do not burn bees or scatter them; do not exploit the spoils and do not be cowardly." Yet the farmhands who had taken up arms against the regime were not going to read books like his.

Even though he did not have media experience, then, ʿUmar sought to turn his sermons into lessons he could transmit on revolutionary television channels (e.g., the now-defunct Sūriyā al-shaʿb). These lessons combined exhortations to specific virtues in the struggle (steadfastness, endurance, sincerity) with religious guidance on practical matters (how to deal with captives). He launched a television program whose episodes lasted at least an hour; many were later uploaded to YouTube. He drew on his network of dissident scholars for guest spots on his program, whether in person or over the phone—including the Egyptian Muslim Brotherhood firebrand Wajdī Ghunayyim (later based in Turkey, having been expelled from Qatar), the Saudi dissident Salmān al-ʿAwda (the reformist now imprisoned in Saudi Arabia), the Syrian exile ʿAdnān al-ʿArʿūr (famous among the rebels for his excoriations of the regime), the Kuwaiti political activist Iḥsān al-ʿUtaybī (who founded an educational charity in north Jordan), the Jordanian quietist ʿAlī al-Ḥalabī (effective successor in the country to the Salafi shaykh al-Albānī), and, in 2013, the charismatic Syrian rebel commander Muḥammad Zahrān ʿAllūsh (killed two and a half years later in the regime siege of Ghouta). The program frequently played video recordings of the aftermath of regime attacks (homes and streets reduced to rubble, wounded children being bandaged) or of Free Army militia chanting God is great! as they sped through the countryside in military jeeps.

They called a Free Army captain from Bābā ʿAmr on-air during the height of the 2012 siege of Homs to describe the condition of the struggle. He picked up the phone frenzied, the pitch of his voice rising, appealing for aid, repeating, "O God, O God." He described his friends and fellow soldiers who had been martyred. "We will be steadfast—we will be steadfast—who are our allies? Where are our allies? We will be steadfast—where are the Muslims? We have to be united." He described in gruesome detail a bus of civilians slaughtered by the Syrian army, exposed bodies they could not bury, a young girl whose limbs had been hacked off with long knives. His voice broke and then dropped off. "I cannot describe the rest of what I have seen here. They are circling us, they are around us everywhere, we will be steadfast, O God. Tell them, shaykh, we need their aid. O God!" 'Umar's son wept but did not avert his gaze from the studio video recorder. The camera shifted to 'Umar himself, who shook his head, muttering "no power or strength except in God," and then harshly imprecated the regime, God's curse upon it and its thugs. "These youth, they are the hope of Syria, who are standing up, fighting for truth," he said.

'Umar's son acted as program host, asking questions for which he had often prepared notes. The television program engaged the most recent developments in the war while rehearsing a series of themes: the depravity and criminality of the regime, the insidious doctrines of the filthy Shi'ites and 'Alawites, the geopolitical machinations of Russia and Iran, and the bravery and heroism of the Free Army. Along the way, they revisited historical analogues to the contemporary situation and returned incessantly to the theological question of divine succor. (The factors [*asbāb*] yielding victory over the enemy was also a section in 'Umar's jurisprudence of jihad, where he enumerated them: sincere faith; preparation; leadership; bravery and steadfastness and sacrifice; unity; and supplication.) In a lengthy 2016 interview on the Saudi-funded Wesal TV, a program host in a dark suit asked 'Umar, dressed in a brown robe and red-checkered kefiyya, what had delayed the victory of God. The Syrian crisis had extended overlong; "With thousands displaced and killed, women widowed and children orphaned," the host said, "many ask themselves: are we not in the right (*alasnā 'alā l-ḥaqq*)? Then we say: indeed (*balā*). So why then is victory delayed (*fa-limādha ta'akhkhara l-naṣr*)?"

'Umar replied that God's victory was not a matter of one army overpowering another: it is the question of the relation of truth and falsehood. The regime has entrenched itself for fifty years, he continued, building itself in through the devils among men, allying itself with the evil of Iran and Russia. And yet God has a practice (*sunna*) regarding victory. It is not rapid. It comes at a price (*thaman*). It will come but it waits, until even the Prophet himself would utter, "When is the victory of God?" (*matā nasru llāh*)—*and verily the victory of God is near* (Q. 2:214). And if you are steadfast in pursuing it, like those who came before you, its reward is paradise. 'Umar turned to face the camera directly, addressing his audience. "I want you listeners,

I want the Syrian people, to believe with certainty, that by God these are good tidings. When the oppressors reach this height of tyranny, of arrogance, of killing and bombardments and torture, when we see our brothers and sisters suffering, starving in the siege, and dying before us, we know that truth and falsehood are clear for all the world to see, and we know that soon, very soon, God's succor will come, and that our beloved land of Syria will be the graveyard of Bashar al-Assad."

In another episode, 'Umar's son asked what he thought of those who claimed that the Syrian crisis delivered a divine trial (*fitna*) from which one should distance oneself. He replied at once. "It's true that there are trials which will submerge everyone they touch. Then, like in the hadith, one can only seek to preserve oneself and one's family, and wait until it passes. But God uses the word *fitna* in five senses in the Quran. It means more than one thing. Those who call this a *fitna* mean that truth and falsehood have become muddled so that they cannot see a clear course of action. Yet all the world sees the crimes and oppression and bloodshed of the regime. They cannot call it a *fitna* and so abandon the obligation of jihad."

There are times of sedition and upheaval in which the most one can do may be to save oneself from strife (*fitna*) and spiritual ruin (*halāk*). In a hadith to this end, the Prophet said, "Before you is a tribulation like a sheet of dark night. In it a person will enter the morning a believer and enter the evening a disbeliever. One who sits during this time is better than one who stands; and one who stands during this time is better than one who walks; and one who walks during this time is better than one who runs." The Companions asked, "What do you command us to do [at that time]?" He replied, "Be like saddle blankets in your homes."[58] Refraining from action, withdrawing from society, and seeking obscurity—being like saddle blankets—is the way to preserve some semblance of integrity and safety in the midst of such broad confusion. The best thing one can do in such times is to retreat to tend sheep in mountain vales or peaks, as in another famous hadith, escaping the tribulation with one's religion whole. These hadiths are well-attested in the chapters of tribulation. But as was clear in 'Umar's televised response, he fundamentally disagreed that the Syrian war called for such a response. There are multiple senses of the term *fitna*, he replied, and one must discern which of these actually applies with reference to the exigencies of our time.

"As long as I've known you," his son said, "you have worked in the way of God through preaching, through proselytizing, through scholarship. Yet now you have joined the ranks of those shaykhs who endorse [military] jihad in the way of God. What has changed?"

'Umar's tone in this video clip is gentle, almost conciliatory. "What do you think, my brother. However peaceful a person, however nonviolent he is, if a monster (*waḥsh*) enters his house, will he remain peaceful? Can one remain peaceful before tyranny? They have made war against our lands, slaughtered our children. It is the most natural human thing to defend oneself. Of course we want peace; Islam came to bring mercy, not the sword. And true change and reform won't happen except through calling to God (*da'wa*). But jihad now has become an individual obligation (*farḍ 'ayn*) in these lands, for those able to resist the regime."

The Scourge of God

As Abū Ḥasan and I readied to leave, 'Umar returned to the topic of the divine trial. He was keen that I understand its role in producing the scenarios of human action. "There is a relationship between tribulation (*ibtilā'*) and examination (*ikhtibār*), which humans in fact benefit from. For humans are created to be tried. Tribulation establishes a proof (*ḥujja*) against people: are they righteous or vicious? Are they to be rewarded or punished? You are going back to Canada, to the lands of the disbelievers; you must know that the infidel deems this world to be the sole abode of life. But this world is not bountiful (*na'īm*) as the infidel thinks it is, that disbeliever who is in pursuit of his appetites (*shahawāt*) and subservient to them. This is not the world of reward (*jazā'*). For the Muslim, this is the world of commands and prohibitions. For the Muslim, these [tribulations] are not surprises: God says in the Quran, *And surely We will try you with something of fear and hunger, and loss of wealth and lives and crops, but give glad tidings to the steadfast* (Q. 2:155). This is a test, all of it, an affliction to gauge our obedience, our response to the divine decrees of poverty and hunger and loss." In summer 2018, when the Syrian regime was methodically reconquering the country and many of the rebel commanders he had hosted on his show had been killed, 'Umar's account of tribulation was more somber than the revolutionary fervor of his television episodes five years prior.

Again and again, in our conversation as on his television program, 'Umar began with the reality of the destruction of the country he had left under duress decades ago. He broadened his perspective to find a precedent from

Muslim history (e.g., that Hafez al-Assad's participation in the 1963 Syrian coup paralleled a military usurpation in the Abbasid empire) or to observe a universal divine habit (e.g., that God delays the victory of truth as a way of beguiling the disbelievers). And then he returned to the specific struggle in Syria to articulate an oppositional political theology. In his analysis, the Syrian conflict was not simply a matter of geopolitical interests and world powers exercising their influence (although it certainly was that). In casting actors in dramatic terms—the evil regime and heroic rebels—he methodically sketched a preternatural struggle between truth and falsehood whose terms were already set. Although its ultimate end was already destined (for to God returns everything), its outcome meantime was certainly not guaranteed.

In a Friday sermon delivered in 2012 and uploaded to a popular religious affairs website (where it had been accessed 54,000 times as of late 2019), 'Umar addressed recent violence in Palestine. In Israel's "Operation Returning Echo," 23 Israelis and 74 Palestinians were wounded and 23 Palestinians were killed. In terms that directly echoed his later commentary on Syria, 'Umar explained that the struggle (*al-ṣirāʿ*) between truth and falsehood reverberated across history—from Abraham and his idolatrous people, to Moses before Pharaoh and his armies, to Muhammad with Abū Jahl and the Qurayshite notables, to Harun al-Rashid facing the Byzantines and Saladin facing the Crusaders, to most recently the Palestinian intifada. It is not merely the result of contemporary events; rather it has successive ancient iterations, as narrated by the wise Reminder (i.e., revelation) and expounded by the generous Lord through its bearers (the prophets) as a vision and reminder for those who remember and as guidance and counsel for the god-wary.

> The decisive battle decreed by God, that its fire not subside nor its flames be extinguished nor its blaze abate, rather that it rages on until God inherits the earth and whoever is upon it—this is the battle of truth with falsehood, guidance with misguidance, and disbelief with faith. This battle is actually, O slaves of God, the uprising of good before the tyranny of evil (*sharr*) in all its forms and colors, regardless of its banners and the number of its soldiers and the greatness of its strength and the imminence of its threat.

Despite the plots and stratagems of the evildoers, God wills the victory of truth. This struggle has its own internal dynamic by which God maintains the presence of His faithful on earth: *Were it not for God's repelling people, some by means of others, monasteries, churches, synagogues, and mosques, wherein God's Name is mentioned much, would have been destroyed. And God will surely help those who help Him—truly God is Strong, Mighty* (Q. 22:40). This was the glory of Islam, so long as the Community upheld the Quran. In the second part of the sermon, ʿUmar buttressed the determination of the faithful:

> The countless lessons of the victory of truth over falsehood, in every one of these battles, strengthens the resolve of the believers to stand firm for the truth they hold to, and to be wary of everything that opposes it or distracts them from it or dissuades them from its path, until God the exalted fulfills His promise of victory—as He did for the predecessors of this Community, for it is a true promise that neither fails nor varies: [*then We took vengeance upon those who were guilty;*] *and it is incumbent upon Us to help the believers* (Q. 30:47).

After the enemy has emerged and his hatred has targeted the Community of Islam, ʿUmar continued, one of the most important factors in attaining victory is remaining united and resolved.

Perhaps this resolve was why ʿUmar had been so vehement in his argument with Abū Ḥasan, the Syrian Quran reciter who had arranged our meeting. The latter had argued, referring to the prominent Salafi scholar who had been ʿUmar's own teacher (al-Albānī), that learning how to articulate the revelation was a personal obligation (*farḍ ʿayn*) incumbent upon anyone who recited the Quran in prayer. ʿUmar recognized that this was necessary—but however virtuous it might be on its own terms, focusing disproportionately on correcting one's glottal stops and extended syllables was ultimately a distraction when one is positioned in the preternatural struggle. This was not quite a claim on behalf of a state of exception outside the normal regime of law, since the battle between truth and falsehood was archaic and iterative, but he did suggest that in a prioritized hierarchy of obligations certain actions supersede others. He repeated the perennial lamentation (common today among Salafis but historically more variegated) that a concern for religious form had become an alibi against attending religious meaning. Abū Ḥasan did not reply to ʿUmar's argument, but it was clear that he considered the formal art of recitation to be integral to properly receiving (safeguarding) the divine revelation. Besides, he had found other ways of engaging the Syrian crisis (helping to coordinate education programs in rebel-held areas and supporting displaced widows and orphans in Jordan; I later visited some of the programs he supported).

ʿUmar's redaction of the jurisprudence of jihad, appearing toward the end of his handbook of Islamic law, cites Q. 2:216: *Fighting has been prescribed for you, though it is hateful to you. But it may be that you hate a thing though it be good for you, and it may be that you love a thing though it be evil for you. God knows, and you know not.* The text states that jihad is a communal obligation (*farḍ kifāya*), such that if enough of the community takes it up, then it is not incumbent on the rest. If none takes it up, the entire community sins. Yet there are four situations in which it becomes an individual obligation (*farḍ ʿayn*), not just a collective one: when two armies meet, it is forbidden to flee; when one's land is invaded, resistance and defense are obligatory; when the leader calls upon one to fight, one must fulfill this demand; and when the Muslims need one's aid, as in the hadith, "Aid your brother, be he oppressed [by defending him] or oppressor [by stopping him]." Although there is today no single legitimate leader of the Muslims to impose a draft (the third of these four cases), the other situations clearly obtain. The section ends with a lengthy quotation from Ibn Taymiyya's *Minhāj al-sunna al-nabawiyya fī naqḍ kalām al-shīʿa wa-l-qadariyya*, a text in which the author asserts the wisdom of God's commands (polemicizing against Shīʿite Muʿtazilites and Ashʿarites, whose excessive formalism on his view respectively implicates God in injustice or evacuates justice of any substantive meaning). "But it may be that you hate a thing though it be good for you," the beginning of that section had cited the Quran.

ʿUmar's response to tribulation consistently pulled analysis and action toward a juridical frame of commandments and prohibitions.[59] Hence his analogy of the Quran to a lawbook to be implemented, not merely chanted (citing al-Ṭanṭāwī). Hence, too, his digital file folders replete with examples of idolatry and deviance in Syria, forming his personal archive furnishing proof of the country's religious corruption; his pedagogical effort at teaching the rebels what they were and were not permitted to do in war; and his notebooks filled with lessons for the masses. But I wondered at how quickly the depths of depravity (torture, rape, indiscriminate slaughter) were transmuted, in the severity of his argument, into evidence for the glory of the coming judgment. By his account, the worst worldly injustice was a sign of the most perfect divine justice. The awful course of the war in Syria was merely the continued beguilement of the infidels. "Tribulation establishes a proof against people," he had said, providing a measure against which they emerge righteous or vicious. But if even the Prophet had been led to ask, "When will God's Help come?" (as in Q. 2:214—though the exegetes differ on the subject and aim of that verse), 'Umar's explanations seemed to turn away from the violence he faced. I felt that his interpretation of history became an alibi against registering that violence. At the same time, I recognized that it is the impossibility of knowing the time of divine victory that also qualifies the possibility of historical interpretation (including his).

The theme of God purifying Syria of its corruption through tribulation echoed an account given by Abū Dharr, one of the founders of the Jam'iyyat al-Kitāb wa-l-Sunna (see the section following and Chapter 1). He was no longer directly involved in the association but remained on cordial terms with its director. Abū Dharr took no pains to soften his perspective. We spoke in his small office in Amman as the Syrian regime and its Russian allies intensified its 2018 campaign to reconquer southern Syria. "This is the test of God (*imtiḥān allāh*)," he said, referring to the most recent battlefront. "Before the war, the Syrian people were not dedicated (*multazimīn*) to their religion—they were seeking intercession at gravesites and practicing Sufism and compromising their monotheism. Now, they call on God alone [not on deceased saints or living spiritual masters]. Now, the call from the countryside and townships of Syria is [merely]: God, God. . . . The ordeal (*miḥna*) and the test (*imtiḥān*) came to clarify truth and falsehood."

He quoted Imam al-Shāfi'ī, the eponym of a Sunni juridical school and as a governor in Yemen no stranger to contentious politics, when he was asked how to discern the partisans of truth (*ahl al-ḥaqq*) in times of upheaval (*fitna*). "Follow the arrows of the enemy," he replied, "for they will guide you to them." He implied that even when confusion spreads such that the upholders of truth are obscured, the enemy will still be identifiable. And that the people of truth inevitably face the violence of the enemy.

Abū Dharr had visited the 'Abdullāh bin al-Mubārak Project in Zaatari Camp, where the topic of his address (later posted to YouTube) was the necessary relationship between preaching (*da'wa*) and wisdom (*ḥikma*). He told the students gathered for his lecture to attenuate their preaching according to the condition of the people they met. "There are those who call to God without wisdom," he had said, "Daesh [ISIS] foremost among them. [That lack of wisdom] nullifies the call to God. Take this as a rule for the seeker of religious knowledge: the best method of calling to God is not through compulsion or commanding. Be wise in your preaching; be appropriate." The Islamic activism to come must be balanced and deliberate. The travails of Syria, which devastated the country, have also prepared the Muslims for the purification of their religion.

For these interlocutors, tribulation is the divine scourge that sweeps aside deviance and heresy. It corrects the relation of form to meaning and rectifies the priority of communal and personal obligations. Although some think the divine trial confuses truth and falsehood—clouding the faculty of discernment and rendering ambiguous the merits of any engagement—affliction in fact is the reckoning that clarifies the struggle and its stakes. Corruption and idolatry drift into virtue and faith and need to be striven against. For these reasons, the ordeal of Syria, as of the *umma* more broadly, is ultimately beneficial.

DISTRIBUTING

My interest in the Jamʿiyyat al-Kitab wa-l-Sunna (The Association of the Quran and Prophetic Practice) had first been piqued by a sector report (discussed in the introduction) which I came across while preparing my fieldwork grant applications. The report notes the growing yet ambiguous influence of Islamist charitable organizations like the association: "Salafist movements and the Muslim Brotherhood gain influence across the region due to the Syrian crisis, and anxiety is rising that these Quran lessons are more than just ordinary religious education, and that they have a long-term impact on the refugees' religious and political thinking in a way that does not comply with international human rights."[60] Although I did not necessarily share this anxiety, being less committed to the normative secularity of humanitarian policy, I was keen to understand how such Islamic organizations' broader reformist visions shaped their charitable activities. The Jamʿiyyat al-Kitab wa-l-Sunna remains one of the largest Islamic charities serving Syrian refugees in the country. Although it has since ended its work in the formal refugee camps, the association was instrumental in coordinating initial funding for the ʿAbdullāh bin al-Mubārak Project in Zaatari (I noticed its logo in faded paint along the side of a trailer on my first visit to the Project site); its director Shaykh Zāyid also claimed responsibility for suggesting that housing in Zaatari be switched to a caravan (trailer) model rather than the tents that UNHCR had originally distributed. Despite donor fatigue since the massive influx of funding in 2012–13 (a common story across all kinds of relief programs in Jordan—and in Lebanon and Turkey as well), in 2025 the association continues to pay for cancer treatments and host orphans, teach Quran and distribute food.

The history of the association illustrates the shifting commitments and internal divisions of the broader Islamic revival. Its first director, Ḥasan Abū Haniyya, had long collaborated with his Palestinian friend ʿUmar Maḥmūd ʿUthmān, now known as the strident preacher Abū Qatāda al-Filasṭīnī.[61] In the late 1970s, Abū Haniyya and Abū Qatāda had together approached the Saudi Ministry of Endowments for religious materials and together studied the work of Ibn Taymiyya and Muḥammad bin ʿAbd al-Wahhāb; together they had attended the religious classes of the exiled Syrian Salafi shaykh Nāṣir al-Dīn al-Albānī before quickly finding his political quietism insufficient for a time when (for example) the Syrian regime to the north had conducted a massacre in the city of Hama. Together they then formed a movement called Ahl al-Sunna wa-l-Jamāʿa ("Adherents to the Prophetic Tradition and Orthodox Community") based in Amman, with the aim of eventually establishing an Islamic state through the activism of a theoretically informed, socially engaged Islamist political vanguard.[62] This movement was the precursor to the Jamʿiyyat al-Kitāb wa-l-Sunna, which Abū Haniyya and others established in 1993 after Jordan permitted the formation of political parties and eased certain media restrictions (all as part of a strategy to manage its Islamist and leftist oppositions).[63] Although the Jordanian Ministry of Culture had authorized it to operate a single branch in Amman, the organization was under close state surveillance. Its founding members seem to have had conflicting agendas, with varied commitments including militancy and agitation for the Palestinian cause, being united mostly by their nonconformance to the quietist approaches that predominate among Salafis in Jordan.[64] State pressure (including constant arrests, interrogation, and harassment by the Jordanian security service)[65] led many of these early members (including a now disillusioned Abū Haniyya) to leave the group; its future was uncertain before Zāyid Ḥammād became its third director in the year 2000.

Ḥammād had known Abū Haniyya and Abū Qatāda since his secondary school days; he joined their Ahl al-Sunna wa-l-Jamāʿa movement and was also a founding member of the association. He, too, had left the association in the brunt of the infighting that characterized Salafism in Jordan in the late 1990s but returned after working privately as an accountant for a few years.[66] He was soon elected to president of the association: a man with shrewd political sensibilities and a talent for working alongside conflicting parties, with a history of religious activism and of seeking religious knowledge (e.g., attending al-Albānī's private hadith classes) but without specific claims to religious scholarship, he represented the promise of effective leadership and administration rather than a partisan position in the intra-Salafi leadership struggles after al-Albānī's death in 1999. In the next few years, amid continued state scrutiny, Ḥammād systematically pushed his more militant colleagues from executive positions in the association, even closing down educational centers where they had influence. He refocused the mandate of the association: reform without revolution; cultivating social change rather than party politics.

When the minister of culture threatened to dissolve the association in 2007, Ḥammād protested that its ethos was firmly aligned with the Amman Message (a royal Jordanian initiative to establish the legitimate scope of moderate Islam)[67] and that its activities mostly comprised Quran education.[68] Be that as it may, its activism was clearly distinct from the "quietist" approach (whether aloof or government-loyalist) of other Jordanian groups. In his 2003 editorial to one of the first issues of the association's journal, *al-Qibla*, Ḥammād argued for a path (*sabīl*) of "openness without dissolution and specificity without yielding" (*infitāḥ min ghayri dhūbān wa khuṣūṣiyya min ghayri inkifā'*). Unlike those Islamists whose dialogues with other religions and ideologies (secular, left, and liberal) undermine their integrity, and unlike those (quietist Salafis) who retreat into a virtuous seclusion, Ḥammād insisted that the way (*manhaj*) of the righteous predecessors was actually to address the exigencies of the age. Those who focus exclusively on questions of personal practice while claiming to uphold the understanding (*fiqh*) of Aḥmad bin Ḥanbal, Ibn Taymiyya, and Muḥammad bin 'Abd al-Wahhāb, he wrote, in fact forget those predecessors' broader understanding of life (*fiqh al-ḥayāt*), their critical engagement with worldly power, and their denouncing of idolatry.[69]

Another article from the same issue lays a course of action for the Muslim community from within the "siege of tribulation" (*ḥiṣār al-fitna*) by which it is currently afflicted.[70] Tribulation, that is, provided a paradigm for the association to conceptualize communal reform well before the Syrian revolution.[71] It continued to use this terminology: in 2012, *al-Qibla* published an article asserting the necessity, from a sharia-reasoning perspective, of continuing the revolution even in the face of its great cost—because in Syria the five universal values of the sharia (preservation of religion, life, reason, progeny, and wealth) were already being utterly destroyed under the corruption of the regime. The legal maxim *lā ḍarar wa lā ḍirār* (no harm inflicted or reciprocated), which in modern Islamic jurisprudential theory yields a principle of public interest (*al-maṣāliḥ al-mursala*), shows that the revolution must continue because the regime's prisons were already full, its torturers were already busy, before the outbreak of the protests. "Thus the trial existed in each of these states" (*fa-l-balā' mawjūd bi-kulli ḥāl min al-aḥwāl*), in peace as in war.[72]

This article posed the question of the Syrian revolution explicitly in terms of tribulation: "Is it true that peaceful protests (demonstrations, rallies) are one of the types of strife (*alwān al-fitan*) that one must caution against?" The outbreak of the Syrian revolution, it continues, was accompanied by widespread debate in religious circles over the legitimacy and politics of the uprising. The two religious scholars cited in this article argue that it is a "complete mistake" (*khāṭi'a tamāman*) to deem such protests unduly divisive. Their arguments in coming to this conclusion differ, however. The first scholar recognized that the tribulation of seditious strife (*fitna*) fractures the orthodox community (*ahl al-sunna wa-l-jamā'a*), setting one party against another, and is a result of faulty religious reasoning (*natījat al-khaṭ' fī-l-ijtihād*); one should indeed warn against inciting such division, as the Prophet warned in reports we now find in the hadith canons under chapter headings like "The Chapter of Tribulations and Fierce Battles" (*bāb al-fitan wa-l-malāḥim*). Yet he insisted that the Syrian revolution is not such a *fitna*. Instead, it is more properly understood as the other term from such chapter-headings—namely, a "fierce battle," for the struggle in such a *malḥama* (as we see in Syria) is not between two groups of Muslims but between the forces of truth and falsehood, between the people of faith (*ahl al-īmān*) and the people of unbelief (*ahl al-kufr*). The other scholar cited Q. 2:193: *And fight them until there is no strife* (*fitna*), *and religion is for God. But if they desist, then there is no enmity save against the wrongdoers.* He interpreted the *fitna* that Muslims are Quranically enjoined to combat as being the overpowering of Islam by unbelief and the domination of the rights and freedoms of Muslims (as clearly seen is the case in

Syria). The uprising is not the *fitna*; rather, the *fitna* is the regime's cruelty and oppression.

Beyond General Equivalence

A gregarious man who had been active in the Jam'iyyat since well before the Syrian uprising, 'Uthmān had witnessed its shift from reformist activism (teaching Quran and organizing youth summer camps) to becoming one of the largest charities serving refugees in the country. As I entered his office in central Amman, I noticed kufic calligraphy hanging on the wall behind his desk. I squinted to decipher the verse in square script: *Truly God provides for whomsoever He wills without reckoning* (Q. 3:37). I was there to discuss how the association's regional branches distributed food and cash to displaced Syrians. But I was curious about how the calligraphy's proclamation of divine provision impacted the charitable work he helped coordinate. Do the association's aid programs reflect this understanding?

"One hundred percent," he replied, "I'll give you a concrete example":

> When the crisis started and Syrians fled to Jordan, we had an operational meeting and decided that we could help 100 refugees. . . . But we also decided to create a database of information, to take data from the Syrians and register their names and addresses, in order that if someone comes to us seeking to offer charity, we would know whom to give to. That database now has more than 300,000 people registered. But we said that their provision lies with the Lord of the worlds, not us.

The first aspect of this work, in 'Uthmān's terms, was employing "administrative" technologies and systems of organization to register hundreds of thousands of Syrians who hold UNHCR registration cards. The database included people's names and contact information as well as a social profile of the household. The second, "faithful" (*īmānī*) aspect seemed to lie in the open-ended nature of the effort. The association itself could not possibly have planned for such a massive budget, he continued; yet they proceeded, with trusting reliance on God (*tawakkul*), as though they would be able to aid these refugees.

> We finished that task—and then God exalted and glorified provided. I did not imagine we could have ever spent so much money on our

charitable projects. People [in the association] objected, they said you are crazy, where will we get money for all these people? We always said: wealth is from the Lord of the worlds, not from us. . . . When the Prophet peace and blessings upon him emigrated from Mecca to Medina, he took with him a Bedouin guide to show him the route in the desert. That is *tawakkul*. God could easily have inspired the Prophet to know the way, but it's by way of *tawakkul* that people must take up the worldly means (*asbāb dunyawiyya*). This is what we did when the Syrian crisis started, in creating our database of recipients. We did that—and waited for donors to come, trusting that they would. And they did.

ʿUthmān saw two aspects as necessary to fulfilling an action: taking up whatever material techniques lay at one's disposal while trusting that God would ensure its outcome. Each of these is alone insufficient, as in the famous hadith that Shaykh Zāyid later cited to me: a man asked the Prophet whether he should tether his camel or leave it be and trust God that it would not wander, and the Prophet replied, "Tie it and trust God" (*aʿqilhā wa tawakkal*).[73] One must do both. Trusting reliance on God was a virtue central to the charitable work of the association, by ʿUthmān's account. Yet I had been curious about other implications of the calligraphed verse. *Truly God provides for whomsoever He wills without reckoning* (Q. 3:37)—but, I stuttered, in the midst of massive inequality, in a world of increasing wealth disparities and crippling poverty (I mentally rehearsed a litany of statistics), doesn't this mean that God provides *unequally* to begin with?

I was embarrassed to frame the question in this way, but ʿUthmān just smiled:

Ah, this leads us into the topic of trials (*ibtilāʾāt*). Well, the first thing is that the trial is for both the rich and the poor. When God the exalted gives a man wealth, it could be a curse upon him, a means by which he enters the hellfire. And conversely for a poor man, his trial [of poverty] could be a means for him to enter paradise. The unequal distribution of provisions is already a trial. But people need to seek their livelihood, because God distributed it separately. The proof (*dalīl*) for this is in Sūrat Maryam, when the voice called to her, "*And shake toward thyself the trunk of the date palm*" (Q. 19:25).

Surely different kinds of trials for rich and poor, I silently demurred, and one harsher than the other; but he was quoting the Quranic verse in which God tells Mary, driven to a palm tree in the throes of childbirth, to shake its trunk toward her for ripe dates to drop down upon her. "The scholars say that one facet of this verse is that she had to shake the tree to get its fruits, even though God could have just directly sent the angel Gabriel to her with provisions. This is something poorly understood today: people would rather sit at home waiting for their provisions [to come to them], be they a Syrian refugee or a Jordanian citizen."

The second aspect of this question, he continued, "is the factor of blessing (*baraka*), which is the most important thing in every effort. If God exalted and glorified evacuated our work of *baraka*, it would exhaust us; if God imbued it with *baraka*, it would grow before us. This isn't the same as the provision itself. Thus one person can find sufficient livelihood in a hundred dinars a month, if God blesses him, while five hundred dinars a month isn't enough for another."

Finally, he continued, people often emphasize worldly means (*asbāb dunyawiyya*) of acquiring their provisions while neglecting godly means (*asbāb allāh*). "Regrettably," he added, "people have become deeply materialist (*mādiyya*). Something may be right before them and yet they do not think of supplicating God for it. They have forgotten everything other than their monthly salaries." The distinction between this factor and the prior one wasn't clear to me. Is this third point the same as the question of *baraka* in one's provision, then? "No," he replied, "I'll give you another example."

> A Syrian woman was sitting at the door of a [medical] center bent over in pain. I saw her sitting there on the ground, on the pavement, so I went to her and asked how she was. She didn't reply, she started to weep—eventually she told me she had cancer and that the center needed 5,000 dollars to treat her. I asked her, "How is your relation (*'alāqatuki*) with your Lord?" She wept again and said, "My relation between me and God glorified and exalted is strong." I told her, "Exert yourself in supplication and God glorified and exalted will send you this amount." I left her then, walked on from her a little, just twenty paces—like she was sitting here [where we were sitting] and I walked just on to there [he gestured to the room down the hall] to get to my car. And I took out my phone to check my email, and as I did so an email arrived from a charitable foundation.

> It said: a donor came to us and donated 5,000 dollars for a cancer patient with leukemia! Imagine, just twenty paces! I mean, her relation with our Lord was strong indeed!

Echoing Quranic idiom (e.g., Q. 2:16, 86, 174, 175; 3:77, etc.), ʿUthmān describes this worldly life as a time of actions and transactions we undertake as we seek out our divinely ordained provisions; if we act righteously in this life, then God will recompense us with good in the afterlife. This is a clear economic theology of merits and demerits, good deeds and bad, in which the hereafter is the domain of divine reward (*ajr, jazāʾ, thawāb*). I later asked ʿUthmān what drove the charitable work he had immersed himself in. "If you ask me, as a Muslim, what I am doing in the world, or what I want, I live for one thing only: to collect good deeds (*ḥasanāt*) in order that God exalted and glorified grant me a good station [in the afterlife]." He also had a strong sense of responsibility, he added, a trait that had accompanied him through his life and that was already a divine "gift" (*mawhiba*).

This latter comment complicates the simple exchange of worldly acts for afterworldly fruits: if the ethical qualities that impel one to action are already a divine gift, then God is on both sides of the balance-sheet of action and consequence. ʿUthmān's account of the divine distribution of provisions (*rizq*) proves more ambiguous yet because God begins by dividing provisions unequally, always already soliciting our action (Mary shaking the date-palm)—but also constantly intervenes into our field of action by imbuing or evacuating blessings, undermining the possibility of general equivalence (100 or 500 dinars can be equally sufficient). And then God further supplements the economic logic by allowing for spiritual means of acquisition that bypass material efforts altogether (answering a cancer-struck worshipper's sincere supplication).[74]

The Moral Economy of Tribulation

ʿUthmān's dynamic apparatus of divine and temporal factors together urging acquisition begins to echo the relationship between Islam and neoliberalism advanced in anthropological literature on modern Muslim charitable practices.[75] Against the neoliberal withdrawal of social services in Egypt, writes Mona Atia, Islamist charities drastically expanded their economic roles—and themselves took on neoliberal logics of discipline and government. This in turn "blurred the boundaries between charity and development, between social welfare and capitalism, as well as between the voluntary, private, and public sectors."[76] Economic privatization produced the conditions for institutional forms of "privatized Islam" (private mosques, private foundations, an Islamic lifestyle market) that cater to new middle-class Muslim consumers.[77] The pious neoliberals who populate these new spaces are self-optimizing subjects who are assiduous about seeking their rewards, both in this life and in the afterlife. Addressing similar developments in Jordan, Sarah Tobin argues that among middle-class Ammanis

> neoliberalism and Islamic piety share similar temporal sensibilities. Both produce a sense of shortcoming and a desire for more—more profit, more gain, and greater expansion into new spaces and new markets. . . . Simply put, there is never enough monetary or spiritual gain, and such pursuits remain unfulfilled even as they prompt further action and new aims. This relentless striving toward profits and blessings and rewards, and the avoidance of punishment and hellfire, is the archetypal reflection of neoliberal piety.[78]

Her middle-class Jordanian interlocutors craft references to sharia as a way of accruing cultural capital; across multiple vernacular sites (Ramadan consumption, hijab debates, Islamic banks), they perform the authenticity, modernity, and cosmopolitanism of their piety, both "Islamiz[ing] their economic selves and economiz[ing] their Islamic selves in the public sphere."[79] 'Uthmān's calculative practice of collecting good deeds would be, by this account, a way of "extend[ing] risk management into the afterlife"—an Islamic ethic for the spirit of capitalism.[80]

However, the economic theology that this literature analogizes to neoliberal acquisition both pervades the archives of Islam and extends well past these middle-class networks. Moreover, 'Uthmān's insistence that they prepare to distribute aid to refugees without knowing if they would be able to do so accords with a much broader contemporary "surplus of deontological reasoning and of actions undertaken from the point of view of eternity, rather than from that of their mundane effects."[81] At the same time, his injunction to both act and have trusting reliance on God (*tawakkul*) expresses an Islamic ethical virtue whose formal telos is not abstracted into deontological terms. In short, although the analogy between neoliberalism and Islamic piety rests on a similar "sense of shortcoming" and "desire for more," positing a convergence around a notion of scarcity does not indicate anything of the *uses* to which that concept is put.[82] Finally, although an emphasis on divine rewards (*thawāb*) in scholarship on "pious neoliberalism" plausibly reflects subjects who seek to optimize future afterworldly profits, their faith inflected by a market orientation, virtuous actions are necessarily intersubjective—meaning that analysis must also attend how the circulation and distribution of *thawāb* within this moral economy establish "accountable flow[s] of moral value" with vectors and logics of their own.[83]

In more resonant terms, Amira Mittermaier analytically contrasts two economic theologies at play in contemporary charitable practices in Egypt: a calculative economy of *thawāb*, by which Muslims collect good deeds like one amasses wealth, maximizing one's rewards through attending to the contexts of virtuous action that can multiply or substitute their merits; and an excessive economy of *baraka*, by which divine abundance effuses past and interrupts whatever calculations one has made. "The discourse of *thawāb* demands of believers to keep count; that of *baraka* reminds them that counting is pointless."[84] Nor are these two economies actually opposed: Marion Katz writes (of a premodern context) that "the mathematics of divine reward (*thawāb*) are magically elastic, and their meaning lies in the wondrous and beneficent incommensurability of meager human actions and bounteous divine reward, rather than in any numerical equivalency."[85] For "since God is the real owner of wealth," Mittermaier continues, "the flow of profits, paybacks, and points is never bound to human rationality. The logic of calculation, investments, and accumulation is always provisional and at any moment can be disrupted by divine excess and divine justice, both of which exceed human understanding."[86]

Both economic models (*thawāb, baraka*) are certainly active within the Muslim projects of refugee support I observed in Jordan and Canada. Donors give expecting a divine "countergift" in the afterlife; volunteers and aid workers seek blessings by implementing relief programs. 'Uthmān himself overlaid an account of the acquisition of provisions with an account of the acquisition of good deeds, suggesting they share a similar logic. Yet he had also couched the entire discussion under the heading of a trial (*ibtilā'*) and had begun by insisting that wealth and poverty are both tests ordained by God. In this way, the trial is what cleaves the undecidable division between linearity (counting) and totality (the uncountable). The ultimate (eschatological) worth of the provisions humans seek is fundamentally withdrawn. Wealth is not a sign of divine favor (it could well be a curse). Blessing and tribulation are interconnected and indeed reversible: they are both sites of possible transformation.[87] In locating divine provision and human action together under the broader heading of tribulation, ʿUthmān destabilizes the basis of academic arguments for a direct relationship between neoliberalism and modern Islamic piety.

The ethics of giving disclosed in ʿUthmān's account of charitable action is based not simply on the sympathy of a benefactor viewing the suffering of another but on a divinely imposed obligation in which both "benefactor" and "beneficiary" are already implicated in the same moral economy of tribulation. Gift/countergift: if one gives in charity, one is receiving the possibility of having one's good deed accepted in the afterlife; in contrast, if one receives some charity, one is giving the giver of that charity the opportunity to receive benefit in the afterlife. These actions (really, these trans-actions) are already circulating in a theological economy whose contours extend past the ambiguous fields of action limited by this world. For this procedure also draws the otherworld (*ākhira*) deeper into this life.[88] And since the scenes of action are emergent (such that, for example, certain acts undertaken in the present may be expiations or recompenses for other acts in the past), collecting good deeds—the stated aim of ʿUthmān's life—is not a simple contract from this life to the next.[89] The temporal lineaments of moral action fractal across past, present, and future.

I had suggested earlier that ʿUthmān put the possibility of general equivalence out of reach because by his account God divides provisions unequally among rich and poor, concentrates abundance (*baraka*) in variegated fashion, and allows for subtle as well as material instruments of acquisition. But even though the exchange value of human actions is essentially unstable—or at least unavailable until Judgment Day, when their final worth will be revealed—one thing that is common across this ambiguous field of action is that these transactions each take time. It takes time for people to give, just as it takes time for others to receive; in Derridean terms, "time already begins to appear as that which undoes the distinction between taking and giving."[90] For ʿUthmān, the divine trial is the secret means by which God temporally distributes the occasions of good and ill. Subjects lack worldly guarantees of the value of their transactions but nonetheless traverse the economies of *thawāb* and *baraka* in time, reiterating the symbolic integrity of the present as that which puts them to the test.

DISCLOSING

I had first met ʿAlī in Damascus nearly fifteen years earlier, in the mosque of Ibn ʿArabī on Mount Qasyoun, when he interceded on my behalf after an older man had scolded me for my shoulder-length hair appearing too feminine. I had been relieved for the intervention by someone whose fluent Arabic, cloak, and already-greying beard marked him as one of the senior student-travelers who had flocked to Damascus over recent decades in search of Islamic knowledge.[91] In speaking afterward, we laughed at the coincidence: he had family in a city near where I had grown up, across the world in Canada. "These kinds of connections happen with Shaykh Muḥyiddīn [Ibn ʿArabī]," he had said, smiling. He was many years into his formal study of Islam, while I was leaving Syria in a few weeks after only a single year. Eventually (before the Syrian revolution began) he, too, moved to Edmonton, where he worked as a home renovations contractor and taught Islamic law on the occasional weekend.

Now he strode into the café I had suggested in northwest Edmonton, wearing a dark blue wool cloak over his long grey robe. I waved to him from the corner where I'd been reading and ordered him a flat white and a croissant, feeling a little self-conscious about my upscale choice of café, and he joked about how long ago our earlier meetings at Tim Horton's seemed. We hadn't met in a few months: I started telling him about my fieldwork from my latest trip to Jordan and how many of my interviews were with people displaced from Daraa. I paused, finding the pop music in the background incongruous. He noticed my hesitation. Then my words came out in a jumble. I told him how painful I found the news of bombings and images of rubble and how utterly disconnected they seemed from my memories of the country where we first met. So many people keep referring to this as a tribulation (*ibtilāʾ*), I said, but what that means isn't always clear to me.

He looked down at the table for a moment. "Your question isn't just about the news," he said quietly. "This is bigger than that, and more subtle."

The Green Man

He sipped his coffee and set it aside to explain what he meant. "What you describe is actually the relationship between *jalāl* and *jamāl*, divine majesty and divine beauty. God has both attributes: both have to be affirmed.

God holds both, and both are related in every thing. *Fī kulli jalālin jamāl*: in every tribulation (*ibtilā'*), every trial (*balā*), every affliction (*shidda*), there is an aspect of divine beauty. This becomes clear in the story of Moses and Khiḍr," he continued, switching back and forth between English and Arabic. "Remember that from Sūrat Kahf? Let's read it together." I fumbled for my phone, recalling the prophet's encounter with the enigmatic figure who is the initiator into the mystical path, who sees into the divine mystery (*ghayb*). I remembered a folktale from my childhood about Khiḍr, the Green Man, guiding Alexander the Great to the Fountain of Life. "Pull it up," he said, and waited for my Quran app to open. "This story shows us that one person can't show anyone else how divine beauty (*jamāl*) and divine majesty (*jalāl*) are connected. The individual has to see this for himself. And how one sees it depends on the spirit (*rūḥ*) of the being, and on the intellect (*'aql*), and how they perceive the real (*ḥaqīqa*). It's not just about whether or not you *believe* God has these qualities. Of course Moses upon him peace had sound belief! He had faith, but he still didn't see what was actually happening until Khiḍr showed him. We'll read it. What's the first verse of the section?"

I scrolled down to the passage and recited haltingly, still distracted by the news media images that had prompted my question:

> (Q. 18:65) *There they found a slave from among Our slaves whom We had granted a mercy from Us and whom We had taught knowledge from Our Presence.*

"Look at this," 'Alī said, "being a slave of God (*'abd*) comes before anything else in the story. It's the purpose of our creation. Then, if God chooses, He gives you mercy (*raḥma*). Remember the hadith in *Bukhārī* about the Prophet saying none will enter paradise by his deeds alone? Not even me, he said, unless God grant me mercy.[92] These divine openings don't depend on whether you believe or not. Then look at this next part of the verse, *and whom We had taught knowledge from Our Presence*—that's where the supplication of the Sufis comes from, 'O God teach me from Your knowledge' (*allāhumma 'allimnī min 'ilmik*): it's not asking for a new revelation—of course not—but for insight."

> (66) *Moses said unto him: Shall I follow thee, that thou mightest teach me some of that which thou hast been taught of sound judgment?*

"*Shall I follow thee*: he is asking for guidance. You follow someone, you learn from them, and then you are guided: this applies even to the great scholars of law (*fiqh*). The Quran is saying be patient, hold on (*istanna shway*), keep going and the answer will be there. Nowadays everyone is so impatient, they just want to ask Shaykh Google for the answers! That's not enough for seeing what God wants from you. In these two verses already the Quran has told us: first, be a slave of God (*'abd*). Then: have patience (*ṣabr*). Only then can you see what happens. You have to make yourself ready."

> (67) *He said: Truly thou wilt not be able to bear patiently with me* (68) *And how canst thou bear patiently that which thou dost not encompass in awareness?*

"Khiḍr is saying you won't be able to put up with me because you can't encompass (*tuḥiṭ*) that knowledge, you can't put it into the light. You might have news of something but you can't perceive its reality. This is the darkness of hearts, when you can't perceive the divine light. Even Moses didn't perceive the divine reality of what was going to happen, and he was a great prophet, of sound intellect, he talked with God. So what then about us?"

> (69) *He said: Thou wilt find me patient, if God wills, and I shall not disobey thee in any matter.*

"This is how you should act when you don't know: realize that you don't know, and shut your mouth!"

I laughed a little, surprised by his vehemence. He was reading the story of Moses and Khiḍr in a distinctly pedagogical key, gleaning from it a set of positions that one could seek out even if one is not, like Moses, being initiated into the realm of the divine mystery (*ghayb*). In doing so, however, he was also foregrounding the problem of capacity. It is not enough to believe that there is a spiritual reality animating the visible world, he had said. Or to affirm that divine beauty and divine majesty are entwined through every aspect of creation. Belief and affirmation are both necessary, of course. But a discursive proposition or affirmation is not sufficient for the aspirant to witness the truth.[93] However authentic and sincere such belief might be, that is, 'Alī insisted that a true witnessing of the interweaving of divine majesty (*jalāl*) and divine beauty (*jamāl*) must be experienced.

> (70) *He said: If thou wouldst follow me, then question me not about anything, till I make mention of it to thee.*

I paused, waiting for him to comment, but he gestured for me to continue.

> (71) *So they went on till, when they had embarked upon a ship, he made a hole therein. He said: Didst thou make a hole in it in order to drown its people? Thou hast done a monstrous thing.* (72) *He said: Did I not say unto thee that thou wouldst not be able to bear patiently with me?* (73) *He said: Take me not to task for having forgotten, nor make me suffer much hardship on account of what I have done.*

"Look at this etiquette (*adab*): nowadays we don't know what to say when we wrong someone. He forgot his pledge, and then remembered it; the nature of the human being is forgetfulness, and everyone makes mistakes. But we've forgotten what to do when we fall into error. Part of true repentance is that you make recompense to the person you've wronged. That's what Moses is doing here. He's saying, excuse me my forgetfulness."

> (74) *So they went on till they met a young boy, and he slew him. He said: Didst thou slay a pure soul who had slain no other soul? Thou hast certainly done a terrible thing!*

"He killed this youth. Elsewhere in the Quran we read that killing a single person without their having killed anyone, *nafsan bi-ghayri nafsin* (Q. 5:32), it is the equivalent of killing all humanity. And that's how horrible it is, *nakira*: a crime against humanity, it's disgusting, reprehensible."

> (75) *He said: Did I not say unto thee that thou wouldst not* (*lan*) *be able to bear patiently with me?*

"The scholars say that the word *lan* here means that you will not be able to do something, even though you want to. You have the will to do something but aren't able to bear it, don't have the ability." Like belief, 'Alī insisted, desire, too, isn't enough. The aspirant cannot, by sheer dint of will, bring herself to witness what she cannot *encompass in awareness* (Q. 18:68). Be a slave of God, he had said; be steadfast. Then see what happens. Whether one can see what one is being shown depends not on one's enthusiasm or the strength of one's commitment (or, as aforementioned, upon one's belief that something is true) but on one's *capacity.* This capacity is variable and depends, at least in part, on the work one does on oneself.

Anthropological literature has described Islamic ritual practices as enacting an ethical pedagogy, a cultivation of the embodied soul. This literature has explored how the repeated performance of outward behavior coordinates inward dispositions to inculcate specific moral virtues. Prayer, veiling, and ritualized weeping, for instance, are not merely virtuous habits that a committed subject may take up; rather, they contribute to a virtuous *habitus* that "takes root in one's character." Saba Mahmood cites Ibn Khaldūn's *Muqaddima*: "A habit[us] (*malaka*) is a firmly rooted quality acquired by doing a certain action and repeating it time after time, until the form of that action is firmly fixed [in one's disposition]."[94] Practices have a durable form of their own, learned within a tradition, and their repeated performance acts on the self. Indeed, these bodily practices "endow the self with particular capacities through which the subject comes to enact the world."[95] Disciplined repetition produces difference: in this Aristotelian model of ethics, virtuous and vicious acts sediment in one's body and in one's character. The embodied practice of a virtue is integral to being virtuous, in that such behavior is less the self's "sign of interiority" as a "means of acquiring its potentiality."[96] The techniques of moral self-cultivation, then, produce the subject through working on the varying capacities she inhabits. The historical range of this Islamic ethical tradition described by Mahmood and others includes modern Islamic reform movements, to be sure, but also precolonial Islamic ethics, Sufism, and even law.[97]

While this model of the ethical self animates much contemporary Islamic education (including among Syrian refugees in both Jordan and Canada), here I note that ʿAlī also underscores the limit of such ethical practice. Being a slave of God and being steadfast: these are aims one can work on, through ritual devotion and self-cultivation, through forming one's will and adhering to pious norms. But bearing with Khiḍr's violent actions in hope of eventually witnessing their reality (*ḥaqīqa*)? That does not depend simply on one's will or desire. And however one might work on one's capacities, ultimately, as Ibn Khaldūn writes elsewhere in the *Muqaddima*, "the power to prepare for a thing is not the same as power over the thing itself."[98] Pious practice makes one ready to witness the intertwining of divine majesty and divine beauty, but such witnessing itself is only possible through initiation or a divine gift.

(76) *He said: If I question thee concerning aught after this, then keep my company no more. Thou hast attained sufficient excuse from me.*

"He's setting a contract: three strikes and I'm out!"

(77) *So they went on till they came upon the people of a town and sought food from them. But they refused to show them any hospitality. Then they found therein a wall that was about to fall down; so he set it up straight. He said: Hadst thou willed, thou couldst have taken a wage for it.* (78) *He said: This is the parting between thee and me. I shall inform thee of the meaning of that which thou couldst not bear patiently.*

"Now Khiḍr will tell him—but he will have to part from him. This shows us that the silent treatment can be good sometimes; you don't want too many answers. If you'd had patience, you would have understood. You couldn't see beyond sinking the boat to the ultimate reality of what was happening. Now Khiḍr will put these events into perspective, beyond the letter of the law."

(79) *As for the ship, it belonged to indigent people who worked the sea. I wished to damage it, for just beyond them was a king who was seizing every ship by force.* (80) *And as for the young boy, his parents were believers and we feared that he would make them suffer much through rebellion and disbelief.* (81) *So we desired that their Lord give them in exchange one who is better than him in purity, and nearer to mercy.* (82) *And as for the wall, it belonged to two orphan boys in the city, and beneath it was a treasure belonging to them. Their father was righteous, and thy Lord desired that they should reach their maturity and extract their treasure, as a mercy from their Lord. And I did not do this upon my own command. This is the meaning of that which thou couldst not bear patiently.*

"There: everything becomes known. Khiḍr has shown Moses the true reality of what he couldn't stand. Because remember, long before Moses met Khiḍr, there were three other episodes in his life that match the confusing ones later. First, his mother put him in a basket to escape the oppression of Pharaoh (Q. 28:7). Second, he killed a man, an Egyptian (Q. 28:15). He killed a man! And he was repentant, of course, but he fled to the desert. And third, he carried water for the two shepherdesses at the oasis, for free (Q. 28:24). So, these three episodes correspond to the three with Khiḍr. Moses was put in a basket [on the water]; Khiḍr put a hole in a boat [on the water]. Moses killed a man; Khiḍr killed a boy. Moses did free service; Khiḍr did free service. But Moses never questioned these things when he was the one doing them, he didn't have this whole crisis searching for the meaning of these things until he saw someone else doing them. This is like us: we don't bear the world with steadfastness.

"We started reading these verses because you had asked about tribulation (*ibtilā'*). I read the news from Ghouta and from Daraa, and I ask myself what we can say. Two things at least: steadfastness is beautiful, *al-ṣabr jamīl*. And God is our refuge, *allāh al-musta'ān*. He is our refuge against all these terrible things happening, the farmers running from their fields, the bombs setting them ablaze. But then I wonder: maybe you would even prefer martyrdom like that to getting sucked into the evil of the world. Or to the material obsessions people get sucked into. Maybe that's my ignorance talking, but Bashar's evil is even a way to populate paradise with the beautiful and the pure."

I sat, looking at the verses on my smartphone screen, thinking for a minute. I appreciated 'Alī's broad insight (that knowledge of the Real is withdrawn from us and that our perception is fundamentally contingent), but the comments he had ended with unsettled me. I remembered my interlocutor 'Umar's insistence on the outskirts of Amman that the destruction in Syria was God rousing the Muslims to shake off their corruption and heresy. I remembered how distasteful I had found it: that it felt like a deflection of the terror and the suffering. Surely 'Alī wasn't saying that the destruction of Syria was like Khiḍr killing the youth to avoid the future grief he would cause his parents? Surely he was not making the rubble and the blood into material for theodicy, fueling the quietism of providential reason! I pulled back from the table, my shoulders starting to clench: So, if you're saying that this might be a way to populate paradise—are you saying that Bashar al-Assad destroying the country is like Khiḍr killing the youth, to avoid him growing into a rebel and a disbeliever?

'Alī was taken aback at my suggestion. "Of course not!" he said. "The very opposite, the very opposite (*bi-l-'aks, bi-l-'aks*)!"

I only brought that up, I said with some relief, because some of the Syrians I talked to in Jordan believed that the destruction was divinely sanctioned, because of the unbelief (*kufr*) and idolatrous (*shirk*) practices that had spread throughout Damascus. And they felt that God was doing this to wake up the Muslims.

He was horrified. "This is the outer meaning of the inner reality," he repeated twice. "The relation to Khiḍr killing the youth is at the level of inner reality (*ḥaqīqa*), not outer meaning (*sharīʿa*). Khiḍr is teaching Moses that there is a difference between *ḥaqīqa* and *sharīʿa*, but both are still true. In this world, in this life, you have to act based on *sharīʿa*. But in the afterlife we are judged by *ḥaqīqa*. So we can't assign people to heaven or hell based on the outer meaning—but that also means you have to defer *ḥaqīqī* judgment even about Bashar."

I was mollified by his explicit rejection of the analogy I had first inferred from his impromptu exegesis—from Khiḍr killing a youth, as a way of preempting future evil, to Bashar al-Assad's killing of Syrians, as a way of populating paradise. I understood, too, that the disclosive relation between *sharīʿa* and *ḥaqīqa* was more oblique than a simple binary of outer form and inner meaning. This much was signaled by his translation of the former as "outer meaning" and the latter as "inner reality," which granted *sharīʿa* an effective status while introducing a hiatus between available *sharʿī* judgments and the witnessing of reality itself. In fact, ʿAlī refused the analogy between Bashar and Khiḍr even though his exegesis of Khiḍr's actions, which initiated Moses into the movement from *sharīʿa* to *ḥaqīqa*, had been prompted by news of Bashar al-Assad's actions. The relation between *sharīʿa* and *ḥaqīqa* judgments, then, may be understood as non-analogical: a judgment is inscribed in each register without these judgments necessarily being aligned. He even allowed for a negative relationship between *sharīʿa* and *ḥaqīqa*. Perhaps the parallel episodes of Moses and Khiḍr he had cited offered possible configurations between them. Moses riding in a basket versus Khiḍr scuttling a ship: inversion. Moses killing a man versus Khiḍr killing a boy: transposition. Moses doing free service versus Khiḍr doing free service: reflection. Taken together, these three cases (inversion, transposition, and reflection) demonstrate the possible range of this relationship. Perhaps ʿAlī was suggesting that the relationship between *sharīʿa* judgments and *ḥaqīqa* judgments is chiasmic, as when terms partake of one another without collapsing into one another. Certainly he was advancing an asymmetry between the terms of this relation, for an interruption (pause, hiatus, lacuna) in the passage from *sharīʿa* to *ḥaqīqa*. But I remained perturbed by his insistence that this hiatus cuts both ways, so that we must still defer *ḥaqīqī* judgment of Bashar. I remembered one of my interlocutors in Jordan taking off his skullcap and showing me the scar all along the side of his head, of where he had been tortured in a Syrian prison. I remembered another interlocutor lifting his robe to show me where the regime's military police had snuffed out their cigarettes on his ankles before tearing his side open. I had difficulty allowing for the retroactive interpretation of these actions—that they helped to populate paradise and so were ultimately turned toward a good outcome.

ʿAlī sensed my reservations. He finished his coffee and glanced at his watch. "Remember," he said, "there is a difference between what God loves and what God wills. Of course everything that happens does so by His power (*qudra*) and His will (*irāda*). But that doesn't mean God prefers these things or loves them. What is God pleased with from me (*riḍāh*)? That's what we should ask." He got up to leave, having redirected our conversation from the broader question of theodicy toward a more immediate question of personal action. This redirection did not dispense with the tribulation altogether, but it certainly reconfigured the basis of our discussion. In doing so, he also invoked a distinction between the divine ontological decree and the divine deontological decree. In the Ashʿarite doctrine ʿAlī had studied in Damascus all those years earlier, God is utterly omnipotent, unbound by the subjective and ultimately self-interested human standards of morality and justice. He brings into being the world as it is through His sovereign will, in all its pain and suffering, without this reflecting on His benevolence in the slightest.[99] Yet at least for later Ashʿarites (and certainly for their critics Ibn Taymiyya and Ibn al-Qayyim), God's normative preference (deontological decree) can be considered separately from his will. "While unbelief and disobedience occur by the will of God (*bi-irādati llāh*)," writes al-Rāzī, "they do not occur according to His love or His pleasure (*laysa bi-maḥabbati llāhi taʿālā wa lā bi-riḍāh*)."[100] Distinguishing between ontological and deontological registers of the divine command allowed the Ashʿarites to insist on divine freedom and human responsibility at once. And, at our meeting in an Edmonton café, this distinction allowed ʿAlī to depict struggling with the theoretical problem of theodicy as ultimately a distraction from how we could concretely act toward meeting God's pleasure.

Before he left, he suggested I read ʿIzz al-Dīn al-Sulamī's short treatise titled *al-Fitan wa-l-balāyā wa-l-miḥan wa-l-razāyā* ("Trials, Tests, Afflictions, and Calamities"). "It won't cover everything we should talk about next time," he said. "But it is a beginning."

Seventeen Benefits of Tribulation

I looked up the text. Its author, 'Izz al-Dīn 'Abd al-'Azīz bin 'Abd al-Salām al-Sulamī (b. 577–78 AH/1181–82 CE), was the leading Shāfi'ite authority of his generation, known even as an independent jurist (*mujtahid*), and was a prominent exponent of Ash'arite theology. His biography is striking, marked by repeated antagonistic encounters with ruling powers: "He avoided praising kings, rather he lectured them," writes one chronicler.[101] He was "the sultan of the scholars" (*sulṭān al-'ulamā'*) rather than "a scholar of the sultans." At the age of sixty, while giving the Friday sermon at the Umayyad Mosque in Damascus, he condemned the city's ruler for a capitulating alliance with the Franks against the Ayyubid ruler of Cairo, and he issued a fatwā prohibiting the sale of arms to the newly allied Crusaders. He was quickly arrested for a few months and left for Egypt upon being released. There he spent the last twenty years of his life (d. 660/1262), though he was soon dismissed from his initial post as chief judge of Cairo due to his continued intransigence. He was also a Sufi who was initiated by Shahāb al-Dīn 'Umar al-Suhrawardī and who frequented the gatherings of Abū Ḥasan al-Shādhilī.[102] His commitment to giving Sufism a privileged (if circumscribed) place can be gauged from how he followed al-Ghazālī and al-Qushayrī in giving saints (*awliyā'*) pre-eminence over scholars (*'ulamā'*), as well as how he allowed for gatherings of Sufi poetry (*samā'*) and ecstatic dance (*raqṣ*).[103] He was a scholar who clearly brooked no compromises, disputing rulers even in their own courts, whose broad popularity already in his lifetime (evidenced by the great throng of his funeral procession) owed less, writes Éric Chaumont, to the "quality of his bibliography or to the originality of his thought than to his exemplary life, to his militancy placed exclusively at the service of the community, to his independence in dealing with political authorities . . . and the zeal with which he conformed to what he regarded as the most important mission of the scholar in society, sc. to command the good and to forbid the reprehensible (*al-amr bi-l-ma'rūf wa-l-nahy 'an al-munkar*)."[104]

The benefits of tribulation, writes Ibn 'Abd al-Salām in the text 'Alī had suggested I read, differ depending on the ranks of the people (*bi-ikhtilāf rutab al-nās*).[105] That is, not all of these seventeen benefits (*fawā'id*) are available to everyone; apprehending them depends on the receptivity of the spiritual aspirant:

(1) realizing the overwhelming power of divine lordship (*rubūbiyya*);
(2) realizing the abjection and brokenness of servanthood (*'ubūdiyya*);
(3) full devotion (*ikhlāṣ*) to God, recognizing that there is no recourse in repelling adversities except Him;
(4) renewed repentance (*ināba*);
(5) entreaty (*taḍarru'*) and supplication (*du'ā'*);
(6) forbearance (*ḥilm*) with those who effect the affliction;
(7) forgiving (*'afw*) those who injure one;
(8) steadfastness (*ṣabr*) through the affliction;
(9) joy (*farḥ*) at the affliction due to the benefits it yields, like at a bitter medicinal draught;
(10) gratitude (*shukr*) for the affliction, like one is grateful to a doctor who amputates a gangrenous limb;
(11) the purification (*tamḥīṣ*) by which affliction expiates one's sins and mistakes;
(12) the mercy (*raḥma*) that a tribulation elicits for those who are afflicted—as in the poetic verse, "only one who has loved passionately has compassion for the lover";
(13) realizing the measure of the blessing of well-being (*qadr ni'mat al-'āfiya*) and gratitude for it;
(14) what God has prepared (*a'adda*) in the afterlife;
(15) what is enfolded (*ṭayy*) in the affliction by way of concealed benefits;
(16) that afflictions preempt (*tamna'*) evil and hubris, tyranny and arrogance; and
(17) satisfaction (*riḍā*).

This short treatise provides a list of possibilities that may obtain in and through an affliction. Again, not all of these will be available at once. In listing seventeen, remarking that they depend upon the receptivity of the aspirant, Ibn 'Abd al-Salām demonstrates that experience of an event is fundamentally contingent. Two people can face the same trial yet come through it to very different outcomes. The nature of experience itself is in question. By providing a roster of these possibilities, without claiming this list to be exhaustive, the author is not suggesting that experience is merely personal (subjectivism). Nor is this a matter of a single material reality being variously construed or interpreted, according to the insight (or "rank") of the individual—it is not as though the remaining benefits from someone's trial wait there unobtained, available to anyone else. Rather, he suggests both that there is a contingency to the nature of the affliction (*muṣība*) and that it can be thematized in its contingency.

The list of seventeen benefits initially seems haphazard, even in their explanation: some cite a Quranic verse or two—the first one is without any gloss whatsoever—while others are supported by multiple hadiths and verses. There is no obvious trajectory to this list; Ibn ʿAbd al-Salām does not present it as a sequential account of the spiritual journey, such that one must apprehend the first benefit before proceeding to the second. Yet the list of seventeen benefits clearly has pedagogic purpose in indicating the broad scope and subtle possibilities of an event. I reread the treatise with a view to its organization. The first two benefits (benefits 1 + 2: realizing the grandeur of divine lordship and the brokenness of human servanthood) clearly mirror one another. The next three benefits (3 + 4 + 5: full devotion, renewed repentance, and entreaty/supplication) all intensify and purify the relation of the aspirant to God. The next two benefits (6 + 7: forbearance and forgiveness) pertain to the relation of the aspirant to the immediate cause of the affliction. The ninth and tenth benefits (9 + 10: joy and gratitude) are reflexive positions taken by the aspirant toward the affliction itself. The next three benefits (11 + 12 + 13: purging one's sins, allowing one to practice mercy, and appreciating the blessing of well-being) are all effects occasioned by the affliction upon the aspirant. The fourteenth and fifteenth benefits (14 + 15: what is prepared in the afterlife and what is concealed in this life) are both withdrawn from outward perception. The sixteenth benefit (16: preempting other evils) suggests unactualized possibilities. Finally, the two remaining benefits (8 + 17: steadfastness and satisfaction) stand apart from the others because Ibn ʿAbd al-Salām writes that they each entail a divine response: steadfastness (*ṣabr*) solicits the love of God the exalted and great reward (*mūjabu maḥabbata llāhi taʿālā wa kathrata thawābih*) while satisfaction (*riḍā*) solicits the good-pleasure of God the exalted (*mūjabu li-riḍwāni llāhi taʿālā*). Steadfastness and satisfaction are also variously paired in the broader Sufi tradition; aligning them here divides Ibn ʿAbd al-Salām's list of the benefits of tribulation into two broad parts (A: 1 – 7; B: 9 – 16; C: 8 + 17) subdivided into parallel groups of two or three (A1: 1 + 2; A2: 3 + 4+5; A3: 6 + 7; C1: 8; B1: 9 + 10; B2: 11 + 12 + 13; B3: 14 + 15; B4: 16; C2: 17). While not providing a sequential account of the spiritual aspirant's journey, then, the author's list of seventeen benefits does form a structure reminiscent of ring compositions.

In this short treatise on tribulation, Ibn ʿAbd al-Salām distinguished steadfastness (*ṣabr*) and satisfaction (*riḍā*) by remarking that each solicited a divine response. In al-Qushayrī's *Risāla*, which Ibn ʿAbd al-Salām had read with al-Suhrawardī in Baghdad, these name two of the mystical stations (*maqāmāt*) that one can traverse through one's own discipline and effort. A station is contrasted with a mystical state (*ḥāl*), which is a divine gift that descends like a flash of lightning; it cannot be earned. The stations must also be ascended sequentially. "A precondition of the station," writes al-Qushayrī, "is that you cannot advance from one station to the next unless you have fulfilled the requirements of the former."[106] In the *Risāla*'s account of the stations, steadfastness and satisfaction occur nearly midway through the mystical journey and are separated by watchful awareness of God (*murāqaba*). Al-Qushayrī cites earlier gnostics: steadfastness is "endurance of the hardships decreed for one by God"[107] while satisfaction is "accepting divine decrees with joy."[108] Across these two stations, then, the divine decree may remain constant. Yet its hardship dissolves in the ascent from one to the other. In the station of steadfastness, you learn to endure the decree. In the station of satisfaction, you receive the decree with joy.[109] By locating steadfastness (8) and satisfaction (17) respectively at the midpoint and end of the benefits of tribulation, Ibn ʿAbd al-Salām gestures to a reality in which the event is worked through: it no longer pains the aspirant; she feels no bitterness at the decree. It ceases to be an affliction.[110]

The Beauty and the Glory

I next met ʿAlī a few months later at the same café. He arrived worried, distracted by the news. A provincial election was looming, and numerous candidates of the United Conservative Party (widely anticipated to win a legislative majority) had recently made local headlines after their prior activities and comments came to light—from lamenting the "demographic replacement of white peoples in their homelands"[111] to posing for photographs with members of anti-Muslim hate group the Soldiers of Odin.[112] (The Edmonton chapter of this right-wing anti-immigration group rebranded itself "Canadian Infidels" after this media exposure, the new group intending to continue activities like street patrols and activism to warn against the danger of Canada becoming a "radical Islamic state."[113]) Other candidates made homophobic and anti-abortion remarks and questioned climate change.[114] Another candidate publicly warned his followers against the United Nations Global Compact on Migration, which he understood to "sign away" Canadian border sovereignty and so to permit mass immigration by Muslims.[115]

A few weeks before we sat together at the café again, the Al Rashid Mosque in north Edmonton had been ostentatiously "patrolled" by members of the Canadian Infidels. Closed-circuit television stills show two burly men in black leather jackets, one wearing a black toque with the word *kāfir* stitched in white, shouldering into the vestibule and then confronting mosque attendees outside.[116] And, shortly before we met, another mosque in south Edmonton had received some mail. "Good day," the letter began. "On behalf of real Albertans, we would like to inform you that you and your religion don't belong here in Alberta. We kindly ask you to close down your fake worship House and leave or accept Jesus as your one true God. We are White. We are Christian. We are Proud. We will fight for our right to exist in our own country. You will not force your savage laws on us."[117] The letter continued like this, promising that United Conservative Party leader Jason Kenney was going to "take Alberta back." In place of a signature, the letter provided an upside-down Canadian flag emblazoned with THE CLANN in gothic font as well as a United Conservative Party logo. The party leader issued a statement condemning this letter and its nativism but did not address why so many of his party's candidates expressed similar politics.

"I just came from a meeting at [an Islamic school near the mosque that received the letter]," ʿAlī said as he sat down. "We're talking about what to do if this threat escalates."

I scoffed a little. These guys are thugs, I said, they're just playing a big game. They want to rile people up, make some noise before the election, but they are braggarts more than anything. I pointed to the random capitalization in THE CLANN's letter and laughed at its internal contradictions.

"I don't know." ʿAlī shook his head. "We don't know what's in their hearts. There is evil around. Remember what happened in Quebec City? People are afraid here now, they think about it every day. Even at the school, we will have new private security. We've been planning what happens if there is a shooter." He had spoken at an Edmonton vigil commemorating the 2017

Quebec City mosque shooting, in which a white nationalist emptied his weapon into a mosque hall, killing six and wounding nineteen.[118] I remembered his phrase from last time we met about martyrdom perhaps populating paradise with the beautiful and the pure. That speculation did not stop him from taking evil seriously or from preparing for it. I felt embarrassed for not taking the letter as seriously as he and for presuming that his talk of enduring a tribulation meant he would not respond proactively.

"I actually wanted to finish what we were saying last time," he said. "What we call a tribulation (*ibtilā'*) isn't always a tribulation. This is something to take note of even before discussing what a tribulation teaches us or what its benefits are. The answer you find will be different from the one I find. I think of what Ḥabīb 'Umar said after Ḥabīb 'Aydarūs was martyred in his own house: that God wanted to ennoble him, to magnify him, to honor him like He had honored others before. Do you know how he died? This was just last year, a man knocked on his door in Tarim and said he was sick, and asked if he would supplicate for him, and then shot him dead in his prayer, right there in front of his wife. They think it was Wahhabis.[119] Or I think about Shaykh Aḥmad Yāsīn. Remember how he was martyred?"

I thought back to how the Hamas leader was killed. It was a rocket, wasn't it?

"That's right, an Israeli rocket just after the fajr prayer, as he was leaving the mosque. Can you think of a better way to die? When some mujahidin returned home from fighting in Bosnia, I remember this myself—maybe you are too young to do so—their parents wept because their sons missed the opportunity to be martyred.[120] These things happen all across the history of Islam—even before the Prophet, if we recall the story of Moses and Khiḍr—but those are just three examples from the last few years. We think that of course these things are tribulations, like the Quran says that God will try you with death and life (e.g., Q. 67:2). But not everyone receives them as tribulations. When you look back at this history, you see there are answers everywhere to the question of divine majesty (*jalāl*) and divine beauty (*jamāl*). *Fī kulli jalālin jamāl*: there is divine beauty in every [revelation of] divine majesty. So again, what we are left with is: what is our assignment (*waẓīfa*)?"

Much as the organization of Ibn 'Abd al-Salām's treatise had implied, there comes a point in one's journey to God at which the events otherwise received as tribulations simply cease hurting. The ontological divine decree is necessarily effective—including whatever death and deprivation it ordains—but how it is lived (how it is begrudged, endured, celebrated) depends on one's striving, one's remaking of one's own body and its capacities, how one educates the body and trains one's desires. 'Alī and the tradition he is speaking from are not suggesting just that everyone's experience of an event is different, in the banal sense that everyone personally interprets what happens, nor are they arguing for a social-constructionist account of historical experience.[121] Rather, they insist that repetition produces difference; self-conscious practices can over time "take root," become unselfconscious, expanding and contracting the potentialities of the self. (This process is only possible because, as Talal Asad writes in another context, "an agent's act is more (and less) than her consciousness of it.")[122] The difficulty of the decree dissipates in the subject's passage from the station of steadfastness to the station of satisfaction. The significance of the event, crucially, hinges on how it is received; how it is received depends, ultimately, upon the striving of the subject; the striving of the subject reclines, finally, upon divine facilitation. Yet *sharī'a* and *ḥaqīqa* are both true and effective at once, which entails allowing for multiple simultaneous registers of a single event.

As 'Alī reprised our earlier conversation, moreover, he extended the range of the sites of disclosure far beyond one's own life. When you consider the history of Islam, he had said, indeed history before Islam as well, you find it replete with the intertwining of divine beauty and divine majesty. This is a theological vision of history whose instances are organized less as chronicle or narrative than through episodes linked by a principle of similarity.[123] Thus he linked disparate episodes of martyrdom drawn from modern Muslim political history (the Bosnian jihad, the Palestinian intifada, sectarianism in Yemen) into a single history of struggle. Whatever else this history depicts of the travails of postcolonial Islamism, that is, he insisted that these are also similar iterations of the same relation (*jamāl* and *jalāl*) instantiated across time.

In the funeral oration 'Alī had cited, the Yemeni scholar Ḥabīb 'Umar bin Ḥafīẓ (b. 1963), founder of the Dār al-Muṣṭafā seminary in Tarim, extolled the life and lineage of the martyred Ḥabīb 'Aydarūs bin 'Abdallāh bin 'Alī bin Sumayṭ, imam of the Miḥḍār Mosque in Tarim, lauding him as a paragon of etiquette (*adab*) and learning (*'ilm*). God wanted to honor him, to ennoble him, he proclaimed, which is why he granted him death on the blessed day of Friday. Ḥabīb 'Aydarūs was a martyr in his own house (*shahīd al-dār*), Ḥabīb ʿUmar continued, like the third caliph ʿUthmān bin ʿAffān, who was assassinated in his own house; and he was martyred while at prayer, like the second caliph ʿUmar bin al-Khaṭṭāb and the fourth caliph ʿAlī bin Abī Ṭālib. He turned the sermon toward moralistic ends, calling on the hundreds gathered at the burial to abandon dissenting practices, to fear God, to accept the difficulty of life. For the world is hardship, and God tests his servants by the measure of their faith. In conclusion, Ḥabīb ʿUmar located the martyrdom of his relative in the broader history of Hadramawt, whose scholars of virtue and learning irrigate the blessed land like water does thirsty plants.[124]

In this funeral oration, Ḥabīb ʿUmar described a contemporary episode (the death of Ḥabīb ʿAydarūs) through reference to far earlier episodes already known to his audience (the deaths of the rightly guided caliphs). The same lessons obtain from each.[125] The meaning of this historical event is disclosed through a typological figure—*shahīd al-dār*, a martyr in his own house—which ʿAlī invoked to the same end. Episodes of this type stand outside the flow of chronometric time, making the historical distance between Ḥabīb ʿAydarūs and the early caliphs irrelevant for how they disclose the same truth. Such episodes, writes Aziz al-Azmeh, form "accents of intensity which manifest an erratic immanence, hence of causal repetition, an allegory along the axis of time." Whatever time separates such events, a "qualitative continuity is maintained . . . by the succession rhythms internal to the purposes of theodicy."[126] While for al-Azmeh typological knowledge of this sort quickly folds into a salvation history, in this section I linger with the relay between *sharīʿa* and *ḥaqīqa* in order to underscore their simultaneous intimacy and asymmetry.

Back to our second meeting at that Edmonton café. If you look across Muslim history, ʿAlī had said, everywhere you see the interweaving of divine majesty and divine beauty. "When we start to see this, we see it everywhere: it removes the veils of disclosure. Do you know the poem? We learned it in Syria." He started to sing.

rufiʿat astār al-bayn	*the curtains of ʿbetween' have been lifted*
wa badiʾta anwār al-ʿayn	*and the lights of oneness have appeared*
tanjalī min ghayri ayn	*disclosed without any ʿwhere'*
fa-shhadūhā yā ṣūfiyya	*so see them, o Sufis!*[127]

"Every time you recite the verses we talked about last time, something new unfolds. Every time I hear this ode, something else opens. No sunrise is the same!" He chanted another stanza from the ode.

akhli qalbaka li-ttajallī	*clear your heart for the theophany*
wa-jlu ʿaynaka li-ttamallī	*open your eye for true joy*
wa-ssiwā yā khillu khalli	*other than the divine, my friend, abandon*
wa-fna fī dhdhāti ʿaliyya	*and be annihilated in the exalted entity*

"Clear your heart, open your eye for true joy! Witness the true joy all around! Remember the miracles our teachers told us about? ʿUmar may God be pleased with him was giving the Friday sermon in the Prophet's mosque in Medina, and shouted to warn the Muslim army—led by Sariyya, a month's ride away—of an ambush. Nowadays, I can pick up this cellphone and call anyone a month's ride away. Flying through the air was among the major miracles (*karamāt*) of the saints (*awliyāʾ*); it was among the miracles (*muʿjizāt*) of Solomon. But now just look around you—what other miracles would you like? You can fly through the air at 1,000 kilometres an hour, with women serving you tea and coffee—what more do you need?" I laughed at this hyperbole, amused by his redescription of modern technology. "So it all depends on two things," he continued, "how you look—with your eye or with your heart—and what you are looking for. In the hadith of Gabriel, the Prophet said that excellence (*iḥsān*) is about knowing that God sees you, even if you cannot see God. If you efface yourself, you will see with your heart. Ultimately this is the difference between the journey to God and the journey in God."

The journey to God, as I understood it, had to do with virtuously striving through the mystical stations, while the journey in God was the experience of the breakdown of the distinction between *sharīʿa* and *ḥaqīqa* altogether.[128] The constant receding of the veils (of multiplicity, of opposition, of unity, and of witness) is the infinite breakdown of this distinction. ʿAlī pressed his point. "One who has experienced the limit of created things encounters a completely different metaphysics. The Muhammadan Reality (*ḥaqīqa muḥammadiyya*) leads to things beyond visible reality: you see everything around you as light (*nūr*), even the difficult divine decrees. But it takes perseverance (*istiqāma*)."

"Well, there's the problem," I joked. "I want to skip the perseverance part to get to the vision of the heart—that sounds nice."

'Alī shook his head. "Hearts are like green mangoes. Some take a long time to ripen while others are ready right away. Look at the men of perseverance and reality. Imam al-Ghazālī only lived 54 years, yet look at what he accomplished. Imam al-Shāfi'ī too was 54 when he passed away. None of this is out of reach. But it begins with facing the tribulation."

The Journey to God, in God

Our conversation drifted to our plans for the weekend, and he soon left to pick up his teenage children. But I mulled over our conversations in the next months. I had started by asking how 'Alī understood what was happening in the land where we first met, where we each had friends and teachers. Yet to my surprise, our discussion began with Quranic exegesis—in the course of which we held out the possibility of redemption even to Bashar al-Assad; then we had ended by celebrating technological advances as modern miracles. A broader question of theodicy was raised and then displaced to foreground one's personal duty. The Syrian war was first affirmed as a collective tribulation but then stripped even of that status through a phenomenological procedure that rendered the nature of the event radically contingent. The importance of virtuous self-cultivation was first underscored but then limited. The presence of evil was acknowledged and prepared against without it cathecting a durable form. The sites of disclosure were multiplied far beyond the span of a single life, but access to them was restricted to those who had been initiated into theophanic vision. The relation between *sharī'a* and *ḥaqīqa* was posited and then dissolved.

Reflecting on why our conversation left me frustrated, I slowly came to understand its relaying movement (stipulation followed by withdrawal) as instructive in its own right. I had been seeking something simpler, something like a mystical condemnation of the Syrian regime, having had some sense of 'Alī's political sensibilities. Instead, he resisted—like Khiḍr in the Quranic passages we read together. The figure of tribulation, for 'Alī, immediately opens onto the asymmetrical relationship between outer meaning (*ẓāhir*) and inner reality (*bāṭin*). These two may reflect one another—but they can equally be inverted or transposed. Their relation bears its own dynamism. In pressing on this relation, one encounters an experience of the limit—which is intolerable and opens up a countermove. Hence 'Alī's constant further elaboration of the same recursive dynamic, which I had heard as a feint.[129] The figure of tribulation cannot be stabilized into a single form of punishment or test. Nor does it yield a reliable worldly politics either of activism or of quietism, for the finitude of interpretation cuts both ways.[130] Rather, this figure is revelatory, rejecting any sequential coordination of the proper lessons to be learned from a historical event.

ʿAlī's account of tribulation as apocalypse—"eschatology can break out at any moment"[131]—also explains his recounting of a history of episodes interweaving divine majesty and divine beauty: "Historical material is fragmented into its archetypal constituents, and then subjected to displacement and condensation, as in dreams."[132] Politics is at stake in the figure of tribulation (worldly judgment of an evil ruler), as too is ethics (virtuous striving and its limits) and history (or at least discrete events like martyrdom, typologically united across time). But also the very possibility of an imaginal vision, of the possibility of still passing from the journey "to God" to the journey "in God," even today when modern technology has released miracles (flying in the air, communicating across vast distances) from the strict purview of the saints.[133] "Quaff the goblet openly / See no disgrace in drinking," the Sufi ode ʿAlī had sung in Damascus continues. "Heed not the words of him who forbids your love / Listening is but tribulation."[134]

A GRAMMAR OF TRIBULATION

The ethnographic articulations of tribulation that have emerged across these four accounts—accepting, reckoning, distributing, disclosing—are not mutually exclusive. They certainly are not exhaustive of the concept of ordeal, nor even of how it makes sense of the Syrian war. But they do demonstrate its broad range and some common coordinates. For each of my learned interlocutors, tribulation is instructive: there is a pedagogy to the ordeal, if one cares to endure it. The ravages of the war are not brute. The divine trial contains an address that requires response. As Talal Asad once commented, "There are different styles of confronting disaster—of explaining, justifying, living it."[135] My interlocutors' styles of confrontation vary widely: from cultivating religious knowledge to the excision of communal deviance to open-ended charitable practices to pursuing mystical vision.

Taken together, these interlocutions offer an ethnographic constellation of contemporary Islamic theology, with the Syrian war debated respectively by a pragmatic pedagogue, a Salafi scholar, a lay activist, and a Sufi mystic.

Taken together, moreover, the contention implicitly leveled by the pseudonyms employed in this chapter comes to the fore. I named these four interlocutors Abū Bakr, ʿUmar, ʿUthmān, and ʿAlī after the first four caliphs, companions of the prophet who exemplify Islamic paradigms (at least within the cultural memory of Sunnism).[136] In doing so, I have implied that my interlocutors' claims on the figure of "tribulation" express and inhabit the sensibilities of those paradigms. Accepting, reckoning, distributing, and disclosing: they express and inhabit such sensibilities in their forms of life, for ethics is "fundamentally a question of form and its making."[137] My interlocutors are variously situated (geographically, socially, economically, ideologically), but their sensibilities are not reducible to these differences. That is, the grammatical affordances of a tradition in its vitality should not be conflated with the historical flourishing of its social institutions. A tradition may wane, it may face an ordeal; its acts of inheritance may be colored by melancholy. But what are their range and efficacy, force and significance? This latter question cannot be answered through histories of the social conditions of a tradition's "survival," whether read as a symbolic order or a regime of social norms.

In this concluding section I move from these four ethnographic accounts of tribulation toward adducing its conceptual grammar.[138] Although I have been calling tribulation a "figure," my inquiry into its grammar presumes that it is not simply a personal or historical trope for social experience. Rather, I treat tribulation as a concept central to (if undertheorized in) the Islamic tradition. Thus, I have been elaborating the "possibilities" of tribulation, the "kinds of statement" made about it rather than claiming to "see right into" it.[139]

In the conclusion to his remarkable book *After Evil*, the political theorist Robert Meister draws on the linguist Émile Benveniste to grammatically model configurations of justice.[140] He explains that the *paradigms* of justice involve the person and declension of nouns (victims, perpetrators, beneficiaries, bystanders), while their *syntagms* involve variations in time, sequence, aspect, and mood. Together these provide a way to explore the poetic forms of politics, whether messianic, utopian, realistic, or prophetic.[141] The "dominant syntagma" of prophetic politics is the present imperative: something more must be done in the present to achieve God's justice. This model of "struggle-as-justice," which Meister reads to obtain in Islam, starkly opposes the model of "justice-as-reconciliation," which Meister reads in Saint Paul and likewise in human rights discourse. (The latter's therapeutic practices—after evil, before justice—"profess faith in a future in which the past will have been different because of increased awareness of the unjustified suffering that occurred."[142]) Considered in these terms, the articulations of tribulation explored in this chapter were also marked by the present imperative. Abū Bakr, 'Umar, 'Uthmān, and 'Alī all saw the ordeal to demand something of them immediately. There was no time outside the divine interpellation: it was neither too soon nor too late.[143] But otherwise their syntagmas varied substantially.

For Abū Bakr, whose articulation of the ordeal I have explored under the heading of "accepting," tribulation questions the relation between accusative and dative cases. In something like Primo Levi's distinction between victims (those true witnesses who touched bottom, "who saw the Gorgon," and did not return) and survivors (those who, at best, bear witness to a missing testimony),[144] the divine trial puts to the test not those who suffer the worst but those who are adjacent to it. Thus, Abū Bakr effectively distinguishes between the event of affliction and that of tribulation. The indirect objects of the former are the direct objects of the latter, for tribulation acts transitively upon everyone who is contiguous to the affliction. In contrast to the moral drama of human rights discourse, which seeks to transform bystanders into compassionate witnesses through viewing the pain of others, his witness is not retrospective. Rather than being situated, as Meister puts it, after evil and before justice, Abū Bakr lives among both.[145] The claims of intertemporal justice endure, grounded in the incommensurable alterity of divine judgment; he cannot distance himself from past and future in order to emerge cleansed through his witness. He cannot deflect the question: Has the affliction affected my capacity? And, with reference to the tribulation: Am I implicated or excused?

For 'Umar, whose articulation of the ordeal I have explored under the heading of "reckoning," tribulation acts as both the spur to change and as its measure. This double role layers the sequence of its syntagma. The present is spatially related to prior episodes of the same struggle while projecting an ultimate victory into the distant future. Tribulation configures the present as the field of militant action. Against the entropic drift of tradition, whose excessive formalism reclines into an optative mood (wish fulfillment), tribulation here reiterates the typological struggle between truth and falsehood. Its paradigm is revolutionary and recursive; its grammatical aspect leaves little conclusive finality to be had (though it might exhaust revolutionaries in the meantime). But the moral clarity so afforded by tribulation (its field of heroes and villains) also troubles its desire for completion, for it ensures that the struggle can only ever be repeated through the end of time. "A faction of my *umma* will continue to fight in defense of truth and prevail until the Day of Judgment," said the Prophet.[146]

For 'Uthmān, whose articulation of the ordeal I have explored under the heading of "distributing," tribulation convenes the divine economies of calculation (*thawāb*) and of excess (*baraka*). Between the commodity and the gift, between restricted and general economies, between scarcity and surplus, we work to acquire what is thus distributed. The grammatical mood of tribulation is here subjunctive, in that we must act as though the metavalue of our exchanges is stable. Its aspect is progressive insofar as such acts are undertaken by finite subjects into whose afterworldly ledgers they are cumulatively inscribed. However intersubjective these acts of acquisition are, that is, however much they are constituted by people acting as conduits for the circulation and flow of abundance and significance, they sediment across the span of single lives. Meanwhile, the present time deepens in intensity: the limit of one's worldly life serves as the approaching horizon, and every action taken modulates the shape of one's passage beyond.

Finally, for 'Alī, whose articulation of the ordeal I have explored under the heading of "disclosing," tribulation sets the symbolic imaginary at play (outer meaning versus inner reality). There is nothing particularly epochal about the ordeal, for the interpenetration of divine beauty (*jamāl*) and divine majesty (*jalāl*) is elemental to creation. Thus, although the sequence of tribulation here is certainly historically layered, its aspect may well be simple (opaque to differentiation). Tribulation is disclosive (revelatory), not of a historical lesson or divine habit but of theophanic vision: a witness that sees through the affliction to the divine decree that gives it shape. "There is no such thing as a properly traumatic event," writes Hayden White.[147] What is key to tribulation rather is likewise "the process of 'working through' (*Durcharbeitung*) the experience of loss"—as when the aspirant facing the divine decree ascends from the mystical station of steadfastness to the station of satisfaction.

Taken alone, one or another of these perspectives might be read as a phenomenological account of local experience mediated through an Islamic political theology. In this vein, historians and anthropologists working in

Muslim contexts have already recognized how naming the present a time of tribulation evokes the disorder and schismatic struggles of early Islamic history (the "great fitna" being the civil war sparked by the murder of the Caliph 'Uthmān in 35 AH/656 CE). For such scholars, this terminology typologically imbues a modern conflict with world-historical significance, making "tribulation" a political instrument that foregrounds sectarian divisions. Along similar lines, commentators on the Syrian war have insightfully observed the "sectarianization" of the uprising cynically manipulated by the Syrian regime (e.g., targeting Sunni areas for collective punishment and releasing Daesh/ISIS prisoners to open another battlefront) as well as the apocalyptic terminology of opposition factions.[148] Regime supporters explicitly labeled rebels as seditious partisans who incite "sectarian discord" (*fitna ṭā'ifiyya*). The rhetoric of tribulation clearly makes a new register available to secular politics. However, my engagements in this chapter push past the observation that this rhetoric is both analeptic and proleptic or that it facilitates the theologico-political objectification of virtue and vice. That is, I am here interested less in the political instrumentalization of tribulation than in tracing variations in its conceptual grammar. These variations are certainly political, in the concrete sense that they articulate different positions in the struggle in Syria, but they are not reducible to this function—not least because they also convene a broader range of political relations and ethical commitments. Rather, the crux of the variations as I explore them has to do with how they disclose our time as a divine ordeal. "Welcoming the event as an ordeal shifts the coordinates of the real," writes Pandolfo.[149]

For these four interlocutors, reckoning with the divine trial does not put our time into proper historical context, in that it does not readily make available a worldly prognosis to be plotted against a given historical trajectory. Instead, it exposes the creational present to the divine command (*amr*) whose work cannot ultimately be determined by historical context. These four variations thus each articulate the present in specific ways, displacing the historicist paradigm whose fundamental coordinates Reinhart Koselleck believed define our modernity. Against that paradigm of crisis/critique/historical consciousness, in which religious phenomena need to be given a proper categorical frame of reference to achieve the fullness of their historical meaning, this chapter has turned to the theological figure of "tribulation" in order to animate another tradition of thinking the difficulty of the present.[150] If, following Koselleck, "crisis" constantly incites decision and epochal division, the figure of "tribulation" rather resists such periodization: according to its grammar, efforts at separating this time from its past are only another form of trial. At minimum it "contains an address, the sign of a divine interpellation," whose meaning may be obscure or withdrawn.[151] Following Koselleck further, we can say that "crisis" and "tribulation" are distinct ways of making sense of the present, affording distinct spaces of experience and horizons of expectation as they release distinct forms of life and death, memory and desire.[152]

Finally, my hope is that developing tribulation as an analytic term may allow for a more adequate conceptualization of the temporal architecture of Islamic forms of life. In doing so, this chapter has joined an ongoing conversation in anthropology on concept-work. The discipline has long worried at the tension between emic and etic concepts, figuring their relationship as one of translation across discursive contexts that are, importantly, structured by linguistic, political, and historical asymmetries.[153] Yet the anthropological translation of concepts still often rests on the assumption either that they are "tools to be manipulated at will" or that they are "equivalent to, or function as, signs" of a more fundamental reality.[154] As developed in this chapter, tribulation neither stands apart from our narrated experience nor serves simply as its medium of representation. As a concept that insists on the opacity of experience, tribulation defamiliarizes historicist explanations by redoubling historical reflection. It presses in on my interlocutors, and on me alongside them.

THRESHOLD

Ambivalence

He set another small cup of sweet tea on the coffee table in front of me and settled back into a plastic chair opposite mine. *Ahlan wa sahlan*, Zāhid smiled. "Welcome." He had finished teaching for the day, and my formal interview with one of his colleagues had just ended. We had already spent the morning together in the small educational complex.

I had taken an early commuter bus an hour and a half from Amman to Mafraq and then waited for the service van to fill at the transit depot. The driver called out his route along the Baghdad Highway. Young men in dusty leather jackets climbed on, then families with suitcases and large clear bags, relieved to be out of the bright sun. I shifted to the corner seat at the end, backpack on my lap, and as the minutes stretched on considered cracking the window despite the exhaust billowing outside. But the longer delay came from Zaatari Camp police, though I'd last visited just a few days earlier. I sat in their military jeep, thankfully parked in the shade of the corrugated metal wall, while the two in the front shared selfies of the women they were talking to on Facebook. I pretended not to understand their jokes and stared out the window across the highway into the desert. Syria lay twelve kilometers north. The occasional motorcycle or farm truck sped across my line of sight. Groups of people presented their exit permits to other guards and waited for the service bus on the highway boulevard. I could see a cluster of buildings and the village minaret back the way we had come. Otherwise, the horizon was utterly bare. Finally, the superior strode over and said he'd confirmed my ministry approval to enter Zaatari. "You leave by 3 P.M.," he added, returning my passport, "or we'll have to come get you. It'll be a big problem. Do you understand?"

I trudged on the uneven shoulder to the checkpoint in the distance and then along the grid of metal trailers. The streets were empty, and the trailers were far less close together on this side of the camp. A boy cycled past, his wheels squeaking. I ducked into the open gate in the chain link fence and met Zāhid at the entrance to the complex. I apologized for being late. "No problem," he said. "The shaykhs are already here." It was a Saturday, when the teachers (some of whom also taught at the camp's mosques and prayer spaces) gathered in the ʿAbdullāh bin al-Mubārak Program office trailer to consult and discuss. Other trailers encircled the spare courtyard, which was covered against the sun by more corrugated metal sheets: a trailer converted to a prayer space, with a pulpit and loudspeakers and rows of red carpet; a library trailer lined with sagging bookshelves organized by scholarly field (law, theology, hadith); classroom trailers filled with red plastic chairs. On this trip I had come to interview the director of the Program (see Chapter 2), which he squeezed between teaching classes on exegesis (*tafsīr*) and the principles of jurisprudence (*uṣūl al-fiqh*). He indulged my questions but soon had to coordinate the curriculum for the week to come.

Some time remaining before I had to leave, I followed Zāhid into the classroom trailer to the right and took a seat in the first row. Three dozen students, mostly teenage boys with some middle-aged men hanging toward the back, opened their notebooks. "The topic today," Zāhid began, his thin voice now projecting to the back of the room, "is the attributes of God (*ṣifāt allāh*). We have discussed how many people deviate into distorting the divine attributes (*taḥrīf*), or presuming to specify their modality (*takyīf*), or divesting God of the attributes (*taʿṭīl*), or likening God to created things (*tamthīl*). None of these is the way of the pious predecessors." He ran his hand twice through his long beard and glanced down at his notes before beginning his lecture in earnest. After the class, which focused on the proper understanding of divine attributes attested in the Quran and Sunna, he called attendance, and we retired to the office trailer. And he made tea.

He had studied to be a civil engineer in Damascus, but when the protests started in 2011, amid news of upheaval across the country, he returned to his family's home near Daraa. Like so many of the Syrians I met, he stayed in Daraa after the early years of the revolution through the regime attacks until shells started landing in his neighborhood. Then he and his family fled south, alongside the nearly 1,000 Syrians who were entering Jordan every day. "When we arrived we were hopeful: we had escaped the siege of Daraa and the Free Army was getting stronger. We thought we would return soon." He even had the chance to join a relative in Canada. "They called me and asked if I would go. I thought about it a lot," he said, "but eventually decided to stay. I thought I would only be here a short time. Yet now it has been two more years since then; the war has lasted seven. The regime is taking back the free territories. So I always ask myself what I should do. I think about it every day." He looked at me directly. "What do you think? You've lived outside the lands of the Muslims—what do you think about leaving? Should I apply to go to Canada?"

I was starting to sweat through my shirt despite the electric fans whirring at us. I had hesitated a few weeks earlier, too, at a Ramadan dinner at a district office barely two kilometers from the Syrian border, when an elderly widow who lived in an informal tent settlement asked if I knew a way for her to get to Canada. Her sister saw me sit down at her table and leaned over. "He could be your new husband," she had joked. Their neighbors overheard and laughed. The woman brushed them away. "Is there a way?"

Zāhid was more ambivalent, less sanguine about the prospect. He asked about the perception of Islam in the West. He asked about the condition of the Muslims in Canada, and what the country was like. The society is more open (*maftūḥa*), he confirmed with me, but that difference made him pause. "That's exactly what I've been thinking. Here we are close to our people, our land. I love my land—around our house in Daraa we had one hundred olive trees. I would walk through them to reach the mosque." His voice broke. He collected himself. "Of course I want to go back. But then I wonder what that means. To return—to what? An entirely unknown (*majhūl*) condition. Whole villages have been entirely demolished to flat rubble, I'm not exaggerating in the slightest, turned to bricks and stone, thrown, scattered across the ground—I would return and not know where I was. To take me, my family (my children, my wife, my brothers)—to live under the regime that has broken us? That has bombed us? That has destroyed us?" His voice rose.

In the years since he arrived in Jordan as an aspiring civil engineer whose professional training had been interrupted by the war, he had committed to the study of Islam. While other new arrivals set up shops along the "Sham-Élysées" main street, or were bailed out of the camp by a Jordanian sponsor (in the *kafāla* system beginning at 15 dinars per person), or even returned to Syria to join the rebels, Zāhid sought out the shaykhs of Zaatari Camp and read with them nearly every day: the principles of jurisprudence, exegesis, technical study of hadith, prophetic biography. But his aptitude was for creed (*'aqīda*), in which he now instructed the intermediate-level students twice each week from a Saudi textbook. And every day, especially as the regime had been retaking Daraa province, he weighed the possibility of returning to Syria against seeking refuge in Canada or staying in Zaatari. But he smiled as he talked about the Institute, where at nearly thirty years old he was the youngest of the teachers. Through the war and his displacement, the destruction of his olive orchard and the dispossession of his former life, God gave him the opportunity to learn his religion and to teach others. "It is necessary for every Muslim to . . . build his religion on a sound foundation," the textbook he had taught from that day begins, "such that he may enjoy its fruits in the world and the afterlife."[1] Without fleeing to Zaatari, he may never have properly understood the divine attributes. "I had studied Quran in Syria, but here I could expand in knowledge (*'ilm*). Of course there are difficulties (*ṣu'ūbāt*) in living here, after the crisis (*azmeh*). But there are benefits (*fawā'id*) through this too—benefits I could not imagine. And this, too, is from the divine decree." I asked if he could be more specific.

"The regime had already destroyed us before the war: it reduced the people to blind incapacitation (*tajhīl al-nās*) by alienating them from religion. But people have a need for knowledge—I mean, religious knowledge (*'ilm shar'ī*)—and gnosis of God (*ma'rifat allāh*)," he replied. "One must drink from the cup of knowledge (*ka's al-'ilm lā budda an nashraba minhu*), or else remain parched. We can do that here, in Zaatari, as we never did before."

By his account and that of many others I would meet at the 'Abdullāh bin al-Mubārak Program and beyond, the Syrian regime's paranoid control of religion was one more expression of its authoritarianism. From state curation of religious institutions to censoring Friday sermons to closing mosques between prayers, the regime saturated the field of religious practice with techniques of discipline and surveillance. These had the double effect of distancing people from religion and incapacitating them, Zāhid had explained: making them unable to appreciate the subtleties of revelation and objectifying religion into a separate social domain instead of a source of sustenance throughout one's life. Studying Islam in Zaatari Camp had quickened his capacity for understanding, he continued, for only drinking from the cup of knowledge of God quenches one's thirst.

I glanced at my phone. It was 3:10 P.M. I remembered the stern captain at the gate and started up. "You have to go?" He held my hand as we walked to the complex entrance, our shoes leaving prints in the yellow dust. Two of the courtyard walls were painted in lush colors: verdant meadows, river reeds, purple and white flowers, clouds in a bright blue sky. A boat on a mountain lake. Someone had calligraphed, "Syria is in our hearts" on posterboard in bright red marker and taped it to the wall. I could hear another instructor's lecture underway from the opposite classroom trailer. I fumbled for words to address Zāhid's ambivalence.[2]

Between return and refuge, religion had opened a space of possibility for his life. Was a return to Daraa worth the name, when the home he would return to was reduced to rubble? How could refuge in Canada measure against the opportunity to learn and teach the truth in Zaatari Camp? Should he tarry in the present (an exile he had not chosen, which yet allowed him to pursue a divine knowledge of God)? Should he return to Daraa (to confront his disorientation from his former middle-class life)? Should he seek refuge in Canada (choosing to leave the lands of the Muslims, to leave a life of intimacy with one's family, land, and religion, for an exposed and potentially disaggregating society)? Each of the latter two horizons promised a blank existence: an unknown condition (*majhūl*), he had said, the grammatical passive participle form effected by the operation of *jahl* (ignorance), whether forcibly imposed by the regime in Syria or as a result of distance from religion in Canada, where its being-unknown (*majhūliyya*) is like traversing a desert without signs of the way (*majhal*)—and this blind incapacitation (*jahl*) in sharp contrast to his present life devoted to knowledge (*'ilm*), albeit stationed in Zaatari in the middle of the desert, without the liberty to come and go from the camp as he might please. For the *jahl* promised by return to Syria or refuge in Canada is not merely the absence of knowledge, as might be ameliorated with greater information, but a further incapacitation that "causes the weakening, if not complete loss, of the function of reason (*'aql*)."[3]

Yet he could not relinquish those alternatives; he weighed them every day. "And this, too, is from the divine decree," he had commented—although so too, strictly speaking, would have been those alternatives. The Saudi textbook he taught from that day noted that affirming the divine decree (*qadr*) is a pillar (*rukn*) of Sunni doctrine, against both the heresies of determinism and free will.[4] He did not flee to Zaatari because he was simply fated to do so, nor because he freely created his own actions. While he located his arrival in Zaatari Camp and his rediscovery of religion in the realm of the divine decree, that is, he had come to understand his fate as more than the narrative logic connecting a series of willed actions. The decree lies in every alternative possibility at once and is actualized in their realization. One's fate needs to be met—the decree needs to be meekly borne—in order to be understood. Hence his constant weighing of these prospects of *jahl* and *'ilm*.

Far from simply being a temporary condition of statelessness or social abjection, the site of Zāhid's displacement had come to sustain him. In expressing this contrast between a life pursuing knowledge of the divine reality (*ṭalab al-'ilm*) against a life incapacitated (*majhūl*), he also opened another perspective on what critical scholars have recently called "refugeetude" or the "humanitarian predicament."[5] Certainly the language of immiseration and precarity, expulsion and abandonment, could well describe the conditions of life in Zaatari.[6] Western news media reports on displaced Syrians emphasize the massive scale of the camp, whose sprawl and sometime squalor is frequently taken as a metonym for the so-called Syrian refugee crisis. Yet Zāhid's effort to inhabit Zaatari as a site of passage from *jahl* to *'ilm*—and thereby his rediscovery of Islam—expanded its space in another sense. The regime had already destroyed Syria before the war, he had commented, through deadening people's capacities for religious knowledge (*tajhīl al-nās*). Now, as the regime was reconquering the country, there was talk of reconciliation agreements under which the displaced could return to the unknown situation (*majhūl*) of their homes (whichever were left).

Yet between the *jahl* produced by the regime before the 2011 uprising (*tajhīl al-nās*, the incapacitation of the people) and the *jahl* produced by the regime since then (the *majhūl* countryside reduced to rubble), the war in all its brutality came to seem less a singular event fracturing an original social integrity than the string of a pendulum that, in displacing Zāhid and his fellows from their beloved homes and olive orchards, had also violently ejected them from the grasp of the regime's various tactics of forcible dispossession. Thus he had acknowledged the difficulties (*ṣu'ūbāt*) and benefits (*fawā'id*) of displacement together—not to rationalize his own exile or to justify the divine decree that he be there, as in a simple theodicy, but to more fully apprehend the situation of his life. He presented his repeated determination to stay in Zaatari as a repudiation of *jahl*, for he could there pursue the religious knowledge (*'ilm*) he was concerned with. In seriously weighing the *majhūl* horizon offered by migration to Canada, he emphasized that his prospective life across the world would be a redoubled exile: both away from his pursuit of *'ilm* and away from the abode of Islam (*dār al-islām*)—that is, into the abode of incapacitation, *jāhiliyya*.[7]

Yet the viability of these terms offered by the archives of Islamic ethics, politics, and theology was fundamentally in question in debates around the Syrian war. How can one insist that devastated villages reduced to rubble by a vicious regime properly belong to the abode of Islam, when they seem to offer only another mode of incapacitation? Or that life in Canada would in fact be barbaric (*jāhil*), if it still released the Muslims from the regime's brutal grip? If the stability of such inherited terms was contested in these interlocutions, however, their implications were not. The very ability to discern the double movement of the war (destroying and opening at once) rests on a calmness of disposition (*ḥilm*) that is the basis for sound judgment (*'aql*). The former virtue (*ḥilm*, meekness) is also the archaic antonym of *jahl*, for one who is intemperate (*jāhil*) "cannot see through things; his sight stops at the surface of things."[8] In reiterating his commitment to the third space opened by the path of learning, Zāhid thus aligned knowledge (*'ilm*) of Islam available in Zaatari Camp also with self-surrender (*islām*) and with meekness (*ḥilm*) in the face of the divine decree, against the multiple horizons of incapacitation (*jahl*) crowding in. Because Zāhid oscillated among three alternatives (remaining in Zaatari Camp, returning to Daraa, migrating to Canada) that were then condensed into a single contrast (knowledge versus incapacitation), this ambivalence does not simply modulate his identification with his exile. It has less to do with realigning a psychic topography, that is, than with the melancholic spatialization of a temporal schema in which the present holds in tension (without ever fully eclipsing) encounters with a devastated past (Daraa) and an abandoned future (Canada).

A quarter hour after the guard had warned that I should have already exited the camp, we were holding hands at the program site gate, sheltered in the shade of the metal awning. And I still had not answered his request for my advice.

I remembered other Syrian friends describing Bashar al-Assad's tyranny as pharaonic. On the morning Pharaoh perished, I said (finding some solace in the delimitation of worldly life), no one imagined that would be the day his reign would end. If God wills, then—

He interrupted me. "Not just if God wills—it is definite, we have certainty about this. We believe this, we affirm it, that *the victory of God is near.*" He quoted Q. 2:214 (*alā inna naṣra llāhi qarīb*). "Someday we will return. And if God wills it, you will visit us next time in Syria." I stepped onto the street, blinking in the sudden sun.

3

THE HEIGHTS

In early 2018 the director of a charitable organization in the northern Jordanian town of Ramtha sent me to visit an orphanage complex to demonstrate the beneficial work of his organization. The building itself belongs to a young Kuwaiti businessman with a large investment company. He constructed it for commercial purposes; when the border was closed and the extensive cross-border trade in the area came to an abrupt halt, he donated it to the support of Syrian widows and orphans. He retains ownership of the building, and it bears the name of his company in large blue tiles, while the Islamic charity manages the building like it does a dozen others (paying utility bills and a 100-dinar monthly stipend for its maintenance). The same Kuwaiti businessman is committed to charitable work well beyond Jordan. His YouTube channel shows him distributing Ramadan dinners to Syrian orphans in Ramtha as well as opening schools for Eritrean refugees and poor Kosovars and overseeing the construction of a well in Kyrgyzstan. (The orphanage, schools, and well are all named after his company.)

The apartment complex is on the outskirts of Ramtha, just off a highway heading northwest. The other highway that intersects the town leads directly to the Daraa border crossing barely two kilometers away, which rebels captured in September 2013 and regime forces retook in July 2018 (see later in this chapter). The apartment building is five stories high, with four apartments on each level, a small square in front of it, and a swing set and a dusty enclosure used for soccer games to its side. It is entirely walled off, with a tall black metal gate at its front.

The orphanage was impressive indeed, though I soon realized that was a result of the efforts of its steward more than of the minimal funding offered by the charity to support the families who lived there. A quiet, slight man with deep-set eyes, of ambiguous middle age and a grey-white beard, Bilāl lived in Zaatari Camp with his family for two years after seeking refuge in Jordan. In 2015 a Jordanian relative of his wife "sponsored" their departure from the camp. Bilāl rented a small apartment in Ramtha, where rent had tripled since the beginning of the revolution,[1] until he was robbed of his savings (1,200 Jordanian dinars, 1,690 USD). Then he heard that this charitable organization was supporting Syrian families in apartment buildings around the town. He and his family have lived in one such building ever since, where he serves as its steward.

WOE TO OUR CONDITION HERE

One of the apartments on the chilly (dug half-underground) lowest level is dedicated to general activities. One of its rooms has a workshop with three donated sewing machines, where the widows sew overcoats and scarves for sale in the Ramtha public market. Another long room, lined with sitting cushions, was dedicated to Quran memorization and religious lessons. Charts on whiteboards tracked the progress of individual children and their mothers. Twenty boys and girls (ages approximately four to twelve) dressed in clean robes and white hijabs and skullcaps, fidgeting along the wall, greeted us in unison when we entered. Shaykh Bilāl asked three of them to recite portions of the Quran they had memorized, which they did in grave tones. He asked the children to recite the assignment of the week; together, they chanted a section on ablutions from the Shāfiʿite manual *Nihāyat al-tadrīb fī ghāyat al-taqrīb*, pantomiming each gesture (*and these ten are all recommended/ first uttering the name of God/ and washing both hands, outside the vessel. . .*).[2] Then the girls sang a song popularized by the Kuwaiti Quran reciter Mishary Alafasy:

Merciful O Merciful
aid me O Merciful
open my heart to the Quran
fill my heart with the Quran
and pour the Quran into my life

"Wonderful," Bilāl said, "Applaud each other!" The children all clapped. "What do you want to be when you grow up?" A little boy, maybe four years old, fell off his cushion and the others giggled at him. One of the older girls raised her hand confidently: a teacher. A boy raised his hand: a doctor. Another said he wanted to be a soldier. "Good, good," Bilāl said. "Who remembers Daraa?" Their hands all shot up. "You do?" He laughed at the littlest ones, who were clearly too young to do so. Some of them had been born in Jordan after their pregnant mothers fled Syria. "Who remembers their father?" Most of the hands shot up again. "You, Maryam?" A girl in a bright pink hijab grinned and said she remembered visiting her father in prison before they left Syria; he had called her "little kitten." "Ah, look at that." He smiled. "All right, you can go, don't run!" The children filed out, and we followed them up the stairs.[3]

A woman in a face-veil greeted us on the landing and went past into her own apartment. "I knew most of the fathers of these children," he said. "For example, this woman we just saw, I knew her husband, he was my friend. Glory be to God. He was walking in the street and a sniper shot him during the siege of Daraa. He was shot here [he gestured to his head] and here [he pointed to his shoulder] and here [he pointed to his heart]. He died in the street—he wasn't holding a weapon, had no connection to the Free Army—now we are here, and I look after his children. When I look at them I feel pity for them—and especially those whose fathers I knew best. Woe to our condition here."

We retired to his apartment's bare living room: floor cushions along the white plaster walls, a tall bookshelf crammed with religious books, and a filing cabinet full of paperwork. I stopped in front of the books, admiring the range of titles. Did you bring these with you from Syria? "No, no. I've slowly gathered them here. I only brought one book from my library in Daraa. Here, this is it." He reached for a thick blue volume: Dr. Muṣṭafā bin Saʿīd al-Khinn's *Athar al-ikhtilāf fī qawāʿid al-uṣūliyya fī ikhtilāf al-fuqahāʾ* (*The Consequence of Divergences in the Legal Maxims on the Divergences of the Jurists*). I paged through it, the author's dissertation from al-Azhar University, a detailed work comparing legal principles across the juridical schools and their consequences for jurisprudence. I asked why he brought this title alone, of all his other books. He had attended his classes in Damascus years ago, he answered, and found a kind of joy in Dr. Khinn's insights into the practical entailments of theoretical differences.

When we sat down, he returned to the double impact of exile. "And the mothers here are under immense psychological pressure, bearing the difficulties of life. They still have regular contact with their families in Syria. I also have family inside. So we continuously hear what is happening. Most of the townships [in Daraa province] do not have electricity, running water. There is severe inflation, unnatural prices, a lack of safety. After sunset, no one can go outside. Before we came here, we didn't know the blessing of a door that closes. Here we can bar the gate and no one will enter. This building is better than others, praise God—we have privacy, a square, a playground. Other buildings [sponsored by the same organization] open directly to the street. And there are emergency services we can call. If someone gets sick, they can go to the [sponsoring] organization's health clinic here in Ramtha. Once there was a fire and the organization sent firemen. I mean, we do feel a sense of safety here. We are secure. But their hearts break to know their brothers are inside, their father is inside. She [the woman we passed] doesn't even know where the grave of her husband is. So they are overwhelmed by feelings of sadness and blessing at once."

I shook my head but didn't say anything. He continued. "Here we are very careful not to violate the laws of the country. Because it can expel us for communicating [with the wrong people]—like if I call someone inside, and he calls suspicious groups, they could expel us, or move us to another camp. So the widows are very cautious only to ever communicate with their fathers, their mothers, their sisters. And they should keep to themselves; I often warn them against taxi drivers, not to say anything that could be manipulated until we know which of them are trustworthy. Don't expose your secrets or personal details, don't go to suspicious places, go together with two or three of you so that no one can accuse you of lewdness. This is how we try to stay safe here."

Bilāl was acutely aware of the tenuous status of Syrians in Jordan. Although a signatory to neither the 1951 UNHCR Refugee Convention nor its 1967 Protocol, the state is committed to the principle of non-refoulement—except on broadly discretionary security grounds. "In the first five months of 2017," reports Human Rights Watch, "Jordanian authorities were deporting about 400 registered Syrian refugees per month," with 300 others returning to Syria voluntarily and 500 others returning under unclear circumstances.[4] Some of these refugees detained had already been approved for resettlement to Canada or elsewhere and had no idea why they were swept up. Others were deported because they kept in contact with family members living in Daesh/ISIS territory. Thus Bilāl was right to be cautious of expulsion—especially because, as I learned on subsequent visits, he and his friends had been there at the beginning of the Syrian uprising. Although he himself did not take up arms against the regime that he condemned, and indeed across the subsequent years of our interlocution he never expressed confidence that the brutality of the regime could in fact be defeated, many of his colleagues and friends had joined revolutionary councils and Free Army militias across Daraa province. He was in near-constant contact with those of them still alive, as well as with other family in Syria, as news of attacks, betrayals, explosions, displacements, and alliances raced along WhatsApp networks in real time.

Under such conditions of precarity, Bilāl saw that preserving one's reputation could also be a means of securing one's safety. Hence the principle of caution by which he advised the widows at his orphanage not to go out at night, to travel with others to avoid the hint of scandal, and not to communicate with those whose family members were involved in rebel groups. Reputation was also effective in other ways. I was sitting with Bilāl a few months later when the director of the charity in Ramtha called him to ask about a widow who had recently sought support from his organization. "Do you know her?" the director asked. "Is she trustworthy (*thiqa*)? How is her character (*akhlāq*)?" Local Islamic charitable organizations (including this one) insisted that their services were open to all, and indeed I never saw them turn anyone away—though their rumored partiality to Muslim beneficiaries rather than Christians was a topic they themselves brought up to dispel in formal interviews. But moral reputation clearly had value in facilitating the degree and kind of aid that was accessible to claimants.[5] After he hung up I joked to Bilāl that there was a kind of *jarḥ* and *taʿdīl* (the formal evaluation of hadith narrators) transposed onto the humanitarian sector. "But of course," he replied.

I remained curious about the ethical infrastructure at stake in these and similar interactions, but our discussions soon exploded in scope. My interlocutions with Bilāl came to inform all my other fieldwork and to shadow all my writing: our conversations over subsequent years accompany me even when I am writing about other sites. The rest of this chapter stays with Bilāl in the borderland between Jordan and Syria, where boundaries and limits turn porous and disorientating. I present his testimony of the violence that has torn his life and opened it to new forms of care, which then redouble into traumatic returns. Once an imam in Daraa, at the mosque celebrated as the birthplace of the Syrian revolution, then tortured and hunted by the Syrian regime, he now serves as steward of this orphanage funded by an Islamic charity. As I follow over the rest of the chapter, his practices of care and memory—the movements of gentleness—bring into stark relief the force of the essentially enigmatic divine decree. His testimony expresses, with an unsentimental lucidity inseparable from his position, the fundamental gestures of creational existence: supplication, submission, insight.

Over the next months, we spent many evenings together discussing recent events with reference to theological concepts (tribulation, community, repair, fate, oppression . . .). Eventually I asked if I could record his story. I have transcribed it here not to document the siege of Daraa (for which one might consult any number of news articles or human rights reports) but to attend the singularity of his narration. He articulated political events and theological principles, relating a tragic outcome within a broader atmosphere of dread.[6] His sensibilities were clearly against the regime: his friends joined revolutionary councils and rebel militias, and he himself was tortured and hunted by the security forces. Yet the most striking quality of his recounting was the accent he placed on his own hesitation. He admitted his own bewilderment in the midst of the revolution. This space of hesitation allows for practices of memory and of care, as I follow later—the movement of gentleness—but is simultaneously incapacitating.

BRUTAL TYRANNY

In the name of God, the merciful, the kind. My name is Bilāl. I am from the Syrian province of Daraa. I am from plain people, farmers and olive workers. I lived in Syria through the era of President Hafez al-Assad, and I witnessed the upheaval that occurred when Bashar al-Assad rose to power. Our family was traditional and the people were close to each other. They lived in fear of the security service due to the state of emergency that had prevailed among us for forty years.

For the slightest of reasons, [state security] would imprison people for ten to twenty years under undeclared charges. I had many friends imprisoned in my youth—some were imprisoned when they were eighteen, and released when they were forty. Others were killed in prison. One was taken on his wedding night. These are the truths of the situation. Others live with us here in Jordan, and if you ask about their imprisonment are unable to speak about the extremity of the torture and the conditions. They would hang people by their necks, by their fingertips. My close friend was imprisoned with 3,000 others in Tadmor prison, the worst prison in the world; only 180 were released with him. He took a bus back to his village—but it had been twenty years, and he did not recognize it at all. Where should he go? What should he do? He is now here in Jordan with us—he keeps only to himself. The others imprisoned with him, teenagers, were executed episodically by the hundreds. And for what reason? We do not know; they did not know. This happened immediately after the events of Hama [in 1982]. It took us twenty years to learn the details of Hama: in a single week they killed nearly 40,000 without cause, after a small group in the city rejected the rule of the Assad family.

*This is a strange kind of oppression (*ẓulm*)—it even reaches children's education, so that by the time a person reaches secondary school he is already a supporter of the Arab Socialist Baath Party. And whoever does not support it or is not a party member, well, he faces consequences and interrogation, he and his parents. Things become difficult. Among us—God bless our master Muḥammad—among us the lowest ranking police officer or intelligence agent could terrify any quarter he entered.*

*I studied sharia in Damascus. [Religious] knowledge in Damascus was moderate (*wasaṭī*), knowledge without fanaticism, without deviance. To the contrary, at the Badr al-Dīn al-Ḥasanī Institute we studied the Shāfiʿī juridical school well-known among all Muslims for being equitable, learned, and far from extremism. I specialized in Quran recitation, mastering the seven canonical modes. I studied there for nearly six years among students of thirty-two nationalities. They were the sweetest days of my life. The security service feared us; I don't know why, as we were always cautious not to speak against them. The very opposite: we always spoke in support of peace and security. But there was great pressure on anyone treading the path of religion. People often consider the shaykh the face of the state, because of how the Friday sermons are [authorized by and monitored by the state], but that identification is not generally accurate.*

I graduated from the Badr al-Dīn al-Ḥasanī Institute in 1999. I was preacher in a village for nearly eleven years, and for around two years I was the imam of the Omari Mosque [in Daraa] and the preacher at another mosque nearby. I had a small salary from that; my wife was a teacher. The Omari Mosque—have you heard of it? It is famous now as the mosque from which the revolution issued, but it was already well-known for its history. The minaret was [one of] the oldest in the world; it used to be a bell tower, because before the building was made into a mosque by our master [the Prophet's Companion] 'Umar bin al-Khaṭṭāb it used to be a church, and before that it was a pagan temple. So it had historical, monumental value. Look, this is it [he showed me a picture on his phone]. These arches are an architectural marvel, see how the black stones are slanted, just there. By the mosque here there was a program called The Assad Institute for the Memorization of the Noble Quran—named that because it needed security service approval, ha! The mosque didn't have an arcade or courtyard at the beginning; those were added under the reign of Ṣalāḥ al-Dīn al-Ayyūbī [rn. 1174–93 CE], so that it could hold around 3,000 worshippers. I was imam there for nearly two and a half years; I was the last imam of the mosque before it was destroyed. When the regime entered the city they desecrated it. They shot tank shells at the minaret because it was the symbol of our dignity. That was painful, so painful, to hear: the call to prayer which had resounded from it for centuries came to an end on April 13, 2013. I had already fled to Jordan; it was my third day here. I mourned it, it affected me intensely.

Toward the end of the events in Syria [before the revolution] we felt that there was such great pressure from the security forces—as though they were the ones inciting the people to go out to the streets and demonstrate. They dismissed the schoolteachers who wore a face-veil. This order increased the tension in the streets. The elders tried to calm things but the state officials lost their minds. They released a directive that any person who wants to pass on his land to his son had to have authorization from the security service. They effectively prohibited buying land, selling land, inheriting it. Then they decreed a municipal law that any person who owned dunums of land—meaning 1,000 square meters—needed authorization to build a house on it; and through this process the state would often expropriate from the people. I mean, this is blatant injustice, clear oppression. As though they were the ones inciting the people into the streets.

*Then the security directorate learned that a young child had written on the wall of one of the schools: hey doctor, you're next (*ajāka l-dawr yā duktūr*)! Meaning, after the events [uprisings] in Tunisia and Egypt and Libya, now it is your turn [to Bashar]. It was just a young child, maybe nine or ten years old, who wrote this on the wall. One of the teachers reported the graffiti [to the police] due to the extremity of his fear. This inflamed the* *security service to madness. It came for every child who had scrawled his name on those walls—even if what he had written had nothing to do with it, if what he had written was about his memories of second grade. They took thirteen [or: fifteen] children and detained them [on March 6, 2011] while their families and relatives pleaded and demanded they be released. They pleaded that the elders go to the security service to ask after them. Courageously, they went to the political security chief [in Daraa], Atef Najib, the cousin of Bashar al-Assad. They said to him, Look, the children are young, you have imprisoned them, we hear they have been tortured. We pledge that they will not repeat this mistake that they committed—even though the children did not actually make a mistake.*

And he replied to them, with all his scorn, forget them, don't you have other children? If not, bring us your women and we'll fuck them and give them more kids.

The elders returned in despair; they didn't know what the youth would do when they heard. We know that the blood of youth is irascible, quickly flung into turmoil. At this response they were inflamed into madness, they said we must go out and revolt, we must. But the elders told them, Don't make mistakes that will have bigger consequences. We then appointed representatives who went to a second official. They said to him, we want the children back. The people are in the streets in uproar, we will calm them, we don't want riots—and he replied, these turbans you wind around your heads, I will throw them all in the trash where they belong. He repudiated them and insulted them. They returned anxious about what the youth would do.

The youth decided that on March 18, 2011, they would rally from the mosque. The people came to the imams and preachers of the mosques [in Daraa], and to me, personally, that I broadcast this message from the pulpit, but I told them it would not benefit anything to do so. Speaking frankly, I was the preacher [at that mosque] and [in my sermon] I did not address the topic of the revolution at all. I spoke about Mothers' Day and Teachers' Day, because I thought it more appropriate. There are those who [because we did not join the struggle then] smear us as traitors and claim that we don't speak the word of truth. But we have always had clarity that the regime is criminal, criminal. . . . After the prayer was over, there were nearly ten thousand in the congregation, under the dome and in the arcade of the mosque and spilling out into the streets. Some of the youth said, we would rather die in the path of God than be silent against such oppression. I tried through suggestions and admonitions to calm them, not to plunge this past a point of no return, but they came out after the prayer chanting Freedom! No fear after today! God is great! Freedom! No fear after today!

Within two hours security forces dressed in black came by helicopter from Damascus and began shooting live rounds at the demonstrators. The people were stunned—these were not rubber bullets or tear gas but real bullets, bullets that explode when they hit the body. One of the two people who died that first day was my neighbor, Ḥussām 'Ayyāsh; the other was Maḥmūd Juwābara. On the first day, two [or: four] died; on the next day, nine youths died; on the third day, eleven youths died; on the fourth day, rage had spread across [the region of] Hauran. The security forces occupied the hospital; we used the Omari Mosque to treat the wounded instead. More people gathered: villagers from across Hauran came to the Great Omari Mosque to demonstrate together demanding political justice, political freedom, demanding the end of this pressure on the people. Forty-five of them died; the regime killed them, snipers aiming for their eyes and shoulders; they died as martyrs.

The army entered the surrounding villages by night, attacking and beating the women and cutting gold rings from their fingers. They captured some of the youth and beat them. That was at the beginning of the revolution. This [showing me a picture on his phone] is my friend, he was walking to the Friday prayer to hear my sermon. A sniper bullet hit him in the neck and paralyzed him, he can't move his legs or his hands. He is now here in Ramtha. Many of my friends were killed at this time; many were disfigured after they were killed, we could see their wounds on their bodies. I documented many of these things. This history needs to be recorded.

Shaykh Aḥmad al-Ṣiyāṣana was our teacher and instructor and role model; he taught me much. He was the preacher of the Omari Mosque where I was the imam. I learned from him; he is a righteous man, a scholar; he would always utter the truth. And he was there leading the protests from the beginning. He addressed the demonstrations, urging them on, guiding the course of the coming revolution, despite the presence in the crowds of the security forces and the Shabiha thugs. But I myself could not perceive what the solution was. I remembered the events of Hama and was afraid of what would come next. I said to the protestors, we are with you, we want to act against the regime, but restrain your fury, let us write down our demands, don't be reckless and ignite everything. Those days were bewildering. I would remember the hadith of the Prophet, God's peace and blessings upon him, that there will *come a time of tribulations (*fitan*) like a dark night. A man will enter the morning a believer and enter the evening a disbeliever, and the mild-tempered will be confounded. . . . I kept to my house; I would leave for the prayer [in the mosque] and then return, because I could not perceive what wisdom [dictated]. I could not perceive where lay the right thing to do. Because we had urged the youth to calm, they maligned us as traitors. But our hearts were with them the whole time.*

Then, because [of] the protests that had started from the mosque [where I was the preacher], the security forces arrested me for four days. They had me taste the types of torment they employ, including punishment on something called the Tire where they bound my head and my feet through it and seven men beat me with bats, with chains, with rifles, with their legs [kicking me] and their hands [striking me]. A perverse brutality. You see here? [He took off his skullcap and parted his short, thinning hair to show me a long scar along the side of his head.] This is the mark of their torture on my head. They brought two people [into the same room]; one of them was a doctor [who had treated wounded demonstrators]; they put him on the German Chair and broke his back from behind. He screamed like an animal from the pain, almost paralyzed.

The news went out, even on Al Jazeera: the imam of the Omari Mosque, Shaykh Bilāl al-Khaṭīb, was arrested. The regime authorities refuted it immediately, they said there is no truth to the arrest of Shaykh Bilāl, and tomorrow [on March 25] he will give the Friday sermon in his mosque [like usual]. They released me from prison in order to deny the claims on Al Jazeera. They told me I had to get up on the pulpit. I told them, what, still bleeding from my beating yesterday? How can I get up there unable to see, blood still dripping from here and here? They gave me sunglasses to cover some of the swelling. I sat on a chair—they sat me on it—and they lifted it onto the pulpit because I couldn't walk. I said to the people, Peace upon you and God's mercy and blessings. And they said, Who is this? They did not recognize me, my face was discolored and swollen, blue and red from the severity of the beatings. When the people saw me like that they left the prayer, they surged from the mosque into the street.

So the demonstrations left, with the youth demanding the fall of the regime. I tried to call them back, as loud as I could, but I was not able to do so. They felled a statue of Hafez al-Assad and they organized popular committees to protect the city against the special forces that were coming. Thus began the series of daily killings; the security forces besieged Daraa, cutting off water and electricity and food and drink and internet. There was no communication with the outside world at all. We were isolated for twenty-three or twenty-four days, by the end of which people would divide and share a single piece of dry bread among them. People did not have candles to light their rooms; babies did not have milk. So many babies were in incubators [at the hospital]. All of them died when the electricity was cut off. They fired mortars into neighborhoods to spread terror through the hearts of the people. Hundreds of youth died from sniper fire—shot in the eye, in the throat, in the ear, in the mouth, in the neck. From quarter to quarter, people were laying their bodies in refrigerators because they could not bury them.

The Lord of the worlds did not create humans to stay at one stage (marḥala*) through their lives. Rather to pass through stages of sweetness and bitterness, to pass through tribulations. What is a trial* (ibtilā')*? It is a test* (imtiḥān)*. Sometimes those who are close to you oppress you, your neighbor oppresses you. What do you do? Do you inflict a greater oppression upon him? Or can you endure it? Why does God impose these trials and these tribulations? The answer is clear in the Quran:* that God may separate the vile from the good *(Q. 8:37). When does the mettle of a person come out? When is a person's faith apparent? In trial, in tribulation, in test:* that He may try you as to which of you is most virtuous in deed, and He is the Mighty, the Forgiving *(Q. 67:2). The problem is not the tribulation—these will necessarily happen in every life, whether of hunger or loss or illness or something else. The problem is how you act undergoing the tribulation.*

*Really, we in Daraa had the greatest trial (*balā'*). It was forbidden to go out onto the street, with the [security forces] roaming. And what did the people do with this trial? They opened their homes to each other. They dug shelters together; whoever had bread gave it to those who did not; whoever had candles shared with those who did not. We felt that the people, all of them, were a single mass, a single body. We endured the siege a duration of twenty-five days; not a single one died of hunger because we stood together, although anyone venturing onto the street was killed by sniper-fire. Women would run into the street to pull the body back; some of them died doing so. Those who had gardens in their houses opened them to us, to bury our dead there because we could not reach the cemetery. Those were arduous days, truly—but magnificent. The people said, praise be to God for this trial that has united our hearts.*

On the twenty-sixth day [on April 25] the regime entered to silence Daraa. The tanks broke through. Then soldiers went house to house, confronting people in their homes. Those who came to my house were polite, but those who went to my neighbors beat them severely. They pulled them out to kick them and stomp on them in the street. They beat women and youth, took their identity papers and interrogated them. . . .

Eventually the security forces broke into the mosque and killed eleven people who were defending it. They threw and trampled more than two thousand Qurans and manuscripts [from the old mosque library], like this [he gestured], scattered across half the mosque courtyard; all torn and trampled upon with the blood of the martyrs and the wounded. The commander of the security forces told me to gather up these pages and burn them far away. He knew what that would mean to the believers; he threatened that if even a photograph or a short clip of this burning comes out on YouTube or Facebook, he would burn us along with them. We went to a far place, a grotto outside the city, and poured gasoline on them. Look, the flames were rising and our tears were falling onto them.

People did not have weapons then, nothing that could defend against the regime's forces. Some of the youth had a little ammunition, a hundred bullets here or there. Slowly these arms grew—but even a thousand bullets would do nothing before tanks, before mortar shells. Then people gradually formed factions. Each one had its own support from a specific country, until we could not see everything happening across the land. The battles started here and there, until the youth had liberated a vast area of Hauran.

You know that they all—Douma, Homs, Hama, Deir ez-Zor, and Damascus—all of them rose to support Daraa because of the injustice we tasted there, which I also felt personally. And all of this was from a social and humanitarian view. They did not then have political demands [i.e., for the fall of the regime]; the people were affected [by what happened to us] and wanted to make the regime accountable. I mean, when a person asks, asks, asks [for reforms] in a civil fashion but [is only repelled]? Glory be to God. If only the regime had been honest, it would have released those it had imprisoned and responded to those who had lost their sons at the beginning, if only the president had come to pray with the people and dismissed the vile security chief, the biggest issue would have been resolved. But instead he had a perverse arrogance, and [in his speech to the People's Assembly on March 30, 2011] replied, War is upon us, and we are ready for it. People felt he was challenging them. What did the security directorate do? It released thugs from prison, criminals, who already had hatred in their hearts because no one had defended them against the regime. They attacked the army—and the army retaliated against civilians. They wanted chaos to erupt. This last thing took the power out of our hands; we would never be able to control its outcome again.

I stayed there [in Daraa] for two years [until April 2013]. Look, this is my friend, on YouTube [showing me a video of a body being shrouded]—you can see how they killed him. Look what they did to him in prison. A terrible picture. They captured him and tortured him for days. Afterward they beat his head with rifles. This is my friend Rabīʿ, and this [opening another video] is my friend Muṣliḥ. Look, you can see how they cut his ears with long knives. These are the marks of torture, here, and of beating. And these bullet holes in his body: on his shoulder, his arm, his belly. They arrested him and I fled from street to street as they chased me. I hid in a building until they gave up on me. God turned them away from me, it was the power of our Lord that saved me from them. They detained him and tortured him while I fled to Jordan. Three days after I arrived, I saw they had done this to him. [He paused.] To God we belong and to Him we are returning.[7]

AS THOUGH IT WERE YESTERDAY

Anthropologists and others have long observed that survivors' testimonies become enscripted, especially as they make claims for restitution or redress.[8] It was clear Bilāl had told his life story before. And he was consistent, even to the extent of repeating the same phrases in detailing his experience across the months that I sat with him. Yet his patterned narration had neither a redemptive arc nor a merely pathetic quality. As our relationship deepened, I came to see the topics of his discourse and reflection through the register of witness. This register does not keep him from acting at all, of course; he still fled Daraa for Jordan when he heard the security forces were coming for him; he still now instructs the orphans (the children of his martyred friends) in religious ethics and Quranic recitation. But in his more formal testimony, as across our conversations, he located himself in the opaque space of receptivity. Thus, he understood the siege of Daraa as a tribulation but, unlike my interlocutors in Chapter 2 (and, indeed, unlike many of his fellows), could not recuperate a revolutionary mandate from this divine address. Our hearts are with you, he had insisted to the demonstrators in 2011; he clearly condemned the oppression and injustice that he himself had tasted. Yet instead of denouncing the crimes of the regime from the mosque pulpit, in seeking to shield his community from the severity of the reprisals he feared, he preached about Mother's Day. Through this time of trials like darkest night, as he recalled the hadith, he could counsel caution but was otherwise confounded. Nor was this a retreat into solipsism or the privacy of his own household, as other Syrians shielded themselves off from the war, for every time we spoke, he read me news from his phone forwarded from other friends or shared on Facebook. He remained engaged with the most recent developments in the war, and he often commented on the geopolitical machinations of Iran or Russia. But this engagement did not provide a constructive program of action.

Our conversations were punctuated by videos and photographs. In the fourteen-second clip he showed me last in the previous narrative, for instance, the body of his close friend Muṣliḥ al-ʿAyyāsh was being shrouded for burial. The security forces had come for Muṣliḥ, Bilāl, and their friend Rabīʿ at once; only Bilāl managed to escape. Three days after he arrived in Jordan he heard that his friends' bodies had been released. In the video clip he showed me multiple times, Muṣliḥ's body is lying on a wooden slat door with peeling green paint. The camera pans up from his waist across his bare chest. Bruises discolor his right side. One large bullet hole under his right armpit, another at his shoulder. Gauze is bunched around his neck. Strips of white cloth are bound around his head; the left half of his face is entirely covered in bandages. Only his right eye is visible, closed, purple. His mouth is open, teeth bared. The man filming says the date, the name of the deceased shaykh, that there is no god but God. Then someone else lowers a white sheet over the body. Bilāl and Muṣliḥ had been friends for over fifteen years, since studying sharia together in Damascus; he later showed me other pictures of them together at his wedding.

Initially, especially when they depicted horrific violence, I understood these images he showed me as a kind of evidence he offered to supplement his testimony. "This history needs to be recorded," he had said. Once, when he recounted his torture in Daraa, he said, "These are the kinds of things we need to tell the world. European countries don't yet know the true nature of the regime." He alluded to the "Caesar photographs": 53,275 images smuggled out of Damascus prisons in August 2013 by a military defector code-named

Caesar. These photographs, taken by the Syrian security apparatus between May 2011 and August 2013, depict sites of insurgency and counterinsurgency; they depict the dead bodies of soldiers (labeled with their names, death dates, and rank); and they depict the emaciated and traumatized dead bodies of at least 6,786 detainees (labeled with distinct identification numbers).[9] An international legal team is using such evidence to bring charges against the key figures in the regime who authorized mass torture.

Although the production of such images may help document the brutality of the regime, however, they do not directly translate into political action that would end it. Thus, at other times Bilāl described disseminating these images as itself a kind of jihad, a way of striving for the truth, as an effort that is worthwhile regardless of the international response. He once recalled the famous hadith in which the Prophet enjoined believers to oppose injustice with their "hand," their "tongue," or their "heart." That is, they must ameliorate it directly, if they are able; or at least denounce it verbally, if they can; or at least oppose it internally, if they only dare risk that much. Bilāl regarded "saying that this is a tragedy, proclaiming it to every part of the world," as a way of opposing evil by one's tongue. "These pictures being shared on Facebook and on social media, that everyone is horrified by—it is a kind of jihad, a way of aiding the Muslims, to distribute the true picture of what is happening, against silence in international media." This publicity might not itself end the regime's evil, but Bilāl saw sharing these images as a religious injunction. "There is no faith left [in one's heart], if one does not oppose that oppression."

At yet other times, Bilāl understood the dissemination of such images not as the gathering of forensic evidence, nor as a meritorious jihad of the tongue, but as itself exerting a technology of terror. Once he showed me a video of two men in their underwear being beaten in a regime detention center. They were from a newly reconquered area, the caption said, and had refused conscription to fight in the regime's army against the remaining rebels in the north. They were hung together by their wrists from the same ring in the ceiling while security members beat them with batons. Blood ran down their backs and their sides. Every time a man in black hit them, they yelped or squealed and contorted themselves away. This meant shielding themselves from the next blow with the likewise suspended body of their companion. Blood dripped onto the floor. We both winced as we watched the video clip. I asked whether this video had been recorded secretly and smuggled out. "Not secretly, no!" Bilāl replied. "These videos are made to spread terror (*ru'b*) through the hearts of people." And they were effective in doing so. The regime's developed repertoire of torture techniques was well-known to displaced Syrians.

The most common method, according to a report that diagrams seventy-two distinct types of torture, is (as in this video) the "ghost" (*shabaḥ*) position by which detainees are hung by their bound wrists from rings in the ceiling, "leading to dislocation of the shoulders and the rupture of the muscles in the arms and upper arms, and severe swelling of the hands."[10] The report does not mention beating two detainees in this position together; that may have been a variation innovated by the security forces at that detention center. The report also illustrates the other methods Bilāl mentioned in his recorded narrative. When he had been detained in Daraa, he had been subjected to "the Tire" (*al-dūlāb*): "The detainee's body is bent over and stuffed into a car tire leaving him squashed with his hands touching his feet and being unable to move before being beaten and kicked on the various parts of his body." The doctor they brought into the same room was subjected to "the German Chair" (*al-kursī al-almānī*): "The detainee is tied by his hands and feet to a metal chair, which has flexible parts. The security members responsible for torture then bend the back of the chair to cause stretching of the spine and neck, which leads to excruciating pain."[11] In publicizing the penalties for resistance, regime forces reminded the populace of lessons it should have learned earlier. Over our conversations, Bilāl variously argued that disseminating such images and videos may document the evil of the regime within the idiom of human rights; that it may comprise a form of striving for the truth (*jihād*); and that it may itself spread terror. Images are certainly powerful, but their effects are ambiguous.[12]

Spreading such images was only one technique of terror practiced by the Syrian regime. Bilāl had begun his account by relating how, as far back as he could remember, the people "lived in fear of the security service." The lowest-ranking member of the security forces could terrify an entire neighborhood, he had said. He had cited Tadmor prison and the Hama massacre together as cases that metonymically represented and rationalized the fear diffused among the people. As Salwa Ismail has written, these sites provide the paradigm for the regime's broader form of rule. State prisons like Tadmor or massacres like the events of Hama were not places or times exceptional to quotidian life in Syria under the Assad family. The camp and massacre "work not only to contain and neutralize opponents, but also to establish conditions of rule and to order citizens' interpretative horizons and understandings of state/regime power."[13] Ismail elaborates:

> Neither the political prison nor the massacre existed on the margin of the polity in Syria. . . . Structurally and operationally, the political prison is continuous with the polity: disciplining and remaking recalcitrant subjects while being a spectre for the purposes of instruction of the wider population. Syrian dissident and former political prisoner Yassin al-Haj Saleh rightly argues that the political prisoner is not the exception but the general rule (*al-mi'yar al-'am*). Spatial arrangements of the edifice of coercive state agencies and acts of violence in the everyday also established the continuity between the space of the prison and its outside. The ubiquitous presence of security-service kiosks on city street corners, of military checkpoints throughout the Syrian landscape and the routine assaults by security services personnel on ordinary citizens going about their daily chores, blurred the boundaries demarcating the camp and the territory beyond it. In tandem with the political prison, the massacres committed in Hama in 1982 came to represent a referential genre in the repertoire of horror managed by the regime. The discursive and symbolic coding of this horror, and affective states and practices it patterned, have all been formative of Syrian political subjectivities.[14]

Bilāl had learned well these "conditions of rule": in his narrative, much of his bewilderment at the early protests stemmed from how they transgressed precisely these "interpretative horizons." "I could not perceive what the solution was," he had said. "I remembered the events of Hama and was afraid of what would come next." In disseminating terror "among the hearts of the people," as Bilāl said, the pedagogical effects of the massacre and the prison camp reconstituted their political subjectivities in the mode of abjection.[15]

Five years later, when I visited him in 2023, Bilāl introduced me to Yūsuf, one of his friends who had been subjected to multiple expressions of the Assad regime's prison system. "You see his face affected by his imprisonment, when you meet him," Bilāl said before Yūsuf arrived. The latter had been detained in Tadmor for fifteen years—the security forces had welcomed him to prison in 1980, a youth of twenty years old, by stubbing out their cigarettes on his ankles. Sitting against the whitewashed wall in the orphanage, Yūsuf pulled up his shalwar to show me the scars, his words slurring slightly. Bilāl offered him tea and the baklawa I had brought, but he demurred, since he was fasting (it was a Thursday). He described the daily schedule in Tadmor dormitories—twelve hours of "sitting" and twelve hours of "sleeping," with each element of the daily routine subject to the cables, batons, and boots of the military police.[16] He had been released in 1995, disorientated. He got off the bus returning to his village and did not recognize it.[17] Only the Quran had sustained him in prison, he said: he memorized it there, and he and his neighbor in the dormitory would recite a sixth of the revelation to each other each day. Ismail describes Tadmor prison as a zone of abandonment—redounding with a "symphony of horror," with some prisoners serving as "exempla of punishment" for others, through "somatic disciplines" whose aim is the breaking of bodies and souls and indeed the "defilement and contamination" of the detainee's personhood, when the purpose of torture practices is precisely the "undoing of the prisoners as political subjects, and their reconstitution in a way that is devoid of dignity and that is incapable of dissenting." And in that space, the memorization and recitation of the Quran served as an "art of human living," as a common "technique of self that is used against the practices aimed at unmaking the subject."[18] "They had sown fear in his mind and everywhere he turns it still bears fruit," Bilāl commented about Yūsuf after he left. He could also have been describing his own bewilderment in the early days of the revolution. "No fear after today!" the crowds had chanted as they coursed out of his mosque in March 2011.

Other images that punctuated Bilāl's narration were less harrowing. He showed me pictures of the Omari Mosque minaret and its prayer hall (large columns made of dark stones, fluorescent lights illuminating the arches, red and white patterned carpet)—as well as pictures of the mosque's destruction that had been sent to him in Jordan. He showed me pictures of himself a decade earlier with his young children and one of him and his mother performing the Hajj pilgrimage. And then, the next time I visited the orphanage in summer 2018, he showed me the same pictures again. I returned to Jordan in February 2019 after being away six months—and once again he pulled up these images and video clips. When he first showed me the clip of Muṣliḥ in the course of our discussion, I had thought he was providing evidence for the brutality of the regime. When he first pulled up a picture of the Omari Mosque prayer hall, I had thought he was complementing his description of the building. But as he returned to these images again and again, I came to understand that these scenes did not supplement whatever conversation we were having so much as organize it. Rather than illustrate his memories, that is, this small visual archive structured them. They had "become the ground of an encounter."[19] *Lā ḥawla wa la quwwata illā bi-llāh*, he repeated as he pulled up another photo: there is no power and no strength except with God. *Ḥasbunā llāhu wa niʿma l-wakīl*, God is our recourse and he is the best of protectors.

The series of images, again: Muṣliḥ's body being shrouded. A much younger Muṣliḥ and Bilāl and their other friends standing together at the latter's wedding. Their elderly teacher at the Badr al-Dīn al-Ḥasanī Institute, the Salafī editor and hadith scholar ʿAbd al-Qādir al-Arnaʾūṭ (d. 2004), speaking at his wedding. Al-Arnaʾūṭ at the Mediterranean Sea at night, speaking toward the camera, his hand raised in greeting, the photograph's flash reflecting his white beard and the blue waves behind him. Bilāl's handsome, three-story home on a quiet street in Daraa. His home in ruins, its cinder blocks crumbling, rebars exposed and bent aside. The Omari minaret before and after its destruction. His children, his mother. A dusty tent in the desert, from his time in Zaatari Camp. He had posted these pictures on Facebook years ago and still now returns to them regularly, posting lines of poetry or reflections or laments as new captions. Sometimes (as with a long obituary he posted for the mufti of Daraa) they were formal statements. Other times they were free-form expressions of his loss. In February 2019 he reposted the picture of the Omari Mosque's prayer hall, writing:

> how the flame of longing stirs the passions yearning to pray in you,
>   O Omari Mosque
> . . .
> at vigil between the hands of God in your prayer-niche O Omari
> how many men have I loved under your roof
> both those who have passed and those who are waiting
> may God gather us in you before He gathers us in highest paradise
> swiftly without delay, O God O most merciful of the merciful

Five months later he reposted the same picture with a new caption: "O God gather us together in prayer at the Omari Mosque after victory. The dawn of victory is near by the will of God." A few months later he reposted it again with some poetic verses about the unwitting return of a longing that cannot be repulsed without denying the realities of one's aching heart.

Once, reposting the photograph of al-Arna'ūṭ (d. 2004) at the seashore, he wrote:

> God witnesses that I loved this scholar for the sake of God
> you felt when he spoke that he was subsumed in knowledge of hadith
> he made you love the prophetic way and the path of sound knowledge and elevated character
> one of the luminaries of calling to God through understanding and wisdom and insight into the prophetic way
> in treading the earth he followed the footsteps of the Prophet, God's blessings and peace upon him
> the hadith-scholar of the Levant, shaykh 'Abd al-Qādir al-Arna'ūṭ
> God envelop him into vast mercy

And on a panoramic image of old Daraa City, simply "Ohhhhhhh Lord. A scene that cleaves the hearts. How I yearn for the people and companions and brethren we would meet there."[20] And on and on.

Bilāl's return to these images contracts the temporal distance between the scenes depicted and the viewer's present. "As though it were yesterday," he repeated to me at various times as we looked at one or another of these pictures, which had been taken many years prior.[21] Such temporal elision is intrinsic to the visual medium, of course, and is elementary to any study of photography.[22] But the passage of time was in fact registered through his accumulation of captions and continuous return to these images. They made clear that the time of Bilāl's visual archive was repeated (punctuated across variations) rather than linear (advancing in regular segments or clear breaks). Meanwhile, the captions to these disparate images or their citation in conversation linked them together within the idiom of his mourning.

■ ■ ■

In our returns to Bilāl's photographs, in his captions and in our conversation, the passage of time was pared into a single binary (then/now) flattened into a spatial opposition (inside/outside Syria). However long passed between then and now was divided into a sharp contrast on either side of his displacement. The temporal binary was overlaid onto a spatial one, which thickened as the years passed. Yet no sooner is this opposition posited than it is undone, not least because the places "inside" Syria no longer exist as they do in his memory and because he nonetheless cleaves to the border that has split his life. He laughed in August 2023 as he pointed to the hills on the horizon. "My house in Daraa is just there," he said, "after the longest ten kilometers in the world." I took his picture.

The ambiguity of this melancholic landscape echoes the broader revolutionary geography that defines political positions in spatial terms (proximity to or distance from the Syrian regime). Rāfiyā Salāma observes a reconfiguration of these positions over the course of the war, such that remaining "inside" had become the currency of steadfastness (*biḍāʿat al-ṣumūd*) while becoming an alibi against political accountability—and fleeing "outside" had become an accusation leveled to disqualify the political activism of those in exile. Taken together, in a perverse transmutation, the depth of one's sacrifice and victimhood became the measure of one's revolutionary politics. "Fear and the wish to remain clash with the desired steadfastness, so that 'remaining' becomes 'distortion' and the steadfast stance becomes meaningless."[23] The division between "inside" and "outside" also structures the discourses of my other interlocutors, whether in political or cultural terms. Zāhid, a teacher in Zaatari Camp's ʿAbdullāh bin al-Mubārak Program, had been ambivalent about leaving for the West because of the religious and cultural gulf he anticipated there. He may be "outside" Syria already, but at least Jordan offered a social context of similar customs and traditions, he said.

The same hesitations led Bilāl to strongly advise a widow at his orphanage not to seek refuge in Canada. At one of our first meetings, he had mentioned to me that a woman and her children who used to live in their building had moved to Canada, and I was eager to speak with her. But when we spoke on the phone, Asmāʾ did not keep bitterness from her voice. She had lived in Jordan for three years, she said, since government forces detained her husband, an apolitical electrician, at his work in Daraa. Two months later they heard he had been killed in prison. Soon thereafter Asmāʾ left to join her natal family in Jordan, where they had already fled after her brother was killed in the shelling of Daraa. She rented an apartment in the northern city of Irbid for a few months until a friend of her deceased husband told her about the building in Ramtha for martyrs' families.

She had been an accomplished seamstress in Syria; since arriving at the orphanage, she worked to supplement the building's meager income by training the other women and by herself sewing clothing for sale in the Ramtha market. "Everything was fine—you did not need to pay rent—but it was like they put me in a cage to work. Then the Canadians called me and said your name came up in the laptop [database of refugees seeking resettlement]." She did not tell anyone at first; she struggled for weeks with her decision to leave. When she broke the news, her family could not accept it. Bilāl and his wife, Umm Mūsā, too pressured her to stay. I was surprised at how adamant they had been, given the hesitation that characterized Bilāl's actions otherwise. "They said they needed me there, that the other women needed me. But I couldn't do it." She also found Bilāl's stewardship stifling. He had told me he advised the women not to unnecessarily leave the orphanage as a means of ensuring their safety in a country where they were already under suspicion. She told me that with five young daughters and no male relatives to facilitate their movements, she was trapped. She even hinted that her proficiency at the sewing machine played a part in Bilāl and his wife's desire that she stay. "I sewed them four hundred overcoats in the years I was there. They just wanted me to stay and work for the building."

When I mentioned her bitterness to him in February 2019, Bilāl qualified his stance against emigrating to the West. "I don't tell everyone they must stay. It depends on their situation, if they have family here; and on their fortitude as well, whether they have some weakness in their character." Seeking refuge across the world may be to one's own gain, he suggested, but it may also result in abandoning one's kin (who have a prior claim to one's attention and commitment) and depriving oneself of the shield of Islamic social norms (which however imperfectly they are practiced still serve a protective function). In contrast, Bilāl continued, "In the West they don't know the meaning of family." He related an anecdote about a Syrian who had emigrated to the United States, who now worked all day and barely saw his own children. "It isn't natural," he said. Again, I was surprised at his authoritative bearing and his objectification of these positions (Islam vs. the West), when otherwise our discussions often seemed to expose their fragility and the evacuation of their significance by the violence that had rent his life. (Along the same lines, once when I sent him some emergency funds collected from friends in Canada, he was surprised that non-Muslims would also donate in aid. "May I ask—what is their objective in doing so?" I said that they too were moved to act and that I thought mercy and compassion [*raḥma*] belonged to the human disposition. "*Mā shā allāh*," he replied, "I am astounded—and will pray that they be guided to the truth.")

Asmā' gave in to the pleading of her natal family, the anger of her in-laws, and the religious reasons of Bilāl and Umm Mūsā: she told the resettlement service she could not go. But her heart was not at rest with her decision to stay; she thought of her children, whom she could not afford to educate in Jordan. She prayed for guidance (*istikhāra*) every night. And then, weeks later, the resettlement service called her back. "Nothing could change God's decree that I leave," she told me from the other side of Canada, "Even if I had told them no." She rejected the meddling of her family, who demanded she keep her children close to them, and the counsel of Bilāl and his wife, who presumed to discern "weakness in [her] character." By his account, she risked too much by exposing herself and her children. In deciding to live outside the bounds of the community, she would intensify the ordeal of her displacement. By her account, in contrast, it was precisely the ordeal that led her to risk that life, far from her natal family and her networks of kin and association, for the sake of her children. "I'm not scared of everything anymore. I only have two friends here [in Ontario], but that is enough: I don't need many people, just my children. My job now is to teach them Arabic, and to learn English for them." Both Asmā' and Bilāl seek to discern and accept the divine decree that shapes their lives; both seek, through their prayers, to make their lives a site of passage. Yet she saw her fate in the aleatory event (the resettlement agency arriving at her name in their database) where he saw only another contingency, another source of danger.[24] She and her children returned to visit Jordan after they gained Canadian citizenship: when I visited Bilāl in 2023, he showed me a picture of her four children in the courtyard of the orphanage. "It was so good to see them again," he said quietly, and then he laughed. "When I saw sister Asmā', I couldn't help asking her: did you forget your face-veil (*khimār*) in Canada?"

Bilāl himself too lives "outside" Syria and has done since 2013. But whether in Zaatari or even since he was permitted to leave the camp in 2015, he has not left the border region. The orphanage building in Ramtha faces Syria. He shares his daily weather with Daraa province. The difference between inside and outside is sharpened, not blurred, by living on its edge. "Walking fifteen or twenty minutes from here," he said, "I can reach the border—but I cannot enter. On this side there is civilization (*'umrān*) and electricity and maintained streets; and inside, ruin (*kharāb*) in every sense of the word. I mean, in some areas, what was there is now nothing but rubble. From the many explosions, the world has become flat. Streets overgrown with grass and weeds and everything ruined, every house bombed or exploded, from one missile here and another there." Bilāl has not seen for himself the full extent of the devastation within; when he left Daraa, his house was yet standing. But friends inside had sent him pictures, and drone footage of ghost cities like east Aleppo was widely circulated among displaced Syrians. Yet this difference in material conditions is further eclipsed by other considerations and mounting regret on every side. "Those who are inside say, would that I had gone to Jordan; and those who are in Jordan say, would that I could return. Others leave for Europe and they regret that too, and it splits families apart." The contrast between "inside" and "outside" Syria thus cannot be simply thematized into the opposition between ruin and civilization. (Even the revolutionary geography cited earlier was mutable, such that the original political symbolism of "inside" and "outside" Syria was reconfigured in the shifting outcomes of the war.)[25]

Although he first contrasts ruin and civilization, Bilāl then confounds the difference between them. Escaping the destruction of Daraa's towns and villages dissolves into a consuming regret that hollows out whatever security is found elsewhere. "When those who are inside visit us here in Ramtha," he told me in 2023, "they say it is like a paradise [compared to Daraa]." But his life in Ramtha, marked by unending dependence and poverty, felt like a captivity of its own. Even when the neighborhood mosque asked him to lead prayers occasionally, he (acutely aware of his own precarity) felt he could not preach from the pulpit or give the advice he felt he should. This only exacerbated his sense of alienation.[26] He wrote on Facebook:

> The difficulty of feeling in exile (*ghurba*): you cannot object. You cannot offer guidance in the mosque or the street when you see an infraction. You cannot counsel (*naṣḥ*) anyone, because they will look at you and say: who are you to counsel me? Always it is you who should apologize. Always you must be polite and manage so that no one bears a grudge against you. . . . Meanwhile those who are inside [in Syria] think you are resting comfortably. By God, yes by God, neither the one in exile nor the one inside is comfortable: God has made both of these a trial (*fitna*) for all people: *and We made some of you a trial for others; will you be patient? And thy Lord is Seeing.* (Q. 25:20)

Being inside and being outside are both trials for the other. One aspect of the trial of exile was the inability to counsel others: as someone only begrudgingly tolerated in Jordan and always under threat of return to Syria, he had no claim on his neighbors. He felt barred from expressing the "everyday concern of friends and kin for the welfare of one another's souls."[27] The difficulty of his estrangement included his sense of being resented and excluded, bound to and by a border that did not release him to a community of refuge.

In 2024, he wrote further: "Every human being believes he is more miserable than others, or he is tried (*mubtalī*) more than others. However, the reality is that each of us has something that disturbs and makes us suffer. But we do differ in our contentment with God's decision and decree. . . ." Bilāl emphasizes the iterative struggle to practice steadfastness (*ṣabr*) and contentment (*riḍā*) with the divine decree, a capacity that is not given but must be unendingly striven for. Hence his repeated supplications every time he opened his memory-images: coming to terms with the divine decree. "God is our recourse and he is the best of protectors" (*ḥasbunā llāhu wa niʿma l-wakīl*), he would repeat. In remarking his proximity to the border, he echoed the terms of Ibn Khaldūn's philosophy of history (*kharāb*, *ʿumrān*), for which recursive cycles of filling and emptying build and lay cities to waste—and in so doing refract the souls of their denizens. What is ruined by the war therefore is not only the external (*khārij*) neighborhoods and shelters of human residence but the internal (*dākhil*) topography as well. Bilāl frequently cited Q. 13:11: *Truly God alters not what is in a people until they alter what is in themselves. And when God desires evil for a people, there is no repelling it; and apart from Him they have no protector.* No refuge from the divine decree except in the divine decree, he would shake his head. Whether inside (*dākhil*) or outside (*khārij*).

Again, he showed me a photograph of his house before its destruction. A proficient gardener, he gestured to where his orchard lay behind the wall; we talked about the plants he used to grow there. He pointed out the vines growing up the front of the building. "They were the sweetest grapes in the world," he said. I remembered seeing a lush grapevine in the courtyard outside. "I taught it to grow up the trellis," he answered. "There are two in the courtyard; I planted them after we arrived here. But one of the vines died, and I don't know why."[28]

IF THE HORIZON BREAKS

A ceasefire of sorts had held in southwest Syria for nearly a year, after fierce fighting resulted in a stalemate, and then a U.S.-Russia brokered "de-escalation agreement" negotiated in Jordan took hold in early July 2017. Israel and Jordan won an agreement that Assad's Iranian militia allies would hold a buffer zone from the Syrian border; at a joint press conference between the Jordanian and Russian foreign ministers in Amman, the former said that his government's priority was ensuring that Daesh/ISIS and other extreme Islamist militias would not establish a presence in southern Syria. But no further details of the de-escalation agreement were publicized. Opposition activists bitterly warned that such ceasefires, though necessary to grant the people relief, "merely free[d] up Syria's army to make territorial gains elsewhere"—and that "Syria's army [would] return to attack them once it [had] consolidated gains in the north and other areas."[29] Less than a year later, that warning held true. The regime used the ceasefire as a deterrent to keep southern rebel groups from trying to break its assault on Ghouta in March 2018. Then, on June 13, Bashar al-Assad told Iranian television, "We've now headed south. We're giving space for the political process; if it doesn't succeed, there will be no choice but liberation by force." Explaining the geopolitical dynamics by which Assad (*asad*) divided and conquered the revolutionaries (*thuwwār*), Bilāl later cited the proverb of the lion (*asad*) eating the bulls (*thīrān*): "The red bull laments: 'I was eaten the day the white bull was eaten.'" The two remaining rebel-held areas of the country had international support (Turkish in the northwest and American in the Kurdish northeast), but the southwest was vulnerable. The ceasefire could not hold, according to Russia and the regime, because half of Daraa was overrun by "terrorists." Thus the regime's steady and methodical campaign to reconquer the country again reached the southern governorate.[30]

The Russian-Syrian bombing started on June 19. Tens of thousands of people fled for the nearest borders (Israel and Jordan), seeking shelter where they could and some kind of surety against the horror raining down from above. They sought a kind of international visibility at the border: to break free of the state that had imprisoned and now hunted them. Some of the displaced found refuge in schools or other large buildings. But most slept open in the streets and in olive groves: "Their mattresses are the ground and their blankets are in the sky." Eventually, nearly one hundred thousand people would reach the border with Jordan, seeking recourse or safe passage.[31]

But the Jordanian government declared that the border would remain closed because the country was already exhausted and depleted. The foreign minister tweeted on June 26, "Jordan engaging all parties to end fighting, protect civilians in south Syria. Host to 1.3million Syrians, we are at capacity. We'll keep doing all we can for them. But we can't host more. UN can help IDPs inside Syria &we'll fully help. We're doing all we can. Others need to do same." Social media streams started filling with supplications and curses in videos sent by Syrians realizing to what extent they had been abandoned, raising their index fingers to heaven, invoking God in an appeal or imprecation. "Between hellfire and a closed border" was the title of one testimony.[32]

I arrived at the orphanage complex shortly before 7 P.M. the next day. I was leaving for Canada again soon and wanted to say farewell. I had heard the explosions as soon as I arrived in Ramtha, low and nearly continuous behind the engines growling and cars honking at the bus depot. I strained to hear the bombardment, my chest already tight. Though I was often embarrassed of the mobility granted me by my accident of birth (Canadian passport) and plane tickets to carry me away (fieldwork funding), and although these flights were booked long ago and I sorely missed my wife and young children after months in Jordan, I shrunk ashamed from the thought of leaving my interlocutors while the shelling was audible on the border. Nausea rose as I walked twenty minutes to the building on the outskirts of town. Bilāl met me at the gate and led me over to the plot of red dirt on the far side of the building. We wove between children playing and shouting: three were on the swing set, a dozen biked in circles, two girls with long braids raced down the slide. He turned to ask if I'd heard the explosions yet. He said they had heard them regularly since the ceasefire ended, once a day or a few times a week, but in the last days they had intensified to the extent that at night the widows living on the upper floors of the apartment building came down, terrified, to huddle in the square. Even when the sound did not carry you could see red-brown flashes on the horizon. "We trust in God, the best of protectors," he sighed. He and his friend (a younger man from a Damascus suburb who had studied at another sharia institute, whom I had met there before) were planting green shoots in rows. Their robes were hiked up and their plastic sandals caked with mud as they placed an irrigation hose. I was impressed—there were dozens of seedlings in already, new since

FIGURE 4. Bilāl walking in his garden at the orphanage, Ramtha, Jordan. Basit Kareem Iqbal, 2023

the last time I had visited two weeks ago. Bilāl explained that the families at the building would eat most of these eggplants, but he would try to sell any remaining produce in the Ramtha market. (Months later he sent me a video of the children harvesting beans with him, from the next crop from the same small plot. When I returned to Jordan in 2023, he proudly showed me the pump he had installed to use grey water from the orphanage—see figure 4. I took notes for my garden at home.)

Four boys played soccer in the bare dust next to the apartment building. A shoulder-height wall separated their game from the rows of eggplants they were putting in. A line of mature olive trees bordered the garden in front of the complex's outside wall. Bilāl called, "Careful of the plants!" The ball had landed among the eggplant shoots. The nearest boy, lanky and lean, hoisted himself over the wall and leapt to where it lay. He threw it back over, where his teammate caught it, but then faced a thick row of plants between himself and the wall again. "Good, now jump!" Bilāl watched the boy clear the plants and grin at us before he turned back to me. The explosions to the northeast started again with low booms, and we squinted at the sky. "We trust in God, the best of protectors," he repeated.

A woman in her apartment above us rapped quickly on the window-frame and called her children in. "Noises, noises in Syria!" a little girl cried as she ran for the building. I shuddered. The red earth, the green plants, the irrigation hose, the men's sweat, the fading heat, the children skipping, the thunder in the cloudless sky. I remembered a hadith about the eschaton: "If you hear that the Antichrist has come while you are planting a young tree, it is not too late to put it in order. . . ."[33] The two men stood by the wheelbarrow, wincing at the horizon. A light wind picked up.

He invited me in for a mostly silent supper he brought in quickly. Cauliflower fried with lemon and onions, tabbouleh, lettuce leaves, bread. "The most unbearable thing—that is the air bombardment," he said. "The bombing when, I mean, it kills entire families at once. Can you imagine—a missile hit the house of one of my neighbors in Daraa City and not a single person remained? The people live in terror and fear . . . their only hope is in the war ending. And for us, that is our only hope of returning." We sat on the floor cushions in his living room. His phone vibrated: a WhatsApp voice recording forwarded from the inside (*al-dākhil*). He played it twice, but I had trouble understanding through the static. It was someone hiding with a group of people in a cellar in a village, he explained. The man on the voice recording said they had been bombed all week, but only one person from their group had died. "All is well, praise God, all is well." His tone was energized and positive.

Bilāl shook his head. We each silently scrolled through news images of the air strikes on our phones. "This bombing, bombing, bombing. . . . I trust in God and He is the best of protectors. . . . Grant them succor. Glory be to God at this fate." We heard another explosion strike, and he winced.

> We hear the raids and shelling, and barrel bombs and rockets and missiles, day and night. The buildings shake, especially at night. We hear the sound of rockets striking our family in Daraa, those who are just two or three kilometers away, and all we can do is raise our hands and pray that God relieve them. I've received so many messages on WhatsApp—they reach to anyone who can send them some money for medicine, for food,

> for water, for gas for their vehicles. We can't aid them or defend them because of this tragic state we ourselves are in—we are weak, depleted, while they are facing the immediate trial. God, release them from it soon!

He showed me a video clip of Iran's PressTV Syria bureau chief: "This is an Iranian, Hossein Mortada, taunting the people of Daraa, telling them, 'We will enter your lands and eat biscuits in your houses.' How vile . . . Now the Russians march through the villages of Hauran, where [the rebels] have laid down their arms and surrendered, except for the city of Daraa. We ask God for protection and relief. When the regime enters a township that has surrendered, they abuse men and women and children, they loot for three days. They kill a man in front of his wife, they rape the women. We ask God for relief." He pulled up another video.

> This is one of the bombed villages in Daraa—see, see its dust cloud. They are saying: who will help us? Then this is the torment (*taʿdhīb*), this is the torment. Ach. This brutality is really the truth of the regime. How can we help our brethren? O God! These people are fleeing in their cars to another area. By God, the elderly at a loss here, they don't know which way to turn or flee. It hits your heart—these people just want safety, they just want to cross [to Jordan]. Why can't they cross? . . . Here, this is a commander in the Free Army who abandoned the youth and fled. I trust in God and He is the best of protectors. I trust in God and He is the best of protectors. We trust in God and He is the best of protectors. I have friends, I have a brother inside, fleeing from place to place. His wife and five children are with him. He doesn't know where to go. I trust in God and He is the best of protectors. We come from God and to Him we return.

His phone vibrated again. Hoping for clemency, a Free Army squadron leader had betrayed his fighters to the advancing ground forces—who killed them all together. Six more WhatsApp messages came in asking if this news was verified and whether they knew anyone among that battalion. Other messages were from people trying to figure out exactly where the bombardments were hitting.

Someone hammered on his apartment door. He sprang up to answer, hearing raised voices outside. When he reached the door, a young girl barged in, nearly in tears. She complained about another child who lived in the building, who had tricked her out of the dinar Bilāl had promised those who practiced their Quran lesson. He heard her out and patted her on the back, sending her on her way with another dinar. "Children's problems just don't end," he commented ruefully as he returned to me. It was unbearable.

We walked on the highway's gravel shoulder into Ramtha, heading to the mosque closest to the edge of town, where he occasionally led prayer. Night had fully fallen. The traffic was intermittent, just a motorcycle or truck heading to a farm nearby. "I have a question," I said. "It's about the shaykh with whom I started Quran lessons in Damascus years ago. When I was in Zaatari Camp, at the 'Abdullāh bin al-Mubārak Project, they said he was still in Damascus, meaning he sided with the regime. Do you—"

CRACK

—there was an explosion on the horizon so loud that we could hear it on both sides of the sky. I jumped and instinctively turned to look across the dark Syrian border. I turned back to Bilāl—but he was no longer next to me. He was crouched down halfway into the ditch with his fingers in his ears. He got up slowly. A baby started wailing in the house nearest the street. He wiped tears from his cheeks. "The children here are playing and they [he gestured to the horizon] are dying," he said after a minute. "Glory be to God." We walked the rest of the way in silence.

I returned to Jordan six months later, long after the regime had reconquered south Syria, and took a service taxi north from Amman as I had so many times before. An older driver with a hacking cough, two women sitting in the backseat, a silent drive past gullies and ravines, the brown hills covered with green, cedar trees and olive shrubs, pottery and strawberry stands along the highway, signs for mosques and restaurants, young men in hoodies and jackets against the cold. . . . Low grey clouds, angry rain, intermittent hail. Bilāl had been glad to hear my voice on the phone but had to delay our meeting till later in the day, as he was arranging his mother's return to Daraa. She had lived with them since his father passed away a decade ago; she had fled with them to Jordan in 2013, had lived with them in Zaatari Camp, then at the orphanage. Now, six years later, she traveled the hour's journey north home to her son who had stayed in Syria. He showed me a video his brother had taken earlier that day when she arrived, weeping. The family crowded around to kiss her hands. Bilāl's brother was crying too, embraced her, called his children to show her how they had grown. "Thank God, thank God I could see you again," she whispered to him.

Bilāl himself, of course, could not return to Daraa: the security forces had been looking for him when he fled, so he would likely be detained at the border crossing. And he had to think of the others with him. He lived in Jordan with his wife and their six children, as well as his sister and her five children. (His sister's husband was detained and disappeared in the first months of the revolution.) If they all somehow did cross the checkpoints and multiplying toll roads to return to Daraa City, to live near his brother while they started to rebuild their houses, his eldest son (eighteen years old, quiet and slim) would almost certainly be conscripted into the regime's ongoing war with the remaining rebels and be bussed up to the Idlib front. Bilāl himself, though he had long ago served his compulsory two and a half years in the military and though he was approaching fifty, might well also be conscripted. Syrians who had returned to Syria warned those who had not of arbitrary arrests and occasional explosions. The Russia-guaranteed reconciliation agreements could not be trusted, that at least was clear. Nor was the infrastructure of normal life restored in Daraa. Electricity was cut multiple times a day. Bilāl's nephew needed special batteries for his inhaler, so his brother had to travel a contorted route across various checkpoints to buy them. The streets were empty after dusk, an effective curfew set by the extreme fear of life inside. Seventy percent of humanitarian aid entering the country was routed to the regime, which distributed it to its partisans in exchange for their loyalty. And the prisons were starting to fill again with new arrests, while tens of thousands of families—including Bilāl's own—still had not heard from their relatives who had disappeared into security detention centers years ago.[34]

On the other hand, Bilāl remaining in Jordan meant enduring an atmosphere of suspicion and resentment. To the Jordanian government, to the different sectors of the humanitarian regime, even to his neighbors in Ramtha, the war in southern Syria was effectively over—and the refugees displaced from there ought to return. Humanitarian funding was drying up. Only eight remained of the twelve buildings for martyrs' families once supported by the Islamic charity in Ramtha. Four had closed for lack of sufficient funds to support them. The families from those four buildings had dispersed: some indeed returned to Syria; others moved to rent in the urban center of Irbid; and a few were amalgamated into the other buildings, which were now overcrowded. The nineteen apartments in Bilāl's orphanage, for example, now hosted twenty-five families. And the hundred-dinar monthly maintenance stipend from the Islamic charity had been reduced to seventy.

He showed me a video of a tall, middle-aged man in a black vest with a high forehead and aquiline nose, smiling at the camera in front of some bushes. "The mourning of my heart will not cease," the man declaimed, "until it receives the glad tidings of arrival / and I see my Book [ledger of life] in my right hand / and my heart's eyes will not rest." He paused and thought for a moment, first quoting the early twentieth-century Tunisian poet Abū l-Qāsim al-Shaʿbī and then extemporizing in verse.

> If, one day, a people desires to live
> then fate will answer their call [he pointed heavenward]
> and their night will then begin to fade
> and their chains break and fall
> with every longing
> and with every sublimity and grandeur
> so we say: O great people of Syria!
> and o proud people of Hauran!
> we say to you: you have endured by the will of God
> and you have extended your power by the will of God glorified and exalted
> such that these youth—show the people [this last to the person recording the video, which panned to show two middle-aged men standing in a courtyard making a V sign]—are firmly committed to the truth (God willing! they replied)
> and that they are certainly of the faction of whom the Prophet spoke, God's peace and blessings upon him, who will continue to hold to the truth and [he called over a short older man who had just entered the courtyard with a cigarette between his fingers] who will not be injured by those who oppose them, until God's command obtains.[35]

The older man was delighted at this comparison; he laughed aloud and made an inaudible joke. The speaker smiled and raised his right index finger again, putting his left arm over the older man's shoulder. "For that reason, for God's pledge, we are coming, O Bashar al-Assad. And we are steadfast." The older man added, "We are coming to free you, O Damascus." The speaker repeated, "We are coming, O Damascus! And our battle will be struck at a set date, by God's will." "Victory in Ramadan," one of the other men chimed in. "And the world will see how the Syrian people deal with their tyrant, Bashar al-Assad," the man concluded.

"This was my friend," Bilāl told me. "We were close, in Daraa together at the beginning of the revolution. He became a Free Army commander. Those other men in the video were shopkeepers and farmers: they were his company. They called their battalion 'Falcons of Quraysh.' He was a hero—he fought bravely, he liberated the village of Dael from the regime. But he was ambushed later. They brought him here for medical treatment, but his wounds were too heavy." I was confused—they brought him here to Jordan? "Yes," he answered, "This was in 2013, so I was here already—I was at the mosque and they announced there would be a funeral after the prayer. The building was packed with thousands of Syrians. I asked who had died and they told me it was Shaykh Anīs and I was confounded. He is buried here in one of the Syrian cemeteries in Ramtha, with the hundreds of other Syrians who were killed across the border and buried here." He paused. "God's curse on you, O Bashar," Bilāl muttered as he put his phone down.

THE DREAD HEIGHTS

The war has moved from that border (there are no more air strikes on the Ramtha horizon) but Bilāl remains implicated in it, raising the children of his martyred friends and anxiously watching the news from Daraa and Idlib. His kaleidoscope of memories fixes scenes in place: his hadith teacher at the Mediterranean; his mother on pilgrimage; the beloved Omari minaret; his shelled house. As the months pass, he returns to his archive of images: the videos of revolutionary promise, the jocular camaraderie of shopkeepers and religious students turned rebel fighters, the hope of the city that dared say "no fear after this day." And their brutal, brutal aftermath. Inside/outside, *juwwa/barra*. Bilāl lives on the border between fear and suspicion, between Syria and Jordan, whose difference is blurred by their common precarity but sharpened by their common weather. What "appears to be an impenetrable boundary (*Schranke*) turns out to be a mobile and porous border (*Grenze*)," writes Rebecca Comay, but this "works simultaneously in both directions," as time and space become disoriented and stagnant.[36] Bilāl does not pass from that border: he lives there. After the revolution but before any substantive relief, his displacement has not been followed by emplacement. The mortified horizon of his orphanage in Ramtha is lined with the images of days gone by and companions who have passed: "The abyss of the irreparable."[37]

According to the methodological nationalism that has conventionally organized refugee studies, life on the border is a protracted experience of liminality. Such social thresholds have been a longstanding topic of anthropology. For Arnold van Gennep, for example, rites of passage are defined by three phases: separation, margin, and aggregation. Victor Turner draws out the transformative importance of the middle phase, of moments both "in and out of time," both "in and out of secular social structure," which "revea[l], however fleetingly, some recognition (in symbol if not always in language) of a generalized social bond that has ceased to be and has simultaneously yet to be."[38] Life on the border, suspended between displacement and emplacement, exposes the conceits of international order: the fragility of the structural isomorphism between nation, state, and territory. But approaching Bilāl's life without grounding reference to the national order of things, without the presumption that either Syria or Jordan offers succor or salvation, provides a different vantage. That perspective returns to the intemporal dimension to which his supplications and imprecations maintain a constant, intimate relation. His prayers, which accompanied our perusal of his photographs and his narration, cut through the empty, homogeneous time of the nation, of state management and intervention, and of bounded, secured territory. Instead they emphasized the ultimate groundlessness of creational existence.

Rather than spatial displacement alone (his movement from Daraa to Ramtha), this suspension also reconfigures the temporal order. Jorge Luis Borges's short story "The Secret Miracle" underscores such a contingency. The story opens with a Quranic epigraph: *And God made him die during the course of a hundred years and then He revived him and said: "How long have you been here?" "A day, or part of a day," he replied* (Q. 2:259). In this parable a man—whom the exegetes identify as Ezra the Scribe, the Babylonian reformer who led Jewish exiles back to the Levant—passes by a hamlet in ruins. How will God resurrect its inhabitants to life, he wonders. By way of answer, God causes him to die there, to remain dead one hundred years, and then restores him to life, as a demonstration of the divine power. He thinks he was gone a single day, or part of a day. The parable goes on to say that his food and drink were still fresh, showing no sign of decay, while his donkey's skeleton had crumbled. But then God recomposes the donkey before his very eyes, and he says, "I know that God has power over all things." God here shows Ezra how the ruins will be restored on Judgment Day and life will return. But resurrecting anything small for the briefest of terms would have served that purpose. Instead, God kills and enlivens Ezra himself, has him lie dead for not a minute or two weeks but a full century, and shows him how he can preserve his food and drink in time, frozen out of time, while subjecting his beast of burden to the wear of time. This is a dramatic parable of divine omnipotence, in the sense of Ezra's proclamation of God "having power over all things," but more specifically it is a parable of the divine power as it acts on time. It demonstrates the contingency of time, in which the bodies of Ezra and his donkey inhabit asymmetrical positions. The world has its time, but God can play with it at will.

That is the lesson that Borges takes up and inverts in his short story, to which the Quranic verse acts as epigraph. In "The Secret Miracle," the writer Jaromir Hladik is arrested and condemned by the Nazis in Prague. In the ten days between his detention and his appointed death by firing squad, he imagines every possible way he will die. He thinks over the body of work he leaves behind and deeply regrets leaving his masterwork unfinished. Finally, on the night before his death, he prays to God that he be granted a year's more time to complete it. The next morning two soldiers come to take him away; they stand him before the firing squad, and the sergeant calls the order to fire. Then the world stands still. "The rifles converged upon Hladik, but the men assigned to pull the triggers were immobile. The sergeant's arm eternalized an inconclusive gesture. Upon a courtyard flagstone a bee cast a stationary shadow. The wind had halted, as in a painted picture. Hladik began a shriek, a syllable, a twist of the hand. He realized he was paralyzed. Not a sound reached him from the stricken world."[39] He first thinks he has entered hell or gone mad, but eventually he remembers his supplication and realizes that God has granted him his prayer. Over the next year he works, suspended, at completing his unfinished play. He chooses its final epithet—and then, his year of reprieve having elapsed, German bullets strike him down. Once again, the world has its time, but God can play with it at will. But in contrast to the Quranic parable, where Ezra was frozen out of time, here it is the world that has been frozen immobile, and it is the individual's time that is extended; it acts as a kind of asymmetrical supplement to the life of the world.

In each of these versions, the pedagogic function of the Quranic parable and the narrative arc of Borges's short story insist that the temporal play of mobility/immobility folds over into another set of coordinates. "Time both contracts and stretches; it simultaneously quickens and thickens."[40] In each of these versions, a heteronomous supplement makes apparent that time is not its own. Neither life nor death offers a stable, reliable relation to the work of time. This fundamental contingency underscores the asymmetry entailed by Bilāl's constant relation to the intemporal: how his prayers work on and through his spatio-temporal displacement. It also pushes past anthropological interpretations of the borderland as a liminal space between forms of social order.

The Quran offers another figure for Bilāl's life at the border. Through its account of "men on the Heights" it becomes possible to articulate suspension as the intemporal procedure that rends worldly forms of life in demanding an orientation to the unbearable. The eponymous Quranic chapter describes ambiguous inhabitants of the Heights (*al-aʿrāf*) who are suspended between Garden and Fire:

> And there will be a veil between them. And upon the Heights are men who know all by their marks. They will call out to the inhabitants of the Garden "Peace be upon you!" They will not have entered it, though they hope. And when their eyes turn toward the inhabitants of the Fire, they will say, "Our Lord! Place us not among the wrongdoing people!" And the inhabitants of the Heights will call out to men whom they know by their marks, "Your accumulating has not availed you, nor has your waxing arrogant. Are these the ones concerning whom you swore that God would not extend any mercy?" "Enter the Garden! No fear shall come upon you, nor shall you grieve." (Q. 7:46–48)

The Quranic exegetes variously identify those who are *upon the Heights*: many hold that they are those whose virtuous deeds do not preponderate over their vicious ones nor vice versa, and so they remain awaiting their fate. Other commentators understand them as being those who have transcended Garden and Fire in their contemplation of the beatific vision, or those in the "intermediate region" (*barzakh*) between outward forms and spiritual reality.[41] Still others interpret their position as that of those exempted from the divine reckoning because they lacked moral accountability.[42] These possible identifications aside, it is the relationship between these suppliants' atopic suspension and the striking lucidity it affords that recalls this verse for me with reference to Bilāl's inhabitation of the border zone. They *know all by their marks*, though they are themselves frozen in place. The inhabitants of the Heights hope and fear between Garden and Fire, but they cannot move from where they are placed. They endure the possibility of divine relief—a possibility that is withheld, not relinquished—and so only *call out to the inhabitants of the Garden* and to their Lord. Suspension itself as a form of life.

Like many of my other interlocutors, however geographically distant they may be from the border itself, Bilāl lives in the Syrian borderland. Their lives, as his, are marked by the division between inside and outside. The place (topos) of such border-life, following Stefania Pandolfo, is "an intermediate zone between the possibility of regeneration and the elasticity of the [destructive] drive."[43] It cannot be localized or confined to one side or the other of the border line. Read this way, the existential border-life of inside/outside may then show "the precarious movement of a being-at-risk, a *sujet risqué*, suspended in a zone between two deaths and two modalities of destruction."[44] At such a moment, what Daniel Knight calls "vertiginous life" is "caught between the impossibility of return and the imponderability of the yet-to-come. Stripped of essence, existence becomes unbearable."[45] Yet the eschatological reference of my interlocutors' gestures shows that this unbearability already belongs to the absolute asymmetry between God and creation.

Facing the incapacitations of crippling inflation and suspicion (on one side of the border) if not outright conscription or detention (on the other side of the border), Bilāl can only repeat the grim gestures of his immobility.[46] This is the refrain of those witnessing the split of inside/outside that determines all their days: God, grant relief! This heteronymous appeal seeks deliverance from the immediate trial but also from the structuring division of inside/outside (*dākhil/khārij, juwwa/barra*) that confounds the difference between civilization and ruin, safety and suspicion. Life at the border problematizes (not accentuates) the opposition between inside and outside.

Exposed and on the edge, memory is brought to a pitch of intensity and efficacy.[47] Bilāl's memory-images, neither simply traumatic nor reparative, splinter into an accelerating series of discontinuous, abbreviated tableaux.[48] As the years pass they generate a form of intemporal witness, expressed through three versions in the Quranic verses and Borges's story, by which "the absence of event" becomes "a negative event."[49] There, writes Comay, as though of Bilāl's returns to his images, "mourning thus becomes the infinite circularity of mortified awakenings and revived mortifications."[50] These repetitions do not generate a new dialogue between past and present. They do not advance a revolutionary politics or abandon one to ruthless pessimism. But they do allow for the practice of what Anne DuFourmantelle calls "gentleness." Such gentleness is not merely a virtue that an ethical subject might develop through habituation and practice. Although it is found through one's capacities (it is not "natural"), it is not owned by the subject. Nor is it merely a principle of relation. "Gentleness does not belong only to the human race. It is a quality whose infinite range extends beyond the realm of the living."[51] It visits us, writes DuFourmantelle.[52] The force of a soft touch: "It takes into account cruelty, the injustice of the world. Being gentle with objects and beings means understanding them in their insufficiency, their precariousness, their immaturity, their stupidity."[53] I remember Bilāl watering the jasmine plants and grape vines growing up the rusted metal bower in the orphanage courtyard; I remember him passing hard candies to even the petulant children as they filed out of the basement classroom.

Gentleness works on time through attending to the insufficiency of creation, through working on the limitation of all things. "God is the best of protectors," he repeated again and again, rearticulating the position of his life. His repeated invocations drew together instances from across his biography: when he fled the Syrian security forces hunting him, when his brother called him from the countryside outside Daraa. Blanchot writes about a young man who also brushed death, as did the characters in the Borges story and the Quranic passages: "A feeling of lightness that I would not know how to translate: freed from life? The infinite opening up? Neither happiness, nor unhappiness. Nor the absence of fear and perhaps already the step beyond."[54] "This lightness," Derrida comments, "neither frees nor relieves of anything; it is neither a salvation through freedom nor an opening to the infinite because this passion is without freedom and this death without death is a confirmation of finitude."[55] This is no alibi or escape. Yet for Blanchot it opens another relation, through its very encounter with death: "the feeling of compassion for suffering humanity, the happiness of not being immortal or eternal."[56] Likewise, gentleness offers "neither redemption nor a possible escape, but words"—and, we may add, in Bilāl's incessant return to his archive of memories, images—"that would come to give shelter to the memory of the dead and recreate space for life among the living."[57] Thus Bilāl's return to the images of life in Daraa and of his murdered friends is not simply a traumatic compulsion. ("It is as if these patients had not yet gotten through with the traumatic situation," declared Freud, "as if it were actually before them as a task which was not yet mastered."[58]) Nor was it readily part of a therapeutic process of healing from trauma (part of the effort to "abreact the intensity of the experience," to defuse the cathected affects that belatedly charge the memories of the wounding events).[59] His return to these images fell neatly neither on the side of trauma nor therapeutics, neither a function of a frozen present nor an effort to set it in motion again. Yet it was *effective*: in this return, the simple force of gentleness expands the present.[60]

There is no knowing whether the grapevines Bilāl plants at the orphanage (recalling his grapes in Daraa) will thrive in his courtyard or that the children he cares for there (the children of his disappeared or murdered fellows) will embody the ethical qualities he seeks. They are bereft of any guarantee of the conditions that would sustain them, exposed to the incapacitations of poverty and still in shadow of the war. He does not move from the border zone; he remains suspended there. Gentleness—tending eggplant shoots and comforting an upset child while the horizon burns—does not itself offer relief from the war or hope for a different future. "The future has become obscure (*ghāmiḍ*)," he told me in 2023.

I wrote earlier that, over our interlocutions, Bilāl listed different senses of images of violence: they have traction in a forensic register, where they could be mobilized as evidence; they serve a virtuous purpose, such that one could wage jihad by spreading news of the regime's terror; and they bear a terror within themselves. But in showing me the same images again, he was not asking that I use them for an international human rights campaign against the Assad regime; nor was he presuming to tell me something I did not know; nor was he seeking to terrify me. Instead, as he has returned me to these same images over the years since we met, I have come to see that gentleness is already there in his returns to the visual archive of his loss. For its images offer among other possibilities the possible glimpse of "a beloved face"[61]—even through the mutilated visages of those tortured unto death. In this way, gentleness confounds the conventional distinction between mourning and melancholia.[62] Pursuing such glimpses, as Bilāl does unremittingly,

> sometimes informs the decision to consent to the worst: to mourning, for example. This ageless sadness, what inside of us also belongs to the missing, the absent, is coiled up, interwoven inside the body and in the hollow of the throat. Is it possible to pass through melancholy? "Thus the shadow of the object fell upon the ego," writes Freud. Might gentleness be deadly? Yes, in melancholy as in sleep, snow, water: all the way to complete self-oblivion.[63]

These returns should themselves be seen as a practice of gentleness, for accompanied by his prayer they open up another relation to his present.

"There are so many things I miss about Syria." This much I had heard Bilāl say before. His friend Muṣliḥ, since tortured to death. His friend Anīs, ambushed by regime thugs. His house in ruins. The Omari Mosque, for which he yearned in passionate verse. His grapes, the sweetest in the world. His hadith teacher, who embodied the prophetic way. Then he continued. "But thank God for the blessing of forgetting."

AFTERWORD

Eternity Has Fallen

In December 2024, the unthinkable occurred. Rumors, acclamations, and tears had been spreading both among those inside and outside Syria as fighters advanced from the north. The rebels of Hauran, who during my fieldwork in 2018 had ostensibly reconciled with the regime under the weight of Russian bombs and Iranian militias, mobilized again from the south. And after fifty-four years, more rapidly than any of my Syrian friends or outside observers thought possible, the regime finally fell. Across the lands of their displacement, my interlocutors and their fellows wept, incredulous. In Ramtha and Irbid and Amman (in Jordan), in Hamilton and Edmonton and Mississauga (in Canada), as elsewhere, they gathered in community centers and mosques and in the streets, with music and sweets and speeches.

A cacophony of pundits in international news media worried about the day "after" the regime. They were anxious about the religiosity of the rebels and the future of minorities in the country. Others explained the swift victory of the rebels with reference to the relative weakness of the regime's allies since Israel's decimation of Hezbollah and Russia's invasion of Ukraine. Some even speculated that the worst for Syrians was yet to come. They condescendingly expressed these concerns while liberated detainees were still streaming out of Sednaya prison.

My interlocutors gave thanks to God for having relieved them.

What was the time of God's relief? It was a time of strange, unfamiliar affects: a language of futurity returned to those who had become unused to it. They circulated videos of those once exiled to the rebel enclave in northwest Syria now returning to their towns and villages: embracing their parents for the first time in a decade, kneeling to the ground as they entered their neighborhoods. Those watching these videos from afar hoped to do as they did. They yearned to kiss the ground and their kin. It was a time of transformation, as when a number of my interlocutors posted on their social media, "I am no longer a Syrian refugee. Today, I am just a Syrian." Regardless of their legal designation or immigration status, they felt released from their abjection and their interpellation as international objects of pity and of fear. It was a time of new mourning: interlocutors from different parts of the country, from Daraa and Aleppo and Homs, started writing (again) about their comrades and companions who did not live to see these days. They circulated their pictures and their memory. And it was a time of joy mixed with deep sorrow: they prayed that the new freedom they tasted would also reach Palestine, after nearly a year and a half of Israel's genocidal campaign to obliterate Gaza.

One striking announcement stated, simply, "Eternity has fallen" (*saqaṭa l-abad*). This extension of the revolutionary chant of the Arab uprisings ("The people demand the fall of the regime," *al-sha'b yurīd isqāṭ al-niẓām*) played on the Syrian regime's declaration of its own eternity. Ubiquitous public posters in Syria, for example, had proclaimed the rhyming slogan "Our leader forever is Hafez al-Assad!" (*qā'idunā li-l-abad ḥāfiz al-asad*) or simply "al-Assad, forever!" (*al-asad ilā l-abad*). Greater than any one man, the regime had laid claim on the rest of time. In fact, the "endlessness" (*abadiyya*) announced by the regime was a theological term naming God as continuous and non-divisible. The exiled Syrian intellectual Yassin al-Haj Saleh had earlier remarked the common etymology of eternity (*al-abad*) and extermination (*al-ibāda*) in order to note that in Syria the former cannot be achieved without the latter. "Killing here is not punitive, nor even retributive; it is destructive and extirpative, aimed at enslaving those not yet killed and immortalizing the killers." Another inflection of its brutality, another sense of the thanatocratic regime's obsessive desire to reproduce itself into infinity.[1] In December 2024, Saleh wrote on Twitter:

> Eternity is over and history is about to begin. The page of a rotten, despicable, son of a bitch has been turned. We do have many difficult pages

ahead of us. But today we celebrate our deliverance as if there is no tomorrow. And tomorrow we return to the heartache, as if deliverance is still far ahead of us.

Granting its difficulty, its ambivalence, and the likelihood of it being obscured, a historical horizon had appeared.

For many of my interlocutors, the time of God's relief was likewise a release from eternity. "These are some of the Days of God," one of Bilāl's friends wrote. "Thank God we could see them." As proclaimed twice in the Quran, the "Days of God" (*ayyām allāh*) are a reminder of the vagaries of creational existence "contrasted with the eternality of God."[2] In the first verse, the phrase may refer to the divine deliverance from Pharaoh: *We indeed sent Moses with Our signs, "Bring thy people out of darkness into light, and remind them of the Days of God. Truly in that are signs for all who are patient, thankful"* (Q. 14:5). In the second verse, the phrase may refer to God's reward and punishment, and thus the passing-away of all creation: *Tell those who believe to forgive those who hope not for the Days of God, that He may requite a people for what which they used to earn* (Q. 45:14). The end of the endless regime was thus a reminder of God's eternity, whose favors and inflictions cannot be accounted for within this life. The fall of the regime as the "end of eternity" recalled the Quranic dictum that everything perishes except the face of God (*kullu shay'in hālikun illā wajhah*) (Q. 28:88). Is this a revolutionary slogan? Yes and no; but in Assad's Syria, it delivered one to a charnel-house.

Bilāl wrote, in summary of the years since the revolution:

Friday March 18, 2011

Friday December 6, 2024

revolution—blood—martyrs—detainees—wounded—disappeared—barrel-bombing—torture—flight—assassination—destruction—widowed—orphaned—sacrificed—jihad—displaced—betrayals—tears of sorrow—faithful fighters who make us proud

difficult stages (*marāḥil ṣaʿba*)

and today, tears of joy

Truly We shall help Our messengers and those who believe during the life of this world and on the Day when the witnesses arise, the Day when the excuses of the wrongdoers will not benefit them, and theirs will be the curse, and theirs will be the evil abode. (Q. 40:51-52)

blessed, blessed, blessed are those who have not been tainted by treachery, betrayal, theft, or exploitation. A difficult test lasting fourteen years

o God, mercy upon the martyrs, heal the wounded, return the distant, and deliver the disappeared; replace our sorrows with joys, O Lord

God grants relief, my interlocutors had repeated over the years of their abandonment, displacement, and exile; but what that means is radically open.[3] It was a time of unfamiliar affects, of transformation, of mourning, and of joys mixed with deep sorrow: as it already had been. For we are all returning to God, whether we will it or not. The position of the dread Heights.

—February 2025

ACKNOWLEDGMENTS

I moved to Damascus twenty-one years ago. I was there for one year: to study Arabic grammar and poetry, to fix my Quran recitation, to attend hadith classes and read theology. I remember the sunrise off Mount Qasyoun and the cool flagstones of my neighborhood mosque. I remember the shopkeepers playing Fairouz in the mornings and the smell of jasmine on the air in the evenings. And I remember the scrutiny of the secret police.

This book was written in solidarity with my Syrian friends and teachers. They are not named in these acknowledgments; nor are my displaced interlocutors, who are given pseudonyms in the text. Even so, they have my full gratitude. Only once I started fieldwork did I realize just how much anthropology as a discipline relies on the grace of strangers—on their patience and the possibility of trust. I hope to have kept that trust.

Saba Mahmood, Charles Hirschkind, Stefania Pandolfo, and Samera Esmeir placed their own kind of trust in me. I went to UC Berkeley at all (and was able to stay there through a family health crisis) due to the efforts of Saba Mahmood. Her commitment to me and my family and my work (even in her most skeptical moments) was sustaining: I miss her every day. Charles Hirschkind is still willing to work through a tangled idea or phrase: in repeating its terms back to me, he practices a generous listening. Stefania Pandolfo insists on the capacity of ethnography to hear the torment of existence: she lets me take this work seriously and pulls me back to it. And Samera Esmeir charts a course through the destruction of loss: other itineraries of land and sky, through her sensibility. I hope to have learned from them.

Discussions with Asad Q. Ahmed, Gil Anidjar, Ovamir Anjum, Judith Butler, Lawrence Cohen, Khaled Furani, Joan Wallach Scott, Jonathan

Sheehan, and Alexei Yurchak shaped the trajectory of my questions and of this text. Thank you. And the kindness of Talal Asad has been a consolation.

My conversations with Kevin Lewis O'Neill, Amira Mittermaier, and Ruth Marshall began at the University of Toronto and continue to be formative: about the practice of anthropology, the demands of imagination, and the politics of critique. And at the University of Alberta before that, my teachers Doug Aoki, Karyn Ball, Christopher Bracken, Andrew Gow, and Marie-Eve Morin introduced me to theoretical and methodological questions to which I still return. Now as I myself try to teach, I appreciate their pedagogy and patience all the more. At McMaster University, I thank especially Ellen Badone, Cal Biruk, Andy Roddick, and Yana Stainova for welcoming me to the department; Faculty 4 Palestine McMaster for solidarity across campus; and Marcia Furtado, Delia Hutchinson, Katie Miller, and John Silva for helping me settle in during the pandemic.

My friendships with Aaron Eldridge, Brent Eng, Ashwak Hauter, Donna Honarpisheh, Jean-Michel Landry, Candace Lukasik, Milad Odabaei, and Yasmina Raiani began at Berkeley. We have scattered since then—but I am honored to think with them, still alongside them, and to call them my peers. Aaron and Brent have long been my stalwart readers: I try not to take them for granted. Discussions with other friends have sustained me over these years: Michael Allan, Tanzeen Doha, Mayanthi Fernando, Rajbir Singh Judge, Zacharia al-Khatib, Harini Kumar, Katherine Lemons, Ali Altaf Mian, Rizwan Mohammad, Nermeen Mouftah, Nada Moumtaz, Junaid Quadri, Walaa Quisay, Jawad Qureshi, Muneeza Rizvi, China Sajadian, Noah Salomon, and the Being Human cohort: Constance Furey, Seçil Dağtaş, Gina Giliberti, C. Libby, Tyrone Palmer, David Maldonado Rivera, Matthew Smith, Yunus Telliel, Andrew Walker-Cornetta, and Tyler Zoanni. Rajbir and Yana have been my companions in navigating the institution of the university, which would have been so much more lonely without their fellowship.

A number of friends and colleagues invited me to present work from this project at their institutions, at a workshop, or on a conference panel. In addition to some named already, these include Joud Alkorani, Abbas Barzegar, Megan Bradley, J. Andrew Bush, Kirill Chepurin, Martijn de Koning, Yazan Doughan, Alex Dubilet, Anver Emon, Veronica Ferreri, David Henig, Cameron Hu, Aisha Ghani, Seema Golestaneh, M. Owais Khan, Setrag

Manoukian, Hannah McElginn, Anne-Marie McManus, Till Mostowlansky, Abdul Rahman Mustafa, Valentina Napolitano, Martin Nguyen, Arzoo Osanloo, Joshua Ralston, Cabeiri Robinson, Marika Rose, Christopher Sheklian, Anthony Paul Smith, Nathan Spannaus, and Winnifred Fallers Sullivan. I am grateful for their assistance and their feedback.

The research, travel, writing, and revision of various stages of this book were supported by a Social Sciences and Humanities Research Council fellowship and Insight Development Grant; a Wenner-Gren Foundation Fieldwork grant; two awards from Alberta Scholarships; grants from the UC Berkeley Center for the Study of Religion, Center for Canadian Studies, Center for Middle Eastern Studies, Department of Anthropology, Graduate Division, Institute for International Studies, Program in Critical Theory, and Townsend Center for the Humanities; and funding from the McMaster University Faculty of Social Sciences and Arts Research Board. To the adjudication committees of these funding bodies, thank you.

In Jordan, I am grateful for the friendship of Christopher Promberger, for some interviews facilitated by Ayat Nashwan, and for Reem el-Momany transcribing some of my Arabic-language interviews.

The series editors of Thinking from Elsewhere, Andrew Brandel, Clara Han, and Bhrigubati Singh, and the Fordham University Press editor, Thomas Lay, welcomed this project and supported its voice. They have made its publication a pleasure. Thanks also to Kem Crimmins and Aldene Fredenburg at the press for their editorial support. I am honored to have an image by Tammam Azzam grace the cover of this book. Aaron Eldridge, Lauren Charman, and two wonderful reviewers (Seema Golestaneh and Darryl Li) read through the manuscript: I am very grateful for their close readings, even (and especially) where I was not able to answer their questions. The lapses that remain are of course my own.

Our family life over these years was given shape, in Toronto, by Adnan Ali, Randy and Anna Boyagoda, Faiza Malik and Syed Ahmed Hussaini, and Youcef Soufi and Sadaf Ahmed; in Berkeley, by Javier Jauregui Lazo and Dominique Dhainaut-Medina, Emad El-Haraty and Zainab Abusbeaa, Shokoofeh Rajabzadeh and Mehdi Jamei, and Melina and Tony Salvador; in Edmonton, by Farooq Maseehuddin and Salwa Elladen, Kyle Robertson and Jane Wodlinger, Omar Yaqub and Azkaa Rahman, and Jairan Gahan; and in Hamilton, by Ian and Lyndsey Copeland, Yana Stainova, and Derek Woods, our neighbors, and Shams.

My parents-in-law, Tom deBeyer and Linda Rogers, and sister-in-law, Michaela, welcomed me more than fifteen years ago. More immediately, the Jordan-side fieldwork for this project (leaving my family for months at a time) could not have happened without their help. Thank you.

My parents, Muzaffar Iqbal and Elma Ruth Harder, planted the seeds of this labor—by sending me to Syria in 2004 but more generally by fostering my curiosity and by raising me with concern for these questions (about the capacities, modes, and limits of tradition), if not in these same terms. I hope they recognize something of its fruits, as too my sister, Noor (and Jed), and Usman.

My wife, Lara, and our children, Rawiya and Bashir, are my joy and have all my love. Her wit, humor, and beauty, and their deliberation and exuberance, bear me along. I thank God for them every day.

NOTES

INTRODUCTION: GOD GRANTS RELIEF

1. For example, see Nick Hopkins and Emma Beals, "How Assad Regime Controls UN's Aid Intended for Syria's Children," *Guardian*, August 29, 2016, https://www.theguardian.com/world/2016/aug/29/how-assad-regime-controls-un-aid-intended-for-syrias-children; Annie Sparrow, "How UN Humanitarian Aid Has Propped Up Assad," *Foreign Affairs*, September 20, 2018, https://www.foreignaffairs.com/articles/syria/2018-09-20/how-un-humanitarian-aid-has-propped-assad; and Carsten Wieland, *Syria and the Neutrality Trap: The Dilemmas of Delivering Humanitarian Aid through Violent Regimes* (London: Bloomsbury, 2021). To be sure, this field was complex: rather than "Western states exerting their hard power under the guise of humanitarian concern (as seen in the wars in Iraq or Libya), or trying to win hearts and minds through the delivery of humanitarian aid (as seen in Afghanistan and Iraq), humanitarian aid delivery in Syria became the battleground itself, the battleground on which the future for the Syrian state was fought"; *Everybody's War: The Politics of Aid in the Syria Crisis*, edited by Jehan Bseiso, Michiel Hofman, and Jonathan Whitall (New York: Oxford University Press, 2021), 11.

2. For a careful exploration of this prayer among Syrian asylum seekers in Jordan, see Hanna Berg, "Waste of Time Is Worse Than Death," *Comparative Studies of South Asia, Africa, and the Middle East* 45, no. 1 (May 2025): 105–20. As she writes, *faraj* (what I am translating as "relief") "does not signify a state or condition of waiting (whether in hope or anticipation) but rather the moment of divine release *from* such a condition" (116).

3. To be clear, the sense of "dread" intended here is not limited to an existentialist account of the relation between anxiety and sin nor a psychological term for extreme fear. Instead, it marks the ongoing apprehension of the struggle of creation as articulated in the Quranic figure of the Heights (God, grant relief!).

For an elaboration of the enigmatic and unsettling aspects of dread (but that, lacking an eschatological referent, refuses the possibility of lucidity), see David Theo Goldberg, *Dread: Facing Futureless Futures* (London: Polity Press, 2021), where "dread is awe absent the possibility of identifying the source, rendering reconciliation irrelevant and redress impossible. . . . Dread expresses the irresolvable tension between the apocalyptic (jihadi, evangelical) promise of afterlife tomorrow and the worldlessness of perpetual flight from global abandonment and ever-present death now" (209). By contrast, the sense of the "dread Heights" developed over this ethnography suggests both that Islamic apocalyptic fractures the present by calling into question the sufficiency of historical time and that "ecologies of care" (210)—for instance, as detailed in this book—are less the antidote to dread than asymmetrical to it. For a similar argument from another archive, see Basit Kareem Iqbal, "The Messiah and the Jurisconsult: Agamben on the Problem of Law in Sunni Islam," *Journal of Religion* 101, no. 3 (July 2021): 351–70.

4. Maurice Blanchot writes that "to live an event as an image" is "to be taken, to pass from the region of the real where we hold ourselves at a distance from things the better to order and use them into that other region where the distance holds us—the distance which then is the lifeless deep, an unmanageable, inappreciable remoteness which has become something like the sovereign power behind all things"; Blanchot, *The Space of Literature*, trans. Ann Smock (Lincoln: University of Nebraska Press, 1982), 261. Stefania Pandolfo quotes this passage to understand the "shift in the coordinates of the real" effected in the divine trial and in the Islamic practice of the remembrance of death (*dhikr al-mawt*), which produces "a temporality of the afterlife in the here and now of presence"; Pandolfo, *Knot of the Soul: Madness, Psychoanalysis, Islam* (Chicago: University of Chicago Press, 2018), 216, 226. I explore this "shift" convened through the heteronomy of the ordeal in Chapters 2 and 3. For anamorphosis, which Pandolfo calls a "revealing element" (*Knot of the Soul*, 134), see Jacques Lacan, *The Ethics of Psychoanalysis, 1959–1960: The Seminar of Jacques Lacan, Book VII*, trans. Dennis Porter, ed. Jacques-Alain Miller (New York: W. W. Norton, 1992): "By means of an optical transposition, a certain form that wasn't visible at first sight transforms itself into a readable image" (135); "it make[s] something emerge that is precisely there where one has lost one's bearings or, strictly speaking, nowhere" (136). For Lacan, what is of interest in anamorphosis (for example, as read in the unbearable splendor of Antigone) is the relation between surface and form: "What we seek in the illusion is something in which the illusion as such in some way transcends itself, destroys itself, by demonstrating that it is only there as a signifier" (136).

5. I refer to the Syrian "revolution" (rather than "civil war," "conflict," "crisis," or "revolt") alongside my displaced interlocutors, from whose courage and political clarity I continue to learn. Among the extensive anglophone literature on

the Syrian revolution, see the following key texts: Robin Yassin-Kassab and Leila al-Shami, *Burning Country: Syrians in Revolution and War* (London: Polity Press, 2016); Yassin al-Haj Saleh, *The Impossible Revolution: Making Sense of the Syrian Tragedy*, trans. Ibtihal Mahmood (Chicago: Haymarket Books, 2017); Salwa Ismail, *The Rule of Violence: Subjectivity, Memory, and Government in Syria* (Cambridge: Cambridge University Press, 2019); Sam Dagher, *Assad or We Burn the Country* (New York: Back Bay Books, 2019); Lisa Wedeen, *Authoritarian Apprehensions: Ideology, Judgment, and Mourning in Syria* (Chicago: University of Chicago Press, 2019); Yasser Munif, *The Syrian Revolution: Between the Politics of Life and the Geopolitics of Death* (London: Polity Press, 2020); and Charlotte al-Khalili, *Waiting for the Revolution to End: Syrian Displacement, Time, and Subjectivity* (London: UCL Press, 2023).

6. Sarah Hasselbarth, "Islamic Charities in the Syrian Context in Jordan and Lebanon" (Beirut: Friedrich-Ebert-Stiftung Foundation, 2014), 6.

7. UNHCR, "Gulf Donors and NGOs Assistance to Syrian Refugees in Jordan" (Amman: UNHCR Jordan, 2015), prepared by Myriam Ababsa and Mamoon Muhsen, http://data.unhcr.org/syrianrefugees/country.php?id=107; Myriam Ababsa, "Islamic NGOs Assistance to Syrian Refugees in Jordan and Gulf Donors Support," *Lajeh: Conflits et migrations*, January 21, 2017, https://lajeh.hypotheses.org/723.

8. Hasselbarth, "Islamic Charities in the Syrian Context," 6. The report offers three conclusions: (1) that Islamic charities "not only fill a gap in humanitarian assistance, but they also function as a parallel system to the UN-coordinated international intervention"—a parallel system whose informality and relative unprofessionalism are both to its effective advantage (in terms of reach) and disadvantage (in terms of scale); (2) that some of these charities are "connected to a huge network of political or religious groups whose ideas of human rights are incompatible"—but that suspicions around this may be addressed through increased transparency and greater international engagement; and (3) that religious and social conservatism does not necessarily lead to violations of human rights (ibid., 40–42). It recommends greater engagement, cooperation, and trust where possible and redoubled efforts to replace the services of those charities with whom coordination is impossible (43). "Neither the international community nor the Islamic charities can afford to fight this crisis on their own" (44). For more on the conceptual translations involved when considering Muslims in these intersecting fields, see "Centering Muslims in Global Humanitarianism and Development," a special issue of *Muslim World* 112, no. 1 (Winter 2022), edited by Nermeen Mouftah and Abbas Barzegar.

9. See Shauna Labman, *Crossing Law's Border: Canada's Refugee Resettlement Program* (Vancouver: University of British Columbia Press, 2019); Shauna Labman and Geoffrey Cameron, eds., *Strangers to Neighbours: Refugee Sponsorship in Context* (Montreal and Kingston: McGill-Queen's University Press, 2020).

10. Cf. Audrey Macklin et al., "A Preliminary Investigation into Private Refugee Sponsors," *Canadian Ethnic Studies* 50, no. 2 (2018): 35–57; and Geoffrey Cameron, *Send Them Here: Religion, Politics, and Refugee Resettlement in North America* (Montreal and Kingston: McGill-Queen's University Press, 2021).

11. Cf. Vappu Tyyskä et al., "The Syrian Refugee Crisis in Canadian Media" (Toronto: Ryerson Centre for Immigration and Settlement, 2017).

12. For a thorough account of Canada's Syrian refugee resettlement program, see Leah K. Hamilton, Luisa Veronis, and Margaret Walton-Roberts, eds., *A National Project: Syrian Refugee Resettlement in Canada* (Montreal & Kingston: McGill-Queen's University Press, 2020). For the details from Statistics Canada, see https://www150.statcan.gc.ca/n1/pub/75-006-x/2019001/article/00001-eng.htm and https://www150.statcan.gc.ca/n1/daily-quotidien/221026/dq221026a-eng.htm.

13. Nor, of course, is this limited to Islam. Christianity has always been central to refugee sponsorship in Canada, even aside from how Trudeau's Liberals abandoned the Conservative policy of prioritizing Christian refugees. On some of the politics this raises, see Paul Bramadat, "Don't Ask, Don't Tell: Refugee Settlement and Religion in British Columbia," *Journal of the American Academy of Religion* 82, no. 4 (December 2014): 907–37. This has resulted in the construction of a particular discursive framework within which refugees are today understood in Canada, a grid of intelligibility whose lines of figuration are difficult for them to escape. The church-based refugee support programs sometimes model their notion of Islam on Christian religion, while other times (invoking the Christian trope of providing hospitality to foreigners in the night) playing up the religious difference of these strangers. One unintended consequence of this development is thus to formalize the role of religion among Syrian refugees coming to Canada. See Lori G. Beaman, Jennifer A. Selby, and Amélie Barras, "No Mosque, No Refugees: Some Reflections on Syrian Refugees and the Construction of Religion in Canada," in *The Refugee Crisis and Religion: Secularism, Security, and Hospitality in Question*, ed. Luca Mavelli and Erin K. Mavelli (London: Rowman & Littlefield, 2017), 77–95; and Mary-Lee Mulholland, "Welcoming the Stranger in Alberta: Newcomers, Secularism and Religiously Affiliated Settlement Agencies," *Canadian Ethnic Studies* 49, no. 1 (2017): 19–42. The Syrian refugee settlement process thus also allows for revisiting the terms of Canadian secularism and Muslim life in Canada, on which more broadly see Anna C. Korteweg and Jennifer A. Selby, eds., *Debating Sharia: Islam, Gender Politics and Family Law Arbitration* (Toronto: University of Toronto Press, 2012); Jennifer A. Selby, Amélie Barras, and Lori G. Beaman, *Beyond Accommodation: Everyday Narratives of Muslim Canadians* (Vancouver: University of British Columbia Press, 2018), chap. 3; and Youcef Soufi, *Homegrown Radicals: A Story of State Violence, Islamophobia, and Jihad in the Post-9/11 World* (New York: New York University Press, 2025), chap. 2.

14. Miriam Ticktin, "Transnational Humanitarianism," *Annual Review of Anthropology* 43 (2014): 275.

15. Trouillot critiques the pervasive "empiricist epistemology" that "equated the object of observation with the object of study"; Michel-Rolph Trouillot, "Making Sense: The Fields in Which We Work," in *Global Transformations: Anthropology and the Modern World* (New York: Palgrave MacMillan, 2003), 122. He insists instead that "localization is part of the process through which I construct my 'field,' it is part of the construction of the object of observation as it relates to the object of study" (128).

16. Andrew Brandel and Marco Motta, eds., *Living with Concepts: Anthropology in the Grip of Reality* (New York: Fordham University Press, 2021). I return to this methodological distinction in Chapter 2. For a detailed elaboration of the complexities of a "grammatical" method, see Talal Asad, "Thinking about Religion through Wittgenstein," *Critical Times: Interventions in Global Critical Theory* 3, no. 3 (December 2020): 403–42.

17. To be sure, I do trace various relations to the revolution over the course of this book. As Charlotte al-Khalili writes, "Revolutionary transformations" should be distinguished from the victory or defeat of historical revolutions. Based on fieldwork in Gaziantep, she powerfully shows how the Syrian revolution "engendered" both "ruptures (intended changes) and disruptions (unexpected shifts) . . . within the self, in the intimate sphere of the home, in Syrians' everyday lives, social relations, and sense of time, and in their experience of Islamic cosmology"; al-Khalili, *Waiting for the Revolution to End*, 4.

18. Basit Kareem Iqbal and Talal Asad, "Thinking About Method: A Conversation with Talal Asad," *qui parle* 26, no. 1 (June 2017): 197, 199.

19. Talal Asad, *Secular Translations: Nation-State, Modern Self, and Calculative Reason* (New York: Columbia University Press, 2018), 93.

20. Saba Mahmood, *Politics of Piety: The Islamic Revival and the Feminist Subject* (Princeton: Princeton University Press, 2005), 180 and 180n23. She then quotes philosopher Ian Hacking: "A concept is nothing other than a word in its sites. That means attending to a variety of types of sites: the sentences in which the word is actually (not potentially) used, those who speak those sentences, with what authority, in what institutional settings, in order to influence whom, with what consequences for the speakers."

21. This formulation and others in this introduction owe to helpful comments by Charles Hirschkind, Clara Han, and Ali Altaf Mian.

22. See, respectively, Katherine P. Ewing, "Dreams from a Saint: Anthropological Atheism and the Temptation to Believe," *American Anthropologist* 96, no. 3 (1994): 571–83; Jione Havea et al., "Dialogues: Anthropology and Theology," *Journal of the Royal Anthropological Institute* 28, no. 1 (March 2022): 297–347; and Amira Mittermaier, "Beyond the Human Horizon," *Religion and Society* 12 (2021): 21–38.

23. See Khaled Furani, *Redeeming Anthropology: A Theological Critique of a Modern Science* (Oxford: Oxford University Press, 2019); Khaled Furani and Joel Robbins, eds., *Religion* 51, no. 4 (2021): "Anthropology Within and Without the Secular Condition."

24. Asad, *Secular Translations*, 148.

25. See Alasdair MacIntyre, *Whose Justice? Which Rationality?* (Notre Dame, Ind.: Notre Dame University Press, 1988), 12; and for the methodological antihistoricism entailed by this approach, see Basit Kareem Iqbal, "Asad and Benjamin: Chronopolitics of Tragedy in the Anthropology of Secularism," *Anthropological Theory* 20, no. 1 (2020): 77–96. Asad comments that MacIntyre's insistence on the "tradition-constituted position" necessary for moral action does not account for the "multiplicity of times" encountered within the space of tradition; nor "*how* we come to argue for or against a particular position from within a tradition"; nor how the disciplined self is also "compelled from inside—passionately, precisely because not in a rationally calculative way"; nor the necessarily embodied practices of historical argument and sensibility. See Asad's response to David Scott and his long interview in *Powers of the Secular Modern: Talal Asad and His Interlocutors*, ed. David Scott and Charles Hirschkind (Stanford: Stanford University Press, 2006), at 234–35 and 286–90.

26. Gil Anidjar reads Jacques Derrida's "Signature Event Context":

> The argument here is therefore not to void the text of all social meaning, nor to argue that texts simply exist "outside" of a context. Rather, it is to interrogate not only the passage (the translation) from inside to outside [as a text traverses contexts], but the very terms of that polarity, and to observe that a text cannot only "break with every given context" but can also "engender infinitely new contexts in an absolutely nonsaturable fashion." In that sense, the particular text we are reading can be seen as taking place as a "social" event, as already "having" a social dimension (there is a social scene of reading, one which we are also trying to read), while also exceeding or resisting ("breaking" with) that dimension or meaning, and thus enabling "an effective intervention in the constituted historic field," a field which is also one of nondiscursive forces ("un champ de forces non-discursives").

Gil Anidjar, *"Our Place in al-Andalus": Kabbalah, Philosophy, Literature in Arab Jewish Letters* (Stanford: Stanford University Press, 2002), 34. In somewhat distinct terms, focusing not on the iterative force of citation (breaking with context) but on its dynamism (citation renewing the force of the original text), Edward Said's 1994 "Traveling Theory Reconsidered" reprises his argument, made twelve years earlier, that the political traction of insurrectionary theories is deflated and diffused as they move outside their original context. Rather, he writes that the radical projects to which Adorno and Fanon variously put Lukács's subject-object dialectic (against the domestication of Lukács outside the immediate context of revolutionary struggle in Hungary) shows "the possibility of actively different locales, sites, situations for theory"; Edward W. Said, "Traveling Theory Reconsidered," in *Reflections on Exile and Other Essays* (Cambridge, Mass.: Harvard University Press, 2000), 452. Whether in Derrida's terms or Said's, "citational acts can open up new social horizons of possibility, signification, and performative power"; Constantine V. Nakassis, "Citation and Citationality," *Signs and Society* 1, no. 1 (Spring 2013): 51–77.

27. Asad, "Thinking about Religion through Wittgenstein," 415. To be clear, the temporality of this expression is not exclusively the time of history or society. Meanwhile, the "circumstances" of reasoning "are unevenly and contingently bound together. . . . To be plausible an argument must therefore resonate with different elements in the network, with the same word used differently, and possibly ambiguously, in ordinary life" (416).

28. As Trouillot observes, "A multisited ethnography is quite reconcilable with an empiricist epistemology if it constructs the object of study as a mere multiplication of the places observed"; "Making Sense," 126.

29. Stefan Helmreich, "Induction, Deduction, Abduction, and the Logics of Race and Kinship," *American Ethnologist* 34, no. 2 (2007): 231, for "abduction" (recalling C. S. Peirce) as "the operations of hope, desire, violence, and the unexpected."

30. Pandolfo, *Knot of the Soul*, 174.

31. Yassin al-Haj Saleh, "Syria's Catastrophe upon Catastrophe," *DAWN*, March 8, 2023, https://dawnmena.org/syrias-catastrophe-upon-catastrophe/.

32. Voltaire's excoriations of the providential order, especially his acerbic 1756 "Poème sur le désastre de Lisbonne," provide the most prominent instance of such movement. For example, Gilles Deleuze in his Leibniz lectures declared that *Candide* shows that "the problem of good and evil cannot be posed as it was a century before. I believe this is the end of the blessed and the damned. . . . After 1755, the problem will be posed differently"; cited in Marie-Hélène Huet, *The Culture of Disaster* (Chicago: University of Chicago Press, 2012), 49. See also Gene Ray, "Reading the Lisbon Earthquake: Adorno, Lyotard, and the Contemporary Sublime," *Yale Journal of Criticism* 17, no. 1 (Spring 2004): 1–18.

33. Huet, *Culture of Disaster*, 7.

34. Didier Fassin, "The Predicament of Humanitarianism," *qui parle* 22, no. 1 (Fall/Winter 2013): 35. Sharon Sliwinski writes that copper engravings of ruined Lisbon were part of "the first modern mass media events in which subjects throughout Europe became spectators to a distant catastrophe. [These representations] helped inaugurate a secular notion of human suffering as well as thoughts about its prevention"; Sliwinski, "The Aesthetics of Human Rights," *Culture, Theory & Critique* 50, no. 1 (2009): 23–39.

35. On sympathy, see Eric Hayot, *The Hypothetical Mandarin: Sympathy, Modernity, and Chinese Pain* (New York: Oxford University Press, 2009), especially the introduction and chapter 2. Luc Boltanski importantly develops the "question of the spectator" into distinct political possibilities, generically divided into three rhetorical "topics" (denunciation, sentiment, aesthetics) through which speech about suffering might articulate a commitment to political action that does not immediately fold into a crisis of pity; Boltanski, *Distant Suffering: Morality, Media, and Politics*, trans. Graham Burchell (Cambridge: Cambridge University Press, 1999).

36. Charles Taylor, *Sources of the Self: The Making of the Modern Identity* (Cambridge, Mass.: Harvard University Press, 1989), 394. In Taylor's intellectual history, the scale and intensity of modern horrors only affirm the singularity (however fragile) of these ideas and ideals.

37. Michael Barnett and Thomas G. Weiss, "Humanitarianism: A Brief History of the Present," in *Humanitarianism in Question: Politics, Power, Ethics*, ed. Michael Barnett and Thomas G. Weiss (Ithaca: Cornell University Press, 2008), 7.

38. Ibid., 19–20. Peter Redfield and Erica Bornstein write that "in temporal terms this secular, contemporary strand of humanitarianism remains inherently presentist; the lives and welfare of those now living fundamentally matter and cannot be conscionably sacrificed in the pursuit of other goals"; Redfield and Bornstein, "An Introduction to the Anthropology of Humanitarianism," in Bornstein and Redfield, eds., *Forces of Compassion: Humanitarianism Between Ethics and Politics* (Santa Fe: SAR Press, 2011), 6. Yet a declarative commitment to "present lives" only mires modern humanitarianism in the sacrificial logic it disavows: see Redfield, "Sacrifice, Triage, and Global Humanitarianism," in Barnett and Weiss, *Humanitarianism in Question*, 196–214; and Didier Fassin, "Inequality of Lives, Hierarchies of Humanity: Moral Commitments and Ethical Dilemmas of Humanitarianism," in *In the Name of Humanity: The Government of Threat and Care*, ed. Ilana Feldman and Miriam Ticktin (Durham, N.C.: Duke University Press, 2010), 238–55. For "legitimacy" as the fundamental problem of a modernity anxiously demanding a self-sufficient present whose "necessity" is independent of its (Christian) history, see Hans Blumenberg, *The Legitimacy of the Modern Age*, 2nd ed., trans. Robert M. Wallace (Cambridge, Mass.: MIT Press, 1983).

39. The career of humanitarianism over the next century and a half is supposed to have moved from a concern with individual suffering (sentimental ethics) to a more sustained involvement with its causes (humanitarian politics). Michael Barnett complicates this narrative arc, arguing that the tensions of modern humanitarianism are constitutive: the relation between universality and particularity, or emancipation and domination, or an irreducible plurality cannot be transcended through a dialectic, nor can they be accommodated between a

pure ideal and compromised reality. Instead, a "double hologram" might be a more appropriate metaphor: "Tilt the picture one way and some parts become prominent and others fade; tilt the other way and there is a reversal"; Barnett, *Empire of Humanity: A History of Humanitarianism* (Ithaca: Cornell University Press, 2011), 8. Barnett recognizes three broad periods of humanitarianism (imperial, neo-humanitarian, and liberal) over the past two centuries, each distinguished by its "constellation of the forces of destruction, production, and compassion" (1).

40. Barnett, *Empire of Humanity*, 21.

41. For another historical "crucible" alongside Lisbon and Solferino, see Keith David Watenpaugh's *Bread from Stones: The Middle East and the Making of Modern Humanitarianism* (Berkeley: University of California Press, 2015), which presents a series of case studies from the interwar Eastern Mediterranean to argue that the Armenian genocide was a critical experience for the troubled formation of modern humanitarianism. For Watenpaugh, humanitarianism is not the extension of compassion to a generic stranger, but helping those "found to be knowable, similar, and deserving" (19)—a distinction borne out through the historical abandonment of Armenian orphans.

42. Barnett, *Empire of Humanity*, 18, 237. Bourgeois revolutions are specifically defined by faith in inevitable moral progress. On the procedures of their partition and disavowal, see Reinhart Koselleck, *Critique and Crisis: Enlightenment and the Pathogenesis of Modern Society* (1959; repr. Cambridge, Mass.: MIT Press, 1988).

43. Didier Fassin, *Humanitarian Reason: A Moral History of the Present*, trans. Rachel Gomme (Berkeley: University of California Press, 2012), 244.

44. Ibid., 247.

45. To be clear, Fassin's critique only reiterates the story that Enlightenment tells about itself, for colonial law requires these distinctions in its production of "the human." See Samera Esmeir, *Juridical Humanity: A Colonial History* (Stanford: Stanford University Press, 2012), 285: "By inscribing the human in its legalities, the law necessitated its own existence and bonded the human to the modern state. The result was the making of juridical humanity—a technology of colonial rule and a modern relationship of bondage. Inscribed in the text of the law, the juridical human had no place to flee. The threat of dehumanization came into being."

46. Fassin, *Humanitarian Reason*, 251, 252.

47. As Robert Meister explains, humanitarian intervention works to "repudiate *past* violence (which always appears as something cyclical and uncontained) by endorsing exceptional violence—that of rescue and occupation." More broadly, humanitarian compassion "*calls* the beneficiary [of historical injustice] a bystander in order to *re*call him as a witness who will *no longer* look away from

those who still suffer. The new, affective bond to be created between them is made possible by an act of memory that makes compassion in the present *discontinuous* with the past." The consequence of both operations is to generate a future affirmation of the present as self-sufficient; see Meister, *After Evil: A Politics of Human Rights* (New York: Columbia University Press, 2011), ix, 230.

48. Fassin, *Humanitarian Reason*, 254, citing Emmanuel Levinas. But even for Levinas the possibility of encountering the face of the other only opens onto the problem of the third and so a necessarily fraught ethical-political scene; see also Meister, *After Evil*, chaps. 4 and 5.

49. Talal Asad, "Reflections on Violence, Law, and Humanitarianism," *Critical Inquiry* 41, no. 2 (Winter 2015): 401–2.

50. See the special issue of the *Journal of Refugee Studies* 24, no. 3 (2011) on this topic, especially Alastair Ager and Joey Ager, "Faith and the Discourse of Secular Humanitarianism," 456–72; Elizabeth Ferris, "Faith and Humanitarianism: It's Complicated," 606–25; and Olivia Wilkinson, *Secular and Religious Dynamics in Humanitarian Response* (London: Routledge, 2019).

51. Moreover, the entanglement of humanitarian and charitable projects demands specific attention to commensuration and conceptual translation across varying formations (e.g., through distinct orientations toward time, hierarchy, motivation, suffering, scale, agency, and more): China Scherz, *Having People, Having Heart: Charity, Sustainable Development, and Problems of Dependence in Central Uganda* (Chicago: University of Chicago Press, 2014), 5. Scherz opens the space for various charitable projects to be seen as alternative forms of ethical practice in their own right. Likewise, Erica Bornstein insists that development, charity, and humanitarianism be seen together as "part of a larger universe of giving marked by notions of global citizenship, relations of social obligation that entail rights and entitlements, and sacred conceptions of religious donation"; Bornstein, *Disquieting Gifts: Humanitarianism in New Delhi* (Stanford: Stanford University Press, 2012), 12.

52. As Pandolfo writes, "The unbearable remains. It can never be overcome." Her interlocutor reminds her that two different modalities of melancholy—one expanding, one constricting; one opening to others, the other choking the soul—are always contiguous. "What does it mean to not forget that risk?"; Pandolfo, *Knot of the Soul*, 330.

53. Saba Mahmood, "Humanism," *HAU: Journal of Ethnographic Theory* 8, nos. 1–2 (2018): 2.

54. For an edited volume that seeks to offer such a simultaneously analytic and constructive account of contemporary displacement, see Ray Jureidini and Said Fares Hassan, eds., *Migration and Islamic Ethics: Issues of Residence, Naturalization and Citizenship* (Leiden: Brill, 2020).

1. REFUGE

1. Myriam Ababsa, "De la crise humanitaire à la crise sécuritaire: Les dispositifs de contrôle des réfugiés syriens en Jordanie (2011–2015)," *Revue européenne des migrations internationales* [online] 31, nos. 3–4 (2015), http://journals.openedition.org/remi/7380. For the charitable work of the Jam'iyyat, see also Sturla Godø Saether, "Humanitarian Salafism: A Contradiction in Terms?" (MA thesis, University of Oslo, 2013); Hanna Röth, Zina Nimeh, and Jessica Hagen-Zanker, "A Mapping of Social Protection and Humanitarian Assistance Programmes in Jordan: What Support Are Refugees Eligible For?" Working Paper 501, Overseas Development Institute (London: ODI, 2017); UNHCR, "Gulf Donors and NGOs Assistance to Syrian Refugees in Jordan" (UNHCR: The UN Refugee Agency, 2014); Olivia Wilkinson and Joey Ager, "Scoping Study on Local Faith Communities in Urban Displacement: Evidence on Localisation and Urbanisation" (London: Refugees & Forced Migration Learning Hub, University College London, 2017); Myriam Ababsa, "Islamic NGOs Assistance to Syrian Refugees in Jordan and Gulf Donors Support," *Lajeh: Migrations et Conflits au Moyen-orient*, January 21, 2017, https://lajeh.hypotheses.org/723.

2. Basit Kareem Iqbal and Talal Asad, "Thinking about Method: A Conversation with Talal Asad," *qui parle* 26, no. 1 (2017): 200.

3. Edward William Lane, *Arabic-English Lexicon* (London: Williams & Norgate, 1863), 90.

4. Cf. Frederick Denny, "The Meaning of Ummah in the Qur'an," *History of Religions* 15, no. 1 (August 1975): 34–70.

5. Taken together, the "distributed authority" and universal mission of the Community (even as granted in the Quran) yield a dynamic vision that, Ovamir Anjum writes, (1) makes the *umma*, the community of all the believers, the "recipient of the Prophet's mission to humankind"; (2) "requires rendering qualified obedience to authorities from among themselves"; (3) "requires *shūrā*, the practice of participation and consultation in collective affairs"; (4) "considers the Community's collective affairs in need of rational human management"; and (5) "considers the caliph answerable to those he rules, the Community"; Ovamir Anjum, *Politics, Law, and Community in Islamic Thought: The Taymiyyan Moment* (Cambridge: Cambridge University Press, 2012), 61–62.

6. Ibid., 133.

7. James Piscatori and Amin Saikal, *Islam Beyond Borders: The Umma in World Politics* (Cambridge: Cambridge University Press, 2019), 1. See also James Piscatori, ed., "Conceptualising the Umma," a special issue of *Muslim World* 109, no. 3 (July 2019).

8. Mohammad Fadel, "International Law, Regional Developments: Islam," in *Max Planck Encyclopedia of Public International Law* (Oxford: Oxford University Press, 2010).

9. Samera Esmeir, "On Becoming Less of the World," *History of the Present* 8, no. 1 (Spring 2018): 88–116; Majid Khadduri, "Islam and the Modern Law of Nations," *American Journal of International Law* 50, no. 2 (1956): 358–72; Khadduri, "The Impact of International Law upon the Islamic World Order," *American Journal of International Law* 66, no. 4 (September 1972): 46–50.

10. Cemil Aydın, "Globalizing the Intellectual History of the Idea of the 'Muslim World,'" in *Global Intellectual History*, ed. Samuel Moyn and Andrew Sartori (New York: Columbia University Press, 2013), 159–86. He argues that it was only after late eighteenth-century reform-minded Ottoman elites sought to participate in the international order that a new Muslim world identity was promulgated, tied to the prestige of the Ottoman sultan ("caliph") as being just as civilized as any European monarch. Then came colonial fears of pan-Islamism and Muslim anticolonial solidarities, which together consolidated the new identity. See further Aydın, *The Idea of the Muslim World* (Cambridge, Mass.: Harvard University Press, 2017), 16, where he writes that prior to the nineteenth century, the notion of Muslim unity was "deterritorialized" ("it urged cross-tribal affiliation, shared legal practices, and a collective eschatological vision")—although his use of the term "deterritorialized" for the precolonial concept, as opposed to simply "nonterritorial," is perplexing. See Mona Hassan's review in the *American History Review* (October 2018): 1294, where she observes the metaleptic rhetoric of this argument: "It is anachronistic, for example, to focus on the specifically modern instruments of politics as evidence for the absence of antecedents to 'Muslim-world thinking' in the premodern era."

11. Aydın, *Idea of the Muslim World*, 26.

12. Faisal Devji, "Against Muslim Unity," *Aeon*, July 12, 2016, https://aeon.co/essays/the-idea-of-unifying-islam-is-a-recent-invention-and-a-bad-one.

13. Militants seek to implement the virtual *umma* in history, Roy writes, but they fight "not to protect a territory but to re-create a community. They are besieged in a fortress they do not inhabit. This empty fortress syndrome is related to the pathological function of their jihad"; Olivier Roy, *Globalized Islam: The Search for a New Ummah* (New York: Columbia University Press, 2004), 289.

14. See, for example, Frédéric Volpi, "Constructing the 'Ummah' in European Security: Between Exit, Voice and Loyalty," *Government and Opposition* 42, no. 3 (2007): 451–70. In contrast, for a more complex account of affective commitments to the *umma*, see Youcef Soufi, *Homegrown Radicals: A Story of State Violence, Islamophobia, and Jihad in the Post-9/11 World* (New York: New York University Press, 2025), chap. 2.

15. Cited in Malcolm H. Kerr, *Islamic Reform: The Political and Legal Theories of Muḥammad ʿAbduh and Rashīd Riḍā* (Berkeley: University of California Press, 1966), 160. Malcolm Kerr comments, "It is not the selection of a candidate that concludes the contract of the Imamate in a constitutive sense, but the ratification of the selection by the [representatives of the] Community." The identity of these representatives is not specified, and Kerr spells out some of the ambiguities this raises.

16. Cited in Kerr, *Islamic Reform*, 164. But see, on the ambiguity of these terms (for in the nineteenth century *umma* also acquired its meaning of "nation"): Florian Zemmin, "Modernity without Society? Observations on the term *mujtamaʿ* in the Islamic Journal *al-Manār* (Cairo, 1898–1940)," *Die Welt des Islams* 56, no. 2 (2016): 223–47.

17. Andrew F. March, *The Caliphate of Man: Popular Sovereignty in Modern Islamic Thought* (Cambridge, Mass.: Harvard University Press, 2019), 59.

18. Aydın, *Idea of the Muslim World*, 71, 100: these themes, he writes, "still shape much of transnational Muslim thought" despite their having outlasted "pan-Islamism's originally symbiotic relationship with the British Empire."

19. Talal Asad, *Formations of the Secular: Christianity, Islam, Modernity* (Stanford: Stanford University Press, 2003), 197.

20. Jérôme Bellion-Jourdan, "Helping the 'Brothers': The Medic, the Militant, and the Fighter," in *The Charitable Crescent*, ed. Jonathan Benthall and Jérôme Bellion-Jourdan (New York: I.B. Tauris, 2003), 69–84.

21. Devji remarks the humanitarian logic adopted by modern Muslim militants, by which the *umma* has come to signify a synchronous body of victims (instead of a transhistorical community of believers). Though once "Christianity" and "humanity" were synonymous, he points to the irony by which the *umma* today is exchangeable with humanity ("claiming the status of global victim, the purity of whose suffering serves as an equivalent of its pure humanity": Devji, "The Terrorist as Humanitarian," *Social Analysis* 53, no. 1 [Spring 2009]: 176). He cites Arendt suggesting that "'the terror of the idea of humanity' resides in the universal responsibility it implies," and argues that militant practices are motivated by the same infrastructure as humanitarianism: each works to embody virtues of courage and sacrifice, thereby redeeming humanity from its division into physical and juridical bodies. Devji's insightful account of how globalized political conditions shape humanitarianism and militancy raises important questions about contemporary *umma* politics. I am not convinced, however, that spatial (synchronous) and temporal (transhistorical) logics of community can be so neatly disarticulated—not least because the hadith about the aching body of the believers already implies a fellow-feeling that cannot be attributed to modern global politics.

22. Tahir Zaman, *Islamic Traditions of Refuge in the Crises of Iraq and Syria* (London: Palgrave Macmillan, 2016), 151. His interlocutors' "position taking" is

done "in relation not only to one another and other material actors but also with their relationship to God in mind." He concludes that "the diffuse solidarity offered through a perceived sense of belonging to the *ummah* or the imagined community of Muslims creates intersections among diasporic and religious actors providing them with the broad canvass of a global imaginary from which to work" (187).

23. Yaḥyā bin Sharaf al-Nawawī, *al-Minhāj sharḥ ṣaḥīḥ muslim bin al-ḥajjāj*, 2nd ed. (Beirut: Dār Iḥyā' Turāth al-'Arabī, 1972), 16:139–40, §2586.

24. Maurice Blanchot, *The Space of Literature*, trans. Ann Smock (Lincoln: University of Nebraska Press, 1982), 135.

25. Marie Juul Petersen, *For Humanity or for the Umma? Aid and Islam in Transnational Muslim NGOs* (London: Hurst, 2015), 163. Petersen does address an aspect of social use when she concludes that, although this secularized culture is contested within those very organizations, it remains an effective means for Muslim NGOs, under countervailing pressures from donors and partners, to maintain simultaneous commitments to secular development and Islamic charity.

26. Abbas Barzegar has attended to how novel configurations of Muslim humanitarianism integrate secular and Islamic humanisms toward what he calls an "emergent, but stable tradition"; Barzegar, "The Living *Fiqh*, or Practical Theology, of Muslim Humanitarianism," in *Migration and Islamic Ethics: Issues of Residence, Naturalization, and Citizenship*, ed. Ray Jureidini and Said Fares Hassan (Leiden: Brill, 2020), 36.

27. Asad, *Formations of the Secular*, 220.

28. Ibid., 256, emphasis added.

29. Iqbal and Asad, "Thinking about Method," 200.

30. "Enjoining good and forbidding evil" is a keystone of Islamic ethics and moral doctrine, based in Quranic injunctions and variously taken up in social practice. For a thorough historical account of the concept, see Michael Cook, *Commanding Right and Forbidding Wrong in Islamic Thought* (Cambridge: Cambridge University Press, 2000); for a political-anthropological exploration of its contemporary traction following the 2011 uprising and 2013 coup in Egypt, see Talal Asad, "Thinking About Tradition, Religion, and Politics in Egypt Today," *Critical Inquiry* 42, no. 1 (Autumn 2015): 179–81. Its rendering as "civic action," as in the presentation under discussion, demonstrates an inventive political vocabulary that moves indifferently across religious and secular forms of social practice.

31. An emphasis on *fiṭra* is key to contemporary Islamic theology. See variously Frank Griffel, "The Harmony of Natural Law and Shari'a in Islamist Theology," in *Shari'a: Islamic Law in the Contemporary Context*, ed. Abbas Amanat and Frank Griffel (Stanford: Stanford University Press, 2007), 38–61; Andrew F. March, "Naturalizing Sharī'a: Foundationalist Ambiguities in Modern Islamic Apologetics," *Islamic Law and Society* 22, nos. 1–2 (2015): 45–81; Yasmin Moll, "Television Is Not

Radio: Theologies of Mediation in the Egyptian Islamic Revival," *Cultural Anthropology* 33, no. 2 (2018): 233–65; Umar F. Abd-Allah, *al-Īmānu fiṭra: dirāsat li-l-īmān al-fiṭrī fī-l-qur'ān wa-l-sunna wa kathīr min al-milal wa-l-niḥal* (Abu Dhabi: Dār al-Faqīh, 2014).

32. A connection between Islamic humanism and Islamic humanitarianism unites the two parts of Jonathan Benthall's anthology: *Islamic Charities and Islamic Humanism in Troubled Times* (Manchester: Manchester University Press, 2016).

33. Although Marcell Mauss described the "gift" as dyadic, Amira Mittermaier writes, "When we keep God in the picture, we must think of the gift as triadic"; Mittermaier, *Giving to God: Islamic Charity in Revolutionary Times* (Oakland: University of California Press, 2019), 8.

34. Charles Hirschkind, *The Ethical Soundscape: Cassette Sermons and Islamic Counterpublics* (New York: Columbia University Press, 2006), 107.

35. Ibid., 115.

36. Dipesh Chakrabarty, *Provincializing Europe: Postcolonial Thought and Historical Difference*, new ed. (2000; repr. Princeton: Princeton University Press, 2008), 71.

37. Darryl Li offers a compelling methodological account of how to anthropologically approach the practice of universalism as a "structure of aspirations," involving a specific "idiom," "horizon of belonging," "mechanisms" to process difference, a "theory of authority," and "institutional formation"; Li, *The Universal Enemy: Jihad, Empire, and the Challenge of Solidarity* (Stanford: Stanford University Press, 2020), 11–15.

38. Read in terms of anthropological discussions of in/commensuration, Shaykh Zāyid can be seen to here offer a kind of ethical "practice upon borders," negotiating affinities while maintaining difference: J. Mair and N. H. A. Evans, "Ethics across Borders: Incommensurability and Affinity," *HAU: Journal of Ethnographic Theory* 5, no. 2 (2015): 215. A more ambivalent (less optimistic) interpretation of Shaykh Zāyid's PowerPoint would read the differences between a regime of Islamic virtues and a regime of rights and values as being grammatical, not just semantic, and thus notices the rough improvisation of its equations. (Rendering *al-amr bi-l-ma'rūf wa-l-nahy 'an al-munkar* as "civic action" speaks to affinities across borders, to be sure, but—so a critic might add—also to the spiritual poverty of a secularized West unaware of the true temporal lineaments of moral action and of the ultimate ground of human authority and history.)

39. Chakrabarty, *Provincializing Europe*, 71. Addressing the methodological problem I am calling "entanglement," though in affective rather than discursive terms, Till Mostowlansky suggests that an affective compulsion can serve as a "link between different, sometimes contradictory humanitarian genealogies"; Mostowlansky, "Humanitarian Affect: Islam, Aid, and Emotional Impulse in Northern Pakistan," *History and Anthropology* 31, no. 2 (2020): 250.

40. Asad, *Formations of the Secular*, 85.

41. Among a large literature, see in particular Wendy S. Hesford, *Spectacular Rhetorics: Human Rights Visions, Recognitions, Feminisms* (Durham, N.C.: Duke University Press, 2011); Sharon Sliwinski, *Human Rights in Camera* (Chicago: University of Chicago Press, 2011); and Pooja Rangan, *Immediations: The Humanitarian Impulse in Documentary* (Durham, N.C.: Duke University Press, 2017).

42. Michael Kimmelman, "The Real Face of War? It May Be This Boy in a Pink Sweater," *New York Times*, March 3, 2018.

43. See Nicolas Guilhot, "The Anthropologist as Witness: Humanitarianism between Ethnography and Critique," *Humanity: An International Journal of Human Rights, Humanitarianism, and Development* 3, no. 1 (2012): 81–101. He concludes:

> The anthropologist seeks to be a witness who refuses the suspension of historical time involved in the idea of "emergency" and who reinscribes humanitarianism within a history that remains political. Yet once it is clear that humanitarianism's bid to transcend politics has failed and generated a humanitarian government whose instruments contribute to reproducing deep inequalities, the question is to decide whether the politics of humanity can be analyzed as the continuation of politics through other means, or whether the temptation to accuse humanitarianism of, alternatively, imperialism or depoliticization simply means that we have not yet developed the proper conceptual tools for analyzing politics once it is translated into biopower. (99)

44. Zāyid Ḥammād, "Ḥulūl li-l-qā'imīn 'alā barnāmij qalbī iṭma'inn li-satr al-muḥtāj," *al-Sā'a*, May 7, 2018, http://alsaa.net/article-85723.

45. Asad, *Formations of the Secular*, 91.

46. How can one learn to be obliged? One classic answer to this question comes in Ibn Ṭufayl's philosophical allegory Ḥayy ibn Yaqẓān, in which a boy raised on an island reasons toward knowledge of God and natural obligation; see Salman H. Bashier, *The Story of Islamic Philosophy: Ibn Tufayl, Ibn al-'Arabi, and Others on the Limit between Naturalism and Traditionalism* (Albany: State University of New York Press, 2012). For a strong relationship between obligation and moral community, see Alasdair MacIntyre, *After Virtue: A Study in Moral Theory*, 3rd ed. (Notre Dame, Ind.: University of Notre Dame Press, 2007), 250: "The notion of desert is at home only in the context of a community whose primary bond is a shared understanding both of the good for man and of the good of that community."

47. For the evocative phrase "making refuge" and a detailed analysis of its collective effort, see Catherine Besteman, *Making Refuge: Somali Bantu Refugees and Lewiston, Maine* (Durham, N.C.: Duke University Press, 2016).

48. See Jill Stauffer, *Ethical Loneliness: The Injustice of Not Being Heard* (New York: Columbia University Press, 2018).

THRESHOLD: NATALITY

1. See a published version in Aksam Alyousef, "Hagar," in *Looking Back, Moving Forward: Fiction, Poetry, Essays*, ed. Julie Robinson (Toronto: Mawenzi House).

2. Dave Breakenridge, "Fringe Review: Hagar," *Edmonton Journal*, August 17, 2019.

3. E.g., "Historical justice, even when it is practiced truly and with pure intentions, is a terrible virtue because it always undermines the living and brings it to ruin: its judging is always annihilating"; Friedrich Nietzsche, *On the Advantage and Disadvantage of History for Life*, trans. Peter Prauss (Indianapolis: Hackett, 1980), 38.

4. David Scott, *Omens of Adversity: Tragedy, Time, Memory, Justice* (Durham, N.C.: Duke University Press, 2014), 121.

5. Ibid., 122–23.

6. Anne-Marie McManus writes that "Syrian cultural production unleashes *al-kharāb* to depict an irredeemable force that spreads across Syria and into the diaspora. Death interrupts the orders of collective life, forcing new, 'palpable intensities' of inhabiting landscapes of death." See McManus, "On the Ruins of What's to Come, I Stand: Time and Devastation in Syrian Cultural Production Since 2011," *Critical Inquiry* 48, no. 1 (Autumn 2021): 54; and more broadly Charlotte al-Khalili, *Waiting for the Revolution to End: Syrian Displacement, Time, and Subjectivity* (London: UCL Press, 2023), chap. 4.

7. On such support movements, see Muneeza Rizvi, "'Strange Affinities': *Iṣlāḥ* and British Muslim Volunteers in the Syrian War," *American Ethnologist* 51, no. 4 (November 2024): 490–501.

8. Hannah Arendt, *The Human Condition* (Chicago: University of Chicago Press, 1958), 9. See also Mavis Louise Biss, "Arendt and the Theological Significance of Natality," *Philosophy Compass* 7, no. 11 (2012): 762–71.

9. Hannah Arendt, *Between Past and Future: Eight Exercises in Political Thought* (New York: Penguin, 2006), 168; essay published in 1960.

10. Revolutions are the paradigmatic miracle in this sense, for they "are the only political events which confront us directly and inevitably with the problem of beginning." A revolution is what introduces a gap, a hiatus, into the linear time of history; revolutions act as a "figure of contingency within historical time"; Hannah Arendt, *On Revolution*, trans. Jonathan Schell (1963; repr. New York: Penguin, 2006).

11. We need a way to be released from the "predicament of irreversibility," that is, "of not being able to undo what has been done though one did not, and could not, have known what he was doing." That "possible redemption" Arendt finds in "the faculty of forgiving"; *Human Condition*, 237. Between the miraculous power

of natality, the redemptive function of forgiveness, and the stabilizing faculty of promise, Arendt's political theology depends on plurality (for one needs others to forgive and bind oneself to in promise). But it is a political theology with a deeply Christian connection. For the Christian-secular ontology of natality, see Daniel Colucciello Barber, "Sense-Making, Affect, and Natality," Senses and Religion: Ontologies and Secularism workshop paper, UC Berkeley, November 2017, e.g., at 12–13: "Whereas Christian natality oriented sense around a specific being, one that appears within the world yet calls forth a beyond of the world, secular natality makes sense a matter of the world as such. What is and must remain definite is the birth of sense, with its corresponding futurity. And so, while this definite birth may be figured in Christological terms, such terms need not be maintained. As long as birth is made definite, the terms of its figuration may change indefinitely." In contrast to the Christian articulation of forgetting as the gift of forgiveness—that is, as the "eschatological horizon of the entire problematic of memory, history, and forgetting" (Paul Ricoeur, *Memory, History, Forgetting*, trans. Kathleen Blamey and David Pellauer [Chicago: University of Chicago Press, 2004], 285)—and unlike Alyousef and Dr. Khālid, my interlocutors over the rest of this book draw on Islamic grammars for which forgetting is a species of blessing already belonging to the unfolding of creation, within which the human (*al-insān*) is mercifully created with a necessary lapse, as tending-to-forgetting (*nisyān*).

12. "Given the nature of human action in time," Scott writes of Arendt, "to use one's freedom is inevitably an *invitation* to tragedy"; Scott, *Omens of Adversity*, 62.

13. Cf. Liane Carlson, *Contingency and the Limits of History: How Touch Shapes Experience and Meaning* (New York: Columbia University Press, 2019).

14. Walter Benjamin, "On the Concept of History," trans. Harry Zohn, in *Selected Writings*, vol. 4, *1938–1940*, ed. Howard Eiland and Michael W. Jennings (Cambridge, Mass: Harvard University Press, 2003), 397.

15. Stéphane Mosès, *The Angel of History: Rosenzweig, Benjamin, Scholem*, trans. Barbara Harshav (Stanford: Stanford University Press, 2009), 125.

16. Stéphane Mosès, "The Theological-Political Model of History in the Thought of Walter Benjamin," trans. Ora Wiskind, *History and Memory* 1, no. 2 (Fall–Winter 1989): 25.

17. For an English translation of another brief text in this genre, see Gibril Fouad Haddad, *The Excellence of Syro-Palestine: al-Shām and Its People; Forty Hadiths*, 2nd ed. ([UK]: Remembrance Publications, 2017).

18. Ibn Mājah, *Sunan*, book 1, 186; Aḥmad, *Musnad*, 26:188 §16201. Cf. Najah Nadi Ahmad, "Despair," *The Integrated Encyclopedia of the Qur'an* (Ardrossan: Center for Islamic Sciences), vol. 3 forthcoming.

2. TRIBULATION

1. Jawad Qureshi, "The Discourses of the Damascene Sunni Ulama during the 2011 Revolution," in *State and Islam in Baathist Syria: Confrontation or Co-Optation?*, by Line Khatib, Raphaël Lefèvre, and Jawad Qureshi (Fife: University of St. Andrews Centre for Syrian Studies, 2012), 59–91.

2. Drawing on and reworking MacIntyre and Foucault, Talal Asad famously argued in the 1980s that Islam is best approached in the discipline of anthropology as a tradition—that is, as a set of "discourses that seek to instruct practitioners regarding the correct form and purpose of a given practice that, precisely because it is established, has a history"; Asad, "The Idea of an Anthropology of Islam," Occasional Papers Series (Washington, D.C.: Center for Contemporary Arab Studies, Georgetown University, 1986), 14.

3. Ami Ayalon, "From *Fitna* to *Thawra*," *Studia Islamica* 66 (1987): 150. For analyses of the Islamic legitimation of rebellion that more closely attend the longer history of this contestation (instead of flattening into an image of classical Sunni quietism), see Khaled Abou El Fadl, *Rebellion and Violence in Islamic Law* (Cambridge: Cambridge University Press, 2001), and Ovamir Anjum, *Politics, Law, and Community in Islamic Thought: The Taymiyyan Moment* (Cambridge: Cambridge University Press, 2012).

4. As surveyed, for instance, in (on *fitna*), Ayalon, "From *Fitna* to *Thawra*" or (on *ibtilā'*), W. Montgomery Watt, "Suffering in Sunnite Islam," *Studia Islamica* 50 (1979): 5–19.

5. As a methodological model, see Stefania Pandolfo, *Knot of the Soul: Madness, Psychoanalysis, Islam* (Chicago: University of Chicago Press, 2018), chap. 6: "The Burning," in which two men debate whether risking passage to Europe is suicidal despair or ethical striving. Pandolfo seeks to understand their theologico-political disagreement by reference to modern reformist and revivalist Muslim thinkers—as well as classical ones, for the link between social critique and eschatological concerns is not limited to the Islamic Revival of the last century. Yet she also shows that her interlocutors' debate is not finally reducible to any of these frameworks, for it is also worked out in the immediacy of their own lives as they confront the limits of belonging and of faith. See also Cabeiri deBergh Robinson, *Body of Victim, Body of Warrior: Refugee Families and the Making of Kashmiri Jihadists* (Berkeley: University of California Press, 2013), 68, where she writes compellingly that "Hijarat and jihād provide moral frameworks through which Muslim refugees interpret the relationships between personal and collective suffering, social responsibility, and political action. . . . People employ the terms in evaluating the conditions under which they are obliged to endure political violence or permitted to perpetrate violent struggle in the name of political and social ideals, such as the sovereignty of the polity or the duty to

protect the community." Robinson traces how these two terms are evaluated and debated within Kashmiri families. Along similar lines, this chapter follows how the Syrian war is variously understood as a trial or ordeal.

6. Edward William Lane, *Arabic-English Lexicon* (London: Williams & Norgate, 1863), 256.

7. Ibid., 2335. See Stefania Pandolfo, *Impasse of the Angels: Scenes from a Moroccan Space of Memory* (Chicago: University of Chicago Press, 1997), esp. "Dialogics of Fitna," 81–103, which provides an ethnographic and conceptual exploration of *fitna* in and of language, its essential conceptual ambivalence, with reference to Ibn Manzur's *Lisān al-ʿarab* and its "spiral textual play between interpreting and interpreted language" (349n104). And see her *Knot of the Soul*, where she explores the "ordeal" of the event with reference to her ongoing conversations with her friend the imam, where "the ordeal is not just what falls upon us, what breaks our lives and hurls us into bereavement or disablement . . . it is the encounter with an event that summons us in our innermost soul to what the Imam calls a 'decision' as for the actualization or the annihilation of an inner potential" (225).

8. Nasrin Rouzati, *Trial and Tribulation in the Qur'an: A Mystical Theodicy* (Berlin: Gerlach, 2015), 10.

9. Of the English terms "trial," "tribulation," and "ordeal," the etymology of the former (examination, experiment, putting to proof) best approaches the concepts I consider here. The etymology of "tribulation" (affliction, oppression, suffering) leans too much toward deprivation; that of "ordeal" (trial by test, verdict, division) is too close to crisis (decision, judgment, division). Yet etymology is not a law; in what follows, I employ these terms as they best fit the context, in the hope of making legible the grammatical variations of the concepts I seek to translate.

10. There is a large literature on Zaatari Camp, much of it from architectural design or psychosociological perspectives. For an introduction to the camp, see Alison Ledwith, "Zaatari: The Instant City" (Boston, Mass.: Affordable Housing Institute, 2014), http://www.affordablehousinginstitute.org/insights/zaatari-the-instant-city. For an account of the transformation of the camp over the years since it was opened, see Ayham Dalal, *From Shelters to Dwellings: The Zaatari Refugee Camp* (Berlin: Transcript Verlag, 2022). From 100 refugee families it grew rapidly as the war intensified, for a time taking in 5,000 refugees per day. In April 2013 its maximum population reached nearly 200,000 people but soon fell back as Syrians left the camp for other urban areas. Images from Zaatari became iconic of the conditions of displaced Syrians. Media attention reflected the attention of NGOs, with international aid organizations hyperfocused on tracking outcomes within the camp (health, education, sanitation, shelter). ReliefWeb and the UNHCR's data portal offer a helpful repository of these reports. Despite this

overwhelming media attention on camp life, four-fifths of the displaced Syrian population in Jordan live outside formal camps (whether in informal tent settlements or in urban areas).

11. Nearly 3,000 such informal shops comprise the camp's market, UNHCR materials state, attesting the "vibrant trade relationship between the peoples of northern Jordan and southern Syria"; UNHCR, "Fact Sheet: Jordan Zaatari Camp" (July 2018), https://data2.unhcr.org/en/documents/download/64690; Myriam Ababsa, "An Urbanizing Camp? Zaatari Syrian Refugee Camp in Jordan," *Conflits et migrations* (May 9, 2018), https://lajeh.hypotheses.org/1076. Those same trade relationships had been key to populating Zaatari itself as fleeing Syrians drew on the routes and networks that had long facilitated the movement of smuggled goods and migrant labor across the border into Jordan and back. For an impressive and detailed account of how these transnational mobilities along the Syria-Jordan border are reconfigured under the pressures of the war, see Ann-Christin Wagner, "Transnational Mobilities during the Syrian War: An Ethnography of Rural Refugees and Evangelical Humanitarians in Mafraq, Jordan" (Ph.D. diss., University of Edinburgh, 2019).

12. Killian Clarke, "When Do the Dispossessed Protest? Informal Leadership and Mobilization in Syrian Refugee Camps," *Perspectives on Politics* 16, no. 3 (September 2018): 617–33; cf. Michael N. Barnett, "Humanitarian Governance," *Annual Review of Political Science* 16 (May 2013): 379–98.

13. Ja'far lived in Abyssinia nearly a dozen years, was famous for his generosity, and later fought bravely in the battle of Mu'ta (east of the river Jordan, much further south from Zaatari) against Byzantine soldiers who cut off his arms. The Prophet wept to hear it; Gabriel consoled him, saying that God had granted him two wings by which to fly in paradise (hence Ja'far's title "the winged," *dhū l-janāḥīn*).

14. In 2012–14, public healthcare was free (i.e., fully subsidized) for Syrian refugees in Jordan; after that, it was subsidized to 35–60 percent (the same rate as for uninsured Jordanians). In early 2018, however, the government decided that Syrians in Jordan must pay 80 percent of healthcare costs up front (the same rate as any other foreigner). This meant that a hospital birth, for example, went from $85 to $338, and a C-section from $338 to $845—an untenable increase when refugees were already spending, on average, 41 percent of their monthly income on healthcare, and when 36 percent of urban refugees could not afford necessary medicine or health services; Human Rights Watch, "Jordan: Step Forward, Step Back for Urban Refugees," *Human Rights Watch*, March 25, 2018, https://www.hrw.org/news/2018/03/25/jordan-step-forward-step-back-urban-refugees; Omer Karasapan, "The Challenges in Providing Health Care to Syrian Refugees," *Brookings Institution*, November 15, 2018, https://www.brookings.edu/blog/future-development/2018/11/15/the-challenges-in-providing-health-care-to-syrian-refugees/. In 2019, based on support from a consortium of international donors,

Syrian refugees were integrated into the public healthcare system at the rate of non-insured Jordanians.

15. To accommodate the massive influx of schoolchildren, the Jordanian Ministry of Education established the "double shift" arrangement by which Jordanian children attend public school in the mornings and Syrian children in the afternoons. While allowing over 126,000 Syrian children to effectively join the public school system within the span of a few years, the double shift system also contributed to deteriorating quality and quantity of education for both Jordanian and Syrian children, while 46 percent of Syrian children living outside camps remain out of school; KidsRights Report, "The Widening Educational Gap for Syrian Refugee Children" (Amsterdam: KidsRights Foundation, 2018), 13–15.

16. Ana V. Ibáñez Prieto, "Jordan Issues More Than 100,000 Work Permits for Syrians," *Jordan Times*, July 18, 2018, http://www.jordantimes.com/news/local/jordan-issues-more-100000-work-permits-syrians.

17. Sophia Hoffmann, "Humanitarian Security in Jordan's Azraq Camp," *Security Dialogue* 48, no. 2 (2017): 97–112.

18. Victoria Mason, "The Im/mobilities of Iraqi Refugees in Jordan: Pan-Arabism, 'Hospitality' and the Figure of the 'Refugee,'" *Mobilities* 6, no. 3 (2011): 353–73; Tahir Zaman, *Islamic Traditions of Refuge in the Crises of Iraq and Syria* (New York: Palgrave Macmillan, 2016); and Dawn Chatty, "The Duty to be Generous (*karam*): Alternatives to Rights-based Asylum in the Middle East," *Journal of the British Academy* 5 (2017): 177–99.

19. Andrew Shryock, "The New Jordanian Hospitality: House, Host, and Guest in the Culture of Public Display," *Comparative Studies in Society and History* 46, no. 1 (January 2004): 36; Shryock, "Breaking Hospitality Apart: Bad Hosts, Bad Guests, and the Problem of Sovereignty," *Journal of the Royal Anthropological Institute* 18, s1 (June 2012): s20–s33.

20. Estella Carpi and H. Pınar Şenoğuz, "Refugee Hospitality in Lebanon and Turkey: On Making 'The Other,'" *International Migration* 57, no. 2 (2018): 126–42. They conclude that "hospitality as a public discourse and 'cultural display' contributes to the further nationalization of host societies (historically in the case of Turkey and a complexly cyclic process in the case of Lebanon)" (138); whatever its value as a moral practice, hospitality as a political discourse now acts as a "societal fragmentation force" and "stems from the nation-state framework and utilises such inter-group tensions as a restoration strategy for the power of the host" (137).

21. Jacques Derrida, with Anne DuFourmantelle, *Of Hospitality*, trans. Rachel Bowlby (Stanford: Stanford University Press, 2000), 77; cf. Andrew Shryock, "Hospitality Lessons: Learning the Shared Language of Derrida and the Balga Bedouin," *Paragraph* 32, no. 1 (March 2009): 32–50. Recent work in refugee studies and the anthropology of humanitarianism cites Derrida either to expose

the ruse of hospitality or to offer a radical alternative to contemporary policies. For Derrida himself, of course, the tension between conditional and unconditional hospitality is constitutive and co-implicative; they cannot be dialectically reconciled.

22. *Ṣaḥīḥ Muslim* 2567.

23. For example, the program curriculum in creed progressed from Khālid bin ʿAlī al-Mushayqaḥ's *al-Mukhtaṣar fī-l-ʿaqīda* to ʿAbd al-Qādir bin Muḥammad ʿAṭā al-Ṣūfī's *al-Mufīd min muhimmāt al-tawḥīd* and then to Muḥammad bin Ṣāliḥ al-ʿUthaymīn's *Sharḥ al-qawāʿid al-muthlā fī ṣifāt allāh wa-asmāʾihi al-ḥusnā*. The notable exception to this staunchly Salafi curriculum was the field of jurisprudence, which included key texts of the Shāfiʿite school as taught in Syria: the contemporary Damascene standard, *al-Fiqh al-manhajī*; Muṣṭafā Dīb Bughā's *al-Tadhhīb fī adillat matn al-ghāyat wa-l-taqrīb*; and al-Suyūṭī's *Ashbāh wa-l-naẓāʾir fī qawāʿid wa furūʿ fiqh al-shāfiʿiyya*.

24. Thomas Pierret, *Religion and State in Syria: The Sunni Ulama from Coup to Revolution* (Cambridge: Cambridge University Press, 2013), chap. 3, "(Re)defining Orthodoxy against Reformist Trends."

25. UNICEF, "Access to Education for Syrian Children in Zaatari Camp, Jordan," Joint Education Needs Assessment Report, Education Sector Working Group (September 2014), 45–46.

26. These numbers are based on a contemporary video recording of Abū Bakr speaking to prospective donors.

27. UNICEF, "Access to Education for Syrian Children in Zaatari Camp, Jordan."

28. On which see Zoltan Pall, "Kuwaiti Salafism and Its Growing Influence in the Levant" (Carnegie Endowment for International Peace, May 7, 2014), https://carnegieendowment.org/2014/05/07/kuwaiti-salafism-and-its-growing-influence-in-levant-pub-55514.

29. UNHCR, "Jordan: Ramadan Prayers for Syrian Refugees," *YouTube*, August 5, 2013, https://www.youtube.com/watch?v=hKWKR5Y7auQ.

30. Pierret, *Religion and State in Syria*, 70–71; for life under the père Assad regime, see generally Lisa Wedeen, *Ambiguities of Domination: Politics, Rhetoric, and Symbols in Contemporary Syria* (Chicago: University of Chicago Press, 1999); and for the continuity in the grammar of violence across the two regimes' styles of government, see Salwa Ismail, *The Rule of Violence: Subjectivity, Memory, and Government in Syria* (Cambridge: Cambridge University Press, 2019).

31. Pierret, *Religion and State in Syria*, chap. 6, "Reforms and Revolution."

32. Christian Jambet, "The Constitution of the Subject and Spiritual Practice," in *Michel Foucault, Philosopher*, trans. Timothy J. Armstrong (1989; repr. New York: Harvester Wheatsheaf, 1992), 241.

33. Peter Singer, "Famine, Affluence, and Morality," *Philosophy and Public Affairs* 1, no. 3 (Spring 1972): 229–43.

34. Amira Mittermaier, *Giving to God: Islamic Charity in Revolutionary Times* (Oakland: University of California Press, 2019), 98.

35. Emmanuel Levinas, *Otherwise Than Being or Beyond Essence*, trans. Alphonso Lingis (Pittsburgh: Duquesne University Press, 1998), 157, cited in Roberto Esposito, *Third Person: Politics of Life and Philosophy of the Impersonal*, trans. Zakiya Hanafi (2007; repr. Cambridge, Mass.: Polity Press, 2012, 124–25.

36. Ibid., 122.

37. Emmanuel Levinas, "Peace and Proximity," trans. Peter Adderton and Simon Critchley, in *Emmanuel Levinas: Basic Philosophical Writings*, ed. Adriaan Peperzak et al. (Bloomington: Indiana University Press, 1996), 168.

38. Marc Crépon, *The Thought of Death and the Memory of War*, trans. Michael Loriaux (Minneapolis: University of Minnesota Press, 2013), 117.

39. Humanitarian contexts are (imagined as) constitutively asymmetrical, "between those whose life is positively sacrificeable, because they are at the mercy of the bombs, and those whose life can be freely sacrificed, because they decided to stay"; Didier Fassin, *Humanitarian Reason: A Moral History of the Present*, trans. Rachel Gomme (Berkeley: University of California Press, 2012), 233; see also Liisa H. Malkki, *The Need to Help: The Domestic Arts of International Humanitarianism* (Durham, N.C.: Duke University Press, 2015), chap. 6.

40. Roberta Dennaro, "From Mars to the *Tugūr*: Ibn al-Mubārak and the Shaping of a Biographical Tradition," *Eurasian Studies* 7, nos. 1–2 (2009): 125–44.

41. Cited in Feryal Salem, *The Emergence of Early Sufi Piety and Sunni Scholasticism: 'Abdullāh bin Mubarak and the Formation of Sunni Identity in the Second Islamic Century* (Leiden: Brill, 2016), 117.

42. 'Abdullāh bin al-Mubārak, *al-Zuhd wa-l-raqā'iq*, ed. Aḥmad Farīd (Riyad: Dār al-Mi'rāj al-Dawliyya li-l-Nashr, 1995), 139.

43. Abū Bakr's account of tribulation registers the force of askēsis—albeit not quite as the Foucauldian "test by which, in the game of truth, one undergoes changes," the "exercise of oneself in the activity of thought"; Michel Foucault, *The Use of Pleasure: The History of Sexuality*, trans. Robert Hurley (New York: Vintage, 1986), 2:9, which Pierre Hadot comments may already be "too much centred on the 'self,'" too "purely aesthetic"; Hadot, "Reflections on the Notion of the 'Cultivation of the Self,'" in *Michel Foucault, Philosopher*, trans. Timothy J. Armstrong (1989; repr. New York: Harvester Wheatsheaf, 1992), 225, 230. Hadot rereads the Stoics and Platonists from whom Foucault elaborates his account of the cultivation of the self, finding that the movements of aesthetic interiorization that Foucault recovers were necessarily accompanied by a universalizing movement that Foucault overlooks.

44. Nauman Naqvi, "Acts of Askēsis, Scenes of Poēisis: The Dramatic Phenomenology of Another Violence in a Muslim Painter-Poet," *diacritics* 40, no. 2 (2012): 52.

45. Ibid., 66n3.

46. See the new translation as Abū ʿĪsa al-Tirmidhī, *Ash-Shama'il al-Muhammadiyya*, trans. Abdul Aziz Suraqah, ed. Mohammed Aslam (Philadelphia: Ghazali Institute, 2020).

47. Cf. Annemarie Schimmel, *And Muhammad Is His Messenger: The Veneration of the Prophet in Islamic Piety* (Chapel Hill: University of North Carolina Press, 1985), 34.

48. Ibid., 46–47.

49. Naqvi, "Acts of Askēsis, Scenes of Poēisis," 64. Naqvi himself is discussing the oeuvre of the Pakistani painter-poet Sadequain, but, as he comments, "the concept of askēsis is, potentially, of virtually limitless applicability in the Islamic field" (66n3).

50. See Umar F. Abd-Allah, *The Islamic Struggle in Syria* (Berkeley, Calif.: Mizan Press, 1983) for tensions between the regime and the "Islamic movement" in the lead-up to the events of Hama; Line Khatib, *Islamic Revivalism in Syria: The Rise and Fall of Baʿthist Secularism* (London: Routledge, 2011), chap. 4: "Conflict with the Muslim Brotherhood," for a broad account of the conflict informed by Social Movement Theory and political economy; Wedeen, *Ambiguities of Domination*, 46–49, for the regime's narrative of rabid Islamist treachery and Assad's infallibility; and Ismail, *Rule of Violence*, chap. 4: "Memories of Violence: Hama 1982" for the long afterlife of these events in social memory, including how they were reactivated in the 2011 Syrian revolution.

51. Ismail, *The Rule of Violence*, 132.

52. ʿAli al-Ṭanṭāwī, *Fuṣūl islāmiyya* (Damascus: Dār al-Manār, 1380/1960), 201–8. He continues in some detail: that one can perfect the Quran's points of articulation (*makhārij al-ḥurūf*), its pharyngealization (*tafkhīm*), extend its syllables (*madd*), assimilate (*idghām*) or dissimilate (*iẓhār*) its consonants, modulate its nasality (*ghunna*)—as though that suffices, when the reciter passes immediately into the most vulgar song or empty talk! What enemy of God, what devilish plot, has made the Quran a verbal plaything for Muslims, although every household has a copy? Al-Ṭanṭāwī insists that proper recitation is not a matter simply of correct articulation nor even of pleasant melody; rather, the reciter must be rationally engaged with and affectively responsive to the meaning of the Quran, to pondering (*tadabbur*) and comprehending (*tafahhum*), to understanding it and acting according to it. By the end of this essay, he recommends Sayyid Quṭb's approach to understanding the Quran. On Quṭb's hermeneutics (*al-taṣwīr al-fannī*), see Lauren E. Osborne, "Feeling the Words: Sayyid Qutb's Affective Engagement with the Qur'an in *Al-Taswir al-Fanni fi al-Qur'an*," *Religion Compass* 13, no. 10 (October 2019). Al-Ṭanṭāwī's essay "Qur'ānakum yā muslimūn" was written the same year that he also argued in the press against hymns praising the Prophet that used to be broadcast from the Umayyad Mosque after Friday

prayer: Pierret, *Religion and State in Syria*, 105. He left Syria seven years later, after the new Baath regime consolidated the judicial system under its mission of secular revolution.

53. See Kristina Nelson, *The Art of Reciting the Qur'an* (1985; repr. Cairo: American University of Cairo Press, 2001), especially chaps. 2, "*Tajwīd*" and 3, "The *Samā*ʿ Polemic."

54. See respectively Pierret, *Religion and State in Syria*, chap. 3, "(Re)defining Orthodoxy against Reformist Trends," and Joas Wagemakers, *Salafism in Jordan: Political Islam in a Quietist Community* (Cambridge: Cambridge University Press, 2016).

55. Al-Būṭī had a complex relationship to the regime over his long career as an academic and public intellectual. A stern critic of scientism, Marxism, and nationalism, his commitments were firmly to Sunni scholasticism—and thus against both the Salafi rejection of the traditions of jurisprudence and theology and the political instrumentalization of religion that he believed characterized the Muslim Brotherhood. He also developed a close personal relationship with Hafez al-Assad, which he was later able to use to secure the release of thousands of political prisoners and to modulate some of the regime's anti-religious measures. His response to the 2011 revolution was marked by a similar approach. In a March 2011 lecture, he called for incrementalist reform rather than mob revolt and largely repeated the regime's narrative of foreign infiltrators instigating the conflict. Yet he also performed the funeral prayer for martyrs over protestors who had been killed by regime forces. He was killed in an attack in 2013 while giving his weekly public class in a mosque. No one immediately claimed responsibility. Rumors spread that he was killed in a false flag attack by the regime to pre-empt his imminent defection to the rebel cause. See Qureshi, "Discourses of the Damascene Sunni Ulama during the 2011 Revolution"; and broadly Jawad Qureshi, "Sunni Tradition in an Age of Revival and Reform: Saʿid Ramadan al-Buti (1929–2013) and His Interlocutors" (PhD diss., University of Chicago, 2019).

56. Translation from Abdal Hakim Murad, *The Mantle Adorned: Imam Būṣīrī's "Burda"* (London: Quilliam Press, 2009). On the broader tradition of "the mantle ode" as an expression of love for the Prophet, see Suzanne Pinckney Stetkevych, *The Mantle Odes: Arabic Praise Poems to the Prophet Muhammad* (Bloomington: Indiana University Press, 2010).

57. This pedagogical impulse extended across sectarian lines (it was not limited to Salafi scholars seeking to exploit the conflict for their own influence, as implied in certain analyses). The Shādhilī Sufi shaykh Muḥammad al-Yaʿqūbī was famously dismissed from the Umayyad Mosque after condemning the brutal regime response to the initial demonstrations; Qureshi, "Discourses of the Damascene Sunni Ulama during the 2011 Revolution." In exile in Morocco, he received requests to rule on the religious legitimacy of killing captured generals

or attacking regime thugs in civilian areas; Matthew Barber, "Sheikh Muhammad al-Yaqoubi Interviewed by Syria Comment," *Syria Comment*, May 30, 2013, https://www.joshualandis.com/blog/sheikh-muhammad-al-yaqoubi-interviewed-by-syria-comment/. He issued a series of fatwas in response to these questions: against killing captives, even if they are soldiers of the Assad regime; against kidnapping foreigners; requiring the permission of one's parents and wife to leave for jihad (except when the enemy is overpowering the land, when it becomes an individual obligation); against "martyrdom operations" (while yet deeming those who carry them out to be martyrs); against bomb attacks that would kill the non-combatant families of the enemy; and more; https://www.joshualandis.com/blog/wp-content/uploads/yaqoubi-fatwas-for-the-uprising.pdf. In 2013, the outcome of the conflict still quite variable, he exhorted the fighters, writing that the hardships of war do not alleviate the obligation of jihad; *shadā'id al-ḥarb lā tasquṭ wājib al-jihād*, https://www.do3atalsham.com/?p=5112. He later wrote a lengthy fatwa legitimizing fighting against Daesh (English version published as Muhammad Al-Yaqoubi, *Refuting ISIS*, 2nd ed. [Herndon: Sacred Knowledge, 2016]), tens of thousands of copies of which were distributed to rebel groups; Matthew Barber, "Sheikh Muhammad al-Yaqoubi Responds to al-Julani's al-Jazeera Interview," *Syria Comment*, May 31, 2015, https://www.joshualandis.com/blog/sheikh-muhammad-al-yaqoubi-responds-to-al-julanis-al-jazeera-interview/.

58. See the Damascene master 'Abd al-Ghānī al-Nābulusī's *The Virtues of Seclusion in Times of Confusion*, trans. Abdul Aziz Suraqah (Toronto: Ibriz Media, 2017), 8.

59. Scholars have rightly troubled hard academic distinctions between Islamic law and Islamic ethics: see, for example, Frederick S. Carney, "Some Aspects of Islamic Ethics," *Journal of Religion* 63, no. 2 (April 1983): 159–74, and A. Kevin Reinhart, "Islamic Law as Islamic Ethics," *Journal of Religious Ethics* 11, no. 2 (Fall 1983): 186–203. In the absence of state enforcement, the fivefold Islamic jurisprudential determination of actions—necessary (*farḍ, wājib*), recommended (*sunna, mandūb*), permissible but neutral (*mubāh*), reprehensible (*makrūḥ*), or forbidden (*ḥarām*)—can well be understood in "moral" terms rather than "legal" ones. Nonetheless, I describe 'Umar as pulling toward a "juridical" frame rather than an "ethical" one based on his concern for the hierarchy of obligations and the interlocking proofs (*ḥujaj*) that convene action.

60. Sarah Hasselbarth, "Islamic Charities in the Syrian Context in Jordan and Lebanon" (Beirut: Friedrich-Ebert-Stiftung, 2014), 15.

61. Joas Wagemakers describes him as one of "the two most important radical Islamist scholars" alive today: *Salafism in Jordan*, 186.

62. Mohammad Abu Rumman, *I Am a Salafi: A Study of the Actual and Imagined Identities of Salafis*, trans. Hassan Barari (Amman: Friedrich-Ebert-Stiftung Foundation, 2014), 202–12.

63. Glenn E. Robinson, "Defensive Democratization in Jordan," *International Journal of Middle East Studies* 30, no. 3 (August 1998): 387–410. Abū Qatāda had already left Jordan for Malaysia and then Pakistan, where he taught sharia to so-called "Afghan Arabs" in Peshawar, before ultimately being granted asylum in London in 1994. In 2013 he was deported to Jordan, where he was tried and acquitted on two separate terrorism charges, and has since returned to prominence as one of the jihadi-Salafi critics of Daesh; Wagemakers, *Salafism in Jordan*, 185–88. Abū Haniyya himself, who always insisted on the integrity of economic and political justice to religious revival, has returned to his leftist roots and no longer calls himself a Salafi; Abu Rumman, *I Am a Salafi*.

64. Abu Rumman, *I Am a Salafi*, 169.

65. Quintan Wiktorowicz, "The Salafi Movement in Jordan," *International Journal of Middle East Studies* 32 (2000): 228: "Of the ten members I met (out of a total of fifty), every one had been arrested or detained by the *mukhābarāt*, prior to and following [the Association's] registration, and during my period of research, all three of my primary informants from the society were brought in by the *mukhābarāt*. This kind of harassment is a constant burden for members."

66. See Wagemakers, *Salafism in Jordan*, chap. 4: "*Fitna*: Quietist Salafi Infighting in Jordan," for a detailed account of the intra-Salafi theological arguments and leadership struggles in the years preceding and then immediately following al-Albānī's death in 1999.

67. On the Amman Message as a strategy of legitimation and political control, see Michaelle Browers, "Official Islam and the Limits of Communicative Action: The Paradox of the Amman Message," *Third World Quarterly* 32, no. 5 (2011): 943–58; and Stacey Gutkowski, "We Are the Very Model of a Moderate Muslim State: The Amman Messages and Jordan's Foreign Policy," *International Relations* 30, no. 2 (2016): 206–26.

68. Ṣaḥafī, "Qarār li-wazīr al-thaqāfa bi-ḥall jamʿiyyat al-kitāb wa-l-sunna," *Ṣaḥafī*, May 7, 2007, http://www.sahafi.jo/arc/art1.php?id=b3d045a789d8905e7786378309858d7f212656dc.

69. Zāyid Ḥammād, "al-Iftitāḥiyya," *al-Qibla* 4–5 (1424/2003): 3–6.

70. Muḥammad Ibrāhīm Shaqra, "Ḥiṣār al-fitna," *al-Qibla* 4–5 (1424/2003): 31–38.

71. Wagemakers (*Salafism in Jordan*, chap. 7: "The Challenge of Political Salafism") writes that what sets the Association apart from other Salafis is the political role it grants "the people": in its emergent ideology, loyalty to rulers is not simply a religious duty (as it is among quietist circles) but rather is contingent on their justice and their adherence to the sharia. Although prudence is a necessary virtue, Muslims need not obey leaders who do not obey God. People are responsible for their communal lives. There are clearly direct political stakes to this position in the era of the Arab uprisings.

72. Bassām Nāṣir, "Thawra sūriyā wa aḥdāthuhā bi-ru'ya wa naẓrāt shar'iyya," *al-Qibla* 9, no. 22 (1433/2012): 68–71.

73. Tirmidhī, *Sunan*, Kitāb Ṣifat al-qiyāma wa-l-raqā'iq wa-l-war', 2517.

74. The "sincerity" of such supplications, as of every (trans)action in this moral economy, is not given but emerges through what Nada Moumtaz calls a "grammar of intent." See her "From Forgiveness to Foreclosure: *Waqf*, Debt, and the Remaking of the Ḥanafī Legal Subject in Late Ottoman Mount Lebanon," *Muslim World* 108, no. 4 (October 2018): 599, which traces how modernizing shifts in late Ottoman Islamic law lead from one grammatical configuration that "takes exterior acts for their apparent meaning" to another that "acts upon the (suspicious) interiority of subjects."

75. For an excellent survey, see Julia Elyachar, "Rethinking Anthropology of Neoliberalism in the Middle East," in *A Companion to the Anthropology of the Middle East*, ed. Soraya Altorki (Chichester: John Wiley & Sons, 2015), 411–33.

76. Mona Atia, *Building a House in Heaven: Pious Neoliberalism and Islamic Charity in Egypt* (Minneapolis: University of Minnesota Press, 2013), 160. Atia considers the productive encounter of Islamism ("a project that seeks to shape the state, economy, and society along Islamic lines") and neoliberalism ("the extension of market logics into all aspects of life," operating as policy, ideology, and governmentality) under the authoritarian Egyptian police state (xvii).

77. According to earlier arguments influenced by Social Movement Theory, Islamic charities and social welfare associations have less to do with serving the poor than with strengthening horizontal ties among middle-class activists; Janine A. Clark, *Islam, Charity, and Activism: Middle-Class Networks and Social Welfare in Egypt, Jordan, and Yemen* (Bloomington: Indiana University Press, 2004). For a detailed study of such welfare associations in Jordan, see Egbert Harmsen, *Islam, Civil Society, and Social Action: Muslim Voluntary Welfare Associations in Jordan between Patronage and Empowerment* (Amsterdam: Amsterdam University Press, 2008).

78. Sarah A. Tobin, *Everyday Piety: Islam and Economy in Jordan* (Ithaca, N.Y.: Cornell University Press, 2016), 6. What may be lost in such analysis, however, is the historical and theological specificity of Atia's "neoliberal piety" as part of a broader set of responses to what Charles Tripp calls "the challenge of capitalism"; Tripp, *Islam and the Moral Economy: The Challenge of Capitalism* (Cambridge: Cambridge University Press, 2006).

79. Tobin, *Everyday Piety*, 21.

80. Cf. Daromir Rudnyckyj, *Spiritual Economies: Islam, Globalization, and the Afterlife of Development* (Ithaca, N.Y.: Cornell University Press, 2014).

81. Joel Robbins, "Causality, Ethics, and the Near Future," *American Ethnologist* 34, no. 3 (2007): 435. Cf. Jane I. Guyer's "Prophecy and the Near Future:

Thoughts on Macroeconomic, Evangelical, and Punctuated Time," in the same issue, 409–21.

82. On social "use," see Ananda Abeysekara, review of Joseph Walser's *Genealogies of Mahayana Buddhism*, in *Religious Theory: The E-Supplement to the Journal of Cultural and Religious Theory*, October 23, 2019, http://jcrt.org/religioustheory/2019/10/23/review-genealogies-of-mahayana-buddhism-ananda-abeysekara/. This literature also tends to read the performance and contestation of everyday piety within middle-class charitable networks as the production/consumption of authentic religiosity—an approach that relies on a concept of authenticity as cultural capital to be publicly accumulated and conspicuously consumed. It follows Aamir Mufti in observing how "authenticity comes to attach itself to the concepts of certain cultural practices as a kind of aura, as the [traditional] practices themselves come to be seen as resources for the overcoming of [modern] forms of alienation"; Aamir Mufti, "The Aura of Authenticity," *Social Text* 18, no. 3 (Fall 2000): 87. Mufti recalls Adorno's critique of the "jargon of authenticity" but also his caution, in *Minima Moralia*, against political sentimentality. Cf. Christa Salamandra, *A New Old Damascus: Authenticity and Distinction in Urban Syria* (Bloomington: Indiana University Press, 2004). In contrast, I would argue that the inheritance of tradition is not simply a matter of a flat present authorized or authenticated through references to "a timeless 'truth,'" as though "authenticity" were merely about "developing connections to the divine past"; Tobin, *Everyday Piety*, 9. Arguing that authenticity is a cultural commodity to be contested or performed is not a sufficient analysis when this authenticity is key to how interlocutors—even those in middle-class charitable networks—inhabit multiple temporalities. That is, I am concerned with the work of authenticity within the specific historicity of a tradition. As Talal Asad writes of Walter Benjamin's concept of aura, "The time employed in the work of tradition is not simply the homogeneous time of modern progressive history. It is the complex time of everyday experience, remembrance, and practice"; "Thinking About Tradition, Religion, and Politics in Egypt Today," *Critical Inquiry* 42, no. 1 (Autumn 2015): 171n11. For aura in Benjamin's broader work, see Miriam Bratu Hansen, "On Benjamin's Aura," *Critical Inquiry* 34, no. 2 (Winter 2008): 336–75.

83. Paul Anderson, "An Abundance of Meaning: Ramadan as an Enchantment of Society and Economy in Syria," *HAU: Journal of Anthropological Theory* 8, no. 1 (2018): 610–24. Anderson comments that an analytic "focus on the individual's attempt to acquire their own salvation" leads the anthropologist away from interlocutors' "notions of the social."

84. Amira Mittermaier, "Trading with God: Islam, Calculation, Excess," in *A Companion to the Anthropology of Religion*, ed. Janice Boddy and Michael Lambek (London: John Wiley and Sons, 2013), 288.

85. Cited in ibid., 285.

86. Ibid., 284.

87. In similar terms (though ʿUthmān himself and his Salafi colleagues at the Association would likely not endorse this author), Abū Ḥāmid al-Ghazālī writes, "Every worldly blessing . . . can also become a tribulation; while every worldly tribulation can also become a blessing"; al-Ghazālī, *On Patience and Thankfulness: Book 32 of the Revival of the Religious Sciences*, trans. H. T. Littlejohn, 2nd ed. (Cambridge: Islamic Texts Society, 2017), 190–91.

88. "The afterlife is now," writes Mittermaier of her charitable volunteer interlocutors in postrevolutionary Cairo. They "enter a dense web of temporalities, one in which they might gain some sense of control over their future . . . and in which they infuse the present moment with meaning by connecting it to the afterlife. Paradise is all at once: located in the future, outside of time, and intertwined with the current moment"; Mittermaier, *Giving to God*, 100.

89. What David Henig calls "performative acts in the moment of exchange" work to maintain the translation between economic value (cash) and halal metavalue (deeds). Such transvaluation allows a broad range of activities (including, but certainly not limited to, charity and alms) to participate in the "mediation of divine abundance and grace"; Henig, "Economic Theologies of Abundance: Halal Exchange and the Limits of Neoliberal Effects in Post-War Bosnia-Herzegovina," *Ethnos* 84, no. 2 (2019): 231.

90. Jacques Derrida, *Given Time, vol. 1: Counterfeit Money*, trans. Peggy Kamuf (Chicago: University of Chicago Press, 1992), 3. The time of giving/receiving, receiving/giving is one that is used together, though it belongs to neither giver/receiver nor receiver/giver. Perhaps the fundamental currency circulated in the moral economy of tribulation is the impersonal time of intersubjectivity. Compare Blanchot: to give "is to give what is always taken, which is perhaps to say time: my time inasmuch as it is never mine, the time which is not at my disposal, the time beyond me and my living particularity, the lapse of time. To give is to give living and dying not at my time but according to the time of the *other*"; Maurice Blanchot, *The Writing of the Disaster*, trans. Ann Smock, new ed. (Lincoln: University of Nebraska Press, 1995), 89; original French published in 1980.

91. For an account of Western Muslims traveling to the Middle East to study and thereby inherit a supposedly authentic Islam, see Zareena Grewal, *Islam Is a Foreign Country: American Muslims and the Global Crisis of Authority* (New York: New York University Press, 2014), chap. 4: "Retrieving Tradition." For an account of Damascus as a modern site of Islamic learning, see Pierret, *Religion and State in Syria*.

92. *Ṣaḥīḥ Bukhārī*, Kitāb al-riqāq, ḥadīth 56; no. 6467.

93. Abū Jaʿfar Muḥammad bin Jarīr al-Ṭabarī, *Jāmiʿ al-bayān wa taʾwīl al-qurʾān*, ed. Aḥmad Muḥammad Shākir, 24 vols. [1420] (N.p.: Muʾassasat al-Risāla, 2000), 18:71, glossing Khiḍr's warning in Q. 18:68: "My actions occur

without an outward proof (*dalīl ẓāhir*) recognizable to your eyes, because it is based on reasons that happen later, not immediately. You cannot attain knowledge [of them] through being told (*bi-l-ḥādith ʿanhā*) because they are unseen."

94. Saba Mahmood, *Politics of Piety: The Islamic Revival and the Feminist Subject* (Princeton: Princeton University Press, 2005), 137.

95. Ibid., 139.

96. Ibid., 147. And see Talal Asad, *Secular Translations: Nation-State, Modern Self, and Calculative Reason* (New York: Columbia University Press, 2018), 75, on how al-Ghazālī's ethics entails that "there is no essential self that can guide itself; there are only potentialities of the soul that can be realized through or against a living tradition."

97. Junaid Quadri, "Moral Habituation in the Law: Rethinking the Ethics of the *Sharīʿa*," *Islamic Law and Society* 26 (2019): 191–226.

98. Cited in Amira Mittermaier, *Dreams That Matter: Egyptian Landscapes of the Imagination* (Berkeley: University of California Press, 2011), 103; and see Mittermaier, "Dreams from Elsewhere: Muslim Subjectivities beyond the Trope of Self-Cultivation," *Journal of the Royal Anthropological Institute* 18 (2012): 247–65, for an occasionally overstated contrast between an ethics of self-cultivation and an ethics of alterity.

99. Thus al-Ghazālī writes with equanimity, "It is permissible [*jā'iz*] for God not to place any obligations upon human beings; and it is permissible for Him to impose upon them obligations beyond their capacity; He may subject them to pain with no offsetting recompense and with no infractions having been committed on their part. And He does not have to do what is in their best interest; nor does He have to reward their obedience or punish their disobedience." Likewise, "If God imposes duties upon humans and they fulfill them all, this does not obligate Him to reward them. Rather, if He wills [*in shā'*], He rewards them; and if He wills, He punishes them; and if He wills, He simply annihilates them with no resurrection. Indeed, it would be all the same were God to forgive all the unbelievers and punish all the believers"; both passages cited in Sherman A. Jackson, *Islam and the Problem of Black Suffering* (New York: Oxford University Press, 2009), 85.

100. Cited in ibid., 190n55.

101. Ibn Qāḍī al-Dimashqī, as cited in Éric Chaumont, "al-Sulamī, ʿIzz al-Dīn ʿAbd al-ʿAzīz b. ʿAbd al-Salām," in *Encyclopedia of Islam*, 2nd ed. (Leiden: E.J. Brill, 1997), 9:812–3.

102. On al-Suhrawardī, see Erik S. Ohlander, *Sufism in an Age of Transition: ʿUmar al-Suhrawardī and the Rise of the Islamic Mystical Brotherhoods* (Leiden: Brill, 2008). On al-Shādhilī, see Elmer H. Douglas, trans., *The Mystical Teachings of al-Shadhili: Including His Life, Prayers, Letters, and Followers*, ed. Ibrahim M. Abu-Rabiʿ (Albany: SUNY Press, 1993).

103. Alexander Knysh traces how polemics around Ibn 'Arabī, at whose tomb in Damascus I had met 'Ali a decade before, took Ibn 'Abd al-Salām as a touchstone, with different camps insisting that the latter variously rejected or secretly admired the former. In these debates, Ibn 'Abd al-Salām came to represent how a staunch Sunnism could either exonerate or censure the doctrines of al-Shaykh al-Akbar. But some of Ibn 'Abd al-Salām's views on the relation between *sharīʿa* and *ḥaqīqa* recounted by Knysh are based on a reading of a text by 'Izz al-Dīn Ibn 'Abd al-Salām al-Maqdisī (d. 678/1279), not his contemporary Ibn 'Abd al-Salām al-Sulamī (d. 660/1262); see Knysh, *Ibn 'Arabi in the Later Islamic Tradition: The Making of a Polemical Image* (Albany: SUNY Press, 1999), 65, 78–79, which paraphrases *Ḥall al-rumūz wa mafātīḥ al-kunūz*, ed. Muḥammad Būkhnayfī (Beirut: Dār al-Kutub al-ʿIlmiyya, 1432/2011), 75–77. In passages directly relevant to 'Alī's impromptu exegesis laid out earlier, Ibn 'Abd al-Salām al-Maqdisī (not al-Sulamī) there considers the case of one given to ecstatic utterances when vacillating (*mutalawwin*) in his spiritual state of annihilation (*fanā'*), of whom observers might opine (1) that he is a heretic (*zindīq*) who should be executed; (2) that he is affirming the truth (*ṣiddīq*) and should be praised; and (3) that he is overwhelmed (*maghlūb*) and should be left alone. The author affirms that those who condemn him to death are justified (*muṣīb*), because the *sharīʿa* has limits, yet also affirms that the *ḥaqīqa* has a vision (*shuhūd*) that transcends the confines of this existence, and so if the gnostic is executed he dies a martyr enfolded into the divine mercy. *Sharīʿa* is concerned with the duties of servanthood (*ʿubūdiyya*) and *ḥaqīqa* with the witnessing of lordship (*rubūbiyya*); the former is the outer (*ẓāhir*) aspect of the path (*ṭarīq*) to God while the latter is the inner (*bāṭin*) aspect. The inner relation between *sharīʿa* and *ḥaqīqa* is like that of milk and its butter, or a trove and its treasure; *sharīʿa* is shallow (*ʿāṭila*) without *ḥaqīqa*, and likewise *ḥaqīqa* is futile (*bāṭila*) without *sharīʿa*; *sharīʿa* is true (*ḥaqq*) and *ḥaqīqa* is its reality (*ḥaqīqatuhā*); *sharīʿa* is establishing the commands (*awāmir*) while *ḥaqīqa* is witnessing the divine command (*amr*) itself, as in (following al-Qushayrī and al-Hujwīrī) the two parts of Q. 1:5. And each of these corresponds to a form of knowledge: *sharīʿa* is given by knowledge of revelation (*ʿilm al-waḥy*), while *ḥaqīqa* is given by knowledge of divine presence (*ʿilm al-ladunnī*). The encounter with Khiḍr discloses to Moses the real configuration of this knowledge.

104. Chaumont, "al-Sulamī."

105. 'Izz al-Dīn 'Abd al-'Azīz bin 'Abd al-Salām al-Sulamī, *al-Fitan wa-l-balāyā wa-l-miḥan wa-l-razāyā aw fawā'id al-balwā wa-l-miḥan*, ed. Iyād Khālid al-Ṭabbāʿ (Damascus: Dār al-Fikr, n.d.), 9; translation occasionally consulting Hamza Yusuf Hanson, "Seventeen Benefits of Tribulation," http://shaykhhamza.com/transcript/17-Benefits-of-Tribulation.

106. Abū l-Qāsim al-Qushayrī, *al-Risāla al-qushayriyya fī ʿilm al-taṣawwuf*, trans. Alexander Knysh as *Al-Qushayri's Epistle on Sufism* (Reading, UK: Garnet, 2007), 77.

107. Ibid., 197.

108. Ibid., 209.

109. Ibn ʿAbd al-Salām, *al-Fitan wa-l-balāyā*, 11n2.

110. al-Qushayrī, *Epistle on Sufism*, 208.

111. Mack Lamoureux, "Alberta Conservative Candidate Caylan Ford Steps Down for Using White Nationalist Talking Points," *VICE*, March 19, 2019, https://www.vice.com/en_ca/article/eve9qe/alberta-conservative-candidate-caylan-ford-steps-down-for-using-white-nationalist-talking-points. UCP candidates had been stepping down for months in the lead-up to this election; for example, in July 2018 one candidate defended comments in which he declared Islam "cruel, revolting, racist, oppressive," an "evil cult"; Rachel Ward, "Disqualified UCP Candidate Stands Behind Calling Islam an 'Evil Cult,'," Canadian Broadcasting Corporation, July 16, 2018, https://www.cbc.ca/news/canada/calgary/todd-beasley-medicine-hat-united-conservative-party-1.4748603.

112. CBC News, "Former UCP Candidate Who Posed with Soldiers of Odin Denied Appeal," *Canadian Broadcasting Corporation*, October 16, 2018, https://www.cbc.ca/news/canada/edmonton/ucp-candidate-lance-coulter-denied-appeal-1.4865661.

113. Mack Lamoureux, "Soldiers of Odin Edmonton Chapter Shuts Down, Rebrands as 'Canadian Infidels,'" *VICE*, October 15, 2018, https://www.vice.com/en_ca/article/xw9pwj/soldiers-of-odin-edmonton-chapter-shuts-down-rebrands-as-canadian-infidels.

114. Press Progress, "Meet 30 Candidates for Jason Kenney's UCP Who Got Caught Promoting Hateful and Extremist Views," *Press Progress*, April 4, 2019, https://pressprogress.ca/meet-30-candidates-for-jason-kenneys-ucp-who-got-caught-promoting-hateful-and-extremist-views/.

115. Press Progress, "UCP Candidate Promoted Far-Right Conspiracy Claiming the United Nations Is Taking Control of Canada's Borders," *Press Progress*, March 31, 2019, https://pressprogress.ca/ucp-candidate-promoted-far-right-conspiracy-claiming-the-united-nations-is-taking-control-of-canadas-borders/.

116. CBC News, "Edmonton Police Investigating After Group Known to Police Visits Al Rashid Mosque," *Canadian Broadcasting Corporation*, January 26, 2019, https://www.cbc.ca/news/canada/edmonton/al-rashid-mosque-police-investigating-1.4994563.

117. CBC News, "Hate Mail Sent to Edmonton Mosque Touches Off Provincial Political Battle," *Canadian Broadcasting Corporation*, February 6, 2019, https://www.cbc.ca/news/canada/edmonton/edmonton-mosque-hate-mail-anti-islam-1.5008013.

118. Sabrina Marandola, Kamila Hinkson, and Kalina Laframboise, "Six Dead, 1 Arrested and a Province in Mourning Following Quebec City Mosque Shooting,"

Canadian Broadcasting Corporation, January 29, 2017, https://www.cbc.ca/news/canada/montreal/six-dead-1-arrested-and-a-province-in-mourning-following-quebec-city-mosque-shooting-1.3957686.

119. News sources note that this was the first such event in Tarim (a city renowned for its seminaries and its political ethic of stability and moderation [*wasaṭiyya*]) but linked his death to the "systematic" killing of imams across southern Yemen: Ahmed El-Haj, "Fear Grips Yemen's Aden as Deadly Attacks Target Clerics," *AP News*, April 5, 2018, https://www.apnews.com/cb514ded-6f284e81b3776575db3ebcd2; Al Arabiya English, "Prominent Cleric Shot Dead While Praying in Yemen's Hadhramaut," *Al Arabiya*, March 2, 2018, https://english.alarabiya.net/en/News/gulf/2018/03/02/Prominent-cleric-shot-dead-while-praying-in-Yemen-s-Hadhramaut.html. And see "Habib Aydarus bin Sumayt," *Muwasala*, March 2, 2018, http://muwasala.org/habib-aydarus-bin-abdullah-bin-sumayt/; Aḥmad Faḍl Bā-Faḍl, "Shahīd al-dār wa-l-maḥārib," *Hunā ʿaden*, March 3, 2018, https://www.hunaaden.com/art19657.html.

120. On some of the transnational relations condensed in the Bosnian jihad, see Darryl Li, "Jihad in a World of Sovereigns: Law, Violence, and Islam in the Bosnia Crisis," *Law & Social Inquiry* 41, no. 2 (Spring 2016): 371–401.

121. On some of the complexities involved in granting experience historiographical weight, and on the analytic lure by which this ostensibly critical move stabilizes the subject, see Joan W. Scott, "The Evidence of Experience," *Critical Inquiry* 17, no. 4 (Summer 1991): 773–97. Scott concludes that "experience is at once always already an interpretation and something that needs to be interpreted. What counts as experience is neither self-evident nor straightforward; it is always contested, and always therefore political. The study of experience, therefore, must call into question its originary status in historical explanation" (797). The point I am arguing here is somewhat distinct but should not be taken to imply a prediscursive space of natural experience.

122. Talal Asad, *Genealogies of Religion: Discipline and Reasons of Power in Christianity and Islam* (Baltimore: Johns Hopkins University Press, 1993), 15.

123. For annals, chronicle, and narrative as three paradigmatic kinds of historical representation, see Hayden White, "The Value of Narrativity in the Representation of Reality," *Critical Inquiry* 7, no. 1 (Autumn 1980): 5–27.

124. For the twenty-five-minute funeral oration delivered by Ḥabīb ʿUmar, see M-Hood Abu-Futaim, "Janāzat al-Ḥabīb ʿAydarūs bin Sumayṭ wa kalimat Ḥabīb ʿUmar bin Ḥafīẓ," YouTube, uploaded March 5, 2018, https://www.youtube.com/watch?v=hp89ZfRTYjc; and on contrasting modes of genealogy and filiation among the Ḥabāʾib of Hadramawt (including the vocabulary of water and irrigation), see Engseng Ho, *The Graves of Tarim: Genealogy and Mobility across the Indian Ocean* (Berkeley: University of California Press, 2006), especially chap. 5. For Ḥabīb ʿUmar's account of how to understand political upheaval in Yemen

through the figure of tribulation, see the transcription of his March 29, 2015, lecture "Prophetic Guidance in Times of Tribulation," at *Muwasala*, March 31, 2015, http://muwasala.org/prophetic-guidance-in-times-of-tribulation/.

125. In speaking of "lessons" from such a history, Ḥabīb 'Umar and 'Alī reject or do not recognize what Reinhart Koselleck describes as the "dissolution of the topos into the perspective of a modernized historical process"; see Koselleck, "Historia Magistra Vitae," in *Futures Past*, 26–42.

126. Aziz al-Azmeh, "Tropes and Temporalities of Historiographic Romanticism, Modern and Islamic," in *The Times of History: Universal Topics in Islamic Historiography* (Budapest: Central European University Press, 2007), 32.

127. 'Abd al-Raḥmān al-Shāghūrī, *Dīwān al-ḥadā'iq al-nadiyya fī-l-nasamāt al-rūḥiyya* ("The Dewy Gardens in the Spiritual Breezes"), 2nd ed. (Damascus: Dār Fajr al-'Urūba, 1998), 84–85; Nuh Ha Mim Keller, ed. and trans., "An Ode by the Gnostic al-Shaghouri," in *Invocations of the Shadhili Order* (n.p.: [Al-Fath for Research and Publishing], [2010]), 104–5.

128. 'Alī bin Muḥammad al-Jurjānī, *Mu'jam al-ta'rifāt*, ed. Muḥammad Ṣiddīq al-Minshāwī (Cairo: Dār al-Faḍīla, n.d.), s.v. *safar*. He describes four "journeys" designated by the Sufis (*ahl al-ḥaqīqa*): (1) lifting the barriers of multiplicity from the face of unicity—and this is the journey "to God," the last station of the heart; (2) the vanishing of the limit between the opposites of inward (*bāṭin*) and outward (*ẓāhir*)—and this is the end of sainthood; (3) lifting the veil of unity from esoteric knowledges, realizing the divine traits (*taḥaqquq bi-asmā'i llāh*)—and this is the journey "in God," the end of presence in divine oneness; and (4) returning from the Real to creation in the station of perseverance (*istiqāma*) that is subsistence (*baqā'*) after annihilation (*fanā'*), witnessing the essence of unity in the form of multiplicity and vice versa—and this is the journey "with God, from God" (103).

129. My thanks to Aaron Eldridge for helping me understand this procedure.

130. See, for instance, al-Ṭabarī's (d. 310 AH/923 CE) commentary on Q. 18:82 (*this is the meaning of that which thou couldst not bear patiently*), where he writes that the story of Khiḍr and Moses served as God "educating" (*ta'dīb*) the Prophet, instructing him to refrain from "urging [God] to hasten the penalty [He has in store for] the polytheists" (*tark al-isti'jāl bi-'uqūbat al-mushrikīn*). This delay only deceptively appears, "to someone who has no knowledge of what God has planned for them [in the future], to be an act of kindness from Him to them, because the [correct] interpretation (*ta'wīl*) of all this ultimately will be [the polytheists'] destruction and annihilation by the sword in the temporal world, along with their well-deserved perpetual abasement from God in the Hereafter"; al-Ṭabarī, *Jāmi' al-bayān*, 18:91; trans. Scott C. Lucas, in *Selections from "The Comprehensive Exposition of the Interpretation of the Verses of the Qur'ān"* (Cambridge: Islamic Texts Society, 2017), 1:317. The true "meaning/interpretation" (*ta'wīl*) of what Moses could not bear patiently is withdrawn into the realm of the

unseen (*al-ghayb*), in that it can only be disclosed to Moses after he has seen Khiḍr's actions; yet it is also temporally fulfilled in the worldly destruction of the idolaters. This Quranic passage and its commentaries do not offer a single, determined politics that is available for emulating when facing the Syrian regime of Bashar al-Assad. Hence why, for ʿAlī, the figure of tribulation is necessarily dynamic.

131. Norman O. Brown, "The Apocalypse of Islam," *Social Text* 8 (Winter 1983–84): 166.

132. Ibid., 167.

133. Brown describes this as the question that opens "silently, majestically, in the heart of the Koran . . . what lies beyond or after the Koran? For Muhammad is like Moses a prophet. Muhammad is the seal of prophecy; what comes after prophecy?"; ibid., 163. Or, otherwise, "What does it mean to be a disciple of Khiḍr?" (170). Cf. Henry Corbin, *Alone with the Alone: Creative Imagination in the Sūfism of Ibn ʿArabī*, trans. Ralph Mannheim (1969; repr. Princeton: Princeton University Press, 1998), "The Disciple of Khiḍr," 53–67, on Khiḍr investing Ibn ʿArabī with the mystical mantle (*khirqa*).

134. Al-Shāghūrī, *Dīwān al-ḥadā'iq al-nadiyya*, 85; Keller, *Invocations of the Shadhili Order*, 105.

135. Talal Asad, response to Scott in *Powers of the Secular Modern: Talal Asad and His Interlocutors*, ed. David Scott and Charles Hirschkind (Stanford: Stanford University Press, 2006), 235.

136. For this phrase, see Ovamir Anjum, "Cultural Memory of the Pious Ancestors (*Salaf*) in al-Ghazali," *Numen* 58 (2011): 344–74.

137. Naqvi, "Acts of Askēsis, Scenes of Poēisis," 66n2.

138. Seeking out the grammatical variations of tribulation in this way does not preclude what Veena Das calls the "failure of grammar" in "the experience of world-annihilating violence"; Das, *Life and Words: Violence and the Descent into the Ordinary* (Berkeley: University of California Press, 2007), 8. Certain forms of loss may indeed be so total that they result in the "end of criteria," something akin to what Jonathan Lear explores as the breakdown of time as it is disclosed—Lear says "experienced"—within a form of life; Lear, *Radical Hope: Ethics in the Face of Cultural Devastation* (Cambridge, Mass.: Harvard University Press, 2006), 40. Nor, of course, should every vicissitude experienced by Muslims be folded back into the grammar of tribulation. Yet when devastation corrodes the paradigms of ethical action, it is explanations of the disaster of this sort that "provid[e] the psychological resources by which one might avoid despair" (135). Lear continues, "But for this hope to count as a constituent of courage, rather than a mere wishful optimism, we must see it as facilitating the capacity to respond well to reality." I follow Stefania Pandolfo in holding that recognizing the divine interpellation in the ordeal is also "a call to accept the event as it is,

confront reality and its hardship; but also, and most important, it is a call to maintain the effort and persist on the path even when our vision is clouded and the world around us is indifferent or hostile"; *Knot of the Soul*, 225–26.

139. Ludwig Wittgenstein, *Philosophical Investigations*, rev. 4th ed. (London: Blackwell, 2009), §90, 47e. And see Talal Asad, *Formations of the Secular: Christianity, Islam, Modernity* (Stanford: Stanford University Press, 2003), 25, where he cites this passage when describing his own effort of an anthropology of the secular as "a matter of showing how contingencies relate to changes in the grammar of concepts—that is, how the changes in concepts articulate changes in practices."

140. Elizabeth Povinelli also turns to Benveniste in the course of her examination of late liberal social tense: *Economies of Abandonment: Social Belonging and Endurance in Late Liberalism* (Durham, N.C.: Duke University Press, 2011). At first glance, tribulation appears to function like the techniques of liberal governance in "deflect[ing] moral sense and practical reason from the durative present to an absolute difference between presence and absence"—for example, in 'Umar's preternatural struggle between truth and falsehood—or "the critical difference between the future anterior and the past perfect"—for example, in 'Uthmān's divine economy (13). Certainly, these events, like crises and catastrophes, are of the type that "seem to demand, *as if authored from outside human agency*, an ethical response" (14, emphasis added). But within this Islamic tradition the authorship of even ordinary events is a theologically complicated question, and tribulation confounds precisely the distinction between ordinary and extraordinary events. Povinelli urges instead an "anthropology of ordinary suffering" that could perceive how "extraordinary events of violence are folded into everyday routines—and vice versa." Yet if, as she writes a little further on, "all subjects are subject to forms of eventualization," then critical purchase on ethical substance as embodied potentiality cannot hinge on asserting the immanence of human agency (that human agency is properly "outside a gesture of transcendental consciousness," 16).

141. Robert Meister, *After Evil: A Politics of Human Rights* (New York: Columbia University Press, 2011), 304–8.

142. Ibid., 301.

143. Arabic (the first language of the revealed Qur'anic imperative) does not employ the tenses of past, present, and future, as broadly in Indo-European languages, instead using verbal aspects of complete and incomplete without decisively distinguishing present from future. "Indeed, from a temporal point of view, the Arabic verb knows only two forms: *madi* (past, finished or perfect act), and *mudari'* (the imperfect act which is currently in progress or which will take place in the future). . . . The present tense comes about while the speaker speaks, which is neither in the elapsed moment, nor in the future one"; Ahmed Achrati,

"Arabic, Qur'anic Speech, and Postmodern Language: What the Qur'an Simply Says," *Arabica* 55 (2008): 176–77.

144. Meister, *After Evil*, 217; Giorgio Agamben, *Remnants of Auschwitz: The Witness and the Archive*, trans. Daniel Heller-Roazen (New York: Zone Books, 1999), 33.

145. Meister, *After Evil*, chap. 7: "Bystanders and Victims."

146. *Ṣaḥīḥ Muslim* 1923.

147. Hayden White, "The Historical Event," *differences: A Journal of Feminist Cultural Studies* 19, no. 2 (2008): 29.

148. See, for example, Fabrice Balanche, "Sectarianism in Syria's Civil War" (Washington, D.C.: Washington Institute for Near East Policy, 2018); Charles Lister, *The Syrian Jihad: Al-Qaeda, the Islamic State, and the Evolution of an Insurgency* (New York: Oxford University Press, 2016); and Lisa Wedeen, *Authoritarian Apprehensions: Ideology, Judgment, and Mourning in Syria* (Chicago: University of Chicago Press, 2019), chap. 5, "Fear and Foreboding."

149. Pandolfo, *Knot of the Soul*, 226.

150. Tribulation offers a means of translating across ostensibly separate historical periods and social domains. It also reprises the rupture conventionally narrated in and of Islamic traditions. See Basit Kareem Iqbal, "Reprising Islamic Political Theology: Genre and the Time of Tribulation," *Political Theology* 23, no. 6 (2022): 525–42, for a fuller methodological argument for attending to "tribulation," a brief illustration of the contours of this figure across certain genres that give it shape, and an exploration of the affordances of genre for such an inquiry. Although Islamicists have similarly relied upon genre in order to reach conclusions about time "in" Islam, to be clear, my broadly anthropological effort is directed less at identifying and recovering technical terms for time (*dawām, zamān, khulūd, waqt, yawm, sāʿa*, etc.) from Islamic genres than at considering how the chronotope of tribulation itself defines generic distinctions. That is, I am not suggesting that a natural time is then "represented" through the concept of tribulation. Instead, much as form is not separate from life, time is encountered in and disclosed through practice: as one inhabits a tribulation. See Dominic Longo, *Spiritual Grammar: Genre and the Saintly Subject in Islam and Christianity* (New York: Fordham University Press, 2017), 23: "Perhaps it could also be said that the genre, conceived of in this way, produces the 'zone' of possibility for an activity, or at least produces the conditions of its possibility. The desire to speak a certain way is a desire to enter into life in a certain way."

151. Pandolfo, *Knot of the Soul*, 225.

152. Cf. the role of prophecy in Reinhart Koselleck, *Futures Past: On the Semantics of Historical Time*, trans. Keith Tribe (New York: Columbia University Press, 2004), chap. 1, "Modernity and the Planes of Historicity"; and see Asad, *Formations of the Secular*, 223, where he describes the complex juncture between

"horizon of expectation" and "space of experience" as being "intrinsic to the structure of time itself"—rather than, as Koselleck writes, being specific to modernity.

153. Among many others on the problem of commensuration and anthropological difference, see Talal Asad, "The Concept of Translation in British Social Anthropology," in *Writing Culture: The Poetics and Politics of Ethnography*, ed. James Clifford and George E. Marcus (Berkeley: University of California Press, 1986), 141–64.

154. Andrew Brandel and Marco Motta, "Introduction: Life with Concepts," in *Living with Concepts: Anthropology in the Grip of Reality*, ed. Andrew Brandel and Marco Motta (New York: Fordham University Press, 2021), 6.

THRESHOLD: AMBIVALENCE

1. Khālid bin ʿAlī al-Mushayqaḥ, *al-Mukhtaṣar fī-l-ʿaqīda* (The Epitome in Creed) (Riyadh: Maktabat al-Rushd, 1431/2010), 5–6; for the material loosely covered in class that day, see 71–79. The author donated dozens of bound photocopies of his book to this program.

2. To be clear, the "ambivalence" encountered here is closer to Butler's reading of Freud (where melancholia, as the "ambivalent reaction to loss, may be coextensive with loss, so that mourning is subsumed in melancholia"; Judith Butler, *The Psychic Life of Power: Theories in Subjection* [Stanford: Stanford University Press, 1997], 174) than to psychologically diagnostic efforts at parsing confusional from depressive anxieties among migrants and exiles (León Grinberg and Rebeca Grinberg, "A Psychoanalytic Study of Migration: Its Normal and Pathological Aspects," *Journal of the American Psychoanalytic Association* 32, no. 1 [1984]: 13–38) or to the paralyzing vacillation between "the attachment to order and the desire for change" that characterized "key populations in Syria" through the years of the war (Lisa Wedeen, *Authoritarian Apprehensions: Ideology, Judgment, and Mourning in Syria* [Chicago: University of Chicago Press, 2019], 7)—not least because what order there was, to be attached to, is already ruined. Much of the academic and clinical psychoanalytic literature on ambivalence approaches it as a problem of identification, but "the historicity of loss is to be found in identification and, hence, in the very forms that attachment is bound to take" (Butler, *Psychic Life of Power*, 194–95). For such identification in Zaatari Camp, see Melissa N. Gatter, "Restoring Childhood: Humanitarianism and Growing Up Syrian in Zaʿtari Refugee Camp," *Contemporary Levant* 2, no. 2 (2017): 89–102.

3. Toshihiko Izutsu, *God and Man in the Qur'an* (1964; repr. Kuala Lumpur: Islamic Book Trust, 2002), 230.

4. al-Mushayqaḥ, *al-Mukhtaṣar fī-l-ʿaqīda*, 114.

5. Vinh Nguyen, "Refugeetude: When Does a Refugee Stop Being a Refugee," *Social Text* 37, no. 2 (June 2019): 109–31; Ilana Feldman, *Life Lived in Relief:*

Humanitarian Predicaments and Palestinian Refugee Politics (Oakland: University of California Press, 2018).

6. See, too, Joel Robbins, "Beyond the Suffering Subject: Toward an Anthropology of the Good," *Journal of the Royal Anthropological Institute* 19, no. 3 (September 2013): 447–62.

7. The Quranic concept of *jāhiliyya* (e.g., Q. 48:26) refers to a kind of obstinate arrogance untempered by faith and came to designate the epoch before Islam. In much contemporary Islamic political theology, notably articulated by Sayyid Qutb but certainly not limited to him, *jāhiliyya* marks a condition that opposes *islām*, not a period that preceded it. For one overview, see William E. Shepard, "Sayyid Qutb's Doctrine of Jāhiliyya," *International Journal of Middle East Studies* 35 (2003): 521–45.

8. Izutsu, *God and Man in the Qur'an*, 231; and chap. 8: "*Jāhiliyyah* and Islam," passim.

3. THE HEIGHTS

1. Khetam Malkawi, "Mafraq, Ramtha Population Doubled Since Start of Syrian Crisis," *Jordan Times*, November 27, 2015, https://www.jordantimes.com/news/local/mafraq-ramtha-population-doubled-start-syrian-crisis%E2%80%99.

2. Sharaf al-Dīn Yaḥyā bin Nūr al-Dīn Mūsā al-ʿAmrīṭī, *Nihāyat al-tadrīb fī naẓm ghāyat al-taqrīb*, ed. Muḥammad Ḥasan Ḥabannaka (Mecca: al-Maktaba al-Makkiyya, 1420/1999), 18. This ninth/fifteenth-century text, which was also taught at the ʿAbdullāh bin al-Mubārak Project in Zaatari Refugee Camp (see Chapter 2), is a popular versification of the Shāfiʿite primer *Matn Abū Shujāʿ*, which covers the breadth of juridical topics from ritual purity to manumission. For a translation of the latter, see Abū Shujāʿ al-Aṣfahānī, *The Ultimate Conspectus: Matn al-Ghāyat wa al-Taqrīb*, trans. Musa Furber (n.p.: Islamosaic, 2007).

3. Much like the children "growing up Syrian in Zaatari Camp," Daraawi orphans here "grow up understanding the importance of their origins at home and cannot ignore their own political histories that tie them to their home city"; Melissa N. Gatter, "Restoring Childhood: Humanitarianism and Growing Up Syrian in Zaʿtari Refugee Camp," *Contemporary Levant* 2, no. 2 (2017): 98.

4. Human Rights Watch, "'I Have No Idea Why They Sent Us Back': Jordanian Deportations and Expulsions of Refugees" (October 2017), https://www.hrw.org/sites/default/files/report_pdf/jordan1017_web.pdf; Alice Su, "Why Jordan Is Deporting Syrian Refugees," *Atlantic*, October 20, 2017, https://www.theatlantic.com/international/archive/2017/10/jordan-syrian-refugees-deportation/543057/.

5. The tractive role played by ethical character here should be seen not as compromising the charities' professionalism (as the policy literature regards relational connections to do) but as analogous to the performance of middle-class

respectability that anthropologists have observed lubricates modern bureaucratic practices across cultural contexts. Each of these forms of comportment convenes a "social space created by the reflexive circulation of discourse" (Michael Warner, *Publics and Counterpublics* (New York: Zone Books, 2002), 90–96), although of course their criteria vary substantively. Literature on how reputation and personal connections facilitate social exchange in the Middle East tends to regard *wāsṭa* as a type of corruption. More recently it has been understood as a network of "social capital." For a more compelling intervention on the "bonds of trust and obligation" that ground practices of *wasṭa*, see Yazan Doughan, "The Rule-of-Law as a Problem Space: *Wāsṭa* and the Paradox of Justice in Jordan," *Comparative Studies in Society and History* 66, no. 1 (2024): 131–54.

6. In similar terms, Veena Das describes the depth of present narration in how the violence of Partition was "incorporated into the temporal structure of relationships," transforming the "patient work" of ongoing kinship into an act of witnessing. "Thus, the memory of the Partition cannot be understood in Asha's life as a direct possession of the past. It is constantly interposed and mediated by the manner in which the world is being presently inhabited. Even when it appears that some women were relatively lucky because they escaped direct bodily harm, the bodily memory of being-with-others makes that past encircle the present as atmosphere"; Das, *Life and Words: Violence and the Descent into the Ordinary* (Berkeley: University of California Press, 2007), 76–77. Later in this chapter I more directly take up the frozen temporality held by scenes from Bilāl's life in Syria.

7. This edited transcription is based primarily on an audio-recording of his life story I made in July 2018, supplemented by details from conversations with him across March 2018–October 2019. I added the dates and the occasional detail in order to locate his story against the early timeline of the Syrian uprising, consulting notably Robin Yassin-Kassab and Leila al-Shami, *Burning Country: Syrians in Revolution and War* (London: Pluto Press, 2016), chap. 3: "Revolution from Below"; and Human Rights Watch, "We've Never Seen Such Horror: Crimes Against Humanity by the Syrian Security Forces" (New York: Human Rights Watch, June 2011), https://www.hrw.org/report/2011/06/01/weve-never-seen-such-horror/crimes-against-humanity-syrian-security-forces.

8. The literature on the narrative emplotment and performance of suffering is vast (especially within medical and psychological anthropology); for an anthology of such work, see Arthur Kleinman, Veena Das, and Margaret Lock, eds., *Social Suffering* (Berkeley: University of California Press, 1997). Some of the most interesting scholarship on humanitarianism takes a similar approach; for an anthology of such work, see Richard Ashby Wilson and Richard D. Brown, eds., *Humanitarianism and Suffering: The Mobilization of Empathy* (Cambridge: Cambridge University Press, 2009). And for two more proximate cases, see

Robert Meister, *After Evil: A Politics of Human Rights* (New York: Columbia University Press, 2011), 65–69, on the melodramatic narrative genre of truth and reconciliation after torture; and Amira Mittermaier, *Giving to God: Islamic Charity in Revolutionary Times* (Oakland: University of California Press, 2019), chap. 4: "Performances of Poverty," on how the bracketing of compassion in Islamic charitable contexts does not always bracket the question of deservingness—and so maintains the cruelty of charity.

9. These images, released to the opposition Syrian National Council and then to Human Rights Watch, even elicited a response from Bashar al-Assad in January 2015: "You can bring photographs from anyone and say this is torture. There is no verification of any of this evidence, so it's all allegations without evidence." For the Human Rights Watch report on the Caesar photographs, composed as precisely the verification Assad disputed, see "If the Dead Could Speak: Mass Deaths and Torture in Syria's Detention Facilities" (HRW, December 2015), https://www.hrw.org/sites/default/files/report_pdf/syria1215web_0.pdf. See also the extensive investigation by Anne Barnard, "Inside Syria's Secret Torture Prisons: How Bashar al-Assad Crushed Dissent," *New York Times*, May 11, 2019, https://www.nytimes.com/2019/05/11/world/middleeast/syria-torture-prisons.html; and, for a full account, Garance Le Caisne, *Operation Caesar: At the Heart of the Syrian Death Machine*, trans. David Watson (Cambridge: Polity Press, 2018).

10. Syrian Network for Human Rights, "Documentation of 72 Torture Methods the Syrian Regime Continues to Practice in Its Detention Centers and Military Hospitals" (SNHR, October 2019), http://sn4hr.org/wp-content/pdf/english/Documentation_of_72_Torture_Methods_the_Syrian_Regime_Continues_to_Practice_in_Its_Detention_Centers_and_Military_Hospitals_en.pdf, 14.

11. Ibid., 18–19.

12. For more on the "assault of images," see the panoply of responses to Susan Sontag's powerful "Regarding the Torture of Others," *New York Times Magazine*, May 23, 2004, https://www.nytimes.com/2004/05/23/magazine/regarding-the-torture-of-others.html—notably Judith Butler's *Frames of War: When Is Life Grievable?* (London: Verso, 2009), chap. 2.

13. Salwa Ismail, *The Rule of Violence: Subjectivity, Memory, and Government in Syria* (Cambridge: Cambridge University Press, 2018), 2.

14. Ibid., 5–6.

15. Ibid., 19–22. And see Allen Feldman, *Formations of Violence: The Narrative of the Body and Political Terror in Northern Ireland* (Chicago: University of Chicago Press, 1991), 112–46, for a remarkable exploration of how "the performance of terror does not apply terror; rather it manufactures it from the 'raw' ingredient of the captive's body. The surface of the body is the stage where the state is made to appear as an effective material force" (115).

16. For a detailed account of Tadmor prison, see Jaber Baker and Uğur Ümit Üngör, *Syrian Gulag: Inside Assad's Prison System* (London: I. B. Tauris, 2023), chap. 7.

17. For a striking reenactment of ex-Tadmor detainees revisiting their incarceration (if not redressing its traumatic alienation), see Monika Borgmann and Lokman Slim, dirs., *Tadmor* (Icarus Films, 2017); for a report on Sednaya prison that graphs psychological and physical impacts of detention and attends particularly to changes in the regime's detention practices since the 2011 revolution, see the Association of Detainees and the Missing in Sednaya Prison, "Detention in Sednaya: Report on the Procedures and Consequences of Political Imprisonment" (Gazientep: ADMSP, November 2019), https://admsp.org/wp-content/uploads/2019/11/sydnaia-en-final-November-s-11-07-2019.pdf.

18. Ismail, *Rule of Violence*, 38–54. This recourse to the Quran is well-attested in the prison literature, including by those who are not pious or even Muslim. For example, see Mustafa Khalifa, *The Shell: Memoirs of a Hidden Observer*, trans. Paul Starkey [Arabic 2006] (Northampton, Mass.: Interlink Books, 2017), 51: "The memorizing started with the beginning of the 'trial,' as the Islamists called it. The older sheikhs would sit and recite chapters and verses of the Qur'an to a group of youths, and the youths would carry on repeating them until they had memorized them. In this way, a mechanism for memorization was generated. There was no one in the dormitory who hadn't memorized the Qur'an from beginning to end. With each new intake a new cycle began"; and Muhammad Saleem Hammad, "Tadmur: Witnessed and Observed," trans. Syrian Human Rights Committee, https://www.shrc.org/en/wp-content/uploads/2017/02/Tadmur-Witnessed-and-Observed-Final-1.pdf: "We quickly returned to the recitation and memorization of the Book of God, our only source of comfort and the cure to our suffering and wounds. A number of weeks later, God blessed our hall with a brother who had the entire Quran memorized. He arrived with a new group of fifteen brothers from Damascus, all from the Mosque of Zayd bin Thaabit. . . . Our pleasure at his arrival in our hall was indescribable, and we learned from him many new Chapters and verses from the Quran" (74). After completing the memorization of the Quran, transmitted orally from one detainee to the next, Hammad then memorized Islamic scholarly texts. His memoir is devastating and frames his incarceration as an ordeal. For more on this intersection, see Walaa Quisay and Asim Qureshi, *When Only God Can See: The Faith of Muslim Political Prisoners* (London: Pluto Press, 2024).

19. Stefania Pandolfo, *Knot of the Soul: Madness, Psychoanalysis, Islam* (Chicago: University of Chicago Press, 2018), 163.

20. As is explored shortly, the significance of the home that Bilāl misses has itself been transformed over the years of his exile, meaning that the "yearning" (*ḥanīn*) he expresses recalls a poetic motif that is decidedly ambivalent. See

Sebastian Günther and Stephan Milich, eds., *Representations and Visions of Homeland in Modern Arabic Literature* (Hildesheim: Georg Olms Verlag, 2016). It also evokes the historical difference underscored in C. Nadia Seremetakis, "Memory of the Senses, Part I," in *The Senses Still: Perception and Memory as Material Culture in Modernity*, ed. C. Nadia Seremetakis (Chicago: University of Chicago Press, 1994), 4: "*Nostalghía* is the desire or longing with burning pain to journey. It also evokes the sensory dimension of memory in exile and estrangement; it mixes bodily and emotional pain and ties painful experiences of spiritual and somatic exile to the notion of maturation and ripening. . . . Nostalgia, in the American sense, freezes the past in such a manner as to preclude it from any capacity for social transformation in the present, preventing the present from establishing a dynamic perceptual relationship to its history. Whereas the Greek etymology evokes the transformative impact of the past as unreconciled historical experience."

21. Das writes, analogously, "Although the Partition was of the past if seen through homogeneous units of measurable time, its continued presence in people's lives was apparent in story, gesture, and conversation. Though of the past, it did not have a *feeling* of pastness about it"; Das, *Life and Words*, 97.

22. "Though photographs freeze a single moment in time," writes Zeynep Devrim Gürsel, "looking together requires observing from the perspective of many points in time to search out not only what photographs show but also what they cannot yet show or can no longer show." See her "Looking Together as Method: Encounters with Ottoman Armenian Expatriation Photographs," *Visual Anthropology Review* 39, no. 1 (Spring 2023): 200–229.

23. Rāfiyā Salāma, "Dākhil wa khārij: kayfa aṣbaḥū 'hum,'" *al-Jumhuriya*, March 22, 2018; trans. Vanessa Breeding as "Syria's 'Inside' and 'Outside': How They Became 'Them,'" *Al-Jumhuriya English*, June 2, 2018, https://aljumhuriya.net/en/2018/03/21/syrias-inside-and-outside-how-they-became-them/. And see Feldman, *Formations of Violence*, for an attention to spatial practices effected through violence: "The command of these spaces is practically achieved and sustained through ideology and violence. . . . The spatial inscription of practices and power involves physical flows, metabolic transactions and transfers—exchanges which connect, separate, distance, and hierarchize one space in relation to another" (9).

24. Pandolfo beautifully elaborates the debate between her interlocutors Kamal and Jawad about the meaning, weight, and stakes of attempting to cross to Europe: see *Knot of the Soul*, chap. 6. Is the risk justified? My conversations, like those related there, "unfolded in a shifting realm between geography and theology, between a disenchanted sociopolitical description of exclusion and a moral account of banishment and transgression; between the violation of the law of states (by the illicit trespassing of frontiers) and that of the law of God; between

a mode of personal narrative and one of moral admonition; between life and death, this world and the other" (195).

25. Charlotte al-Khalili writes that "spatial disruption (the creation of *juwwa* and the displacement to *barra*) appears as engendering a specific kind of subject: the revolutionary self"; al-Khalili, *Waiting for the Revolution to End: Syrian Displacement, Time, and Subjectivity* (London: UCL Press, 2023), 78.

26. On the relentless and unsettling tropics of contemporary estrangement, see Aaron Eldridge and Basit Kareem Iqbal, "A Tropics of Estrangement: *Ghurba* in Four Scenes," *diacritics: A Review of Contemporary Criticism* 50, no. 1 (March 2022): 112–40.

27. Talal Asad, "Thinking About Tradition, Religion, and Politics in Egypt Today," *Critical Inquiry* 42, no. 1 (Autumn 2015): 179n28, for an anthropological engagement with the Islamic practice of "commanding right" (*amr bi-l-maʿrūf*).

28. Seremetakis writes that "an entire past sensory landscape" may be "translated into a present act." Such "sensory stasis is not always cultivated . . . it can occur through forced experiences of crisis, separation and cross cultural contact. For these moments release hidden substances of the past. It is the very absence of referents, surfaces and textures that lifts them out of the banality of structural silence imposed by a culture or social order and allows a previously by-passed contact to be released as history"; Seremetakis, "Memory of the Senses, Part I," 16–17.

29. Suleiman Al-Khalidi, "Russia, Jordan Agree to Speed De-Escalation Zone in South Syria," *Reuters*, September 11, 2017, https://www.reuters.com/article/us-mideast-crisis-jordan-russia/russia-jordan-agree-to-speed-de-escalation-zone-in-south-syria-idUSKCN1BM2A5.

30. International Crisis Group, "Keeping the Calm in Southern Syria," Report 187 (Brussels: ICG, June 21, 2018), https://www.crisisgroup.org/middle-east-north-africa/eastern-mediterranean/syria/187-keeping-calm-southern-syria.

31. Patrick Wintour, "Syrian Forces' Push into East Daraa 'Could Spark Humanitarian Crisis,'" *Guardian*, June 27, 2018, https://www.theguardian.com/world/2018/jun/27/syria-assad-forces-eastern-daraa-humanitarian-crisis-un; Emma Graham-Harrison, "Syria: Southern Towns Surrender to Assad Forces after Thousands Flee Homes," *Guardian*, June 30, 2018, https://www.theguardian.com/world/2018/jun/30/syria-southern-towns-surrender-to-assad-forces; and Hussein Akoush and Elizabeth Hagedorn, "'Their Blankets Are the Sky': Syrian Civilians Flee Deraa," *Guardian*, July 5, 2018, https://www.theguardian.com/global-development/2018/jul/05/blankets-sky-syrian-civilians-flee-daraa.

32. Ṣādiq ʿAbd al-Raḥmān, "Jaḥīm wa ḥudūd mughlaqa: shahādat min ḥawrān," *Al Jumhuriyya*, June 29, 2018, trans. Alex Rowell, at https://www.aljumhuriya.net/en/content/between-hellfire-and-closed-border.

33. *Al-Adab al-mufrad*, hadith 480. For this hadith within the genres of Islamic apocalyptic, see Basit Kareem Iqbal, "The Messiah and the Jurisconsult: Agamben on the Problem of Law in Sunni Islam," *Journal of Religion* 101, no. 3 (July 2021): 351–70.

34. Once, as Bilāl was describing the thousands detained and disappeared since the revolution, I remembered studying (in Damascus) the jurisprudential case of the absent merchant whose family had not heard from him for over a year. Bilāl noted that the analogy was complicated, but that there were some overlaps in how jurists approached these questions. Then he sent me a 2014 responsum by the Islamic Organization of Syria (Hay'at al-Shām al-Islāmiyya) about the situation of a woman whose husband was disappeared by the regime without news of whether he was alive or dead. Is she married or not? Can a judge rule upon their effective divorce to release her from the marriage? How should inheritance be distributed? The "jurisprudence of the revolution" responsa issued by Hay'at al-Shām al-Islāmiyya were later collected in three volumes freely available online. See *Fatāwā al-thawra al-sūriyya* (N.p.: al-Maktab al-'Ilmī li-l-Hay'at al-Shām al-Islāmiyya, 2019), https://www.islamicsham.org/versions/796, 2:55–72, "Aḥkām zawjat al-ghā'ib wa-l-mafqūd."

35. See "The Politics of Translating al-Shabbi's 'If the People Choose to Live One Day,'" *ArabLit*, January 22, 2011, https://arablit.org/2011/01/22/the-politics-of-translating-al-shabbis-if-the-people-choose-to-live-one-day/. For this hadith, see Abū Dāwūd, *Sunan*, Kitāb al-fitan wa-l-malāḥim, bāb dhikr al-fitan wa dalā'ilihā.

36. Rebecca Comay, "Deadlines (Literally)," Gillian Rose Memorial Lecture (London: CRMEP Books, 2020), 16, 12.

37. Rebecca Comay, "Mourning Work and Play," *Research in Phenomenology* 23 (1993): 111.

38. Victor Turner, *The Ritual Process: Structure and Anti-Structure* (New Brunswick, N.J.: AldineTransaction, 1969), 95–96.

39. Jorge Luis Borges, "The Secret Miracle," in *Labyrinths: Selected Stories and Other Writings*, ed. Donald A. Yates and James E. Irby (1943; repr. New York: New Directions Books, 1964).

40. Comay, "Deadlines (Literally)," 14.

41. The Quranic term *barzakh* has been productively invoked in anthropology as a figure for a limit that constitutes at once barrier and bridge, partition and passage, separation and mediation. Stefania Pandolfo crafts an ethnography that traverses the "hiatus which destabilizes the assignment of places and parts, which displaces the categories of classical and colonial reason and opens a heterological space of intercultural dialogue—an atopical intermediate region that might be called a *barzakh*." There, "a certain listening becomes possible"; Pandolfo, *Impasse of the Angels: Scenes from a Moroccan Space of Memory* (Chicago: University of Chicago Press, 1997), 5–6. Vincent Crapanzano gives the disjunctive time of

liminality an epistemological significance in its own right, where invention and negation together reveal that "moment of transition that resists articulation"; Crapanzano, *Imaginative Horizons: An Essay in Literary-Philosophical Anthropology* (Chicago: University of Chicago Press, 2004), 60–61. He approaches the Islamic concept of *barzakh* as one such term of liminality. Likewise, Amira Mittermaier writes that the concept of *barzakh* may provide "an analytical tool that circumvents the rule of the either/or . . . [it] ruptures binary outlooks and invites us to think beyond the present and the visible. It invites us to dwell on the in-between"; Mittermaier, *Dreams That Matter: Egyptian Landscapes of the Imagination* (Berkeley: University of California Press, 2011), 3–4. Each of these anthropologists approaches the *barzakh* as both an ethnographic object and as a methodological term of analysis. Whether allowing for heterological dialogue (Pandolfo) or revealing the play of nonbeing (Crapanzano) or reprising the role of imagination (Mittermaier), the *barzakh* splices the sites of encounter. The ethnography offered here is deeply inspired by these works even as it emphasizes the violence of such encounters with and of liminality.

42. For some of these interpretations, see *The Study Quran: A New Translation and Commentary*, ed. Seyyed Hossein Nasr et al. (New York: HarperCollins, 2017), 423–25.

43. Pandolfo, *Knot of the Soul*, 322. Perhaps such life exposes what is always already at work to show at last an intimate exteriority—an "extimacy"—"that is always lurking and comes to be exposed in trauma." In Pandolfo's "possible conversation" between psychoanalysis and Islamic psychology, this "return to the inorganic state, beyond the subject and beyond life," resonates with the project of Jacques Lacan's ethics seminar. In its final session, Lacan describes his proposal simply as seeking "the point of view of the Last Judgment" (*The Ethics of Psychoanalysis, 1959–1960: The Seminar of Jacques Lacan*, Book VII, trans. Dennis Porter, ed. Jacques-Alain Miller [New York: W. W. Norton, 1992], 313)—perhaps the perspective of those suspended between Garden and Fire—or the extimate presence of the real in the symbolic; cf. Jacques-Alain Miller, "Extimité," trans. Françoise Massardier-Kenney, *Prose Studies: History, Theory, Criticism* 11, no. 3 (1988): 122. Although the tradition of Islamic ethics is frequently assimilated into a broadly Aristotelian model of virtue, Pandolfo shows that "Lacan's moving 'beyond' of the Aristotelean ethics of the good, and towards an ethics of the vulnerable struggle," may well take place through "daily confrontations" on "the battlefield of the *nafs*."

44. Pandolfo, *Knot of the Soul*, 321–22.

45. Daniel M. Knight, *Vertiginous Life: An Anthropology of Time and the Unforeseen* (New York: Berghahn Books, 2021), 133.

46. Blanchot describes the "'hollowing out' of the present, a 'hollowing infinitely distended,' as of a present to which we are no longer present"; Gerald L. Bruns, *Maurice Blanchot: The Refusal of Philosophy* (Baltimore: Johns Hopkins

University Press, 1997), 127. In writing of the temporality of the defeat of the Syrian revolution, Charlotte al-Khalili similarly quotes the historian Elias Sanbar on the equation of spatial and temporal displacement for exiled Palestinians: "They found themselves trapped in an ephemeral dimension, and for half a century they would live in limbo, achieving a very special relationship with the concept of duration. Since the present was forbidden to them, they would occupy a temporal space made up of both a past preserved by a memory afflicted by madness and a dreamt-of future which aspired to restore time"; quoted in al-Khalili, *Waiting for the Revolution to End*, 111.

47. Comay, "Deadlines (Literally)," 15.

48. Ibid., 20.

49. Ibid., 23–24.

50. Comay, "Mourning Work and Play," 125.

51. Anne DuFourmantelle, *Power of Gentleness: Meditations on the Risk of Living*, trans. Katherine Payne and Vincent Sallé (New York: Fordham University Press, 2018), 7.

52. Ibid., 81.

53. Ibid., 15.

54. Maurice Blanchot, *The Instant of My Death*/Jacques Derrida, *Demeure: Fiction and Testimony*, trans. Elizabeth Rottenberg (Stanford: Stanford University Press, 2000), 7–9.

55. Ibid., 90. See Christopher Fynsk, *Last Steps: Maurice Blanchot's Exilic Writing* (New York: Fordham University Press, 2013), 118: "The narrator testifies not to dispersion and loss of self in a community of affliction, but rather to the opening of another relation via a secret bond with death that he does not hesitate to name *friendship* and that allows him to affirm being with, and in some measure, for the other."

56. Blanchot, *The Instant of My Death*, 5.

57. DuFourmantelle, *Power of Gentleness*, 77.

58. Sigmund Freud, "Traumatic Fixation—the Unconscious," in *A General Introduction to Psychoanalysis*, trans. Edward L. Bernays (New York: Boni and Liveright, 1920), 237. See also Yassin al-Haj Saleh's comments on ISIS destroying the Assad regime's infamous Tadmor prison: "I dreamt that I would visit it someday. . . . This visit would redeem me . . . it would be a closure. . . . The destruction of a prison that was the symbol of our slavery is the destruction of our freedom"; BBC Magazine, "Inside Tadmur: The Worst Prison in the World?" *British Broadcasting Corporation*, June 20, 2015, https://www.bbc.com/news/magazine-33197612.

59. Sigmund Freud, "Beyond the Pleasure Principle" (German 1920), in *Beyond the Pleasure Principle and Other Writings* (New York: Penguin, 2003), 55; as also in Eric Santner's account of homeopathic mourning by which the symbolic introduction of poison becomes an effective cure, empowering the subject to

master its potentially traumatic effects: Santner, *Stranded Objects: Mourning, Memory, and Film in Postwar Germany* (Ithaca, N.Y.: Cornell University Press, 1990); but also Jean Laplanche's more enigmatic account of mourning in which he notes that Penelope's nocturnal weaving/unweaving for Ulysses "does not cut the threads, as in the Freudian theory of mourning; she patiently unpicks them, to be able to compose them again in a different way": Laplanche, *Essays on Otherness* (London: Routledge, 1999), 256.

60. DuFourmantelle, *Power of Gentleness*, 10. The expansion of the present obtains variously but is already familiar to psychoanalysis, for instance through the intensifying relay implied by Laplanche's account of afterwardsness (*Nachträglichkeit*): "Right at the start, there is something that goes in the direction of the past to the future, from the other to the individual in question . . . this message is then retranslated, following a temporal direction which is, in an alternating fashion, by turns retrogressive and progressive"; Laplanche, *Essays on Otherness*, 269.

61. DuFourmantelle, *Power of Gentleness*, 85.

62. For Freud, mourning is a normalizing relation to loss: it offers a freeing of the ego from its libidinal attachment to the lost object. By contrast, melancholia occurs through a narcissistic identification with the lost object—an attempt to devour the object and loss into oneself. "In mourning it is the world which has become poor and empty; in melancholia it is the ego itself." Mourning reorients the longing for the lost object, even though there is understandable opposition to the withdrawing of such attachments. As Freud writes, "People never willingly abandon a libidinal position, not even, indeed, when a substitute is already beckoning to them"; Sigmund Freud, "Mourning and Melancholia," in *The Standard Edition of the Complete Psychological Works of Sigmund Freud*, trans., ed. James Strachey (London: Hogarth, 1953), 14:244, 246.

63. DuFourmantelle, *Power of Gentleness*, 98–99.

AFTERWORD: ETERNITY HAS FALLEN

1. Yassin al-Haj Saleh, "State Extermination, Not a 'Dictatorial Regime'," trans. Alex Rowell, *Aljumhuriya*, April 30, 2018; see also Eylaf Bader Eddin, "*Al-Abad*: On the Ongoing," *Middle East Journal of Culture and Communication* 15 (2022): 367–76.

2. Bilal Ali, "Days of Allah," in *Integrated Encyclopedia of the Qur'ān*, vol. 3 (Ardrossan: Center for Islamic Sciences), forthcoming.

3. As Charlotte al-Khalili writes about an earlier moment, "The meaning of the present as the revolution's defeat, the finished revolutionary past, and the uncertain future is supposed to be understood not only by the return of the revolution but also in the afterlife on Judgement Day"; al-Khalili, *Waiting for the Revolution to End: Syrian Displacement, Time and Subjectivity* (London: UCL Press, 2023), 132.

BIBLIOGRAPHY

Quran translations are from *The Study Quran: A New Translation and Commentary*, ed. Seyyed Hossein Nasr et al. (New York: HarperCollins, 2017). All other translations are my own, unless otherwise noted. Since editions vary, hadith references are given by book and chapter in the text.

Ababsa, Myriam. "De la crise humanitaire à la crise sécuritaire: Les dispositifs de contrôle des réfugiés syriens en Jordanie (2011–2015)." *Revue européenne des migrations internationales* [online] 31, nos. 3–4 (2015). http://journals.openedition.org/remi/7380.

———. "Islamic NGOs Assistance to Syrian Refugees in Jordan and Gulf Donors Support." *Lajeh: Migrations et Conflits au Moyen-orient*, January 21, 2017, https://lajeh.hypotheses.org/723.

———. "An Urbanizing Camp? Zaatari Syrian Refugee Camp in Jordan." *Conflits et migrations* (May 9, 2018), https://lajeh.hypotheses.org/1076.

Abd-Allah, Umar F. *The Islamic Struggle in Syria*. Berkeley, Calif.: Mizan Press, 1983.

———. *al-Īmānu fiṭra: dirāsat li-l-īmān al-fiṭrī fī-l-qur'ān wa-l-sunna wa kathīr min al-milal wa-l-niḥal*. Abu Dhabi: Dār al-Faqīh, 2014.

'Abd al-Raḥmān, Ṣādiq. "Jaḥīm wa ḥudūd mughlaqa: shahādat min ḥawrān." *Al Jumhuriyya*, June 29, 2018, translated by Alex Rowell at https://www.aljumhuriya.net/en/content/between-hellfire-and-closed-border.

Abou El Fadl, Khaled. *Rebellion and Violence in Islamic Law*. Cambridge: Cambridge University Press, 2001.

Abeysekara, Ananda. Review of Joseph Walser's *Genealogies of Mahayana Buddhism* (Routledge, 2018). In *Religious Theory: The E-Supplement to the "Journal of Cultural and Religious Theory*," October 23, 2019, http://jcrt.org/religioustheory/2019/10/23/review-genealogies-of-mahayana-buddhism-ananda-abeysekara/.

Abu Rumman, Mohammad. *I Am a Salafi: A Study of the Actual and Imagined Identities of Salafis*. Translated by Hassan Barari. Amman: Friedrich-Ebert-Stiftung Foundation, 2014.

Abū Shujā' al-Aṣfahānī. *The Ultimate Conspectus:* Matn al-Ghāyat wa al-Taqrīb. Translated by Musa Furber. n.p.: Islamosaic, 2007.

Achrati, Ahmed. "Arabic, Qur'anic Speech, and Postmodern Language: What the Qur'an Simply Says." *Arabica* 55 (2008): 176–77.

Agamben, Giorgio. *Remnants of Auschwitz: The Witness and the Archive.* Translated by Daniel Heller-Roazen. New York: Zone Books, 1999.

Ager, Alastair. and Joey Ager. "Faith and the Discourse of Secular Humanitarianism." *Journal of Refugee Studies* 24, no. 3 (2011): 456–72.

Ahmad, Najah Nadi. "Despair." In *The Integrated Encyclopedia of the Qur'an*, vol. 3. Ardrossan: Center for Islamic Sciences, forthcoming.

Akoush, Hussein, and Elizabeth Hagedorn. "'Their Blankets Are the Sky': Syrian Civilians Flee Deraa." *Guardian*, July 5, 2018, https://www.theguardian.com/global-development/2018/jul/05/blankets-sky-syrian-civilians-flee-daraa.

Ali, Bilal. "Days of Allah." In *Integrated Encyclopedia of the Qur'ān*. Vol. 3. Ardrossan: Center for Islamic Sciences, forthcoming.

Alyousef, Aksam. "Hagar." In *Looking Back, Moving Forward: Fiction, Poetry, Essays*. Edited by Julie Robinson. Toronto: Mawenzi House.

al-'Amrīṭī, Sharaf al-Dīn Yaḥyā bin Nūr al-Dīn Mūsā. *Nihāyat al-tadrīb fī naẓm ghāyat al-taqrīb*. Edited by Muḥammad Ḥasan Ḥabannaka. Mecca: al-Maktaba al-Makkiyya, 1420/1999.

Anderson, Paul. "An Abundance of Meaning: Ramadan as an Enchantment of Society and Economy in Syria." *HAU: Journal of Anthropological Theory* 8, no. 1 (2018): 610–24.

Anidjar, Gil. *"Our Place in al-Andalus": Kabbalah, Philosophy, Literature in Arab Jewish Letters*. Stanford: Stanford University Press, 2002.

Anjum, Ovamir. "Cultural Memory of the Pious Ancestors (*Salaf*) in al-Ghazali." *Numen* 58 (2011): 344–74.

———. *Politics, Law, and Community in Islamic Thought: The Taymiyyan Moment.* Cambridge: Cambridge University Press, 2012.

Al Arabiya English. "Prominent Cleric Shot Dead While Praying in Yemen's Hadhramaut." *Al Arabiya*, March 2, 2018, https://english.alarabiya.net/en/News/gulf/2018/03/02/Prominent-cleric-shot-dead-while-praying-in-Yemen-s-Hadhramaut.html.

ArabLit. "The Politics of Translating al-Shabbi's 'If the People Choose to Live One Day.'" *ArabLit*, January 22, 2011, https://arablit.org/2011/01/22/the-politics-of-translating-al-shabbis-if-the-people-choose-to-live-one-day/.

Arendt, Hannah. *The Human Condition*. Chicago: University of Chicago Press, 1958.

———. *Between Past and Future: Eight Exercises in Political Thought*. New York: Penguin, 2006. Originally published in 1960.
———. *On Revolution*. Translated by Jonathan Schell. New York: Penguin, 2006. Originally published in 1963.
Asad, Talal. "The Concept of Translation in British Social Anthropology." In *Writing Culture: The Poetics and Politics of Ethnography*, edited by James Clifford and George E. Marcus, 141–64. Berkeley: University of California Press, 1986.
———. "The Idea of an Anthropology of Islam." Occasional Papers Series. Washington, D.C.: Center for Contemporary Arab Studies, Georgetown University, 1986.
———. *Genealogies of Religion: Discipline and Reasons of Power in Christianity and Islam*. Baltimore: Johns Hopkins University Press, 1993.
———. *Formations of the Secular: Christianity, Islam, Modernity*. Stanford: Stanford University Press, 2003.
———. "Thinking about Religion, Belief, and Politics." In *The Cambridge Companion to Religious Studies*, edited by Robert A. Orsi, 36–57. New York: Cambridge University Press, 2012.
———. "Thinking About Tradition, Religion, and Politics in Egypt Today." *Critical Inquiry* 42, no. 1 (Autumn 2015): 166–214.
———. "Reflections on Violence, Law, and Humanitarianism." *Critical Inquiry* 41, no. 2 (Winter 2015): 390–427.
———. *Secular Translations: Nation-State, Modern Self, and Calculative Reason*. New York: Columbia University Press, 2018.
———. "Thinking about Religion through Wittgenstein." *Critical Times: Interventions in Global Critical Theory* 3, no. 3 (December 2020): 403–442.
Association of Detainees and the Missing in Sednaya Prison. "Detention in Sednaya: Report on the Procedures and Consequences of Political Imprisonment." Gazientep: ADMSP, November 2019. https://admsp.org/wp-content/uploads/2019/11/sydnaia-en-final-November-s-11-07-2019.pdf.
Atia, Mona. *Building a House in Heaven: Pious Neoliberalism and Islamic Charity in Egypt*. Minneapolis: University of Minnesota Press, 2013.
Ayalon, Ami. "From *Fitna* to *Thawra*." *Studia Islamica* 66 (1987): 145–74.
Aydın, Cemil. "Globalizing the Intellectual History of the Idea of the 'Muslim World.'" In *Global Intellectual History*, edited by Samuel Moyn and Andrew Sartori, 159–86. New York: Columbia University Press, 2013.
———. *The Idea of the Muslim World*. Cambridge, Mass.: Harvard University Press, 2017.
al-Azmeh, Aziz. "Tropes and Temporalities of Historiographic Romanticism, Modern and Islamic." In *The Times of History: Universal Topics in Islamic Historiography*, 3–38. Budapest: Central European University Press, 2007.

Bader Eddin, Eylaf. "*Al-Abad*: On the Ongoing." *Middle East Journal of Culture and Communication* 15 (2022): 367–76.

Baker, Jaber, and Uğur Ümit Üngör. *Syrian Gulag: Inside Assad's Prison System*. London: I.B. Tauris, 2023.

Balanche, Fabrice. "Sectarianism in Syria's Civil War." Washington, D.C.: Washington Institute for Near East Policy, 2018.

Barber, Daniel Colucciello. "Sense-Making, Affect, and Natality." Senses and Religion: Ontologies and Secularism workshop paper, UC Berkeley, November 2017.

Barber, Matthew. "Sheikh Muhammad al-Yaqoubi Interviewed by *Syria Comment*." *Syria Comment*, May 30, 2013, https://www.joshualandis.com/blog/sheikh-muhammad-al-yaqoubi-interviewed-by-syria-comment/.

———. "Sheikh Muhammad al-Yaqoubi Responds to al-Julani's al-Jazeera Interview." *Syria Comment*, May 31, 2015, https://www.joshualandis.com/blog/sheikh-muhammad-al-yaqoubi-responds-to-al-julanis-al-jazeera-interview/.

Barnard, Anne. "Inside Syria's Secret Torture Prisons: How Bashar al-Assad Crushed Dissent." *New York Times*, May 11, 2019, https://www.nytimes.com/2019/05/11/world/middleeast/syria-torture-prisons.html.

Barnett, Michael. *Empire of Humanity: A History of Humanitarianism*. Ithaca: Cornell University Press, 2011.

———. "Humanitarian Governance." *Annual Review of Political Science* 16 (May 2013): 379–98.

Barnett, Michael, and Thomas G. Weiss. "Humanitarianism: A Brief History of the Present." In *Humanitarianism in Question: Politics, Power, Ethics*, edited by Michael Barnett and Thomas G. Weiss, 1–48. Ithaca: Cornell University Press, 2008.

Barzegar, Abbas. "The Living *Fiqh*, or Practical Theology, of Muslim Humanitarianism." In *Migration and Islamic Ethics: Issues of Residence, Naturalization, and Citizenship*, edited by Ray Jureidini and Said Fares Hassan, 28–46. Leiden: Brill, 2020.

Bashier, Salman H. *The Story of Islamic Philosophy: Ibn Tufayl, Ibn al-'Arabi, and Others on the Limit between Naturalism and Traditionalism*. Albany: State University of New York Press, 2012.

BBC Magazine. "Inside Tadmur: The Worst Prison in the World?" *British Broadcasting Corporation*, June 20, 2015, https://www.bbc.com/news/magazine-33197612.

Beaman, Lori G., Jennifer A. Selby, and Amélie Barras. "No Mosque, No Refugees: Some Reflections on Syrian Refugees and the Construction of Religion in Canada." In *The Refugee Crisis and Religion: Secularism, Security, and Hospitality in Question*, edited by Luca Mavelli and Erin K. Mavelli, 77–95. London: Rowman & Littlefield, 2017.

Bellion-Jourdan, Jérôme. "Helping the 'Brothers': The Medic, the Militant, and the Fighter." In *The Charitable Crescent*, edited by Jonathan Benthall and Jérôme Bellion-Jourdan, 69–84. New York: I.B. Tauris, 2003.

Benjamin, Walter. "On the Concept of History." Translated by Harry Zohn. In *Selected Writings*, vol. 4, *1938–1940*, edited by Howard Eiland and Michael W. Jennings, 389–400. Cambridge, Mass.: Harvard University Press, 2003.

Benthall, Jonathan. *Islamic Charities and Islamic Humanism in Troubled Times.* Manchester: Manchester University Press, 2016.

Berg, Hanna. "Waste of Time Is Worse Than Death." *Comparative Studies of South Asia, Africa, and the Middle East* 45, no. 1 (May 2025): 105–20.

Besteman, Catherine. *Making Refuge: Somali Bantu Refugees and Lewiston, Maine.* Durham, N.C.: Duke University Press, 2016.

Biss, Mavis Louise. "Arendt and the Theological Significance of Natality." *Philosophy Compass* 7, no. 11 (2012): 762–71.

Blanchot, Maurice. *The Space of Literature.* Translated by Ann Smock. Lincoln: University of Nebraska Press, 1982.

———. *The Writing of the Disaster.* Translated by Ann Smock. New ed. Lincoln: University of Nebraska Press, 1995. Originally published in 1980.

———. *The Instant of My Death*/Jacques Derrida, *Demeure: Fiction and Testimony.* Translated by Elizabeth Rottenberg. Stanford: Stanford University Press, 2000.

Blumenberg, Hans. *The Legitimacy of the Modern Age.* Translated by Robert M. Wallace. 2nd ed. Cambridge, Mass.: MIT Press, 1983.

Boltanski, Luc. *Distant Suffering: Morality, Media, and Politics.* Translated by Graham Burchell. Cambridge: Cambridge University Press, 1999.

Borges, Jorge Luis. "The Secret Miracle." In *Labyrinths: Selected Stories and Other Writings*, edited by Donald A. Yates and James E. Irby. New York: New Directions Books, 1964. Originally published in 1943.

Borgmann, Monika, and Lokman Slim, dirs. *Tadmor.* Icarus Films, 2017.

Bornstein, Erica. *Disquieting Gifts: Humanitarianism in New Delhi.* Stanford: Stanford University Press, 2012.

Bramadat, Paul. "Don't Ask, Don't Tell: Refugee Settlement and Religion in British Columbia." *Journal of the American Academy of Religion* 82, no. 4 (December 2014): 907–37.

Brandel, Andrew, and Marco Motta, eds. *Living with Concepts: Anthropology in the Grip of Reality.* New York: Fordham University Press, 2021.

Breakenridge, Dave. "Fringe Review: *Hagar.*" *Edmonton Journal*, August 17, 2019.

Browers, Michaelle. "Official Islam and the Limits of Communicative Action: The Paradox of the Amman Message." *Third World Quarterly* 32, no. 5 (2011): 943–58.

Brown, Norman O. "The Apocalypse of Islam." *Social Text* 8 (Winter 1983–84): 155–71.

Bruns, Gerald L. *Maurice Blanchot: The Refusal of Philosophy.* Baltimore: Johns Hopkins University Press, 1997.

Bseiso, Jehan, Michiel Hofman, and Jonathan Whitall, eds. *Everybody's War: The Politics of Aid in the Syria Crisis.* New York: Oxford University Press, 2021.

Butler, Judith. *The Psychic Life of Power: Theories in Subjection.* Stanford: Stanford University Press, 1997.

———. *Frames of War: When Is Life Grievable?* London: Verso, 2009.

Cameron, Geoffrey. *Send Them Here: Religion, Politics, and Refugee Resettlement in North America.* Montreal and Kingston: McGill-Queen's University Press, 2021.

Carlson, Liane. *Contingency and the Limits of History: How Touch Shapes Experience and Meaning.* New York: Columbia University Press, 2019.

Carney, Frederick S. "Some Aspects of Islamic Ethics." *Journal of Religion* 63, no. 2 (April 1983): 159–74.

Carpi, Estella, and H. Pınar Şenoğuz. "Refugee Hospitality in Lebanon and Turkey: On Making 'The Other.'" *International Migration* 57, no. 2 (2018): 126–42.

CBC News. "Former UCP Candidate Who Posed with Soldiers of Odin Denied Appeal." *Canadian Broadcasting Corporation*, October 16, 2018, https://www.cbc.ca/news/canada/edmonton/ucp-candidate-lance-coulter-denied-appeal-1.4865661.

———. "Edmonton Police Investigating after Group Known to Police Visits Al Rashid Mosque." *Canadian Broadcasting Corporation*, January 26, 2019, https://www.cbc.ca/news/canada/edmonton/al-rashid-mosque-police-investigating-1.4994563.

———. "Hate Mail Sent to Edmonton Mosque Touches Off Provincial Political Battle." *Canadian Broadcasting Corporation*, February 6, 2019, https://www.cbc.ca/news/canada/edmonton/edmonton-mosque-hate-mail-anti-islam-1.5008013.

Chakrabarty, Dipesh. *Provincializing Europe: Postcolonial Thought and Historical Difference.* New ed. Princeton: Princeton University Press, 2008. Originally published in 2000.

Chatty, Dawn. "The Duty to be Generous (*karam*): Alternatives to Rights-Based Asylum in the Middle East." *Journal of the British Academy* 5 (2017): 177–99.

Chaumont, Éric. "al-Sulamī, 'Izz al-Dīn 'Abd al-'Azīz b. 'Abd al-Salām." In *Encyclopedia of Islam*, 2nd ed., edited by C. E. Bosworth et al. Leiden: E. J. Brill, 1997. 9:812–13.

Clark, Janine A. *Islam, Charity, and Activism: Middle-Class Networks and Social Welfare in Egypt, Jordan, and Yemen.* Bloomington: Indiana University Press, 2004.

Clarke, Killian. "When Do the Dispossessed Protest? Informal Leadership and Mobilization in Syrian Refugee Camps." *Perspectives on Politics* 16, no. 3 (September 2018): 617–33.

Comay, Rebecca. "Deadlines (Literally)." Gillian Rose Memorial Lecture. London: CRMEP Books, 2020.

———. "Mourning Work and Play." *Research in Phenomenology* 23 (1993): 105–30.

Cook, Michael. *Commanding Right and Forbidding Wrong in Islamic Thought*. Cambridge: Cambridge University Press, 2000.

Corbin, Henry. *Alone with the Alone: Creative Imagination in the Sūfism of Ibn 'Arabī*. Translated by Ralph Mannheim. Princeton: Princeton University Press, 1998. Originally published in 1969.

Crapanzano, Vincent. *Imaginative Horizons: An Essay in Literary-Philosophical Anthropology*. Chicago: University of Chicago Press, 2004.

Crépon, Marc. *The Thought of Death and the Memory of War*. Translated by Michael Loriaux. Minneapolis: University of Minnesota Press, 2013.

Dagher, Sam. *Assad or We Burn the Country*. New York: Back Bay Books, 2019.

Dalal, Ayham. *From Shelters to Dwellings: The Zaatari Refugee Camp*. Berlin: Transcript Verlag, 2022.

Das, Veena. *Life and Words: Violence and the Descent into the Ordinary*. Berkeley: University of California Press, 2007.

Dennaro, Roberta. "From Mars to the *Tugūr*: Ibn al-Mubārak and the Shaping of a Biographical Tradition." *Eurasian Studies* 7, nos. 1–2 (2009): 125–44.

Denny, Frederick. "The Meaning of Ummah in the Qur'an." *History of Religions* 15, no. 1 (August 1975): 34–70.

Derrida, Jacques. *Given Time*. Vol. 1, *Counterfeit Money*. Translated by Peggy Kamuf. Chicago: University of Chicago Press, 1992.

Derrida, Jacques, with Anne DuFourmantelle. *Of Hospitality*. Translated by Rachel Bowlby. Stanford: Stanford University Press, 2000.

Devji, Faisal. "The Terrorist as Humanitarian." *Social Analysis* 53, no. 1 (Spring 2009): 173–92.

———. "Against Muslim Unity." *Aeon*, July 12, 2016, https://aeon.co/essays/the-idea-of-unifying-islam-is-a-recent-invention-and-a-bad-one.

Doughan, Yazan. "The Rule-of-Law as a Problem Space: *Wāsṭa* and the Paradox of Justice in Jordan." *Comparative Studies in Society and History* 66, no. 1 (2024): 131–54.

Douglas, Elmer H., trans. *The Mystical Teachings of al-Shadhili: Including His Life, Prayers, Letters, and Followers*. Edited by Ibrahim M. Abu-Rabiʿ. Albany: SUNY Press, 1993.

DuFourmantelle, Anne. *Power of Gentleness: Meditations on the Risk of Living*. Translated by Katherine Payne and Vincent Sallé. New York: Fordham University Press, 2018.

Eldridge Aaron, and Basit Kareem Iqbal. "A Tropics of Estrangement: *Ghurba* in Four Scenes." *diacritics: A Review of Contemporary Criticism* 50, no. 1 (March 2022): 112–40.

Elyachar, Julia. "Rethinking Anthropology of Neoliberalism in the Middle East." In *A Companion to the Anthropology of the Middle East*, edited by Soraya Altorki, 411–33. Chichester: John Wiley & Sons, 2015.

Esmeir, Samera. *Juridical Humanity: A Colonial History*. Stanford: Stanford University Press, 2012.

———. "On Becoming Less of the World." *History of the Present* 8, no. 1 (Spring 2018): 88–116.

Esposito, Roberto. *Third Person: Politics of Life and Philosophy of the Impersonal*. Translated by Zakiya Hanafi. Cambridge: Polity Press, 2012. Originally published in 2007.

Ewing, Katherine P. "Dreams from a Saint: Anthropological Atheism and the Temptation to Believe." *American Anthropologist* 96, no. 3 (1994): 571–83.

Fadel, Mohammad. "International Law, Regional Developments: Islam." *Max Planck Encyclopedia of Public International Law*. New York: Oxford University Press, 2010.

Faḍl Bā-Faḍl, Aḥmad. "Shahīd al-dār wa-l-maḥārib." *Hunā 'aden*, March 3, 2018, https://www.hunaaden.com/art19657.html.

Fassin, Didier. "Inequality of Lives, Hierarchies of Humanity: Moral Commitments and Ethical Dilemmas of Humanitarianism." In *In the Name of Humanity: The Government of Threat and Care*, edited by Ilana Feldman and Miriam Ticktin, 238–55. Durham, N.C.: Duke University Press, 2010.

———. *Humanitarian Reason: A Moral History of the Present*. Translated by Rachel Gomme. Berkeley: University of California Press, 2012.

———. "The Predicament of Humanitarianism." *qui parle* 22, no. 1 (Fall/Winter 2013): 33–48.

Feldman, Allen. *Formations of Violence: The Narrative of the Body and Political Terror in Northern Ireland*. Chicago: University of Chicago Press, 1991.

Feldman, Ilana. *Life Lived in Relief: Humanitarian Predicaments and Palestinian Refugee Politics*. Oakland: University of California Press, 2018.

Ferris, Elizabeth. "Faith and Humanitarianism: It's Complicated." *Journal of Refugee Studies* 24, no. 3 (2011): 606–25.

Fiddian-Qasmiyeh, Elena. *Faith-Based Humanitarianism in Contexts of Forced Displacement*. Edited special issue of the *Journal of Refugee Studies* 24, no. 3 (2011): 429–633.

Foucault, Michel. *The Use of Pleasure: The History of Sexuality*. Volume 2. Translated by Robert Hurley. New York: Vintage, 1986.

Freud, Sigmund. "Traumatic Fixation—the Unconscious." In *A General Introduction to Psychoanalysis*, trans. Edward L. Bernays. New York: Boni and Liveright, 1920.

———. "Beyond the Pleasure Principle." In *Beyond the Pleasure Principle and Other Writings*. New York: Penguin, 2003. Originally published in German in 1920.

———. "Mourning and Melancholia." In *The Standard Edition of the Complete Psychological Works of Sigmund Freud*, translated and edited by James Strachey, 14:243–58. London: Hogarth, 1953.

Furani, Khaled. *Redeeming Anthropology: A Theological Critique of a Modern Science*. Oxford: Oxford University Press, 2019.

Furani, Khaled, and Joel Robbins, eds. "Anthropology Within and Without the Secular Condition." *Religion* 51, no. 4 (2021).

Fynsk, Christopher. *Last Steps: Maurice Blanchot's Exilic Writing*. New York: Fordham University Press, 2013.

Gatter, Melissa N. "Restoring Childhood: Humanitarianism and Growing Up Syrian in Zaʿtari Refugee Camp." *Contemporary Levant* 2, no. 2 (2017): 89–102.

al-Ghazālī, Abu Hamid. *On Patience and Thankfulness: Book 32 of the Revival of the Religious Sciences*. 2nd ed. Translated by H. T. Littlejohn. Cambridge: Islamic Texts Society, 2017.

Goldberg, David Theo. *Dread: Facing Futureless Futures*. London: Polity Press, 2021.

Graham-Harrison, Emma. "Syria: Southern Towns Surrender to Assad Forces after Thousands Flee Homes." *Guardian*, June 30, 2018, https://www.theguardian.com/world/2018/jun/30/syria-southern-towns-surrender-to-assad-forces.

Grewal, Zareena. *Islam Is a Foreign Country: American Muslims and the Global Crisis of Authority*. New York: New York University Press, 2014.

Griffel, Frank. "The Harmony of Natural Law and Shariʿa in Islamist Theology." In *Shariʿa: Islamic Law in the Contemporary Context*, edited by Abbas Amanat and Frank Griffel, 38–61. Stanford: Stanford University Press, 2007.

Grinberg, León, and Rebeca Grinberg. "A Psychoanalytic Study of Migration: Its Normal and Pathological Aspects." *Journal of the American Psychoanalytic Association* 32, no. 1 (1984): 13–38.

Guilhot, Nicolas. "The Anthropologist as Witness: Humanitarianism between Ethnography and Critique." *Humanity: An International Journal of Human Rights, Humanitarianism, and Development* 3, no. 1 (2012): 81–101.

Günther, Sebastian, and Stephan Milich, eds. *Representations and Visions of Homeland in Modern Arabic Literature*. Hildesheim: Georg Olms Verlag, 2016.

Gürsel, Zeynep Devrim. "Looking Together as Method: Encounters with Ottoman Armenian Expatriation Photographs." *Visual Anthropology Review* 39, no. 1 (Spring 2023): 200–29.

Gutkowski, Stacey. "We Are the Very Model of a Moderate Muslim State: The Amman Messages and Jordan's Foreign Policy." *International Relations* 30, no. 2 (2016): 206–26.

Guyer, Jane I. "Prophecy and the Near Future: Thoughts on Macroeconomic, Evangelical, and Punctuated Time." *American Ethnologist* 34, no. 3 (August 2007): 409–21.

Ḥabīb ʻUmar. "Prophetic Guidance in Times of Tribulation." *Muwasala*, March 31, 2015, http://muwasala.org/prophetic-guidance-in-times-of-tribulation/.
Haddad, Gibril Fouad. *The Excellence of Syro-Palestine: al-Shām and Its People; Forty Hadiths*. 2nd ed. [UK]: Remembrance Publications, 2017.
Hadot, Pierre. "Reflections on the Notion of the 'Cultivation of the Self.'" In *Michel Foucault, Philosopher*, translated by Timothy J. Armstrong, 225–32. New York: Harvester Wheatsheaf, 1992. Originally published in 1989.
El-Haj, Ahmed. "Fear Grips Yemen's Aden as Deadly Attacks Target Clerics." *AP News*, April 5, 2018, https://www.apnews.com/cb514ded6f284e81b3776575db3ebcd2.
Hamilton, Leah K., Luisa Veronis, and Margaret Walton-Roberts, eds. *A National Project: Syrian Refugee Resettlement in Canada*. Montreal & Kingston: McGill-Queen's University Press, 2020.
Hammad, Muhammad Saleem. "Tadmur: Witnessed and Observed." Syrian Human Rights Committee, https://www.shrc.org/en/wp-content/uploads/2017/02/Tadmur-Witnessed-and-Observed-Final-1.pdf.
Ḥammād, Zāyid. "al-Iftitāḥiyya." *al-Qibla* 4–5 (1424/2003): 3–6.
———. "Ḥulūl li-l-qā'imīn ʻalā barnāmij qalbī iṭma'inn li-satr al-muḥtāj." *al-Sāʻa*, May 7, 2018, http://alsaa.net/article-85723.
Hansen, Miriam Bratu. "On Benjamin's Aura." *Critical Inquiry* 34, no. 2 (Winter 2008): 336–75.
Harmsen, Egbert. *Islam, Civil Society, and Social Action: Muslim Voluntary Welfare Associations in Jordan between Patronage and Empowerment*. Amsterdam: Amsterdam University Press, 2008.
Hassan, Mona. Review of Aydın, *The Idea of the Muslim World* in the *American History Review* (October 2018): 1294–95.
Hasselbarth, Sarah. "Islamic Charities in the Syrian Context in Jordan and Lebanon." Beirut: Friedrich-Ebert-Stiftung Foundation, 2014.
Havea, Jione, et al., "Dialogues: Anthropology and Theology." *Journal of the Royal Anthropological Institute* 28, no. 1 (March 2022): 297–347.
Hay'at al-Shām al-Islāmiyya. *Fatāwā al-thawra al-sūriyya*. 3 vols. N.p.: al-Maktab al-ʻIlmī li-l-Hay'at al-Shām al-Islāmiyya, 2019.
Hayot, Eric. *The Hypothetical Mandarin: Sympathy, Modernity, and Chinese Pain*. New York: Oxford University Press, 2009.
Helmreich, Stefan. "Induction, Deduction, Abduction, and the Logics of Race and Kinship." *American Ethnologist* 34, no. 2 (2007): 230–32.
Henig, David. "Economic Theologies of Abundance: Halal Exchange and the Limits of Neoliberal Effects in Post-War Bosnia-Herzegovina." *Ethnos* 84, no. 2 (2019): 223–40.
Hesford, Wendy S. *Spectacular Rhetorics: Human Rights Visions, Recognitions, Feminisms*. Durham, N.C.: Duke University Press, 2011.

Hirschkind, Charles. *The Ethical Soundscape: Cassette Sermons and Islamic Counterpublics*. New York: Columbia University Press, 2006.
Ho, Engseng. *The Graves of Tarim: Genealogy and Mobility across the Indian Ocean*. Berkeley: University of California Press, 2006.
Hoffmann, Sophia. "Humanitarian Security in Jordan's Azraq Camp." *Security Dialogue* 48, no. 2 (2017): 97–112.
Hopkins, Nick, and Emma Beals. "How Assad Regime Controls UN's Aid Intended for Syria's Children." *Guardian*, August 29, 2016, https://www.theguardian.com/world/2016/aug/29/how-assad-regime-controls-un-aid-intended-for-syrias-children.
Huet, Marie-Hélène. *The Culture of Disaster*. Chicago: University of Chicago Press, 2012.
Human Rights Watch. "We've Never Seen Such Horror: Crimes Against Humanity by the Syrian Security Forces." HRW, June 2011, https://www.hrw.org/report/2011/06/01/weve-never-seen-such-horror/crimes-against-humanity-syrian-security-forces.
———. "If the Dead Could Speak: Mass Deaths and Torture in Syria's Detention Facilities." HRW, December 2015, https://www.hrw.org/sites/default/files/report_pdf/syria1215web_0.pdf.
———. "'I Have No Idea Why They Sent Us Back': Jordanian Deportations and Expulsions of Refugees." HRW, October 2017, https://www.hrw.org/sites/default/files/report_pdf/jordan1017_web.pdf.
———. "Jordan: Step Forward, Step Back for Urban Refugees." HRW, March 2018, https://www.hrw.org/news/2018/03/25/jordan-step-forward-step-back-urban-refugees.
Ibáñez Prieto, Ana V. "Jordan Issues More Than 100,000 Work Permits for Syrians." *Jordan Times*, July 18, 2018, http://www.jordantimes.com/news/local/jordan-issues-more-100000-work-permits-syrians.
Ibn ʿAbd al-Salām (al-Maqdisī), ʿIzz al-Dīn. *Ḥall al-rumūz wa mafātīḥ al-kunūz*. Edited by Muḥammad Būkhnayfī. Beirut: Dār al-Kutub al-ʿIlmiyya, 1432/2011.
Ibn ʿAbd al-Salām (al-Sulamī), ʿIzz al-Dīn. *al-Fitan wa-l-balāyā wa-l-miḥan wa-l-razāyā aw fawāʾid al-balwā wa-l-miḥan*. Edited by Iyād Khālid al-Ṭabbāʿ. Damascus: Dār al-Fikr, n.d. Translated by Hamza Yusuf Hanson as "Seventeen Benefits of Tribulation." http://shaykhhamza.com/transcript/17-Benefits-of-Tribulation.
Ibn al-Mubārak, ʿAbdullāh. *al-Zuhd wa-l-raqāʾiq*. Edited by Aḥmad Farīd. Riyad: Dār al-Miʿrāj al-Dawliyya li-l-Nashr, 1995.
International Crisis Group. "Keeping the Calm in Southern Syria." Report 187. Brussels: ICG, June 21, 2018, https://www.crisisgroup.org/middle-east-north-africa/eastern-mediterranean/syria/187-keeping-calm-southern-syria.

Irom, Bimbisar. "Mediating Syria's Strangers through Levinas: Communication Ethics and the Visuals of Children." *Communication Theory* 29, no. 4 (November 2019): 441–62.

Iqbal, Basit Kareem. "Asad and Benjamin: Chronopolitics of Tragedy in the Anthropology of Secularism." *Anthropological Theory* 20, no. 1 (2020): 77–96.

———. "The Messiah and the Jurisconsult: Agamben on the Problem of Law in Sunni Islam." *Journal of Religion* 101, no. 3 (July 2021): 351–70.

———. "Reprising Islamic Political Theology: Genre and the Time of Tribulation." *Political Theology* 23, no. 6 (2022): 525–42.

Iqbal, Basit Kareem, and Talal Asad. "Thinking About Method: A Conversation with Talal Asad." *qui parle* 26, no. 1 (June 2017): 195–218.

Ismail, Salwa. *The Rule of Violence: Subjectivity, Memory, and Government in Syria*. Cambridge: Cambridge University Press, 2019.

Izutsu, Toshihiko. *God and Man in the Qur'an*. Kuala Lumpur: Islamic Book Trust, 2002. Originally published in 1964.

Jackson, Sherman A. *Islam and the Problem of Black Suffering*. New York: Oxford University Press, 2009.

Jambet, Christian. "The Constitution of the Subject and Spiritual Practice." In *Michel Foucault, Philosopher*, translated by Timothy J. Armstrong, 233–47. New York: Harvester Wheatsheaf, 1992. Originally published in 1989.

Jureidini, Ray, and Said Fares Hassan, eds. *Migration and Islamic Ethics: Issues of Residence, Naturalization, and Citizenship*. Leiden: Brill, 2020.

al-Jurjānī, ʿAlī bin Muḥammad. *Muʿjam al-taʿrifāt*. Edited by Muḥammad Ṣiddīq al-Minshāwī. Cairo: Dār al-Faḍīla, n.d.

Karasapan, Omer. "The Challenges in Providing Health Care to Syrian Refugees." *Brookings Institution*, November 15, 2018, https://www.brookings.edu/blog/future-development/2018/11/15/the-challenges-in-providing-health-care-to-syrian-refugees/.

Kerr, Malcolm H. *Islamic Reform: The Political and Legal Theories of Muḥammad ʿAbduh and Rashīd Riḍā*. Berkeley: University of California Press, 1966.

Khadduri, Majid. "Islam and the Modern Law of Nations." *American Journal of International Law* 50, no. 2 (1956): 358–72.

———. "The Impact of International Law upon the Islamic World Order." *American Journal of International Law* 66, no. 4 (September 1972): 46–50.

al-Khalidi, Suleiman. "Russia, Jordan Agree to Speed De-Escalation Zone in South Syria." *Reuters*, September 11, 2017, https://www.reuters.com/article/us-mideast-crisis-jordan-russia/russia-jordan-agree-to-speed-de-escalation-zone-in-south-syria-idUSKCN1BM2A5.

Khalifa, Mustafa. *The Shell: Memoirs of a Hidden Observer*. Translated by Paul Starkey. Northampton, Mass.: Interlink Books, 2017. Originally published in Arabic in 2006.

al-Khalili, Charlotte. *Waiting for the Revolution to End: Syrian Displacement, Time, and Subjectivity.* London: UCL Press, 2023.
Khatib, Line. *Islamic Revivalism in Syria: The Rise and Fall of Ba'thist Secularism.* London: Routledge, 2011.
KidsRights Report. "The Widening Educational Gap for Syrian Refugee Children." Amsterdam: KidsRights Foundation, 2018.
Kimmelman, Michael. "The Real Face of War? It May Be This Boy in a Pink Sweater." *New York Times*, March 3, 2018.
Kleinman, Arthur, Veena Das, and Margaret Lock, eds. *Social Suffering.* Berkeley: University of California Press, 1997.
Knight, Daniel M. *Vertiginous Life: An Anthropology of Time and the Unforeseen.* New York: Berghahn Books, 2021.
Knysh, Alexander. *Ibn 'Arabi in the Later Islamic Tradition: The Making of a Polemical Image.* Albany: SUNY Press, 1999.
Korteweg, Anna C., and Jennifer A. Selby, eds. *Debating Sharia: Islam, Gender Politics and Family Law Arbitration.* Toronto: University of Toronto Press, 2012.
Koselleck, Reinhart. *Critique and Crisis: Enlightenment and the Pathogenesis of Modern Society.* Cambridge, Mass.: MIT Press, 1988. Originally published in 1959.
———. *Futures Past: On the Semantics of Historical Time.* Translated by Keith Tribe. New York: Columbia University Press, 2004.
Labman, Shauna. *Crossing Law's Border: Canada's Refugee Resettlement Program.* Vancouver: University of British Columbia Press, 2019.
Labman, Shauna, and Geoffrey Cameron, eds. *Strangers to Neighbours: Refugee Sponsorship in Context.* Montreal and Kingston: McGill-Queen's University Press, 2020.
Lacan, Jacques. *The Ethics of Psychoanalysis, 1959–1960: The Seminar of Jacques Lacan.* Book VII. Translated by Dennis Porter. Edited by Jacques-Alain Miller. New York: W.W. Norton, 1992.
Lamoureux, Mack. "Soldiers of Odin Edmonton Chapter Shuts Down, Rebrands As 'Canadian Infidels.'" *VICE*, October 15, 2018, https://www.vice.com/en_ca/article/xw9pwj/soldiers-of-odin-edmonton-chapter-shuts-down-rebrands-as-canadian-infidels.
———. "Alberta Conservative Candidate Caylan Ford Steps Down for Using White Nationalist Talking Points." *VICE*, March 19, 2019, https://www.vice.com/en_ca/article/eve9qe/alberta-conservative-candidate-caylan-ford-steps-down-for-using-white-nationalist-talking-points.
Lane, Edward William. *Arabic-English Lexicon.* London: Williams & Norgate, 1863.
Laplanche, Jean. *Essays on Otherness.* Edited by John Fletcher. London: Routledge, 1999.

Le Caisne, Garance. *Operation Caesar: At the Heart of the Syrian Death Machine.* Translated by David Watson. Cambridge: Polity Press, 2018.

Lear, Jonathan. *Radical Hope: Ethics in the Face of Cultural Devastation.* Cambridge, Mass.: Harvard University Press, 2006.

Ledwith, Alison. "Zaatari: The Instant City." Boston, Mass.: Affordable Housing Institute, 2014. http://www.affordablehousinginstitute.org/insights/zaatari-the-instant-city.

Levinas, Emmanuel. *Otherwise than Being, or Beyond Essence.* Translated by Alphonso Lingis. Pittsburgh: Duquesne University Press, 1998.

———. "Peace and Proximity." Translated by Peter Adderton and Simon Critchley. In *Emmanuel Levinas: Basic Philosophical Writings*, edited by Adriaan Peperzak et al. Bloomington: Indiana University Press, 1996.

Li, Darryl. "Jihad in a World of Sovereigns: Law, Violence, and Islam in the Bosnia Crisis." *Law & Social Inquiry* 41, no. 2 (Spring 2016): 371–401.

———. *The Universal Enemy: Jihad, Empire, and the Challenge of Solidarity.* Stanford: Stanford University Press, 2020.

Lister, Charles. *The Syrian Jihad: Al-Qaeda, the Islamic State, and the Evolution of an Insurgency.* New York: Oxford University Press, 2016.

Longo, Dominic. *Spiritual Grammar: Genre and the Saintly Subject in Islam and Christianity.* New York: Fordham University Press, 2017.

MacIntyre, Alasdair. *After Virtue: A Study in Moral Theory.* 3rd ed. Notre Dame, Ind.: University of Notre Dame Press, 2007.

———. *Whose Justice? Which Rationality?* Notre Dame: University of Notre Dame Press, 1988.

Macklin, Audrey, et al. "A Preliminary Investigation into Private Refugee Sponsors." *Canadian Ethnic Studies* 50, no. 2 (2018): 35–57.

Mahmood, Saba. *Politics of Piety: The Islamic Revival and the Feminist Subject.* Princeton: Princeton University Press, 2005.

———. "Humanism." *HAU: Journal of Ethnographic Theory* 8, nos. 1–2 (2018): 1–5.

Mair, Jonathan, and N. H. A. Evans. "Ethics across Borders: Incommensurability and Affinity." *HAU: Journal of Ethnographic Theory* 5, no. 2 (2015): 201–25.

Malkawi, Khetam. "Mafraq, Ramtha Population Doubled Since Start of Syrian Crisis." *Jordan Times*, November 27, 2015. https://www.jordantimes.com/news/local/mafraq-ramtha-population-doubled-start-syrian-crisis%E2%80%99.

Malkki, Liisa H. *The Need to Help: The Domestic Arts of International Humanitarianism.* Durham, N.C.: Duke University Press, 2015.

Marandola, Sabrina, Kamila Hinkson, and Kalina Laframboise. "Six Dead, 1 Arrested and a Province in Mourning Following Quebec City Mosque Shooting." *Canadian Broadcasting Corporation*, January 29, 2017, https://www.cbc.ca/news/canada/montreal/six-dead-1-arrested-and-a-province-in-mourning-following-quebec-city-mosque-shooting-1.3957686.

March, Andrew F. "Naturalizing Sharīʿa: Foundationalist Ambiguities in Modern Islamic Apologetics." *Islamic Law and Society* 22, nos. 1–2 (2015): 45–81.

———. *The Caliphate of Man: Popular Sovereignty in Modern Islamic Thought.* Cambridge, Mass.: Harvard University Press, 2019.

Mason, Victoria. "The Im/mobilities of Iraqi Refugees in Jordan: Pan-Arabism, 'Hospitality' and the Figure of the 'Refugee.'" *Mobilities* 6, no. 3 (2011): 353–73.

McManus, Anne-Marie. "On the Ruins of What's to Come, I Stand: Time and Devastation in Syrian Cultural Production Since 2011." *Critical Inquiry* 48, no. 1 (Autumn 2021): 45–67.

Meister, Robert. *After Evil: A Politics of Human Rights.* New York: Columbia University Press, 2011.

M-Hood Abu-Futaim. "Janāzat al-Ḥabīb ʿAydarūs bin Sumayṭ wa kalimat Ḥabīb ʿUmar bin Ḥafīẓ." YouTube, uploaded March 5, 2018, https://www.youtube.com/watch?v=hp89ZfRTYjc.

Miller, Jacques-Alain. "Extimité." Translated by Françoise Massardier-Kenney. *Prose Studies: History, Theory, Criticism* 11, no. 3 (1988): 122.

Mittermaier, Amira. *Dreams That Matter: Egyptian Landscapes of the Imagination.* Berkeley: University of California Press, 2011.

———. "Dreams from Elsewhere: Muslim Subjectivities beyond the Trope of Self-Cultivation." *Journal of the Royal Anthropological Institute* 18 (2012): 247–65.

———. "Trading with God: Islam, Calculation, Excess." In *A Companion to the Anthropology of Religion*, edited by Janice Boddy and Michael Lambek, 274–93. London: John Wiley and Sons, 2013.

———. *Giving to God: Islamic Charity in Revolutionary Times.* Oakland: University of California Press, 2019.

———. "Beyond the Human Horizon." *Religion and Society* 12 (2021): 21–38.

Moll, Yasmin. "Television Is Not Radio: Theologies of Mediation in the Egyptian Islamic Revival." *Cultural Anthropology* 33, no. 2 (2018): 233–65.

Mosès, Stéphane. "The Theological-Political Model of History in the Thought of Walter Benjamin." Translated by Ora Wiskind. *History and Memory* 1, no. 2 (Fall–Winter 1989): 25.

———. *The Angel of History: Rosenzweig, Benjamin, Scholem.* Translated by Barbara Harshav. Stanford: Stanford University Press, 2009.

Mostowlansky, Till. "Humanitarian Affect: Islam, Aid, and Emotional Impulse in Northern Pakistan." *History and Anthropology* 31, no. 2 (2020): 236–56.

Mouftah, Nermeen, and Abbas Barzegar, eds. "Centering Muslims in Global Humanitarianism and Development." Special issue of *Muslim World* 112, no. 1 (Winter 2022): 1–204.

Moumtaz, Nada. "From Forgiveness to Foreclosure: *Waqf*, Debt, and the Remaking of the Ḥanafī Legal Subject in Late Ottoman Mount Lebanon." *Muslim World* 108, no. 4 (October 2018): 593–612.

Mufti, Aamir. "The Aura of Authenticity." *Social Text* 18, no. 3 (Fall 2000): 87–103.

Mulholland, Mary-Lee. "Welcoming the Stranger in Alberta: Newcomers, Secularism and Religiously Affiliated Settlement Agencies." *Canadian Ethnic Studies* 49, no. 1 (2017): 19–42.

Munif, Yasser. *The Syrian Revolution: Between the Politics of Life and the Geopolitics of Death*. London: Polity Press, 2020.

Murad, Abdal Hakim. *The Mantle Adorned: Imam Būṣīrī's "Burda."* London: Quilliam Press, 2009.

al-Mushayqaḥ, Khālid bin ʿAlī. *al-Mukhtaṣar fī-l-ʿaqīda* (The Epitome in Creed) [1431]. Riyadh: Maktabat al-Rushd, 2010.

Muwasala. "Habib Aydarus bin Sumayt." *Muwasala*, March 2, 2018, http://muwasala.org/habib-aydarus-bin-abdullah-bin-sumayt/.

al-Nābulusī, ʿAbd al-Ghānī. *The Virtues of Seclusion in Times of Confusion*. Translated by Abdul Aziz Suraqah. Toronto: Ibriz Media, 2017.

Nakassis, Constantine V. "Citation and Citationality." *Signs and Society* 1, no. 1 (Spring 2013): 51–77.

Naqvi, Nauman. "Acts of Askēsis, Scenes of Poēisis: The Dramatic Phenomenology of Another Violence in a Muslim Painter-Poet." *diacritics* 40, no. 2 (2012): 50–71.

Nāṣir, Bassām. "Thawra sūriyā wa aḥdāthuhā bi-ru'ya wa naẓrāt sharʿiyya." *al-Qibla* 9, no. 22 (1433/2012): 68–71.

al-Nawawī, Yaḥyā bin Sharaf. *al-Minhāj sharḥ ṣaḥīḥ muslim bin al-ḥajjāj*. 2nd ed. Beirut: Dār Iḥyā' Turāth al-ʿArabī, 1972.

Nelson, Kristina. *The Art of Reciting the Qur'an*. Cairo: American University of Cairo Press, 2001. Originally published in 1985.

Nguyen, Vinh. "Refugeetude: When Does a Refugee Stop Being a Refugee." *Social Text* 37, no. 2 (June 2019): 109–31.

Nietzsche, Friedrich. *On the Advantage and Disadvantage of History for Life*. Translated by Peter Prauss. Indianapolis: Hackett, 1980.

Ohlander, Erik S. *Sufism in an Age of Transition: ʿUmar al-Suhrawardī and the Rise of the Islamic Mystical Brotherhoods*. Leiden: Brill, 2008.

Osborne, Lauren E. "Feeling the Words: Sayyid Qutb's Affective Engagement with the Qur'an in *Al-Taswir al-Fanni fi al-Qur'an*." *Religion Compass* 13, no. 10 (October 2019): e12338.

Pall, Zoltan. "Kuwaiti Salafism and Its Growing Influence in the Levant." Carnegie Endowment for International Peace, May 7, 2014, https://carnegieendowment.org/2014/05/07/kuwaiti-salafism-and-its-growing-influence-in-levant-pub-55514.

Pandolfo, Stefania. *Impasse of the Angels: Scenes from a Moroccan Space of Memory.* Chicago: University of Chicago Press, 1997.
———. *Knot of the Soul: Madness, Psychoanalysis, Islam.* Chicago: University of Chicago Press, 2018.
Papailias, Penelope. "(Un)seeing Dead Refugee Bodies: Mourning Memes, Spectropolitics, and the Haunting of Europe." *Media, Culture, & Society* 41, no. 8 (2019): 1048–68.
Petersen, Marie Juul. *For Humanity or for the Umma? Aid and Islam in Transnational Muslim NGOs.* London: Hurst, 2015.
Pierret, Thomas. *Religion and State in Syria: The Sunni Ulama from Coup to Revolution.* Cambridge: Cambridge University Press, 2013.
Piscatori, James, ed. "Conceptualising the Umma." Special issue of *Muslim World* 109, no. 3 (July 2019): 193–307.
Piscatori, James, and Amin Saikal. *Islam Beyond Borders: The Umma in World Politics.* Cambridge: Cambridge University Press, 2019.
Povinelli, Elizabeth. *Economies of Abandonment: Social Belonging and Endurance in Late Liberalism.* Durham, N.C.: Duke University Press, 2011.
Press Progress. "UCP Candidate Promoted Far-Right Conspiracy Claiming the United Nations Is Taking Control of Canada's Borders." *Press Progress,* March 31, 2019, https://pressprogress.ca/ucp-candidate-promoted-far-right-conspiracy-claiming-the-united-nations-is-taking-control-of-canadas-borders/.
———. "Meet 30 Candidates for Jason Kenney's UCP Who Got Caught Promoting Hateful and Extremist Views." *Press Progress,* April 4, 2019, https://pressprogress.ca/meet-30-candidates-for-jason-kenneys-ucp-who-got-caught-promoting-hateful-and-extremist-views/.
Quadri, Junaid. "Moral Habituation in the Law: Rethinking the Ethics of the *Sharī'a.*" *Islamic Law and Society* 26 (2019): 191–226.
Quisay, Walaa, and Asim Qureshi. *When Only God Can See: The Faith of Muslim Political Prisoners.* London: Pluto Press, 2024.
Qureshi, Jawad. "The Discourses of the Damascene Sunni Ulama during the 2011 Revolution." In *State and Islam in Baathist Syria: Confrontation or Co-Optation?,* by Line Khatib, Raphaël Lefèvre, and Jawad Qureshi, 59–91 Fife: University of St. Andrews Centre for Syrian Studies, 2012.
———. "Sunni Tradition in an Age of Revival and Reform: Sa'id Ramadan al-Buti (1929–2013) and His Interlocutors." Ph.D. diss., University of Chicago, 2019.
al-Qushayrī, Abū l-Qāsim. *al-Risāla al-qushayriyya fī 'ilm al-taṣawwuf.* Translated by Alexander Knysh as *Al-Qushayri's Epistle on Sufism.* Reading, UK: Garnet, 2007.
Rangan, Pooja. *Immediations: The Humanitarian Impulse in Documentary.* Durham, N.C.: Duke University Press, 2017.

Ray, Gene. "Reading the Lisbon Earthquake: Adorno, Lyotard, and the Contemporary Sublime." *Yale Journal of Criticism* 17, no. 1 (Spring 2004): 1–18.

Redfield, Peter. "Sacrifice, Triage, and Global Humanitarianism." In *Humanitarianism in Question: Politics, Power, Ethics*, edited by Michael Barnett and Thomas G. Weiss, 196–214. Ithaca: Cornell University Press, 2008.

Redfield, Peter, and Erica Bornstein. "An Introduction to the Anthropology of Humanitarianism." In *Forces of Compassion: Humanitarianism between Ethics and Politics*, edited by Erica Bornstein and Peter Redfield, 3–30. Santa Fe: SAR Press, 2011.

Reinhart, A. Kevin. "Islamic Law as Islamic Ethics." *Journal of Religious Ethics* 11, no. 2 (Fall 1983): 186–203.

Ricoeur, Paul. *Memory, History, Forgetting*. Translated by Kathleen Blamey and David Pellauer. Chicago: University of Chicago Press, 2004.

Rizvi, Muneeza. "'Strange Affinities': *Iṣlāḥ* and British Muslim Volunteers in the Syrian War." *American Ethnologist* 51, no. 4 (November 2024): 490–501.

Robbins, Joel. "Causality, Ethics, and the Near Future." *American Ethnologist* 34, no. 3 (2007): 433–36.

———. "Beyond the Suffering Subject: Toward an Anthropology of the Good." *Journal of the Royal Anthropological Institute* 19, no. 3 (September 2013): 447–62.

Robinson, Cabeiri deBergh. *Body of Victim, Body of Warrior: Refugee Families and the Making of Kashmiri Jihadists*. Berkeley: University of California Press, 2013.

Robinson, Glenn E. "Defensive Democratization in Jordan." *International Journal of Middle East Studies* 30, no. 3 (August 1998): 387–410.

Röth, Hanna, Zina Nimeh, and Jessica Hagen-Zanker. "A Mapping of Social Protection and Humanitarian Assistance Programmes in Jordan: What Support Are Refugees Eligible for?" Working Paper 501. London: Overseas Development Institute, 2017.

Rouzati, Nasrin. *Trial and Tribulation in the Qur'an: A Mystical Theodicy*. Berlin: Gerlach, 2015.

Roy, Olivier. *Globalized Islam: The Search for a New Ummah*. New York: Columbia University Press, 2004.

Rudnyckyj, Daromir. *Spiritual Economies: Islam, Globalization, and the Afterlife of Development*. Ithaca, N.Y.: Cornell University Press, 2014.

Ṣaḥafī. "Qarār li-wazīr al-thaqāfa bi-ḥall jam'iyyat al-kitāb wa-l-sunna." *Ṣaḥafī*, May 7, 2007, http://www.sahafi.jo/arc/art1.php?id=b3d045a789d8905e778637 8309858d7f212656dc.

Said, Edward W. "Traveling Theory Reconsidered." In *Reflections on Exile and Other Essays*. Cambridge, Mass.: Harvard University Press, 2000.

Salāma, Rāfiyā. "Dākhil wa khārij: kayfa aṣbaḥū 'hum.'" *al-Jumhuriya*, March 22, 2018. Translated by Vanessa Breeding as "Syria's 'Inside' and 'Outside': How They Became 'Them,'" *Al-Jumhuriya English*, June 2, 2018.

Salamandra, Christa. *A New Old Damascus: Authenticity and Distinction in Urban Syria*. Bloomington: Indiana University Press, 2004.

Saleh, Yassin al-Haj. *The Impossible Revolution: Making Sense of the Syrian Tragedy*. Translated by Ibtihal Mahmood. Chicago: Haymarket Books, 2017.

———. "State Extermination, Not a 'Dictatorial Regime'." Translated by Alex Rowell. *Aljumhuriya*, April 30, 2018.

———. "Syria's Catastrophe upon Catastrophe." *DAWN*, March 8, 2023. https://dawnmena.org/syrias-catastrophe-upon-catastrophe.

Salem, Feryal. *The Emergence of Early Sufi Piety and Sunni Scholasticism: 'Abdullāh bin Mubarak and the Formation of Sunni Identity in the Second Islamic Century*. Leiden: Brill, 2016.

Santner, Eric L. *Stranded Objects: Mourning, Memory, and Film in Postwar Germany*. Ithaca: Cornell University Press, 1990.

Saether, Sturla Godø. "Humanitarian Salafism: A Contradiction in Terms?" M.A. thesis, University of Oslo, 2013.

Sayyid, Salman. *Recalling the Caliphate*. London: Hurst, 2015.

Scherz, China. *Having People, Having Heart: Charity, Sustainable Development, and Problems of Dependence in Central Uganda*. Chicago: University of Chicago Press, 2014.

Schimmel, Annemarie. *And Muhammad Is His Messenger: The Veneration of the Prophet in Islamic Piety*. Chapel Hill: University of North Carolina Press, 1985.

Scott, David. *Omens of Adversity: Tragedy, Time, Memory, Justice*. Durham, N.C.: Duke University Press, 2014.

Scott, David, and Charles Hirschkind, eds. *Powers of the Secular Modern: Talal Asad and His Interlocutors*. Stanford: Stanford University Press, 2006.

Scott, Joan W. "The Evidence of Experience." *Critical Inquiry* 17, no. 4 (Summer 1991): 773–97.

Selby, Jennifer A., Amélie Barras, and Lori G. Beaman. *Beyond Accommodation: Everyday Narratives of Muslim Canadians*. Vancouver: University of British Columbia Press, 2018.

Seremetakis, C. Nadia. "Memory of the Senses, Part I." In *The Senses Still: Perception and Memory as Material Culture in Modernity*, edited by C. Nadia Seremetakis, 1–18. Chicago: University of Chicago Press, 1994.

al-Shāghūrī, 'Abd al-Raḥmān. *Dīwān al-ḥadā'iq al-nadiyya fī-l-nasamāt al-rūḥiyya* ("The Dewy Gardens in the Spiritual Breezes"). 2nd ed. Damascus: Dār Fajr al-'Urūba, 1998. Translated by Nuh Ha Mim Keller as *Invocations of the Shadhili Order*. n.p.: [Al-Fath for Research and Publishing], [2010].

Shaqra, Muḥammad Ibrāhīm. "Ḥiṣār al-fitna." *al-Qibla* 4–5 (1424/2003): 31–38.

Shepard, William E. "Sayyid Qutb's Doctrine of Jāhiliyya." *International Journal of Middle East Studies* 35 (2003): 521–45.

Shryock, Andrew. "The New Jordanian Hospitality: House, Host, and Guest in the Culture of Public Display." *Comparative Studies in Society and History* 46, no. 1 (January 2004): 35–62.

———. "Hospitality Lessons: Learning the Shared Language of Derrida and the Balga Bedouin." *Paragraph* 32, no. 1 (March 2009): 32–50.

———. "Breaking Hospitality Apart: Bad Hosts, Bad Guests, and the Problem of Sovereignty." *Journal of the Royal Anthropological Institute* 18, s1 (June 2012): s20–s33.

Singer, Peter. "Famine, Affluence, and Morality." *Philosophy and Public Affairs* 1, no. 3 (Spring 1972): 229–43.

Sliwinski, Sharon. "The Aesthetics of Human Rights." *Culture, Theory & Critique* 50, no. 1 (2009): 23–39.

———. *Human Rights in Camera*. Chicago: University of Chicago Press, 2011.

Sontag, Susan. *Regarding the Pain of Others*. New York: Picador, 2003.

———. "Regarding the Torture of Others." *New York Times Magazine*, May 23, 2004, https://www.nytimes.com/2004/05/23/magazine/regarding-the-torture-of-others.html.

Soufi, Youcef. *Homegrown Radicals: A Story of State Violence, Islamophobia, and Jihad in the Post-9/11 World*. New York: New York University Press, 2025.

Sparrow, Annie. "How UN Humanitarian Aid Has Propped Up Assad." *Foreign Affairs*, September 20, 2018, https://www.foreignaffairs.com/articles/syria/2018-09-20/how-un-humanitarian-aid-has-propped-assad.

Statistics Canada. "Results from the 2016 Census: Syrian Refugees Who Resettled in Canada in 2015 and 2016." February 12, 2019. https://www150.statcan.gc.ca/n1/pub/75-006-x/2019001/article/00001-eng.htm.

———. "Immigrants Make Up the Largest Share of the Population in Over 150 Years and Continue to Shape Who We Are as Canadians." October 26, 2022. https://www150.statcan.gc.ca/n1/daily-quotidien/221026/dq221026a-eng.htm.

Stauffer, Jill. *Ethical Loneliness: The Injustice of Not Being Heard*. New York: Columbia University Press, 2018.

Stetkevych, Suzanne Pinckney. *The Mantle Odes: Arabic Praise Poems to the Prophet Muhammad*. Bloomington: Indiana University Press, 2010.

Su, Alice. "Why Jordan Is Deporting Syrian Refugees." *Atlantic*, October 20, 2017, https://www.theatlantic.com/international/archive/2017/10/jordan-syrian-refugees-deportation/543057/.

Syrian Network for Human Rights. "Documentation of 72 Torture Methods the Syrian Regime Continues to Practice in Its Detention Centers and Military Hospitals." SNHR, October 2019, http://sn4hr.org/wp-content/pdf/english/Documentation_of_72_Torture_Methods_the_Syrian_Regime_Continues_to_Practice_in_Its_Detention_Centers_and_Military_Hospitals_en.pdf.

al-Ṭabarī, Abū Jaʿfar Muḥammad bin Jarīr. *Jāmiʿ al-bayān wa taʾwīl al-qurʾān*. Edited by Aḥmad Muḥammad Shākir, 24 vols. [1420]. N.p.: Muʿassasat

al-Risāla, 2000. Excerpts translated by Scott C. Lucas as *Selections from "The Comprehensive Exposition of the Interpretation of the Verses of the Qur'ān."* Cambridge: Islamic Texts Society, 2017.
al-Ṭanṭāwī, 'Ali. *Fuṣūl islāmiyya*. Damascus: Dār al-Manār, 1380/1960.
Taylor, Charles. *Sources of the Self: The Making of the Modern Identity*. Cambridge, Mass.: Harvard University Press, 1989.
Ticktin, Miriam. "Transnational Humanitarianism." *Annual Review of Anthropology* 43 (2014): 273–89.
al-Tirmidhī, Abū 'Īsa. *Ash-Shama'il al-Muhammadiyya*. Translated by Abdul Aziz Suraqah. Edited by Mohammed Aslam. Philadelphia: Ghazali Institute, 2020.
Tobin, Sarah A. *Everyday Piety: Islam and Economy in Jordan*. Ithaca, N.Y.: Cornell University Press, 2016.
Tripp, Charles. *Islam and the Moral Economy: The Challenge of Capitalism*. Cambridge: Cambridge University Press, 2006.
Trouillot, Michel. "Making Sense: The Fields in Which We Work." In *Global Transformations: Anthropology and the Modern World*, 117–39. New York: Palgrave Macmillan, 2003.
Turner, Victor. *The Ritual Process: Structure and Anti-Structure*. New Brunswick, N.J.: AldineTransaction, 1969.
Tyyskä, Vappu, et al. "The Syrian Refugee Crisis in Canadian Media." Toronto: Ryerson Centre for Immigration and Settlement, 2017.
UNHCR. "Jordan: Ramadan Prayers for Syrian Refugees." *YouTube*, August 5, 2013, https://www.youtube.com/watch?v=hKWKR5Y7auQ.
———. "Gulf Donors and NGOs Assistance to Syrian Refugees in Jordan." Amman: UNHCR Jordan, 2015, prepared by Myriam Ababsa and Mamoon Muhsen, http://data.unhcr.org/syrianrefugees/country.php?id=107.
———. "Fact Sheet: Jordan Zaatari Camp." July 2018, https://data2.unhcr.org/en/documents/download/64690.
UNICEF. "Access to Education for Syrian Children in Zaatari Camp, Jordan." Joint Education Needs Assessment Report, Education Sector Working Group September 2014, 45–46.
Volpi, Frédéric. "Constructing the 'Ummah' in European Security: Between Exit, Voice and Loyalty." *Government and Opposition* 42, no. 3 (2007): 451–70.
Wagemakers, Joas. *Salafism in Jordan: Political Islam in a Quietist Community*. Cambridge: Cambridge University Press, 2016.
Wagner, Ann-Christin. "Transnational Mobilities during the Syrian War: An Ethnography of Rural Refugees and Evangelical Humanitarians in Mafraq, Jordan." Ph.D. diss., University of Edinburgh, 2019.
Ward, Rachel. "Disqualified UCP Candidate Stands Behind Calling Islam an 'Evil Cult.'" Canadian Broadcasting Corporation, July 16, 2018, https://www.cbc.ca/news/canada/calgary/todd-beasley-medicine-hat-united-conservative-party-1.4748603.

Warner, Michael. *Publics and Counterpublics*. New York: Zone Books, 2002.
Watenpaugh, Keith David. *Bread from Stones: The Middle East and the Making of Modern Humanitarianism*. Berkeley: University of California Press, 2015.
Watt, W. Montgomery. "Suffering in Sunnite Islam." *Studia Islamica* 50 (1979): 5–19.
Wedeen, Lisa. *Ambiguities of Domination: Politics, Rhetoric, and Symbols in Contemporary Syria*. Chicago: University of Chicago Press, 1999.
———. *Authoritarian Apprehensions: Ideology, Judgment, and Mourning in Syria*. Chicago: University of Chicago Press, 2019.
White, Hayden. "The Value of Narrativity in the Representation of Reality." *Critical Inquiry* 7, no. 1 (Autumn 1980): 5–27.
———. "The Historical Event." *differences: A Journal of Feminist Cultural Studies* 19, no. 2 (2008): 9–34.
Wieland, Carsten. *Syria and the Neutrality Trap: The Dilemmas of Delivering Humanitarian Aid through Violent Regimes*. London: Bloomsbury, 2021.
Wiktorowicz, Quintan. "The Salafi Movement in Jordan." *International Journal of Middle East Studies* 32 (2000): 219–40.
Wilkinson, Olivia. *Secular and Religious Dynamics in Humanitarian Response*. London: Routledge, 2019.
Wilkinson, Olivia, and Joey Ager. "Scoping Study on Local Faith Communities in Urban Displacement: Evidence on Localisation and Urbanisation." London: Refugees & Forced Migration Learning Hub, University College London, 2017.
Wilson, Richard Ashby, and Richard D. Brown, eds. *Humanitarianism and Suffering: The Mobilization of Empathy*. Cambridge: Cambridge University Press, 2009.
Wintour, Patrick. "Syrian Forces' Push into East Daraa 'Could Spark Humanitarian Crisis.'" *Guardian*, June 27, 2018, https://www.theguardian.com/world/2018/jun/27/syria-assad-forces-eastern-daraa-humanitarian-crisis-un.
Wittgenstein, Ludwig. *Philosophical Investigations*. Rev. 4th ed. London: Blackwell, 2009.
al-Yaqoubi, Muhammad. *Refuting ISIS*. 2nd ed. Herndon: Sacred Knowledge, 2016.
Yassin-Kassab, Robin, and Leila al-Shami. *Burning Country: Syrians in Revolution and War*. London: Polity Press, 2016.
Zaman, Tahir. *Islamic Traditions of Refuge in the Crises of Iraq and Syria*. London: Palgrave Macmillan, 2016.
Zemmin, Florian. "Modernity without Society? Observations on the Term *mujtamaʿ* in the Islamic Journal *al-Manār* (Cairo, 1898–1940)." *Die Welt des Islams* 56, no. 2 (2016): 223–47.

INDEX

abandonment: in creation, 17, 61; of the future, 27, 156; humanitarian, 22, 155, 217n41; of Syrians, 5, 19, 59–62, 185, 188, 203; of the *umma*, 18, 62, 68, 96, 108; zone of, 176, 210n3
ʿAbdullāh bin al-Mubārak Program, 83–100, 113–114, 150–57, 179, 189, 249n2; curriculum, 87–89, 100. *See also* Ibn al-Mubārak
Abeysekara, Ananda, 238n82
abjection, 66, 155, 175, 201
abode: evil, 202; of Islam, 32, 36, 156; of life, 109; of war, 32, 36
Abū Bakr (caliph), 50, 51, 106, 145
Abū Bakr (interlocutor), 80–100, 146
Abū Dharr (interlocutor), 113
Abū Haniyya, Hasan, 115
Abū Ḥasan (interlocutor), 100–5, 109, 111
Abū Qatāda, 115
Achrati, Ahmed, 246n143
Adorno, Theodor, 215n26, 238n82
Afghanistan, 68, 209n1
afterlife (*ākhira*), 79–80, 91, 104, 121–24, 132, 135–36, 153, 210n3–4, 239n88, 244n130, 254n24, 258n3
agency: and consciousness, 140; divine, 45, 47, 73–74; human, 58, 73, 155, 218, 246n140
ākhira. *See* afterlife
Al Jazeera, 78, 168
al-Albānī, Nāṣir al-Dīn, 100, 103, 106, 111, 115–116, 236n66
Aleppo, 25–26, 69–70, 75, 182, 201
ʿAlī (caliph), 141
ʿAlī (interlocutor), 73, 81, 125–47
alienation, and trauma: of modernity, 238n82; from politics, 33; from religion, 153. See also *ghurba*
Alyousef, Aksam, 70–77
ambivalence: conceptual, 223n38; of creation, 17; of loss, 72, 252n20; and melancholia, 248n2; of refuge, 63, 150–57, 179; of translation, 223n38; of victory, 201
Amman Message, 116, 236n67
Ammar (interlocutor), 64–68
amnesty (by Assad regime), 20, 86, 94, 155, 190
anamorphosis, 8, 210n4
Anderson, Paul, 238n83
angel, 13, 42, 60, 69, 72, 87; Gabriel, 73, 120, 142, 229n13; of history, 75
Anidjar, Gil, 214n26
Anjum, Ovamir, 31, 219n5
anthropology, 17, 149, 193; of humanitarianism, 14, 16, 25, 29, 155, 230n21;

anthropology (*cont.*)
of Islam, 16, 40, 47, 129, 227n2, 247n150; of secularism, 17, 25, 29, 47, 246n139; of suffering, 246n140, 249n6. *See also* ethnography of theology; methodology; translation
apocalyptic, 5, 81, 102, 144, 148, 210n3, 255n33
Arab uprisings, 165, 201, 236n71
Arendt, Hannah, 20, 26, 74, 221n21, 225n10–11, 226n12
Aristotle, 129, 256n43
al-Arna'ūṭ, ʿAbd al-Qādir, 177, 178
al-Arna'ūṭ, Shuʿayb, 100
arrogance, 7, 108, 135, 170, 195, 249n7
Asad, Talal: on agency and obligation, 58–59, 140, 144, 240n96; on the Community, 34; on grammar, 213n16; on humanitarianism, 23; on secularization, 40–41, 246n139, 247n152; on tradition, 16, 18, 30, 40–41, 214n25, 227n2, 238n2, 240n96, 254n27; on translation, 248n153. *See also* methodology
asceticism, 98, 232n43, 233n49
Ashʿarī theology, 112, 133–34
Asmā' (interlocutor), 179–81
al-Assad, Bashar: defeat of, 108, 191–92; judgment upon, 131–33, 143, 244n130; sanction of, 20, 94; tyranny of, 92, 157, 163, 165–66, 184, 251n9
al-Assad, Hafez, 92, 101, 110, 163, 168, 201, 234n55
asymmetry: of global power, 43, 47, 149, 232n39; God and not-God, 7, 196; of the intemporal, 194–96, 210n3; *sharīʿa* and *ḥaqīqa*, 132, 141, 143
Atia, Mona, 121, 237n76, 237n78
authenticity, 52, 122, 127, 238n82, 239n91
Aydın, Cemil, 32–34, 36, 220n10, 221n18
al-Azhar University, 81, 85, 97, 160
al-Azmeh, Aziz, 141
Azraq Refugee Camp, 48–49, 85–86

Baath, 92, 164, 234n52. *See also* Assads
Bābā ʿAmr, 106
baraka. *See* blessing
Barnett, Michael, 22, 216n39
barzakh (liminal zone), 195, 255n41
Barzegar, Abbas, 222n26
bāṭil. *See* falsehood
bāṭin (inner reality), 81, 132, 143, 147, 241n103, 244n128. See also *ẓāhir*
beauty (*jamāl*), 70, 72, 79, 131, 139; divine, 125–29, 139–41, 144, 147
belief/faith (*īmān*): actions shaped by, 118; market orientation of, 123; necessary for victory, 107; requirements of, 4, 60, 173; struggle of, 110, 114, 157; test of, 141, 169; and witness, 126–28
believer (*mu'min*): and divine abundance, 123; and fate, 3, 240n99; Khiḍr and, 130; under obligation, 4, 60, 93; parable of the, 18, 35, 37–39, 93; prayers for, 5; and the Prophet, 42; relying on God, 6; in struggle, 111, 173, 202; trial confounding, 108, 168; and the *umma*, 30–31, 35, 221n21
benefactor, 6, 14, 43, 46, 61, 124. *See also* donor
beneficiary, 6, 14, 39, 43, 46, 50–52, 124, 145, 162, 217n47
benefit (*fā'ida*): by charity, 124; of displacement, 153, 155; by knowledge, 98, 102; of protest, 166; of tribulation, 109, 134–39
Benjamin, Walter, 73–75, 238n82
Benthall, Jonathan, 223n32
Benveniste, Emile, 145, 246n140

betrayal, 36, 40, 67; of religious knowledge, 40, 100; of the Community, 5, 36, 67, 96, 202; of the revolution, 162, 166, 168, 188, 202
Bilāl (interlocutor), 3–6, 52, 58–62, 73, 76, 158–99, 201–2
Blanchot, Maurice, 37, 197, 210n4, 239n90, 256n46, 257n55
blessing (*baraka, ni'ma*): in action, 120–24, 147; of forgetting, 199, 226n11; through knowledge, 103, 252n18; of places, 76, 141; of safety, 161; of times, 4, 64, 140; and tribulation, 124, 202, 239n87; of well-being, 135–36
Blumenberg, Hans, 216n38
Boltanski, Luc, 216n35
border crisis (2018), 1–6, 8, 21, 63, 182–89
Borges, Jorge Luis, 193–95, 197
Bornstein, Erica, 216n38, 218n51
Bosnia, 139–40, 243n120
brotherhood (*ukhuwwa*), 4, 60, 71, 85–87, 90–91, 96, 108–9, 112, 252n18
Brown, Norman O., 245n133
Bukhārī (hadith canon). *See* hadith
bureaucracy, 6, 10, 12, 14, 19, 90, 250n5
al-Būṣīrī, Muḥammad, 104
al-Būṭī, Sa'īd Ramaḍān, 78, 104, 234n55
Butler, Judith, 248n2, 251n12

Caesar photographs, 172–73, 251n9
caliph, 31–34, 50, 141, 145, 148, 219n5, 220n10
calling to God (*da'wa*), 44–46, 92, 109, 113–114
capacity: of acting, 58–59, 95–97, 127–29, 140, 146, 153–56, 183, 197, 240n99, 245n138, 253n20; to begin, 74; of humanity, 43; of theology, 17
cash support, 10, 50, 54, 118
ceasefire, 1–6, 8, 21, 63, 182–89
Chakrabarty, Dipesh, 45–47
character, 26, 44, 62, 129, 162, 178, 181, 249n5
charitable organization, 1–2, 5, 8–11, 24, 61, 71, 90, 101, 158–59, 162–63, 190–91, 238n82. *See also* Jam'iyyat al-Kitāb wa-l-Sunna
Christianity: and Canadian nativism, 138; and charitable organization, 42, 45, 64–65, 162; and humanitarianism, 22–24, 216n38, 221n21; and Islamic history, 83; and refugee support (Canada), 12, 212n13; and secularism, 226n11
citizen and citizenship, 6, 44, 120, 181, 218n51
coherence, 16, 30, 41
colonial and postcolonial, 31–32, 34, 37–38, 40–41, 67, 140, 217n45, 220n10, 255n41
Comay, Rebecca, 192, 195–97
commanding good. *See* enjoining right
Community (*umma*): as affective symbol, 32; and Canadian refugee support, 14; hadiths about the, 4–6, 14, 18–19, 35–36, 147; and humanitarianism, 30–39, 46, 221n21; and Islamic law, 32; in Islamic political thought, 31–33, 219n5; as local, 36; and militancy, 33, 35, 81, 111, 134, 220n13–14, 221n21; modern enclosure of, 30, 32–38, 220n10, 221n18; and nation, 221n16; obligation to the, 80–81, 96; in the Quran, 31, 35; repair of, 44–45; the ruined, 36–38, 47–48, 62–63, 67, 75; tribulation and the, 81
companion (of the Prophet), 20, 83, 88, 98, 106, 108, 145, 165, 229n13

compassion: for the afflicted, 135, 181, 197; among the believers, 5–6, 18, 35, 37; humanitarian, 5–6, 22–23, 39, 43, 49, 146, 216n39, 217n41, 217n47; in Islamic charity, 39, 43, 51–53, 251n8. *See also* gentleness; mercy; sympathy
confounding: of human measure, 21, 63, 246n140; of inside and outside, 182, 196; of sovereignty, 8, 198; in tribulation, 167–68, 172, 192
conscription: by Assad regime, 173, 190, 196; by international aid regime, 14, 40; by international geopolitics, 34
contentment (*riḍā*), 135–37, 183. *See also* divine pleasure
contingency: of experience, 9, 80, 131, 135–36, 143, 193–95; miracle of, 73–75, 225n10; as threat, 181; and tradition, 9, 215n27, 246n139
Corbin, Henry, 245n133
corruption (*fisq*): humanitarian, 35, 58; pedagogy against, 60–62, 88, 112; social, 250n5; of Syria, 67–68, 112, 117; tribulation and, 113–114, 131; of the *umma*, 36, 45, 68, 131. *See also* deviance; heresy
Crapanzano, Vincent, 255n41
curse (*la'na*): at abandonment, 1, 5, 185; at the regime, 107, 192; at the war, 69; of wealth, 119, 124

da'wa (calling to God), 44–46, 92, 109, 113–114
Daesh (ISIS), 66, 113, 148, 161, 184, 235n57, 236n63, 257n58
dār al-islām. *See* abode
Daraa, 81–82, 85, 125, 131, 151, 153–54; protests in, 9, 75, 78; siege of, 5, 151–52, 160, 163, 169–71. *See also* Bilāl; border crisis; Omari Mosque
Das, Veena, 245n138, 250n6, 253n21
Day of Judgment: awful justice on, 5, 31, 59, 95, 98, 100, 124, 202; the Community adhering until, 6, 147; destruction of, 67–68, 102; inflecting the present, 18, 59, 256n43, 258n3; resurrecting for, 194; tribulation and, 79. *See also* eschatology
Days of God (*ayyām allāh*), 201–2
defeat, 80, 162, 213n17, 257n46, 258n3
demonstration. *See* protest
deportation, 86, 161, 236n63
Derrida, Jacques, 86, 97, 124, 197, 214n26, 230n21, 239n90
desire, 149, 215n29, 247n150; acquisitive, 66, 69, 122, 140; for freedom, 191, 248n2; for God, 128–29; for release, 23, 147, 253n20; for revenge, 72
despair (*ya's, qanaṭ*), 13, 53, 66, 73, 76–77, 166, 227n5, 245n138
deviance, 100, 105, 112, 114, 144, 164. *See also* corruption; heresy
devil, 56, 67–68, 107, 233n52
Devji, Faisal, 33, 221n21
dignity (*karāma*), 35, 42, 50–52, 165, 176
disappeared (*mafqūd*), 9–10, 20, 88, 190, 198, 202, 255n34
disbelief. *See* unbelief
discernment (*firāsa*), 97, 108, 113–114, 156, 181
discipline, 56, 121, 129, 137, 153, 175–76, 214n25
disclosure: divine, 17, 31, 132, 141, 241n103, 245n130; and history, 140–41, 143; and tribulation, 27, 80–81, 98, 144–45, 147–48, 247n150; violence and, 37, 52, 245n138
dislocation, 7, 62, 193
divine beauty (*jamāl*), 125–29, 139–41, 144, 147

divine command (*amr*), 79, 112, 133, 148, 191, 241n103
divine decree (*qaḍā', qadar*): accepting, 137, 140, 147, 153–56, 181, 183; battle between truth and falsehood, 110; enigmatic, 9, 25, 27, 155, 163; grievous, 109, 137, 142, 147, 187; and human action, 21, 133; inexorable, 3, 6–7, 9, 139, 154, 181
divine majesty (*jalāl*), 125–27, 129, 139
divine mystery (*al-ghayb*), 105, 126–27, 244n130
divine pleasure (*riḍā, riḍwān*), 46, 63, 133, 136
divine power (*qudra*), 55–56, 73, 133, 135, 171, 193, 194
divine provision (*rizq*), 118–24
divine punishment (*'adhāb*), 67, 80, 109, 122, 144, 202, 240n99
divine refuge, 68, 131
divine reward (*ajr, jazā', thawāb*), 4, 41, 61, 107, 109, 121–23, 136, 153, 202, 240n99
divine victory (*naṣr*), 105–13, 146, 157, 177, 192
divine will (*irāda, mashī'a*), 92, 133, 177, 191–92
divine wrath (*ghaḍab*), 52, 97
Dr. Khalid (interlocutor), 71–77
donor, 3–5, 10–11, 53, 61–62, 82, 88, 97, 115, 119–23, 222n25, 231n26. *See also* benefactor
dread, 7, 25, 27, 49, 163, 203, 209n3
DuFourmantelle, Anne, 197–99
dunya (this world), 19, 26, 33, 74, 79–81, 91, 104, 119–21, 124, 147, 157, 239n87, 245n130. *See also* afterlife

earth, 37, 68, 79, 110–111, 178, 187
earthquake, 19–22, 96
economic theology, 121–23, 147
Edmonton, 8, 13, 18, 52, 63–68, 76, 125, 137–38, 141
embodiment, 129, 198–99, 214n25, 246n140
emergency, 2–4, 6, 19–20, 66, 163, 224n43
enemy, 107, 111, 113, 117, 233n52, 235n57. *See also* Assads; evil; truth
enjoining right (*amr bi-l-ma'rūf*), 31, 35, 43–45, 47, 134, 222n30, 223n38, 254n27. *See also* forbidding wrong
Enlightenment, 22–23, 217n45
epistemology, 17, 213n15, 215n28, 256n41
eschatology: as disclosure, 144, 210n3; and gift, 226n11; and the incommensurable, 6, 196; and judgment, 67–68, 77, 79, 100, 220n10, 227n5; obligation and, 58–59, 91, 187; and withdrawal, 123. *See also* Day of Judgment; Heights
Esmeir, Samera, 217n45
estrangement. See *ghurba*
eternity (*abad*), 58, 122, 194, 197; of Assad regime, 200–2
ethnography of theology, 15–19, 144
etiquette (*adab*), 62, 87, 89, 128, 140
events of Hama (1982), 101, 115, 164, 167, 174–75, 233n50
everyday: humanitarianism, 21, 66; piety, 9, 16, 44, 183, 238n82; revolution, 213n17; violence, 68, 175, 238n140; witness, 49
evil (*sharr, munkar, bi's*): abode, 202; acting against, 56–57, 62, 139, 173, 183; duplicity of, 112, 215n32; future, 132; in human rights discourse, 145–46; natural vs. moral, 21; in Syria, 76, 88, 107, 110, 131, 144, 173–74; and tribulation, 79–80, 110, 135–36; in the world, 76, 131, 138, 143. *See also* divine punishment; forbidding wrong

excommunication (*takfīr*), 59, 88
excuse (before God), 94–96, 128, 146, 202
exile. *See ghurba*
experience: contingency of, 80, 135, 140, 243n121; everyday, 21, 145, 147, 238n82; and of limit, 142–43, 193, 245n138; of loss, 59, 72, 147, 245n138, 253n20, 254n28; narrated, 149, 171; space of, 149, 248n152; tradition, 41, 213n17, 238n82; traumatic, 48–49, 198; of tribulation, 98, 149
extremism, 59, 61, 88, 104–5, 164, 184
Ezra the Scribe, 193–94

Face of God, 24, 38, 195, 202
faith (*īmān*). *See* belief
faith-based organization, 12, 14, 40–41
fall of the regime, 9, 91–92, 108, 168, 170, 177, 200–3
falsehood (*bāṭil*) and truth, 78, 103–14, 117, 146, 246n140
Fassin, Didier, 21, 23, 217n45, 218n48, 232n39
fate. *See* divine decree
fear (*khawf, ru'b*): of the Assad regime, 3, 67, 101, 165, 169, 172, 174, 176, 179, 187, 190, 192, 198; for children, 71; of God, 51, 141; of the Hour, 68; images spreading, 173–75; of refugees, 59, 201; rejecting, 55, 57, 167, 176; relief from, 7, 195, 197; in torture, 251n15; as trial, 79, 109, 209n3. *See also* confounding
Feldman, Allen, 251n15, 253n23
finitude and the infinite: action between, 74, 147, 256n46; critique of, 25; divine mercy enfolding, 76; gentleness between, 197; of interpretation, 144, 214n26; veils between, 142. *See also* disclosure
Fire, 6–7, 55, 60, 119, 122, 185, 195–96, 256n43. *See also* divine punishment; Garden
fitna (trial), 35, 78–80, 94, 108, 113, 116–118, 148, 182, 228n7. See also *ibtilā'*
fiṭra (human disposition), 42–46, 181, 222n31
forbidding wrong (*nahy 'an al-munkar*), 31, 35–36, 43–45, 47, 134, 222n30, 223n38, 254n27. *See also* enjoining right
forgetting: as blessing, 199, 226n11; on Day of Judgment, 67; the duality of existence, 218n52; as human nature, 128, 226n11; kin, 67, 166; obligation, 4, 97, 120, 181; the other, 97; religious knowledge, 35, 60; the war, 71–72
forgiveness, 93, 97, 136, 202, 225n11, 240n99
form of life, 7, 145, 196, 245n138
Foucault, Michel, 227n2, 232n43
Fraser, Nancy, 44
Free Syrian Army. *See* rebels
freedom: from the Assad regime, 5, 49, 64, 67, 76, 92–93, 167, 184, 191, 201, 257n58; human, 74, 133, 155, 197, 226n12, 258n62; from sin, 37. *See also* agency; rebels
Freud, Sigmund, 198–99, 248n2, 257n59, 258n62
funeral, 68, 134, 140–41, 192, 234n55

Gabriel, 73, 120, 142, 229n13
Garden, 4, 6, 84, 107, 119, 126, 132, 133, 139, 177, 182, 239n88. *See also* divine reward; Fire
Gatter, Melissa, 249n3
Gaza, 29, 201
general equivalence, 47, 118–21

generation, 18, 66–68, 71–75, 99
genocide (*ibāda*), 20, 24, 49, 201, 217n41
genre, 216n35, 247n150
gentleness, 27, 76, 109, 163, 197–99
geopolitics, 30–34, 36, 107, 110, 172, 184
ghayb (divine mystery), 105, 126–27, 244n130
al-Ghazālī, Abū Ḥāmid, 31, 134, 143, 239n87, 240n96, 240n99
Ghouta, 49, 55, 75, 106, 131, 183–84
ghurba (exile): appropriating, 155, 254n26; constriction of, 182, 257n46; memory in, 76, 252n20; pedagogy in, 59–60, 62; theology and, 9, 16, 203
gift: affect of the, 51–52; charity and, 123–24, 147, 223n33; divine, 121, 129, 137; of forgiveness, 226n11
globalization, 32, 33, 36, 47
Goldberg, David Theo, 210n3
good (*khayr, ma'rūf*): calling to, 31; in the Community, 5–6, 224n46; divinely distributed, 26, 124; duplicity of, 112, 215n32; struggle between evil and, 108–110, 256n43; and tribulation, 79–80, 124, 169; in the world, 76. *See also* divine reward; enjoining right
good deeds (*ḥasanāt*), 37, 50–52, 60, 79, 91, 93, 96, 121–24, 126
government assisted refugees (Canada), 11–12
grammar: of concepts, 15, 17–18, 213n16, 223n38, 228n9, 237n74, 246n139; failure of, 245n138; of geopolitics, 30, 33–34, 37; of humanitarianism, 24, 40, 44, 46; secular, 44; of tribulation, 26, 79, 144–49, 245n138
gratitude (*shukr*): to Canada, 64–65; to donors, 4, 50–51, 82; to God, 76, 85, 135–36, 189, 199–200, 202; to Jordan, 85, 87
Grewal, Zareena, 239n91
guest, 44, 85–87, 97, 212n13, 230n20–21. *See also* hospitality politics
guidance (*hidāya*), 16, 87–88, 97, 100, 106, 110, 127, 181–82
Guilhot, Nicolas, 224n43

Ḥabīb 'Umar, 139–41, 243n124, 244n125
Hacking, Ian, 213n20
hadith: the believers are an aching body, 4, 14, 18–40, 221n21; on brotherhood, 87; on divine mercy, 126; on the eschaton, 147, 187; faith and acts, 4, 103; of Gabriel, 142; God replaces despair, 76, 113; goodness in the Community, 6, 147, 191; inheritance of the prophets, 98; on knowledge and action, 93; my Community is like rain, 35; on oppression, 112, 147, 173; about the Prophet, 99; punished for starving a cat, 60; reward for serving others, 41; scum upon a torrent, 68; study and transmission, 59–60, 89, 98–101, 116, 151, 153, 162, 177–78, 192, 199; on tribulation, 35, 78, 108, 117, 136, 167–68, 172, 255n35; on trusting God, 119
Hadot, Pierre, 232n43
Hagar (play), 69–75
Hagar (Quran), 73
Hama, 170
Hama massacre (1982), 101, 115, 164, 167, 174–75, 233n50
Ḥammād, Zāyid, 2, 30, 34–37, 41–47, 50–53, 114–116, 119
ḥaqīqa (the real), 126, 129, 132–33, 140–43, 241n103, 244n128
Harper, Stephen, 12
Hassan, Mona, 220n10
Ḥassūn, Badr al-Dīn, 78

Hauran (region of southern Syria), 82, 167, 170, 188, 191, 200
Hayot, Eric, 216n35
heart (*qalb*): hatred held in the, 171; jihad of the, 173; pained, 4–5, 47, 50, 161, 188, 201; in solidarity, 168, 172; spiritual readiness and, 127, 138, 142–43, 159, 244n128; spreading terror through the, 169, 174–75; Syria in the, 154; tribulation uniting the, 169; unsettled, 181; wounded, 160; yearning, 178, 191
heaven. *See* Garden
Heights (*aʿrāf*), 6–7, 25, 27, 195–96, 203, 209n3
hellfire. *See* Fire
Henig, David, 239n89
hereafter. *See* afterlife
heresy, 100, 105, 114, 131, 151, 154, 241n103. *See also* corruption; deviance
Hezbollah, 200
Hirschkind, Charles, 44
historicism, 9, 18–19, 30, 34, 40–41, 58, 145, 147–49, 210n3, 214n25–26, 224n43. *See also* methodology
Homs, 106, 170, 201
hope, 64, 66, 71–77, 107, 192, 196, 198
hospitality politics, 44, 85–87, 97, 212n13, 230n20–21
Hour. *See* Day of Judgment
Huet, Marie-Helene, 21
human disposition (*fiṭra*), 42–46, 181, 222n31
human rights, 114, 146, 174, 198, 211n8
human, concept of, 6, 23, 217n45
humanitarian: faith, 22–24; field, 38, 42–46, 49; funding, 48, 190; government, 23, 48, 83, 86, 224n43; media, 38–40, 48–50; objects, 7; principles, 2, 5, 10, 21, 23, 30, 39, 41–43, 46, 58, 86, 161; reason, 6, 23–25, 63; sacrifice, 98, 216n38, 221n21, 232n39. *See also* spectatorship
humanitarianism: anthropology of, 25, 29, 216n38, 230n21; and charity, 26, 46, 211n8, 218n51; critique of, 14, 16, 24; failures of, 5, 21; history of, 22, 216n39; and militancy, 33, 221n21; and religion, 22, 24, 35, 40–41, 45–47, 54, 63, 114, 216n38; as war, 209n1

Ibn ʿAbd al-Salām al-Sulamī, ʿIzz al-Dīn, 133–37, 139, 241n103
Ibn ʿAbd al-Wahhāb, Muḥammad, 115–116
Ibn ʿArabī, Muḥammad, 125, 241n103, 245n133
Ibn al-Mubārak, ʿAbdullāh, 91, 98
Ibn Ḥanbal, Aḥmad, 116
Ibn Khaldūn, ʿAbd al-Raḥmān, 129, 183
Ibn Taymiyya, Aḥmad, 102, 112, 115–116, 133
Ibn Ṭufayl, Muḥammad, 224n46
ibtilāʾ (trial), 26, 77, 79–80, 94–95, 109, 119, 123, 125–26, 131, 139, 169. See also *fitna*
Idlib, 64, 94, 190, 192
idolatry. *See* unbelief
IFSSA (Islamic Family and Social Services Association), 13, 36, 76
ignorance (*jahl*), 45, 105, 131, 154–56
image: of an aching body, 37; in Bilāl's archive, 192–93, 196, 198; Blanchot on the, 210n4; on book cover, 7–8; of emergency, 1, 12, 21–22, 25, 75, 125; and (non)humanitarian witness, 47–53; of violence, 52, 172–74, 251n9
impartiality, 10, 14, 21, 30, 39, 46, 162

individual: and agency, 58–59, 238n83; and humanitarianism, 23, 216n39; and the real, 126; and religious knowledge, 87–88; and temporality, 194, 258n60; and tribulation, 79–81, 136. *See also under* obligation
inheritance, 89, 110, 165, 255n34; of tradition, 15, 31–32, 34, 38, 61–62, 98–100, 145, 156, 238n82, 239n91; of traumatic experience, 8, 72
injustice, 32, 112, 173, 197, 217n47. *See also* justice; oppression
inner reality. See *bāṭin*
inside and outside Syria, 4–5, 53, 67, 161, 178–92, 196, 200
instrumentalization, 32, 41, 48, 52, 61–62, 148, 234n55
insufficiency (*faqr, naqṣ*), 6, 8–9, 24, 63, 80, 98, 115, 119, 197
intention (*niyya*), 3, 39, 41, 50, 60, 213n17, 225n3
international aid sector, 1, 5, 10–12, 14, 19–21, 24, 38–40, 43–44, 46–47, 54, 63, 87, 90, 97
Iran, 20, 107, 172, 184, 188, 200
Iraq, 12, 68, 86, 209n1
Irbid, 4, 10, 18, 179, 190, 200
Ishmael (prophet), 73
ISIS. *See* Daesh
Islamic Revival, 29, 33, 44–45, 91, 115, 227n5, 236n63
Islamism: and charity, 45, 114, 121–22, 237n76; in Jordan, 115–116, 235n61; and the modern enclosure of the *umma*, 32–38, 220n10, 221n18; postcolonial, 140; in Syria, 92, 101, 184, 233n50, 252n18
Ismail, Salwa, 101, 174–76, 231n30, 233n50
Israel, 1, 29, 110, 139, 184, 200–1. *See also* Palestine
Izutsu, Toshihiko, 248n3, 249n8
Jackson, Sherman, 240n99
jāhiliyya, 156, 249n7
jahl (ignorance), 45, 105, 131, 154–56
Jamʿiyyat al-Kitāb wa-l-Sunna, 2, 29–30, 34–37, 41–47, 50–57, 62, 81, 113–24, 219n1
Jambet, Christian, 231n32
Jesus (prophet), 76, 138
JHCO (Jordan Hashemite Charity Organization), 2, 82
jihad: as apocalyptic, 210n3, 220n13; Bosnian, 140; hadiths on, 98; law of, 105, 107, 112, 234n57; obligation of, 108–9, 227n5; stage of, 202; of the tongue, 52, 173–74, 198. *See also* militancy
jinn, 42, 57, 60
Jordan Hashemite Charity Organization (JHCO), 2, 82
journey, 7–8, 37; spiritual, 136–37, 139, 142–44, 244n128
judgment: abandonment and, 68; humanitarian, 21, 146; loss of, 75, 156; by *sharīʿa* and *ḥaqīqa*, 132–33, 144; teaching from, 126; violence and, 112. *See also* Day of Judgment
jurisprudence (*fiqh*): curriculum in Zaatari, 89, 231n23; as ethics, 235n59; of jihad, 105, 107, 112; patience in, 127; principles of, 117, 151–52, 160; Salafi, 101, 234n55; of the revolution, 255n34; as understanding, 116; of worship, 59, 88
al-Jurjānī, ʿAlī, 244n128
justice (*ʿadl*), 31–32, 36, 38, 58, 96, 112, 123, 145, 225n3. *See also* Day of Judgment; injustice; oppression

Kashmir, 14, 227n5
Katz, Marion, 123
Kenney, Jason, 138

Kerr, Malcolm, 221n15–16
khalīfa. *See* caliph
Khalifa, Mustafa, 252n18
al-Khalili, Charlotte, 213n17, 254n25, 257n46, 258n3
khayr. *See* good
Khiḍr (the Green One), 126–33, 139, 239n93, 241n103, 244n130, 245n133
al-Khinn, Muṣṭafā, 160
Khulūd (interlocutor), 54–57
kinship. *See* brotherhood
Knight, Daniel, 196
Knysh, Alexander, 241n103
Koselleck, Reinhart, 148–49, 217n42, 244n125, 247n152
Kuwait, 10–11, 91, 106, 158–59

Lacan, Jacques, 210n4, 256n43
Lane, Edward-William, 219n3, 228n6
Laplanche, Jean, 258n59, 258n60
Le Caisne, Garance, 251n9
Lear, Jonathan, 245n138
Lebanon, 9, 18, 53–54, 83, 86, 115, 230n20, 237n74
leftist, 68, 115, 236n63
legitimacy: of humanitarianism, 22, 24, 42, 44, 46; of modernity, 216n38; of opposing the ruler, 78–79, 94, 112, 117, 227n3; and scope of religious difference, 88, 116, 236n67
Levi, Primo, 146
Levinas, Emmanuel, 96, 97, 218n48
Li, Darryl, 223n37, 243n120
liberalism, 24, 116, 217n39, 246n140. *See also* neoliberalism
Libya, 165, 209n1
liminality, 193, 195, 255n41
Longo, Dominic, 47n150
loss: of caliph, 34; of Community, 36, 38; inhabiting, 71, 147, 177, 198, 257n55, 258n62; inheriting, 72; of judgment, 154, 245n138; multiple registers of, 75, 248n2; as tribulation, 79, 109, 169. *See also* melancholia; mourning; pain; suffering; trauma
lucidity, 7, 19, 25, 27, 66, 163, 196, 210n3

MacIntyre, Alasdair, 214n25, 224n46, 227n2
Mafraq, 4, 82, 150, 229n11
Mahmood, Saba, 17, 24–25, 129, 213n20
Malkki, Liisa, 232n39
Marjān (interlocutor), 76–77
martyr (*shahīd*): beloved to God, 64, 131, 139–41, 241n103; families of, 10, 88, 171, 179, 190, 192; in history, 140–41, 144; opposing Assad regime, 106, 167, 170, 202, 235n57; prayer for, 4, 202–3, 234n55
Mary (Quran), 119–21
Mauss, Marcel, 223n33
McManus, Anne-Marie, 225n6
meekness (*ḥilm*), 135, 156
Meister, Robert, 145–46, 217n47, 251n8
melancholia: and constriction, 218n52; and gentleness, 198–199; and inherited loss, 72, 75, 248n2, 258n62; and spatial division, 156, 179; and tradition, 145; yearning to exit the law, 23. *See also* mourning
memorization. *See under* Quran
memory, 27, 72, 76, 198, 201
mercy (*raḥma*): affirming divine, 7, 76, 97, 159, 177, 195, 241n103; among the believers, 4, 36, 181; enigma of, 130, 226n11; supplicating for, 73, 178, 202; and tribulation, 131, 135–36; to the worlds (the Prophet), 42, 60, 109. *See also* compassion; gentleness; sympathy
methodology: ethnography of tribulation, 16–18, 25, 147–49, 227n5,

247n150, 256n41; grammar and, 213n16; objects of observation and study, 15; in refugee studies, 193; tradition-oriented inquiry, 16, 18, 30, 32, 214n25, 215n27; universal vs. particular, 45–47. *See also* historicism
migration (*hijra*): ambivalence about, 152–56, 179–81, 248n2; and Canadian nativism, 137–38; of the Prophet, 105, 119; to Canada, 9–14
militancy: and Salafism, 45, 115–116, 236n63; and tribulation, 146; and the *umma*, 33, 35, 134, 220n13–14, 221n21. *See also* jihad; terrorism
Ministry: of Culture (Jordan), 115; of Education (Jordan), 230n15; of Endowments (Jordan), 101; of Endowments (Saudi Arabia), 115; of Endowments (Syria), 92; of Immigration (Canada), 14; of Interior (Jordan), 86
miracle, 73–75, 103, 142–44, 193–94, 225n10–11
mistake (*khaṭ'*, *ḍalāl*), 54–55, 77, 102–3, 105, 117, 128, 135, 166
Mittermaier, Amira, 43, 123, 223n33, 239n88, 240n98, 251n8, 256n41
modernity: as crisis, 148, 247n152; and humanitarianism, 21–24, 215n34, 216n35–36, 216n38–39, 217n41, 217n45; Islamic legal maxim in, 117; and legitimacy, 216n38; martyrdom in, 140; and media, 50, 215n34; and miracle, 73, 142–44; neoliberal piety in, 121–24; and tradition, 40–41, 44, 129, 227n5, 237n74, 238n82, 253n20; tribulation in, 148, 244n125; and the *umma*, 30, 32, 36, 220n10, 221n21
moral economy, 6, 26, 121–24, 237n74, 237n78, 239n90
Moses (prophet), 110, 124–32, 139, 202, 241n103, 244n130, 245n133
mosque: in Canada, 12–13, 68, 138–39, 200; in the Islamic Revival, 44, 122; in Jordan, 4, 102, 182, 189, 192, 200; in Medina, 142; in Palestine, 139; in Quran, 111; in Ramtha, 4; in Syria, 85, 92, 104–5, 125, 152–53, 234n55, 252n18; in Yemen, 140; in Zaatari Refugee Camp, 83, 89–90, 93, 151. *See also* Omari Mosque; Umayyad Mosque
Mostowlansky, Till, 223n39
Moumtaz, Nada, 237n74
mourning: circular, 197–99, 248n2, 258n59, 258n62; fallen companions, 171–72, 176–77, 191–92, 199, 201, 203; image as site of, 52, 178; the Omari Mosque, 165; poetry as site of, 191; protest, 64. *See also* melancholia
Mu'tazilī theology, 112
Mufti, Aamir, 238n82
Muhammad, peace be upon him: biography of (*sīra*), 89, 153; hejira of, 119; in history, 110, 139, 244n130; mercy to the worlds, 42, 60; praise of, 104–5, 233n52, 234n56; qualities of, 21, 99, 178, 199; revelation to, 55, 107, 219n5, 245n133; salutations upon, 164. *See also* companion; hadith; Quran
Muslim (hadith canon). *See* hadith
Muslim Brotherhood, 92, 101, 106, 114, 233n50, 234n55
Muslim world (concept), 32, 34, 36, 220n10
mystical state (*ḥāl*), 137
mystical station (*maqām*), 137, 140, 147, 244n128

al-Nābulsī, Rātib, 42
al-Nābulusī, 'Abd al-Ghānī, 235n58

Naqvi, Nauman, 99, 233n49
narrative: decline, 34, 36; of divine punishment, 80; and fate, 155; and genre, 254n24; and history, 140, 243n123; humanitarian, 51, 216n39, 250n8; regime, 233n50, 234n55; singular, 163, 171, 193, 250n6, 257n55; and tribulation, 149, 247n150; and violence, 251n15, 257n55. *See also* Bilāl; hadith
naṣr (divine victory), 105–13, 146, 157, 177, 192
natality, 26, 74–75, 225n11
nation, 5, 7, 30, 34, 193, 221n16, 230n20
al-Nawawī, Yaḥyā bin Sharaf, 37, 60
neighbor: attacking one's, 33, 169; fear and the, 56, 59, 169; hadith about, 4; killed, 167, 187; obligation to, 59–60, 62, 68, 95–96, 183; *umma* and, 36
neoliberalism, 15, 46–47, 121–24, 237n75–78, 239n89
Nietzsche, Friedrich, 71, 225n3

obligation: in charity, 43, 124, 218n51; communal (*farḍ kifāya*), 112, 114; and community, 224n46; competing, 96–97, 111; enigma of divine, 240n99; of hospitality, 86–87; of jihad, 108–9, 112; personal (*farḍ ʿayn*), 87, 97, 103, 109, 111–112, 114, 133, 143, 235n47; of repair, 78; through tradition, 58–62; to the *umma*, 35–38, 62–63, 95–97. *See also* agency
ode, 104, 142, 144
Omari Mosque (Daraa), 76, 162–68, 170, 176–77, 198–99
oppression (*ẓulm*): afflictions preempt, 135; of the Assad regime, 60, 108–9, 118, 157, 164–66, 172–73; opposing, 44, 55, 67, 78, 106, 109–12, 169, 172–73; overwhelming, 20–21, 108; of Pharaoh, 130, 157; rewards of, 14
orphan: at the ʿAbdullāh bin al-Mubārak Program, 88–89; and humanitarianism, 217n41; and Khiḍr, 130; serving, 50–51, 54, 61, 74, 112, 115, 158; in Syrian war, 107, 202
orphanage (Ramtha), 27, 58–62, 158–63, 171, 176, 179–81, 185–93, 197–98
Ottoman empire, 4, 32–33, 82, 220n10, 237n74
outer meaning. *See* *ẓāhir*

pain: body in, 120, 168, 174; creation in, 133, 240n99; and humanitarianism, 23, 146; images bearing, 52, 125, 165; as inherited loss, 72, 253n20; and tribulation, 26, 137; *umma* as a body in, 4, 34, 36, 38, 47–48, 63. *See also* suffering
Palestine, 68, 86, 110, 115, 140, 201, 257n46. *See also* Israel
pan-Islamism, 34, 36, 38, 220n10, 221n18
Pandolfo, Stefania, 19, 148, 196, 210n4, 218n52, 227n45, 228n7, 245n138, 253n24, 255n41, 256n43
parable (*mathal*), 18, 50, 93, 193–95
paradise. *See* Garden
patience. *See* steadfastness
peace, 64, 71–72, 93, 109, 117, 164
pedagogy: embodied, 129; in exegesis, 127, 195; to humanitarian counter-public, 44; of obligation, 53–63; to the ordeal, 136, 144; to rebels, 112; of violence, 101, 175; in Zaatari Refugee Camp, 88–90, 96. *See also* religious knowledge
Petersen, Marie-Juul, 40, 222n25
Pharaoh, 110, 130, 157, 202
Pierret, Thomas, 92, 239n91

pilgrimage (*ḥajj*, *'umra*), 4, 44, 48, 71–72, 176, 192
Piscatori, James, 219n7
poetry, 105, 134–35, 141–42, 177–78, 191, 215n32, 234n56, 252n20
poor and needy (*fuqarā'*): aiding the, 44, 119–20, 124, 158, 237n77; precarity since the Syrian war, 20, 62, 71, 198; representing the, 50–53; trial of the, 109, 119–20, 124. *See also* moral economy
postcolonial. *See* colonial
poverty. *See* poor
Povinelli, Elizabeth, 246n140
prayer (*ṣalāt*): afternoon, 39, 83; dawn, 50, 139; dusk, 59–60; Friday, 168; funeral, 68, 134, 140–41, 192, 234n55, 243n124; at humanitarian site, 39; jurisprudence of, 59, 88, 101, 111; martyred at, 139, 141; night, 61, 189; at Omari Mosque, 168, 176–77; practice of, 67, 102–3, 129; in Ramtha, 189; as technology of control, 92, 153; at Umayyad Mosque, 102. *See also* mosque; supplication
preacher (*khaṭīb*), 85, 92, 94, 97, 164, 166–68, 172, 182
precarity, 62, 71, 155, 162, 182, 192, 196–97
prison: Assad regime, 94, 117, 133, 160, 163–64, 168, 170–76, 179, 190, 200, 234n55, 251n9, 252n16–18, 257n58; children in, 166; and immobility, 94, 184; refugee camp as, 85; scholars in, 102, 106, 168; torture in, 133, 164, 168, 171–76, 251n9; and tribulation, 117. *See also* Sednaya prison; Tadmor prison
privately sponsored refugees (Canada), 11–12, 14, 66
progress, 23, 146, 217n42
proof (*dalīl*, *ḥujja*), 5, 100, 109, 112–113, 119, 228n9, 235n59, 240n93
prophecy, 91, 245n133, 247n152
Prophet. *See* Muhammad, peace be upon him
prophets, 73, 80, 98, 104, 110. *See also* individual prophets
protest: in Canada, 63–68; in Syria, 9–10, 75, 78, 117, 151, 165–68, 172, 175, 234n55; in Zaatari Refugee Camp, 83, 85–87. *See also* Arab uprisings
proverb, 60, 75, 86, 91, 184
provision. *See* divine provision
purification: of knowledge, 85, 97; of the Community, 33, 113–114; of the self, 94, 98, 105, 135–36; of wealth, 97

al-Qaraḍāwī, Yūsuf, 78
Qatar, 10, 20, 92, 106
quietism, 24, 115–116, 131, 144, 227n3, 236n71
Quran exegesis (*tafsīr*), 195; between form and content, 102; of divine victory, 113; of the enigmatic Khiḍr, 132; of the Heights, 7, 195; of ruins, 193; study of, 89, 151, 153; of tribulation, 79
Quran memorization (*ḥifẓ*): in Daraa, 165; between form and content, 102; in prison, 176, 252n18; at Ramtha orphanage, 59–60, 159; at Zaatari Refuge Camp, 83, 88–92
Quran recitation (*qira'ā*, *tajwīd*): in Amman, 54–57; children's programs, 54–57, 60, 83; between form and content, 100–3, 111, 233n52; in prison, 176, 252n18; at Ramtha orphanage, 60, 159, 171; at sharia institute, 164; and theophany, 142; in Zaatari Refugee Camp, 83, 89, 92–93

al-Qushayrī, Abū l-Qāsim, 134, 137, 241n103
Quṭb, Sayyid, 233n52, 249n7

Ramadan: battle during, 64, 67, 192; in Canada, 8, 13; charity during, 152, 158; consumption in, 122; in Zaatari Refugee Camp, 93, 99
Ramtha, 2–6, 10–11, 18, 54, 60, 158–59, 161–62, 167, 179–82, 185–86, 189–93, 200
al-Rāzī, Fakhr al-Dīn, 133
rebels: and 2018 border crisis, 1–2, 184–85, 188, 190; enclaves of, 19–21, 53, 101, 152, 162, 192; extremist, 59–60; instructing, 26, 105–7; victorious, 91, 200, 202
recitation. *See under* Quran
reconciliation, 145, 210n3, 251n8. *See also* amnesty
redemption: in art, 49; of evil, 143; through forgiveness, 225n11; gentleness is not, 197; of humanity, 23, 221n21; in narrative, 171; ruin and, 74, 225n6; of/in suffering, 23, 36; of trauma, 257n58
Redfield, Peter, 216n38
reform. *See* Islamic Revival; repair
refuge, 15, 24–27, 70, 86–88, 131, 153–54, 159, 179–80, 183–84
refugee art, 48–49
refugee camp. *See* Azraq Refugee Camp; Zaatari Refugee Camp
refugee education (Jordan), 85, 89–90, 97, 230n15
refugee healthcare (Jordan), 10–11, 85, 229n14
refugee sponsorship (Canada), 11–14, 64, 66
refugee status, 9, 11, 29, 85, 118, 201
refugee studies, 155, 193, 230n21
reliance on God (*tawakkul*), 3, 16, 118–119, 122, 185, 187–88
relief (*faraj*): before, 193, 198; ceasefire as, 184; God grant, 3–7, 9, 15, 19, 24, 27, 63, 187–88, 196, 203, 209n2–3; time of, 200–1
religious knowledge (*al-ʿilm al-sharʿī*): capacity for, 153, 155–56; as corrupted, 61–62; empty without practice, 103; as guide, 87–88, 153; moderate, 53, 114, 164; as obligation, 97; pay zakat on, 85, 97; as perilous, 99–100; as revolutionary project, 90–92, 144. *See also* ʿAbdullāh bin al-Mubārak Program
repair (*iṣlāḥ*), 26, 45, 63, 78, 87, 163, 196, 198
repentance (*tawba*), 128, 130, 135–36. *See also under* return
resettlement, 8, 11–13, 16, 161, 180–81, 212n12
responsibility. *See* obligation
resurrection (*qiyāma*), 5–6, 18, 59, 67–68, 95, 98, 100, 102, 146, 202. *See also* Day of Judgment; eschatology
return: to God, 31, 188, 203; to Syria, 61, 76, 90–93, 153–57, 182, 187, 200
Ricoeur, Paul, 226n11
Riḍā, Rashīd, 33–34
Robbins, Joel, 249n6
Robinson, Cabeiri deBergh, 227n5
Roy, Olivier, 33, 220n13
rubble, 7, 19, 75, 92, 106, 125, 131, 152, 154–56, 182
ruin (*kharāb, halāk*), 37, 66, 70–76, 182, 194, 196, 225n3, 225n6; spiritual, 108
Russia, 1, 20, 37, 49, 64, 67, 94, 105, 107, 113, 172, 184, 188, 190, 200

sacrifice: facing the trial, 26, 81, 98, 107; humanitarian, 216n38, 221n21,

232n39; in messianic time, 74; in revolutionary politics, 179
safety, 1, 108, 161–62, 180, 188, 196
Said, Edward, 214n26
saints (*awliyā'*), 73, 113, 134, 142, 144, 244n128
Salafism, 15, 45, 89, 100–3, 111–116, 231n23, 234n57, 236n66, 236n71, 239n87
Ṣalāḥ al-Dīn al-Ayyūbī, Yūsuf, 165
al-Saleh, Raed, 19
Saleh, Yassin al-Haj, 19–21, 175, 201, 257n58
Sanbar, Elias, 257n46
Santner, Eric, 257n59
satisfaction (*riḍā*), 135–37, 183. *See also* divine pleasure
Saudi Arabia, 10, 106–7, 115, 153–54
Scherz, China, 218n51
Scott, David, 72, 226n12
Scott, Joan Wallach, 243n121
secret police (*mukhābarāt*), 92, 236n65
sectarianism, 61, 140, 148, 234n57
secular: anxiety, 10, 40–41, 53, 114, 200; humanitarianism, 10, 14, 22–24, 39–40, 44–45, 215n34, 216n38, 222n25, 222n26; translation, 25, 31, 36, 45–47, 148, 193, 222n30, 226n11
secularism, 17; anthropology of, 17, 25, 29, 40–41, 47, 246n139; in Canada, 212n13; in Syria, 92
security forces: in Syria, 9, 73, 75, 163–75, 190, 197; at Zaatari Camp, 82
security studies, 33
Sednaya Prison, 200, 252n17
Seremetakis, C. Nadia, 253n20, 254n28
sermon (*khuṭba*): in Jordan, 110–111; in Medina, 142; revolutionary, 78, 91, 105–6, 134, 166; in Syria, 78, 91–92, 134, 153, 164, 166–68; in Yemen, 141
al-Sha'bī, Abū l-Qāsim, 191
al-Sha'rāwī, Muḥammad, 35, 42
al-Shādhilī, Abū Ḥasan, 134
Shāfi'ī juridical school, 134, 159, 164, 231n23, 249n2
al-Shāfi'ī, Muḥammad, 113, 143
al-Shāghūrī, 'Abd al-Raḥmān, 141–42
sharī'a and *ḥaqīqa*, 132, 140–43, 241n103, 244n130
sharia studies institute, 15, 88–89, 164, 177, 185. *See also* 'Abdullāh bin al-Mubārak Program
sharr. See evil
Shryock, Andrew, 86
siege (*ḥiṣār*), 5, 9, 108; of Community, 81; of Daraa, 5, 151–52, 160, 163, 169–71; of Ghouta, 106; of Homs, 106; militancy and, 220n13; of tribulation, 116
sin (*dhanb, ithm*): anxiety and, 209n3; despair as, 76; disqualifying solidarity, 37; expiating, 135–36; failing communal obligation as, 112; God forgives, 93; and humanitarian concern, 23; religious knowledge a shield against, 87–88; suffering not a sign of, 80, 95
sincerity (*ikhlāṣ*): in charity, 39, 50; in faith, 127; hadith about, 60; in jihad, 106–7, 202; in prayer, 121, 237n74
Singer, Peter, 96
al-Ṣiyāṣana, Aḥmad, 167
Sliwinski, Sharon, 215n34
Sontag, Susan, 251n12
soul (*nafs, rūḥ*): burden on, 96–97; constriction of, 68, 218n52; exile and, 9; killing a, 128; loss of, 79; pedagogy of, 63, 129, 176, 183, 240n96; servility in, 67; tribulation and, 79, 228n7
sovereignty, 5, 8, 21, 32–33, 38, 86, 133, 138, 210n4, 227n5

spatiality: displacement, 70, 178–79, 193, 254n25, 257n46; and governmentality, 86, 175; and melancholy, 156; and tradition, 41; and tribulation, 146; and *umma*, 34, 36, 221n21; and violence, 253n23. *See also* inside and outside; temporality
spectatorship, 5, 21–22, 43, 50, 53, 215n34, 216n35
Sponsorship Agreement Holder (Canada), 12–14
starvation, 9, 24, 60, 67, 108
steadfastness (*ṣabr, ṣumūd*): Quran on, 79, 109, 127–31, 182, 202, 244n130; recourse to, 3, 183; revolutionary, 106–8, 179, 191; station of, 135–37, 140, 147
stranger, 57, 59–60, 90, 96, 212n13, 217n41. *See also* brotherhood; neighbor
suffering: hadith about, 35, 38–39; and humanitarianism, 5, 20–23, 43, 50, 124, 215n34, 216n35, 216n39, 217n47, 218n51, 221n21, 250n8; images of, 49–52; magnitude of, 20–21, 197; redemptive, 36, 131, 146; sin and, 80, 128; social, 48, 246n140, 249n6, 250n8; tribulation and, 108, 131, 133, 183, 227n5, 228n9. *See also* pain
Sufism, 101, 103, 105, 113, 125–44, 234n57, 244n128
al-Suhrawardī, ʿUmar, 134, 137
al-Sulamī, Ibn ʿAbd al-Salām, 133–37, 139, 241n103
Sunnism, 8, 31, 99, 145, 148, 154, 227n3, 234n55, 241n103
supplication (*duʿā*ʾ): of Abraham, upon him peace, 31; benefit of tribulation, 135–36; for divine knowledge, 126; gesture of creation, 7, 27, 163, 203; of gratitude, 50; for guidance, 181; opening the present, 183, 193–96, 199; for provision, 120–21; for relief (*faraj*), 1, 4–7, 27, 95, 185, 187, 209n2; request for, 139; sincerity and, 120–21, 237n74; strength through, 55, 107
suspension, 7, 59, 73, 86, 193–98, 256n43
suspicion: of Islamic charities, 14, 46, 211n8; of Syrians in Jordan, 59, 161, 190, 192, 196; in war, 88
sympathy, 22, 35, 124, 216n35. *See also* compassion; gentleness

al-Ṭabarī, Ibn Jarīr, 239n93, 244n130
Tadmor Prison, 164, 174–76, 252n16–17, 257n58
al-Ṭanṭāwī, ʿAlī, 102–3, 112, 233n52
Taylor, Charles, 22, 216n36
temporality: and the intemporal, 7, 124, 193, 210n4, 225n11, 239n88, 256n46; and melancholy, 156, 178, 193, 254n28, 257n46; and tradition, 16, 41, 215n27, 238n82; and trauma, 72, 250n6, 253n21, 258n60
territory, 5, 7, 14, 19, 31–33, 37–38, 63, 175, 193, 220n10, 220n13
terror. *See* fear
terrorism (*irhābiyya*), 2, 33, 184, 221n21, 236n63
test (*imtiḥān*): affliction and, 94–96, 146, 169; as enigmatic, 144; Ibn ʿAbd al-Salām on, 133–37; by measure of faith, 141; and moral economy, 123–24; Quran on trial and, 79–80, 169; Syrian crisis as, 94–96, 109, 113, 169, 202; translating, 228n9; and truth, 232n43
testimony, 18, 22, 27, 52, 146, 162–72. *See also* Bilāl; Day of Judgment; witness
theodicy, 21–22, 24, 131, 133, 141, 143, 155
al-Tirmidhī, Muḥammad, 99

Tobin, Sarah, 122, 237n78, 238n82
torture (*ta'dhīb*): of Bilāl, 163, 168, 172; of children, 9, 75, 166; and divine judgment, 108, 112; images of, 52, 172–73, 198, 251n9, 251n12; magnitude of, 20, 112, 164, 173–76; marks of, 133, 168, 171, 176, 198; news of, 37, 199; and tribulation, 117, 202
translation: conceptual, 18–19, 149, 214n26, 223n38, 248n153; of *faraj*, 209n2; of humanitarianism, 38–47, 63, 211n8, 218n51, 223n38; of *iṣlāḥ*, 45; of obligation, 59; of the past, 254n28; of religion, 18; secular, 25; of tribulation, 228n9, 247n150; of *umma*, 32; of value, 239n89
trauma: ambivalence of, 147, 162, 196, 198, 256n43; image and, 49, 173, 196, 198; transformation of, 72, 252n17, 257n58–59
tribulation, 15, 26, 37, 63, 77, 163, 168–69, 171
Tripp, Charles, 237n78
Trouillot, Michel-Rolph, 15, 18, 213n15, 215n28
Trudeau, Justin, 12
trust (*amāna*), 39, 58, 85, 87. *See also* reliance
trust in God. *See* reliance
trustworthy (*amīn, ṣādiq, thiqa*), 83, 94, 102, 161–62
truth (*ḥaqq, ṣaḥīḥ*): ambiguation of, 31, 117, 223n38; demands of, 98–100, 147, 166–67, 173–74, 191, 232n43; everything perishes, 24; and falsehood, 78, 103–14, 117, 146, 246n140; guidance to the, 181; historical disclosure of, 141; simultaneous, 130, 132, 140, 241n103, 244n130; about Syria, 62, 163, 172, 188; teaching the, 130, 154; and tradition, 238n82; witnessing the, 127–29. *See also* religious knowledge
Tunisia, 165, 191
Turkey, 9, 12–13, 15, 18–19, 33, 53–54, 64, 69–70, 75, 83, 86, 106, 115, 184, 230n20
Turner, Victor, 193
typology: of heresies, 100; of historical events, 73, 141, 144, 146, 148; social-scientific, 45
tyranny. *See* oppression

Umayyad Mosque, 76, 102, 134, 233n52, 234n57
'Umar (caliph), 50, 51, 141, 165
'Umar (interlocutor), 100–14, 146
umma. *See* Community
unbelief (*kufr, shirk*): battling belief/faith, 54, 83, 97, 110–14, 116, 131; corrosive drift of, 81, 103, 114, 132, 146; despair as, 76; enigma of, 108, 130, 168, 240n99, 245n130; and worldly delusion, 109
UNHCR, 9–11, 82–83, 85–86, 92, 115, 118, 161, 229n11
union (*fanā'*), 142, 241n103, 244n128
United Arab Emirates, 14
United Conservative Party (Alberta), 137–38, 242n111
United Nations, 12, 19, 41, 85–86, 138, 185, 211n8. *See also* UNHCR
United States, 39–40, 180
unity: in jihad, 106–7, 111; of truth and obligation, 100; of the *umma*, 31–34, 37–40, 46, 95, 111, 169, 220n10. *See also* union
universality: of culture, 45, 47, 223n37, 232n43; humanitarian, 2, 5, 14, 22–25, 29, 216n39, 221n21; of Islam, 34, 46, 219n5
'Uthmān (caliph), 141
'Uthmān (interlocutor), 118–24, 147

van Gennep, Arnold, 193
victory (*naṣr*), 105–13, 146, 157, 177, 192
Voltaire, 215n32

Wagemakers, Joas, 234n54, 235n61, 236n63, 236n66, 236n71
Warner, Michael, 250n5
Watenpaugh, David, 217n41
wealth: donating, 4, 11, 85, 97; loss of, 79, 109; preserving, 117, 123; as trial, 35–38, 80, 98, 119
White Helmets, 19
White, Hayden, 147, 243n123, 247n147
widow, 107, 152, 202; charity to, 10, 51, 61, 88, 112; at Ramtha orphanage, 158–62, 179–81, 185, 190
Wiktorowicz, Quintan, 236n65
will of God (*irāda, mashīʾa*), 92, 133, 177, 191–92
witness: to border-life, 171, 196; God as, 68, 178; humanitarian, 217n47, 224n43; of images, 48–49, 52–53, 63; on Judgment Day, 202; to the real, 127–29, 132, 142, 147; to the trial, 26, 81, 100, 146; *umma* as, 31. *See also* Heights; testimony
Wittgenstein, Ludwig, 246n139

al-Yaʿqūbī, Muḥammad, 78, 234n57
Yassin, Ahmad, 139
Yemen, 24, 55, 113, 140, 243n119, 243n124
Yūnus (interlocutor), 13–14
Yūsuf (interlocutor), 175–76

Zaatari Refugee Camp, 16, 81–83, 177, 181, 189, 228n10, 229n11, 249n3. *See also* ʿAbdullāh bin al-Mubārak Program
Zāhid (interlocutor), 84, 94, 99, 150–57, 179
ẓāhir (outer meaning), 143, 240n93, 241n103, 244n128. See also *bāṭin*
zakat, 39, 85, 97–98
Zaman, Tahir, 36, 221n22
ẓulm. *See* oppression

Basit Kareem Iqbal is Assistant Professor of Anthropology at McMaster University.

THINKING FROM ELSEWHERE

Robert Desjarlais, *The Blind Man: A Phantasmography*

Sarah Pinto, *The Doctor and Mrs. A.: Ethics and Counter-Ethics in an Indian Dream Analysis*

Veena Das, *Textures of the Ordinary: Doing Anthropology after Wittgenstein*

Clara Han, *Seeing Like a Child: Inheriting the Korean War*

Vaibhav Saria, *Hijras, Lovers, Brothers: Surviving Sex and Poverty in Rural India*

Richard Rechtman, *Living in Death: Genocide and Its Functionaries.* Translated by Lindsay Turner, Foreword by Veena Das

Jérôme Tournadre, *The Politics of the Near: On the Edges of Protest in South Africa.* Translated by Andrew Brown

Cheryl Mattingly and Lone Grøn, *Imagistic Care: Growing Old in a Precarious World*

Heonik Kwon and Jun Hwan Park, *Spirit Power: Politics and Religion in Korea's American Century*

Mayur R. Suresh, *Terror Trials: Life and Law in Delhi's Courts*

Thomas Cousins, *The Work of Repair: Capacity after Colonialism in the Timber Plantations of South Africa*

Hélène Dumas, *Beyond Despair: The Rwanda Genocide against the Tutsi through the Eyes of Children.* Translated by Catherine Porter. Foreword by Louisa Lombard

Elizabeth Anne Davis, *The Time of the Cannibals: On Conspiracy Theory and Context*

Basit Kareem Iqbal, *The Dread Heights: Tribulation and Refuge after the Syrian Revolution*

www.ingramcontent.com/pod-product-compliance
Lightning Source LLC
Chambersburg PA
CBHW020356080526
44584CB00014B/1036
* 9 7 8 1 5 3 1 5 1 0 3 2 9 *